Aga*year*
365 seasonal recipes

Acknowledgements

My love of good food has to come from my parents, George and Molly Lunt. I now appreciate the love and care that went in to preparing good simple meals that as children my brother John and I took for granted.

Many thanks to all my friends who get to sample test recipes and give me ideas; to all the keen and novice Aga cooks that I meet who encourage me to write and give them tips and hints; and not least to the team at Absolute Press: Jon, Meg, Matt, Andrea and Claire, who work so hard to get these beautiful books together; and to Cristian Barnett who made my food look so good in all the photographs.

My special thanks to Geoff my husband who supports me not just by eating all the samples, but by helping with the washing-up, and keeping the kitchen and me in order!

I would like to dedicate this book to my children Hanna, Dominic and Hugo and all their generation, in the hope that they will appreciate good food and have as much fun round the kitchen table, enjoying good food with family and friends as I have.

About the author

In 1994, Louise Walker's *The Traditional Aga Cookery Book* was published. It marked the beginning of a remarkable series of titles that have been consistent sellers and a source of inspiration and reassurance for tens of thousands of Aga owners all over the world.

Louise has written seven Traditional Aga titles to date. Louise runs Aga cookery classes from around the four-oven Aga from her home in Bath, and travels to Aga shops all over the United Kingdom to demonstrate to both new and seasoned Aga owners.

Aga Year is her tenth book.

Aga*year*
365 seasonal recipes
Louise Walker

Absolute Press

First published in Great Britain in 2008
by Absolute Press, an imprint of
Bloomsbury Publishing Plc.

Absolute Press
Scarborough House,
29 James Street West, Bath BA1 2BT
Phone 44 (0) 1225 316013
Fax 44 (0) 1225 445836
E-mail info@absolutepress.co.uk
Website www.absolutepress.co.uk

Reprinted 2010, 2012
Text copyright © Louise Walker, 2008
This edition copyright © Absolute Press
Photography copyright © Cristian Barnett

Publisher Jon Croft
Commissioning Editor Meg Avent
Editorial Assistant Andrea O'Connor
Designer Matt Inwood
Design Assistant Claire Siggery
Photographer Cristian Barnett
Food Styling Louise Walker
Indexer Pam Scholefield

ISBN 13: 9781904573999
Printed in China by C&C Printing Ltd.

Bloomsbury Publishing Plc
50 Bedford Square, London WC1B 3DP
www.bloomsbury.com

A catalogue record of this book is available from
the British Library.

A note about the text
This book was set using Century. The first Century
typeface was cut in 1894. In 1975 an updated
family of Century typefaces was designed by
Tony Stan for ITC.

6 Introduction

9 January
44 February
78 March
114 April
150 May
188 June

224 July
260 August
296 September
332 October
368 November
404 December

440 Index

As a child growing up outside Oxford we never spoke of 'seasonality' but that is certainly how we ate. The cookery year and the food involved was defined by seasons.

My father grew all our vegetables and most of our fruit, other than of course lemons and oranges. I don't recall my mother buying any fruit and vegetables or even eggs. We had chickens for their eggs and for the table in the garden: when the fox didn't get them first. And I do remember buckets of eggs preserved in waterglass for the periods when the hens weren't laying.

Summer, of course, was not only busy as a growing season, but also for preserving the glut of produce for enjoyment later in the year.

There were preparations for seasonal events and family occasions – Easter, Hallowe'en, Bonfire Night, Christmas, not to mention birthdays – all with seasonal food as part of the celebrations.

Sadly, my children have not been brought up with all home grown seasonal produce, but for me that start to my cooking life has lasted and I find it hard to buy and prepare vegetables and fruits which are out of season.

Writing now about seasonal cooking is becoming more difficult because our British climate is so changeable. It can be chilly in August and fairly warm in December, so though this book should give you ideas about what to cook when, a lot of the dishes will fit in to many different times of the year. Go by the feel of the day, on a cold and chilly day, it is just right to make bread and warming soup and on a hot day stay distant from the Aga and make a quick goat's cheese and rocket slice.

Farmers' markets have been a great gift for those of us interested in shopping and eating seasonally and locally, but we are a very small portion of the nation's shoppers. As I write this, oil prices are rising rapidly and a knock on effect is the rapid rise in food prices. Everyone now needs to shop more carefully and not waste what they buy.

There seems to be an obsession amongst many to bash supermarkets. I think many fail to appreciate that food of a high standard has been brought to us at a cheap price led by supermarkets. We are now having to get used to higher prices and if it keeps our local producers in business I will accept that. The problem with supermarkets is that their buyers think we want everything available to us all year round, hence the tasteless strawberries, the flavourless asparagus and the leeks from Australia in July!

It is not realistic for most families to shop daily for all their needs at the local shops like our mothers did. So the art that we all need to learn is how to shop well. Use the supermarkets for some of the basics and then visit farmers' markets and farm shops to buy as much local produce as possible or have a local vegetable box delivered. Here I do have a gripe with a lot of farm shops. As they expand, produce is bought in but it is not necessarily local produce, so again be wary about where your food is coming from. The more local and fresher the ingredients the better they will taste and anything picked from your own garden should be the best of all.

Aga *year*

A few notes about the recipes. They have all been tested by me on my Aga, so they work for me and I hope they will do for you! Agas do vary, so you may need to adapt cooking times slightly. I have tried to use ingredients in season that should be easy to source. I try to buy British fresh produce wherever possible. The eggs I have used for cakes are large and butter is used for most things, as I am not a fan of margarine. I know it is more expensive, but the flavour and texture of butter is superior. Buy the best quality ingredients that you can afford. I do believe that if you use really good food you will need less because the flavours satisfy so completely. Most of the meat for testing these recipes has come from my butcher, Brian Mitchard. He is one of those traditional family butchers and knows where all the animals come from. He butchers and cures and his son Chris makes wonderful sausages. Butchers like Mitchards need supporting.

Another major source of ingredients has been the Bath Farmers' market. This market, the first in the country, is now a weekly event selling everything from fish to local cheeses, mushrooms and herbs and in the summer months, Cheddar strawberries – a real bonus!

A few notes on cookware. A new Aga comes with a selection of roasting tins, a cold shelf and a toast bat. A lot of new owners think they will have to spend a fortune on additional new equipment, this is not the case. What follows is a list of equipment that I use on a regular basis.

Saucepans. The size you need depends upon who you cook for. A large one for pasta and a non-stick one for sauces and porridge are a must. As long as water will boil quickly on the boiling plate any saucepan will work on the Aga. It is useful if the handle is either detachable or stainless steel so that it will go in the simmering oven.

Frying pan. A really good one is essential. My Berndes pans were expensive, but they are tough enough to stand up to constant use. They are non-stick and have detachable handles. I also have a sauté pan the same size as the frying pan and one lid to fit both pans.

Ridged pan. I have a very old Aga cast-iron ridged pan which heats brilliantly in the roasting oven and cooks evenly.

Baking trays. When Aga introduced the baking trays to fit on the runners I thought they wouldn't be used much as we all had roasting tins. It turns out that I was wrong. Mine are in constant use for roast vegetables, biscuit baking, crisping bacon, making roulades and so on.

Bake-O-Glide. Last, but certainly not least, this wonderful liner can be washed and re-used. It saves having to scrub tins and makes turning out cakes and other goodies virtually foolproof. I have had some sheets for years. Just don't cut foods up on it with a sharp knife or let helpful guests who are washing up for you throw it away!

Louise Walker, Bath, August 2008

January

1st Japanese Style Salmon 2nd Polenta Shortcake with Raisins and Dried Figs 3rd Parmesan and Mustard Parsnips 4th Wrapped Cod Fillet with Fennel Saffron Butter 5th Beef Tagine with Prunes 6th Soft and Chewy Cranberry Biscuits 7th Apple Porridge 8th Winter Minestrone with Pesto Croûtons 9th Cherry and White Chocolate Cookies 10th Raisin Bread for Cheese 11th Bakewell Tart 12th Somerset Cider Hotpot 13th Jerusalem Artichokes with Cheese 14th French Rice Pudding 15th Seville Orange Marmalade 16th Fricaséed Chicken with Rosemary and Lemon Juice 17th Macaroni Cheese 18th Individual Ginger Puddings 19th Pheasant Breasts with Orange and Walnut 20th Orange Drizzle Tray Bake 21st Braised Sausages with Chestnuts 22nd Spicy Red Cabbage 23rd Chocolate Mousse 24th Chestnut Soup 25th Chicken in Red Wine with Raisins 26th Orange and White Chocolate Sponge 27th Sweet Potato and Ham Soup 28th Turkey and Leek Crumble 29th Three-Chocolate Millefeuille 30th Blue Stilton Soup 31st Lemon Ricotta Puddings

January
1

Japanese Style Salmon

After the excess of the Christmas period it is time for some fresh tastes. If you are entertaining on New Year's day it is easy to multiply this recipe for more than 2 people. Serve with a light green salad to help all those beginning their New Year's diet!

4 tablespoons dark soy sauce
4 tablespoons mirin
2 tablespoons sake, rice wine or dry sherry
$2^1/_2$ cm /1-inch piece fresh ginger, peeled and slivered
2 salmon fillets
1 tablespoon vegetable oil

Serves 2

Put the soy sauce, mirin, sake and half the slivered ginger in a bowl and mix together. Place the salmon fillets on a non- metallic plate and pour over the mixed marinade ingredients. Marinade for 20–30 minutes.

Heat the oil in a frying pan. Drain the fish from the marinade and fry in the pan, starting with the skin side down in the pan first. Turn the fish after 4–5 minutes and cook through. For the last minute, pour over the remaining marinade and serve garnished with the remaining slivers of ginger.

Serve with plain boiled rice.

Cook's notes
If cooking larger quantities of this recipe, put the fish on an oiled baking tray on the floor of the roasting oven to cook.

January
2

Polenta Shortcake with Raisins and Dried Figs

This is a shortcake a world away from the one we know from Scotland. But it is still scrummy! I tend to cook this recipe after Christmas when I have plenty of dried fruits left over, sometimes adding dates as well, and serve it with plain yoghurt for a pudding.

140g/5oz polenta
pinch salt
1$\frac{1}{2}$ tablespoons extra-virgin olive oil
110g/4oz caster sugar
50g/2oz pine nuts
50g/2oz lexia or muscat raisins
110g/4oz dried figs, chopped
50g/2oz butter plus a little for smearing the tin
1 egg, beaten
2 teaspoons fennel seeds
110g/4oz plain flour

Cuts into 8 triangles

Butter well a 23cm/9-inch round cake tin. Base line with Bake-O-Glide.

Put 500ml/16 fl oz water into a large saucepan and bring to the boil. Move to the simmering plate and pour in the polenta in a continuous stream, beating all the time. I find this easiest if pouring from a jug. Stir until the polenta thickens and pulls away from the sides of the saucepan. Remove from the heat. Add the flour and mix in well. Add the sugar, pine nuts, raisins, figs, butter, egg and fennel seeds. Stir in well to mix the ingredients evenly.

Spoon the batter into the tin and level off the top.

Hang the shelf on the bottom set of runners of the roasting oven, put in the cake tin. Slide the cold shelf onto the second set of runners from the top of the oven and bake the polenta cake for 40–50 minutes until set and dry.

When cool turn onto a wire rack and serve cold.

Cook's notes
If you can't find polenta you can use semolina instead. It is worth using one or other as it adds a wonderful texture to the shortbread.

Parmesan and Mustard Parsnips

Parsnips are a great favourite simply roasted, but adding the mustard and parmesan gives them a crunch and special flavour. They are particularly good served with a grilled pork chop for example.

700g/1$^{1}/_{2}$lbs small parsnips, peeled
  and halved
50g/2oz butter
2 tablespoons olive oil
110g/4oz Parmesan cheese, grated
5 teaspoons mustard powder

Serves 8

Place the parsnips in a saucepan. Pour enough water in the pan to come 2.5cm/1-inch up the sides of the pan. Bring to the boil and simmer for 2–3 minutes. Drain well.

Put the butter and oil in a small roasting tin. Place the tin on the floor of the roasting oven while preparing the parsnips.

On a plate, mix together the Parmesan and mustard powder. Coat the parsnips in the mixture. Place in the hot roasting tin, turning in the hot oil. Hang the tin on the second set of runners from the top of the roasting oven and roast for 30–40 minutes, until cooked and golden brown.

Cook's notes
To freeze: after coating the parsnips in the cheese mixture place on a baking tray and freeze. Once frozen, remove from tray and pack them into a freezer bag. Roast from frozen.

Parsnips belong to the same family as carrots and parsley and are traditionally dug up after the first hard frosts of the season, although they can be enjoyed fresh throughout all of the winter. When buying parsnips, look for the slightly smaller roots as these are sweeter and less fibrous than the larger ones. They should have unblemished skin and a firm texture too. Parsnips are native to Eurasia and are available all year round with a peak in the winter months. Much of the parsnip's early use in cooking is obscured in literary records due to its uncanny similarity to carrots which in ancient times were also white in appearance.

Wrapped Cod Fillet with Fennel Saffron Butter

Fennel is a shockingly under-used vegetable, though in recent times it has become much more readily available. I love it in salads, finely shredded, or as here where the flavour of the fish is delicately enhanced when sautéed in a sweet, buttery sauce. The saffron adds colour and a subtle Mediterranean flavour.

500g/1lb 2oz cod fillet, skinned
50ml/2fl oz double cream
salt and pepper
juice 1 lemon
4 thin slices pancetta
50g/2oz butter

For the fennel saffron butter
1 large fennel bulb

10g/$^1/_2$oz butter
2 tablespoons Pernod or
    vermouth
150ml/$^1/_4$ pint dry white wine
125ml/4fl oz fish stock
good pinch saffron strands
1 tomato, cored, skinned and
    diced
50g/2oz butter, diced and cold

Serves 4

Cut 4 even-sized portions of cod, each about 125g /4$^1/_2$ oz. Reserve the trimmings.

Place the portions in a shallow, non-metallic dish. Squeeze the lemon juice over the fish and season with salt and pepper. Set aside.

Mix the cod trimmings with the cream and chill well in the fridge or freezer for 30–40 minutes. When well chilled, whiz in a blender or food processor until very smooth. Season with salt and pepper. Spread the puréed fish over the fish fillets and then wrap each fillet with a slice of pancetta. Chill to firm.

Trim any green from the fennel and chop. Set aside to garnish. Slice the fennel bulb lengthways into thin strips. Heat the butter in a sauté pan and sauté the fennel for 3–4 minutes, do not allow to brown. Add the Pernod or vermouth, the wine, the stock and the saffron. Bubble the mixture until the fennel is just cooked. Remove the fennel and keep warm.

Put 50g/2oz of butter in an ovenproof frying pan and put it on the floor of the roasting oven. When the butter is melted and bubbling, put the fish in the pan. Cook for 4 minutes, turn over and then cook for a further 2 minutes.

Meanwhile, whisk the cold cubes of butter into the remaining stock and stand the pan on the simmering plate. Stir in the fennel greens and the diced tomato.

Spoon the cooked fennel onto serving plates and lay a portion of fish alongside. Spoon the sauce over the fennel.

Cook's notes
Be sure to chill the fish well first to prevent the filling coming out during cooking.

Beef Tagine with Prunes

This wonderful North African tagine, like most casserole dishes, seems to taste better if made the day before and then reheated through just before serving. Add the prunes when heating through, just before serving.

3 tablespoons olive oil
2 onions, peeled and finely
   chopped
3 cloves garlic, peeled and
   chopped
2 teaspoons ground coriander
2 teaspoons ground cumin
1/4 teaspoon ground cayenne
   pepper
1.25kg/2lbs 12oz chuck steak,
   cubed
1 tablespoon tomato purée

2 teaspoons honey
300ml/1/2 pint beef stock
250g/9oz pitted prunes
salt and pepper
3 tablespoons chopped coriander
3 tablespoons chopped parsley

To serve
600g/1lb 3oz couscous
410g can chickpeas, drained
2–3 pickled lemons, finely
   chopped

Serves 6

Heat the oil in a casserole and add the onion, garlic and spices. Fry gently for 4–5 minutes until the onion is softening but don't let the spices burn. Add the beef, tomato purée, honey and stock. Bring to the boil, cover and move to the simmering oven for 2–3 hours. Stir in the prunes, check the seasoning and return to the oven for 15–20 minutes while preparing the couscous.

Place the couscous, chick peas and lemons in an ovenproof serving dish. Pour over enough boiling water to cover the couscous by 2.5cm/1-inch. Cover with a lid or plate and leave to stand at the back of the Aga for 10–15 minutes. Fork through to loosen the grains before serving.

Stir the parsley and coriander into the beef and serve with the couscous.

Cook's notes
If the casserole seems dry, add more liquid along with the prunes. As casseroles don't evaporate much in the simmering oven I tend to start off with a reduced amount of liquid and add more later if needed.

January
6

Soft and Chewy Cranberry Biscuits

Soft and chewy cookies are very much the American style and have become popular on this side of the Atlantic over the last few years. The reason they are so soft and chewy is because of the amount of sugar used!

250g/9oz plain flour	1/2 teaspoon salt
1/2 teaspoon baking powder	2 teaspoons vanilla essence
200g/7oz butter, softened	2 eggs
110g/4oz granulated sugar	150g/5oz dried cranberries
200g/7oz soft brown sugar	50g/2oz chocolate chips

Makes about 36 biscuits

The best time to buy cranberries is from late autumn through until early January. Cranberries are firm, small red berries with quite a thick skin and a bitter flavour. They grow on a small shrub and thrive in damp climates, especially around areas of marsh and bog land. Whilst the majority of berries are imported from across the Atlantic, a range of wonderfully tasty smaller varieties can be found across northern Europe.

Place the flour, bicarbonate of soda, butter, sugars, salt, vanilla essence and eggs in a mixing bowl. Mix well with either a wooden spoon or a mixer until well mixed. Add the cranberries and the chocolate chips and mix in well (these can be added at the beginning if mixing by hand).

Line a large baking tray with Bake-O-Glide.

Place teaspoons of mixture on the baking tray, spacing about 5cm/ 2 inches apart.

For a two-oven Aga, hang the tray on the bottom set of runners of the roasting oven and put the cold shelf on the third set of runners from the bottom.

For a three- or four-oven Aga, hang the tray on the second set of runners from the bottom of the baking oven.

Bake the biscuits for 10–12 minutes until golden round the edges. Cool on the tin for 2–3 minutes and then cool on a wire rack.

Cook's notes
Take care not to bake these cookies for too long if you want them chewy and just tinged with colour round the edge. They will be soft when straight out of the Aga so let them set firm on the tray for a minute or two before cooling on a wire rack.

You can experiment with a range of alternative flavours. Try substituting the cranberries for any of the following: 110g/4oz chopped nuts; 2 tablespoons cocoa powder; 75g/3oz chopped crystallised ginger; 150g/5oz rolled oats.

January

7

Apple Porridge

Over the years I have received so many questions about the technique for making successful porridge in the Aga. It really isn't a mystery or indeed difficult. Years ago I used to slow cook it in the simmering oven overnight, but now I find the bran too often comes to the surface and forms a crust, which is neither pleasing to look at nor enjoyable to eat. So simply soak the oats in water on the back of the simmering oven overnight or just make the porridge on the simmering plate in the morning, it really doesn't take more than a few minutes.

1 mugful porridge oats
2 mugs apple juice
1 eating apple, grated
2 tablespoon sultanas

Serves 2

Measure the porridge oats into a saucepan and add the apple juice. Stand the saucepan on the simmering plate and stir the porridge for a few minutes until it is creamy and piping hot. Stir in the sultanas and serve with the grated apple on top.

Cook's notes
Use a heavy based non-stick saucepan so that the porridge doesn't burn and the pan is easy to clean afterwards!

Winter Minestrone with Pesto Croûtons

I am not the most patient cook in the world but I do spend time carefully chopping the vegetables for this soup so that it looks attractive and appealing when served. The pesto croûtons add both crunch and that essential Italian flavour.

For the croûtons
4 slices crusty bread cut into cubes
3 tablespoons olive oil
1 tablespoon pesto

For the soup
2 tablespoons olive oil
1 onion, peeled and chopped
100g/3^1/$_2$oz unsmoked bacon lardons
3 large carrots, chopped

2 sticks celery, chopped
1 medium potato, peeled and chopped
2 cloves garlic, peeled and chopped
400g can chopped tomatoes
1 litre/1^3/$_4$ pints vegetable stock
2 teaspoons chopped sage leaves
2–3 cabbage leaves, shredded
400g can haricot beans, drained
a handful of parsley, chopped

Serves 4

First make the croûtons. Mix together the olive oil and pesto. Pour over the bread cubes and toss well. Tip onto a small baking tray lined with Bake-O-Glide. Slide the tray onto the third set of runners from the top of the roasting oven and bake for 8–10 minutes until crisp.
Heat the olive oil in a large pan and add the onion and the lardons. Fry gently for about 5 minutes until the onion is just turning a golden colour. Add the carrot, celery, potato and garlic, stir well and cook for 2–3 minutes.

Add the tomatoes, stock and sage, cover and bring to the boil. Move to the simmering oven for 30–40 minutes.

Remove the pan from the oven and place on the simmering plate. Stir in the cabbage and cook for 5 minutes before adding the beans and the parsley. Heat through and then ladle into warmed bowls topped with the pesto croûtons.

Cook's notes
If you double the quantity of croûton mixture any spare left over can be stored in an airtight box or in the freezer for other soups and salads.

January
9

Cherry and White Chocolate Cookies

Cookies and biscuits are really satisfying to make and always very popular. I've put some dried fruit into these, ever mindful of the inevitable post-Christmas glut, which give the cookies a certain chewiness and a little tang.

110g/4oz unsalted butter, softened
50g/2oz Demerara sugar
75g/3oz soft brown sugar
$^1/_2$ teaspoon vanilla extract
1 egg, beaten
160g/5$^1/_2$oz plain flour
$^1/_4$ teaspoon bicarbonate of soda
110g/4oz dried cherries (or blueberries or cranberries)
110g/4oz white chocolate, chopped into small chunks

Line 2 large baking trays with Bake-O-Glide.

Put the butter and sugars in a bowl and beat until light and fluffy. Beat in the vanilla extract and the beaten egg. Mix the flour and the bicarbonate of soda together and fold into the creamed butter mixture. Fold in the dried cherries and the white chocolate.

These cookies can be made any size you like. Place spoonfuls of mixture onto the baking tray, allowing room for spreading during baking.

For a two-oven Aga hang the baking tray on the bottom set of runners of the roasting oven and slide the cold shelf onto the second set of runners from the top. Bake the cookies for 18–20 minutes, until golden brown. Carefully lift onto a cooling rack and continue to bake all the mixture.

For the three or four-oven Aga hang the baking tray onto the second set of runners from the bottom of the baking oven and bake the cookies for 18–20 minutes, until a pale golden brown. Lift carefully onto a rack to cool.

Cook's notes
Remember to cool the cold shelf if using it for more than 40 minutes, after that time it won't be effective.

January
10

Raisin Bread for Cheese

I love the combination of fruit and cheese for lunch and this fruit loaf makes a great alternative to the usual bread and cheese. I've used Lexia raisins because they are very plump and moist but any type will do. If the raisins you have are a little dry, just soak them in warm water for half an hour before use.

350g/12oz wholemeal flour
350g/12oz strong white flour
2 teaspoons salt
15g/¹/₂oz yeast
1 tablespoon treacle
150g/5oz Lexia raisins
425ml/³/₄ pint water

Makes 2 loaves

Place the flours and the salt in a mixing bowl and stir in the raisins. In a basin, blend the yeast, treacle and a little water together. Add to the flours along with the remaining water. Mix to a dough, ensuring no flour is left at the bottom of the bowl. Knead the dough for 10 minutes. Place in an oiled mixing bowl, cover with oiled clingfilm and put to rise on the Aga lid, insulated with a trivet or an Aga Chef's Pad, until doubled in size.

Tip the dough out onto a lightly floured worktop and gently knock back. Cut the dough in half, and shape each half into an oblong loaf. Place on a lightly greased and floured baking tray or one lined with Bake-O-Glide. Cover with oiled clingfilm or a damp tea-towel. Place on top of the Aga and allow the loaves to rise until doubled in size.

Hang the tin on the bottom set of runners of the roasting oven and bake for 25–30 minutes, until golden brown and sounding hollow when tapped on the bottom. Cool on a wire rack.

Cook's notes
If you make this bread in a Kitchen Aid mixer or similar, don't put the raisins in at the beginning but after the first rising as otherwise the mixer will mash up the raisins during the kneading.

Bakewell Tart

There is a continuing debate in certain circles about what constitutes a genuine Bakewell tart. I am sure that my recipe would not be considered authentic but it still tastes good and is very easy to make!

500g/1lb 2oz packet puff pastry
250g/9oz raspberry jam
110g/4oz ground almonds
110g/4oz caster sugar
50g/2oz softened butter
3 eggs
3 drops almond essence

Serves 8

Roll the pastry to fit a large pie plate or 28cm/11-inch flan dish. Trim and flute the edges.

Spread the base of the pastry with the jam, leaving a small border of pastry.

Put the remaining ingredients in a mixing bowl and beat with a wooden spoon, until the batter is smooth – it will be soft. Spread the batter over the jam.

Hang the shelf on the third set of runners from the top of the roasting oven and put in the tart and bake for 10 minutes. Then move the dish to the floor of the roasting oven and slide in the cold shelf onto the second set of runners from the bottom of the oven if the tart is browning a lot. Bake for a further 10–15 minutes, until the filling is golden brown and firm to the touch.

Serve with custard or cream.

Cook's notes
Always give pastry dishes some cooking time on the floor of the roasting oven so that they don't have a soggy base.

Somerset Cider Hotpot

Here is a recipe to assemble in advance and then leave for long slow cooking in the simmering oven. These days I don't bother to brown the meat for casseroles such as this but I do make sure it is bubbling hot before putting it to cook gently in the Aga, as the heat of the simmering oven is not fierce enough to start the cooking of the meat.

700g /1¹/₂ lbs cubed pork
1 tablespoon seasoned flour
700g/1¹/₂ lbs potatoes, peeled and sliced
450g/1lb leeks, trimmed, sliced and washed
salt and pepper
300ml/¹/₂ pint Somerset cider
2 tablespoons tomato purée

Serves 4

Coat the cubes of meat in seasoned flour.

Cover the base of a flameproof casserole with a layer of half the sliced potatoes and then a layer of half the leeks. Season. Spoon in the floured pork and top with the remaining leeks and then finally the potatoes. Mix together the cider and the tomato purée and pour over the potatoes.

Stand the casserole on the simmering plate and bring to the boil. Boil for 1–2 minutes and then transfer to the simmering oven for 3–4 hours. If after that time the potatoes need further browning, put the shelf on the bottom set of runners of the roasting oven and put in the casserole for 20–30 minutes or until the potatoes are crispy on the top.

Cook's notes
I find that after 4–4¹/₂ hours cooking in a casserole the meat and vegetables can loose their peak of flavour, so be careful not to cook your casseroles for too long!

Jerusalem Artichokes with Cheese

When I was growing up I remember clearly my father growing vast quantities of Jerusalem artichokes and my mother continually trying to think of new ways of preparing them. Now I buy them as I need them. Jerusalem artichokes are a member of the sunflower family and no relation to the globe artichoke. They are a knobbly root vegetable that can be cooked like parsnips, and may only require scrubbing.

450g/1lb Jerusalem artichokes,
 peeled, if liked
300ml/¹/₂ pint milk
25g/1oz butter
25g/1oz flour
salt and pepper
grated nutmeg
110g/4oz Emmental cheese, grated

Serves 4

Despite their name, Jerusalem artichokes have no connection to Jerusalem. They are native to North America and are not even in fact artichokes, but root vegetables. In fact, the Jerusalem artichoke is the root of a type of sunflower. Jerusalem artichokes have a sweet, nutty flavour and soft flesh once cooked, which makes them ideal for use in soups and stews.

Place the Jerusalem artichokes in either a saucepan with a heatproof handle or a flameproof casserole, with about 2.5cm/1 inch of water and a pinch of salt. Cover and bring to the boil. Drain off the water and place the covered pan in the simmering oven for about 30 minutes, until the artichokes are tender. Butter an ovenproof dish. Slice the artichokes and put in the dish.

Make a sauce by placing the butter, flour and milk into a saucepan and whisk on the simmering plate until boiling. When the sauce has thickened and is smooth, season with pepper and nutmeg. Stir in half the cheese and pour the sauce over the artichokes. Sprinkle on the remaining cheese and bake on the second set of runners from the top of the roasting oven for about 10 minutes, until bubbling and golden-brown.

Cook's notes
If you do decide to peel the artichokes before cooking, pop them into a bowl of water with some lemon juice added to prevent them browning.

French Rice Pudding

If you are fond of rice pudding without crispy skin then this recipe will be more to your liking than traditional rice pudding. A perfect winter pudding which can, of course, be served cold in the summer.

1.2 litres/2 pints whole milk
110g/4oz caster sugar
2 vanilla pods
3 bay leaves
$1/_4$ teaspoon ground cinnamon
175g/6oz pudding or Arborio rice

Serves 6

Place the rice in a saucepan and cover with plenty of water. Bring to the boil and boil for 5 minutes. Drain well.

Place the milk, sugar, vanilla pods, bay leaves and cinnamon in a large saucepan and bring to a simmer. Add the drained rice, stir well. Cover with a lid and, when just coming to the boil, move to the simmering oven for $1-1^1/_2$ hours, until the rice is cooked but the pudding is still moist.

Remove the bay leaves. Take out the vanilla pods, split open and scrape the seeds into the rice pudding.

Serve warm with apricot sauce.

To make the sauce, empty a jar of apricot jam into a saucepan and thin with 2 tablespoons hot water. Stir well and warm through.

Cook's notes
Rice pudding must be made with whole milk – skimmed varieties do not work!

January
15

Seville Orange Marmalade

Homemade marmalade is a world away from the commercial variety. Sadly, I am the only one in my family who eats marmalade. I simply can't resist buying Seville oranges when I see them appear in the shops after the New Year. My jars never go to waste, though, as marmalade makes a lovely present and is always gratefully received!

1kg/2lb 2oz Seville oranges
1 lemon
1.5 litres/2^1/$_2$ pints water
2 kg/4lbs 4oz preserving sugar
a little butter

Makes about 2.5 kg/4lbs 4oz

Scrub the oranges and lemons and put in a large saucepan. Pour on the water and cover with a lid. Stand on the boiling plate and bring to the boil. When boiling, move the pan to the simmering oven for 1–1^1/$_2$ hours, until the fruit is soft.

Remove the pan from the oven and leave until the fruit is cool enough to handle. Stand a sieve over a basin. Line the sieve with muslin. Cut the oranges and lemon in half and scoop out the insides of the fruit with a spoon into the sieve. Shred the fruit rinds finely.

Rub some butter over the base and sides or a preserving pan, this helps to stop a scum forming when the marmalade is boiling. Pour the cooking liquid into the pan and add the preserving sugar, shredded rind and the muslin, tied with string.

Stand the pan on the simmering plate and stir constantly until the sugar has dissolved completely. Move the pan to the boiling plate and allow the marmalade to boil rapidly for 10 minutes. Watch that it does not boil over! Remove the pan from the heat and spoon some of the marmalade on to a cold plate. Leave to set for a few minutes. If the marmalade wrinkles well when pushed with your little finger then the marmalade has reached setting point. If necessary, return to the boil for 2–3 more minutes and re-test.

Squeeze out the muslin bag and discard. Allow the marmalade to cool before potting up otherwise the shreds will all rise to the top of the jar.

Pot the marmalade and, when cold, seal and label.

Cook's notes
Try to keep attractive jars for your marmalade – clean off all labels and wash in the dishwasher. They are then ready for when you need them and make lovely gifts.

January
16

Fricaséed Chicken with Rosemary and Lemon Juice

Rosemary is a hardy herb and handy to use all year round. I have some growing in a pot near the kitchen door so it is always available, even to use as greenery with a few flowers on the kitchen table.

a 2kg/4^1/$_2$lb chicken, jointed
2 tablespoons olive oil
25g/1oz butter
1 large sprig fresh rosemary, finely chopped
3 cloves garlic, peeled
salt and pepper
150ml/^{1}/$_4$ pint dry white wine
rind and juice 1 lemon

Serves 6

Put the oil and butter into a shallow sauté pan and heat on the simmering plate. When the butter foams add the chicken pieces and brown on all sides. Add the rosemary, garlic and a seasoning of salt and pepper. Toss the chicken to flavour evenly and then add the wine. Bubble briskly and then cover with a lid and move to the simmering oven.

Cook the chicken for 1–1^1/$_2$ hours and then check that the chicken is cooked and tender. When the meat is coming from the bone, move the chicken portions to a warm serving plate.

Grate or cut the lemon rind into julienne strips. Squeeze the juice. Skim any excess fat from the pan juices. Add the lemon juice and rind to the pan removing the rosemary sprig. Heat the pan juices, scraping any residue from the base of the pan. Pour the juice over the chicken and serve.

Cooks notes
It is always more economical to buy a whole chicken and joint it yourself. The meat cooked on the bone will have more flavour than the boneless joints that are so popular these days.

January
17

Macaroni Cheese

This must be the ultimate 'comfort food'. I can remember learning to make Macaroni Cheese at school and it has become a great standby ever since. When my children were small I often added cooked vegetables, such as broccoli, as a devious way of getting them to eat more greens. And it worked!

225g/8oz macaroni
600ml/1 pint milk
50g/2oz butter
50g/2oz flour
salt and pepper
1 teaspoon mustard
175g/6oz grated west country Cheddar cheese

Serves 4

Put a large saucepan of water on the boiling plate and bring to the boil. Add a pinch of salt and, when boiling, pour in the macaroni. Return to the boil and cook without a lid for the time on the packet, usually 12 minutes. You may have to pull the pan half off the boiling plate to stop the water boiling over. When the pasta is cooked, drain well through a colander.

Meanwhile make the sauce. Put the milk, butter and flour into a saucepan, non-stick is best. Stand the saucepan on the simmering plate and whisk constantly until a smooth, creamy and glossy sauce has formed. Whisk in the mustard and remove from the heat. Whisk in two-thirds of the grated cheese.

Return the macaroni to the saucepan and pour on the cheese sauce. Stir to coat all the macaroni with the sauce and have a taste adding salt and pepper as needed. Pour the macaroni into an ovenproof serving dish and scatter over the remaining grated cheese.

Hang the oven shelf on the third set of runners from the top of the roasting oven and put in the dish of Macaroni Cheese. Cook for 10–15 minutes until bubbling on the top and golden brown.

Serve immediately.

Cook's notes
Don't be afraid to experiment with different cheeses. You will find though that hard cheeses are best, such as Red Leicester or Double Gloucester.

Aga *year*

January
18

Individual Ginger Puddings

Ginger is a favourite and versatile winter warming ingredient of mine and can be found in a variety of forms, fresh, powdered or crystallised. For this recipe I use crystallised ginger and add some of the luscious syrup from the jar.

4 balls crystallised ginger
2 tablespoons ginger syrup
3 eggs
175g/6oz self-raising flour
175g/6oz caster sugar
175g/6oz softened butter

Serves 6

Butter well the insides of 6 individual pudding basins. Cut a small circle of baking parchment and put in the base of each pudding basin. Stand in the small roasting tin.

Take two of the ginger balls and cut into long thin needles. Divide these between the basins. Spoon a teaspoon of syrup onto the ginger. Chop the remaining ginger into small pieces.

Put the eggs, flour, sugar and butter into a mixing bowl and beat well until smooth, either with a wooden spoon or an electric mixer. Fold in the chopped ginger and the remaining syrup.

Divide the sponge mixture between the basins.

Pour enough boiling water into the roasting tin to cover the base by about 1cm/^{1}/$_2$-inch. Cover the tin with a sheet of foil, sealing on the long sides. Cook.

For the two-oven Aga, hang the roasting tin on the bottom set of runners of the roasting oven and slide the cold shelf on to the third set of runners from the top of the roasting oven. Bake for 25–30 minutes.

For a three- or four-oven Aga, hang the roasting tin on the second set of runners from the bottom of the baking oven. Bake for 30–35 minutes.

To test that the pudding is cooked, insert a skewer into the middle of the pudding and it should come out clean.

Remove the puddings from the oven and leave to stand for 2–3 minutes. Slide a knife round the side of the basin and invert the pudding onto a serving plate.

Cook's notes
Serve the puddings with cream or custard, with 1–2 tablespoons of ginger syrup stirred in just before serving.

January
19

Pheasant Breasts with Orange and Walnut

Pheasant breasts are readily available from most supermarkets now, or if you are lucky enough to have a number to hand, you can use just the breast meat for this recipe and make a wonderful stock with the rest of the bird.

4 pheasant breasts, from 2 birds
2 tablespoons seasoned flour
2 oranges
50g/2oz walnut pieces
1 tablespoon walnut oil
150ml/$^1/_4$ pint stock
15g/$^1/_2$oz cold butter
salt and pepper

Serves 4

The pheasant season runs from the beginning of October through to the end of January. Pheasant tends to be a lean bird and so requires careful cooking to produce meat that is succulent and tender. In order to achieve this, pheasant is commonly wrapped in streaky bacon or basted regularly with butter throughout the cooking process. Due to its rich, full-bodied flavour, pheasant pairs with fresh citrus flavours wonderfully well.

Put the seasoned flour onto a plate and grate the rind of one orange into the flour. Coat the pheasant breasts with the flour. Squeeze the juice from the rindless orange and reserve. Peel and segment the remaining orange. Set aside.

Stand a sauté pan on the simmering plate and add the walnuts. Shake the walnuts in the pan for a minute and then set aside. Heat the walnut oil in the pan and, when hot, add the floured pheasant breasts, skin side down. Move the pan to the floor of the roasting oven and cook for about 6 minutes. Remove the pheasant from the pan and keep warm.

Add the stock and the reserved orange juice to the pan, scraping up any bits, and then return the pheasant breasts to the pan, skin side uppermost. Allow the juices to bubble and return the pan to the floor of the roasting oven for a further 5–8 minutes, until cooked. Remove the pheasant breasts from the pan and keep warm. Strain the pan juices into a clean saucepan and bring to the boil. Reduce the sauce until it has become syrupy. Whisk in the cold butter to make a glossy sauce.

Cut the pheasant breasts into slices and serve with the orange segments, walnuts and a little sauce.

Cook's notes
Pheasant breasts are now very readily available and should be used more often. They don't take a lot of cooking and are a very healthy option. Be sure they aren't overcooked as they easily become dry.

Orange Drizzle Tray Bake

This lazy way of doing a drizzle cake was given to me by David Pengelly, an Aga demonstrator from Cornwall. It takes no time to make and no time to eat!

4 eggs
225g/8oz self-raising flour
225g/8oz caster sugar
225g/8oz soft butter
75g/3oz sultanas
1 large orange
2 tablespoons caster sugar for the topping

Line the small roasting tin with Bake-O-Glide.

Put the eggs, flour, caster sugar and soft butter in a mixing bowl and beat well with a wooden spoon or electric beater until smooth. Finely grate the rind of the orange into the cake mixture and add the sultanas. Stir in gently. Spoon the mixture into the roasting tin and level the surface. Bake.

For the two-oven Aga, hang the tin on the bottom set of runners of the roasting oven and slide the cold shelf onto the second set of runners from the bottom of the oven. Bake for 20–25 minutes.

For a three- or four-oven Aga, hang the tin on the second set of runners from the bottom of the baking oven. Bake for 25–30 minutes.

The cake will be baked when it is risen and golden and firm to the touch when pressed in the middle.

Remove the cake from the oven and scatter over the 2 tablespoons of caster sugar. Squeeze the orange juice and pour evenly over the top of the cake. Leave to cool in the tin. Cut into squares to serve.

Cook's notes
Take care not to beat the cake mix too much – a light touch is always best with cakes! Be sure to have the orange slightly warmed to extract maximum juice.

January
21

Braised Sausages
with Chestnuts

I like to make this dish using any chestnuts left over from Christmas.
It is a good hearty dish for a cold winter day.

4 onions, peeled
1 tablespoon olive oil
8 chunky good quality pork sausages
2 cloves garlic, peeled and chopped
150ml/¹/₄ pint red wine
200ml/7fl oz chicken or vegetable stock
1 tablespoon tomato purée
6 sage leaves
3 bay leaves
salt and pepper
200g/7oz chestnuts, cooked and peeled

Serves 4

Leaving the root intact, quarter the onions.

Heat a frying pan, this is best done on the floor of the roasting oven.
When the pan is really hot, add the oil and fry the onions until well
browned. Remove from the pan and set aside. Add the sausages to the
hot pan and brown them well. Scatter in the chopped garlic and cook
for 2–3 minutes before adding the wine, stock, tomato purée and the
sage and bay leaves.

Simmer for 20 minutes and then stir in the chestnuts and cook for a
further 5 minutes.

Serve straight from the oven with creamy mashed potatoes.

Cook's notes
A frying pan with a detachable handle is really useful when frying in the
Aga. All the smells will go out through the flue and the top of the Aga
won't get dirty!

Spicy Red Cabbage

Sometimes it is useful to have a few items tucked away in the freezer for busy times ahead. Here is a seasonal vegetable recipe that freezes well and can be used with any roast meat.

75g/ 3oz butter
2 red onions, peeled and finely chopped
1 small red cabbage, finely sliced
1 large or 2 small cooking apples
juice 1 lemon
2 tablespoon balsamic vinegar
2 teaspoons soft brown sugar
1 cinnamon stick
4 cloves
2 star anise

Serves 8

Melt the butter in a large casserole or saucepan. Add the onions and cook gently until soft, but not brown.

Add the cabbage, apples, sugar, lemon juice, vinegar, sugar and spices. Season well and then cover with a lid. Heat for 2–3 minutes and then move to the simmering oven for about 1 hour, or until the cabbage is soft.

This dish can be frozen after cooking. Thaw overnight in the fridge and reheat on the simmering plate.

Cook's notes
Red cabbage usually turns a deep purple-blue colour during the cooking process. Be sure to include the balsamic vinegar to help keep its colour.

Chocolate Mousse

I always regard chocolate mousse as one of the great standby puddings
– the key ingredients are always to hand. It can be served on its own, of
course, though I like to accompany it with seasonal fruits, either fresh
or poached.

5 eggs, separated
75g/3oz caster sugar
200g/7oz dark plain chocolate
4 tablespoons hot strong coffee
150ml/¹/₄ pint double cream

Serves 4

Put the chocolate in a basin and stand at the back of the Aga to melt.
   Whisk the egg whites until stiff and slowly whisk in 50g/2oz of sugar.
   Whisk the egg yolks and 25g/1oz sugar together until light and airy.
   Stir the hot coffee into the melted chocolate and then stir into the egg
yolk mixture.
   Lightly whip the double cream until it is just holding its shape. Fold into
the chocolate mixture, followed by the egg whites.
   Pour into a serving bowl, cover with clingfilm and chill for not much
more than 2 hours.
   Serve with a little whipped cream.

Cook's notes
Take care not to be heavy handed when folding together all the whipped
ingredients.

Chestnut Soup

After Christmas, during the dull days of January or February I like to set to and clean out cupboards. The kitchen cupboards reveal all sorts of goodies put away usually in case needed for the festive season or extras bought but not used. Chestnuts are a good case in point.

1 tablespoon vegetable oil
1 onion, peeled and chopped
2 sticks celery, chopped
600ml/1 pint water or turkey stock
1 bouquet garni
salt and pepper
200g pack whole roasted chestnuts
    (Merchant Gourmet are good)
300ml/^{1}/$_2$ pint milk
1–2 teaspoons lemon juice

Serves 6

Chestnuts can be found throughout autumn and winter. They belong to the beech and oak tree family. The majority of chestnuts available in supermarkets today are commercially imported but wild chestnut trees do still grow in England, predominantly in the south. There is confusion between horse chestnuts – more commonly known as conkers – and chestnuts. The latter have a slightly tapered end, unlike conkers, which are round. Chestnuts are a great addition to hearty winter dishes; cooking brings out their sweet, nutty flavour. They can be eaten boiled, roasted, candied or puréed.

Heat the oil in a saucepan and sauté the onion and celery until soft but not browned. Add the water, bouquet garni, salt and pepper and the chestnuts. Bring to the boil and place in the simmering oven for 10 minutes to allow the flavours to infuse.

Return to the simmering plate and add the milk. Bubble for 1–2 minutes and then remove the bouquet garni.

Blend the soup and add enough lemon juice to take off the very rich edge.

Heat through and serve with fresh crusty bread.

Cook's notes
If you happen to have some turkey stock leftover from last month, it makes an ideal base for this soup. Replace the water with the stock and enjoy a heavenly taste.

25

Chicken in Red Wine with Raisins

The sauce for this casserole dish is rich and spicy and makes a lovely winter dish. During cooking the raisins and apricots become plump and juicy. Serve with crispy-skinned jacket potatoes.

300ml/¹/₂ pint red wine
3 tablespoon red wine vinegar
50g/2oz seedless raisins
110g/4oz no-soak dried apricots,
  halved
1 teaspoon ground ginger
1 teaspoon ground cinnamon
1 cm/¹/₂-inch piece fresh root
  ginger, peeled and grated

4 cloves
4 juniper berries, lightly crushed
4 chicken portions
2 tablespoons flour
salt and pepper
knob of butter
1 tablespoon vegetable oil
300ml/¹/₂ pint chicken stock

Serves 4

Put the wine, vinegar, raisins, apricots, ground ginger, cinnamon, fresh ginger, cloves and juniper berries in a non-metallic dish. Add the chicken pieces and cover with the marinade. Cover and leave to marinate for at least 3–4 hours or overnight.

Remove the chicken from the marinade and pat dry on kitchen paper. Season the flour with salt and pepper then coat the chicken with the flour. Heat the oil and butter in a flameproof casserole dish, add the chicken, skin side down, and fry until golden brown. Turn and brown the other side. Lift the chicken out and put to one side. Pour off any excess fat. Pour the marinade and stock into the casserole dish, bring to the boil, stirring, and return the chicken. Boil for 2–3 minutes and then transfer, covered, to the simmering oven for 1–1¹/₂ hours until the chicken is tender. Transfer the chicken to a warm plate. Boil the liquid to reduce to a thicker sauce. Pour over the chicken.

Cook's notes
Chicken portions with the bone in will taste better for this dish as the dark meat is best with the robust flavours, and of course is cheaper than chicken breasts.

Orange and White Chocolate Sponge

Orange and chocolate go very well together, but this recipe is a little different as it uses white chocolate. The orange rind makes the cake beautifully moist.

175g/6oz butter, softened
175g/6oz caster sugar
finely grated zest 4 oranges
juice 1 orange
4 eggs, separated
110g/4oz self-raising flour
1 teaspoon baking powder
110g/4oz ground almonds

For the icing
150g/5$^1/_2$oz white chocolate
150ml/5fl oz crème fraîche
50g/2oz white chocolate to
  decorate

Butter and base-line two 23cm/9-inch spring-release cake tins. Put the butter, sugar and orange zest in a bowl and beat well. Then beat in the egg yolks. Fold in the flour and baking powder, followed by the ground almonds and orange juice. Whisk the egg whites until stiff and fold into the cake mixture. Spoon the mixture into the two tins. Bake.

For the two-oven Aga, put the oven shelf on the floor of the roasting oven and put in the cakes. Slide the cold shelf onto the second set of runners from the bottom of the oven. Bake for 25–30 minutes until risen and golden brown.

For a three- or four-oven Aga, put the shelf on the bottom set of runners of the baking oven, put in the cakes and bake for 30–35 minutes until risen and golden brown.

Slide a knife carefully round the side of the tins and release the sides. Remove the base and cool both sponges on a wire rack.

Put the white chocolate in a basin and stand at the back of the Aga to melt. Whisk the crème fraîche until thick and fold in the melted chocolate.

Place one cake upside-down on a serving plate and spoon some of the icing on top. Smooth over the cake, going right to the edge. Lay the second cake on top and spoon on the remaining icing. Swirl over the top and leave to set. Grate over the remaining chocolate to decorate.

Cook's notes
If you can only find waxed oranges, they will need a scrub in hot water before finely grating the rind.

27

Sweet Potato and Ham Soup

Sometimes you just need a thick, warming soup to serve with freshly baked wholemeal bread. I cook this recipe if I have some leftover pieces from a gammon joint (see page 300).

1 large onion, peeled and roughly chopped
1kg/2lbs 4oz sweet potato, peeled and cut
    into chunks
50g/2oz butter
1 tablespoon plain flour
300g/10$^1/_2$ oz ham, in one piece, cut into cubes
leaves from a small bunch basil, chopped
salt and pepper

Serves 4

Melt the butter in a roomy saucepan and add the onion and the sweet potato. Toss in the butter and cook for 4–5 minutes, until the vegetables are starting to soften. Stir in the flour and mix well to absorb the butter. Gradually pour in 600ml/1 pint water. Bring to the boil, stirring. Cover with a lid and move to the simmering oven for 30 minutes.

Remove the pan from the heat and blend the soup until smooth. Return to the pan. Stir in the ham and the basil. Season with salt and pepper. Bring to the boil and then return the pan to the simmering oven for 20–30 minutes until piping hot.

Divide the soup between four large warm bowls and serve with warm wholemeal bread.

Cook's notes
The sweet potato can be substituted with squash or pumpkin.

Turkey and Leek Crumble

I know many people only eat turkey at Christmas but it is often such a good buy in January and this dish bears no resemblance to a traditional roast turkey. The leg meat has more flavour as well as being cheaper but you may need to cook it a little longer than breast meat.

25g/1oz butter
450g/1lb boneless turkey, skinned and cubed
25g/1oz flour
450ml/³/₄ pint milk
salt and pepper
450g/1lb leeks, trimmed, sliced and washed
110g/4oz mushrooms, wiped and sliced

For the crumble topping
110g/4oz wholemeal flour
75g/3oz butter, chilled and cubed
1 teaspoon paprika
1 teaspoon mustard powder
50g/2oz grated hard cheese such as
*   Cheddar or Double Gloucester*
50g/2oz porridge oats

Serves 4–6

Melt the butter in an ovenproof sauté pan and add the turkey. Fry for 5 minutes, turning to evenly brown the meat. Stir in the flour and, when evenly mixed, add the milk. Stir until the sauce thickens and then allow to bubble for 1–2 minutes before adding the leeks and mushrooms. Allow the sauce to bubble again and then cover with a lid and move the pan to the simmering oven for 30–40 minutes, until the meat is tender.

Meanwhile make the crumble topping. Put the flour in a mixing bowl and add the butter. Rub the butter into the flour until the mixture resembles breadcrumbs. Stir in all the remaining ingredients.

Spoon the turkey mixture into a shallow ovenproof dish and scatter over the crumble mixture.

Hang the shelf on the third set of runners from the top of the roasting oven and slide in the turkey crumble. Bake for 25–30 minutes until crisp on the top and bubbling hot.

Cooks notes
The turkey can always be replaced with chicken if you prefer.

Three-Chocolate Millefeuille

I think this should be called 'lazy cook's spectacular dessert' it is so simple to make. Do use ready-rolled puff pastry as you will then get an even rise for the millefeuille. Serve with bowls of fresh fruit and cream.

2 packets chilled ready-rolled puff pastry
1 egg yolk, beaten
100g/3$^1/_2$oz plain dark chocolate
100g/3$^1/_2$oz milk chocolate
100g/3$^1/_2$oz white chocolate
150ml/$^1/_4$ pint single cream
icing sugar, to finish

Serves 6

Unroll the pastry. Cut each sheet in half. Lay two pieces on a large baking tray and brush one piece only with the beaten egg. Hang the baking tray on the third set of runners from the top of the roasting oven and bake for 15–20 minutes, until risen and evenly golden brown. Cool the pastry on a wire rack. Repeat with the remaining pastry but do not glaze with the egg.

Meanwhile put the chocolate into three separate basins and stand at the back of the Aga until the each has melted. Stir 3 tablespoons of cream into the plain chocolate and beat well until thick and smooth. Repeat the process with the other two chocolates.

Stand one of the plain pieces of pastry on a serving board or plate. Spread with the plain chocolate cream. Spread the white chocolate cream on another plain pastry piece and then lay on top of the plain chocolate cream. Repeat with the milk chocolate and the remaining plain piece of pastry. Top with the glazed sheet of pastry.

Dust with icing sugar and serve.

Cook notes

When the cream is added to the melted chocolate the mixture will thicken, don't panic, you are simply making a ganache.

When cooking with chocolate, try to use the same quality chocolate that you would like to eat on its own – using it in a dish with other ingredients won't compromise (or disguise!) its flavour.

Blue Stilton Soup

I cannot understand why we are so wedded to packet soups in this country. Soup is so easy to make, especially in the Aga and a fresh soup is nutritious and warming. Seasonal vegetables will give you fresh ideas for soups or simply look in the chill counter of the supermarket and see what flavours they are selling and then go home and replicate them. I assure you yours will taste much nicer, and be cheaper!

25g/1oz butter
2 onions, peeled and chopped
1 head broccoli
25g/1oz flour
1 litre/1³/₄ pints vegetable stock
salt and pepper
225g/8oz blue Stilton, crumbled

Serves 6

The town of Stilton, in Leicestershire, gives its name to this slightly soft, slightly tangy, crumbly, creamy cheese. It was so named after a landlord of the town fell in love with its distinctive flavour. Traditionally, Stilton is eaten with port and or pears, and is typically a key food item at Christmas. There are two main types of Stilton: blue and the younger, lesser-known white. Like so many traditional English cheeses, the history of Stilton is steeped in culture and has been much loved through the ages, as this line from G.K. Chesterton's poem, 'Sonnet to a Stilton Cheese', suggests: 'England has need of thee, and so have I'.

Melt the butter in a saucepan and add the onion. Toss in the butter and cook gently until softening but not browning. Break the broccoli florets into the saucepan and chop the stalk finely and add to the pan. Cook for 4–5 minutes until the vegetables are softening and then stir in the flour. Cook the flour, coating the vegetables for 1 minute, and gradually pour in the stock. Bring the pan contents to the boil, cover and move to the simmering oven for 20–25 minutes, until the broccoli is cooked.

Remove the soup from the oven and add half the crumbled Stilton. Blend until smooth. Adjust the seasoning. Re-heat gently.

Ladle the soup into bowls and sprinkle the remaining Stilton over the soup as garnish.

Cook's notes
Don't cook the broccoli for too long as it will begin loose colour.

Lemon Ricotta Puddings

These little puddings have become a winter standby for me. They are light in texture and the lemon juice gives a fresh, zingy taste. I like to serve them warm, but they are just as delicious eaten cold.

110g/4oz ground almonds
400g/14oz Ricotta cheese
110g/4oz caster sugar
2 tablespoons lemon juice
3 eggs

For the lemon syrup
150g/5 oz caster sugar
100ml/4 fl oz lemon juice
15g/$^1/_2$ oz toasted, flaked almonds

Serves 6

Butter 6 x 150ml/5fl oz individual metal pudding basins.

Place the ground almonds in a mixing bowl and add the ricotta. Beat together. Add the caster sugar and 2 tablespoons lemon juice. Beat well and then beat in the eggs, one at a time, until the mixture is light and fluffy. Spoon the mixture into the buttered pudding basins. Place the tins on a baking tray and bake on the third set of runners from the top of the roasting oven for 25–30 minutes, until just firm to the touch. Cool slightly before turning out to serve.

Make the syrup while the puddings are cooking. Place the sugar in a saucepan with 6 tablespoons of water. Place on the simmering plate and heat gently until the sugar has dissolved. Bring the syrup to the boil and bubble until the mixture is a pale golden colour, taking care not to allow it to colour too much. Remove from the heat and allow to cool slightly before adding the lemon juice.

Loosen the puddings from the basins and invert onto a plate. Spoon over some syrup and scatter over the flaked almonds.

Cook's notes
If you have used the rind of a lemon for a dish, squeeze the juice, pour into a plastic box and freeze. Remember to label how many lemons you have put in the box! This recipe is perfect for using saved juice.

February

1st Classic Beef Casserole 2nd Bread and Butter Pudding
3rd Chilli Salt Squid 4th Goat's Cheese Croustade
5th Thin Pancakes with Lemon 6th Chicken and Egg
Oriental Rice 7th Cup Cakes 8th Roast Swede
9th Slow Roast Pork 10th Almond Crusted Salmon Fillet
11th Butter Digestive Biscuits 12th Spice-Crusted Chicken
with Rose Harissa 13th Cauliflower Soufflés
14th Passion Cake 15th Braised Carrots with Parmesan
16th Venison Casserole with Parsley Dumplings
17th Smoked Fish Risotto with Poached Egg
18th Fudge Nut Tranche 19th Middle Eastern Shepherd's Pie
20th Chicken Noodle Soup 21st Chelsea Buns
22nd Roquefort Feuilleté 23rd Oriental 'Paella'
24th Almond Marmalade Tart 25th Sultana and Nut Pilaf
26th Mascarpone and Gorgonzola Tart with Balsamic Onions
27th Orange and Vanilla Custard Tart 28th Cheese Ramekins

February

1

Classic Beef Casserole

The Aga is ideal for cooking casseroles slowly, as it develops rich flavours and tenderises the meat. This recipe has a strong French influence and can easily be adapted to suit whatever ingredients are to hand. Serve with crisp baked potatoes and very fresh green vegetables, or have a crispy salad to follow.

900g/2lb good braising steak or skirt,
  cut into large squares
175g/6oz unsmoked streaky bacon,
  in one piece if possible, then diced
2 onions, peeled and sliced
2 carrots, peeled and sliced
2 tomatoes, skinned and sliced
2 cloves garlic, peeled
bouquet garni
2 tablespoons olive oil
150ml/$^1/_4$ pint red wine

Serves 6–8

In the bottom of a flameproof casserole pour the olive oil, then place in the bacon and prepared vegetables. Lay the meat on top. Bury the garlic and the bouquet garni in the centre.

Stand the casserole, uncovered, on the floor of the roasting oven.

After about 10–15 minutes put the wine in a small pan on the boiling plate. When it is boiling, set the wine alight and allow the alcohol to burn off. When the flames have died down pour the wine over the casserole. Cover with a lid and allow the casserole to come to the boil. Transfer to the simmering oven for 3 hours.

To serve, dish the meat, bacon and vegetables onto a warm serving platter. Skim off most of the fat from the liquid, and remove the bouquet garni. Heat the sauce to bubbling on the simmering plate and pour over the meat.

Cook's note
Ask your butcher for beef skirt, it makes the most wonderful casserole but it can also be slow roasted.

February
2

Bread and Butter Pudding

Bread and butter pudding was traditionally made as a way of using up leftovers. Over recent years this pudding has been changed into something smarter. I now want to return to the idea of using leftover bread. I sometimes use plain yoghurt if I have some in the fridge, sometimes I put cream in if I have that to hand or if not I use all milk. Cooked gently in a bain-marie in the simmering oven, the custard will be just set and smooth. Before starting, be sure to check that your dish will fit in the roasting tin!

8 slices stale bread
50g/2oz butter
50g/2oz sultanas
8fl oz/225ml milk
8fl oz/225ml Greek-style yoghurt
2 eggs
50g/2oz caster sugar
1 teaspoon vanilla extract
1 tablespoon caster sugar, for the topping

Serves 6–8

Butter the sides and base of a shallow 1 litre/2 pint ovenproof dish.

Spread the bread slices with butter on one side and cut each slice into four triangles. Arrange the bread in the dish, buttered side up and sprinkle with the sultanas. Bring the milk to the boil.

Gently stir in the yoghurt and mix well. Beat the eggs, caster sugar and vanilla extract together. Add the milk and yoghurt and mix well. Strain and pour over the bread. Sprinkle over the caster sugar.

Stand the dish in the roasting tin. Pour hot water round the dish to about halfway up the side. Slide the roasting tin into the roasting oven on the bottom set of runners and bake for 10 minutes.

Transfer the tin to the simmering oven for 30–45 minutes until set.

Serve warm with cream or ice cream.

Cook's notes
After pouring over the egg mixture, it is best to leave this pudding to stand for at least half an hour before baking, This allows time for the bread to absorb the liquid – the staler the bread the longer it needs to soak.

Aga *year*

Chilli Salt Squid

Fresh squid is easy to prepare and slice, but if you don't fancy the idea, just ask your fishmonger to do it for you. Alternatively, you can use calamari rings, though beware as sometimes they can be sliced rather thickly – thin is best. Try serving these spicy rings either in a salad or as finger food for nibbles.

300g/10$^1/_2$oz squid, cleaned and cut into rings
cornflour for dusting
2 teaspoons salt
1 teaspoon Chinese five-spice
good grinding pepper
4 tablespoons sunflower oil for frying

Serves 6 as nibbles or as a starter

Toss the cleaned squid rings with the cornflour.
    Mix together the salt, Chinese five-spice and pepper and put to one side.
    Heat the oil in a small frying pan and when hot drop the squid in, in small batches, and fry until crisp and golden. Remove from the pan and drain on kitchen paper. Continue to fry the remaining squid in the same way. Tip into a bowl and toss in the salt and spice mixture.

Cook's notes
Take care not to overcook the squid as it will become rubbery. Keep the pan hot throughout the cooking.
    Chilli is a favourite accompaniment to squid and is used a lot in mediterranean cooking. Try adding a little de-seeded chopped red chilli when frying the squid to enhance the flavour of the pepper and add a little zing to the dish.

February
4

Goat's Cheese Croustade

February seems to me a slightly dull month in the culinary calender so I often like to catch up on some informal entertaining. Instead of making starters I sometimes serve substantial nibbles with drinks and then serve a hearty main course to follow. Here is a simple-to-make nibble.

1/2 thin French stick
olive oil
100g/3 1/2 oz soft, rindless goat's cheese
chives

Goat's cheese is a soft and creamy cheese made from goat's milk. Slightly piquant and musky in flavour, goat's cheese has the same fat content as cow's milk and is renowned for its subtle flavour and consistency. It can be served warm or cold.

Slice the bread into thin, mouth-size rounds. Put them on the simmering plate and toast until golden brown. Turn over to toast on the reverse side. When toasted, place on a baking tray. Drizzle olive oil over them. Lay on a slice of goat's cheese. When ready to serve put the tray on the bottom set of runners of the roasting oven for 4–5 minutes, just to heat through. Garnish with strips of fresh chives.

Cook's notes
The bread can be toasted and stored in an airtight container a couple of days ahead of use. Spread the cheese up to 2 hours before heating through.

Thin Pancakes with Lemon

Shrove Tuesday comes but once a year and how often is it asked 'Why don't we have pancakes more often?'. They are so moreish and I never seem to make enough. Having a good non-stick pan makes tossing the pancakes easy – everyone should have a go! Tip the pancake almost half out of the pan and flip or toss to turn the pancake out of the pan and over. It becomes quite easy after you have done it once or twice.

110g/4oz plain flour
pinch salt
1 egg
300ml/^{1}/$_2$ pint milk
a little melted butter or oil, for frying
lemon juice and caster sugar, to serve

Makes about 6–8

Put the flour and salt in a mixing bowl and break in the egg. Add about a quarter of the milk and start whisking. Add more milk, beating and whisking to make a smooth batter about the thickness of single cream.

Heat the frying pan on the boiling plate and, when hot, add a little butter or oil to the pan and wipe round with a piece of kitchen paper. There should be a thin smear of fat in the pan.

Pour a ladleful of batter into the pan and swirl round. If there is too much batter, pour out the excess. Cook until the pancake will move freely in the pan when eased with a table knife. Slide the pancake away from you so that it is about one third of the way out of the pan and then toss over. Cook the second side until just browning. Slide the pancake onto a plate and serve with lemon juice and sugar to sprinkle over and roll up.

Cook's notes

There is no need to stand the batter before cooking. Either make the batter and cook immediately or leave in the fridge until ready to use.

Chicken and Egg Oriental Rice

This is a very simple and tasty recipe that can be enhanced with different vegetables in season and is an excellent starting point for novice wok cooks.

1¹/₅ litres/2 pints chicken or vegetable
  stock, hot
4 tablespoons vegetable oil
2¹/₂cm/1-inch cube fresh ginger, grated
2 cloves garlic, peeled and thinly sliced
4 spring onions, trimmed and sliced
3 lemongrass stalks, tender cores sliced
300g/10oz chicken breast, skinned and
  cut into fine strips
2 tablespoons soy sauce
400g/14oz basmati rice
4 eggs
salt and pepper
1 tablespoon sesame oil

Serves 6

Remove 5 tablespoons of stock from the measured amount and set aside to cook the chicken in. Put the remaining stock in a saucepan and add the rice. Bring to the boil and transfer the covered pan to the simmering oven for 12–15 minutes, until the rice is cooked.

Heat 2 tablespoons oil in a frying pan or wok and stir-fry the ginger, garlic, spring onions and lemongrass for 2–3 minutes. Add the chicken and stir-fry for 3–4 minutes. Add 4–5 tablespoons of stock and the soy sauce and continue cooking for 4–5 minutes. Set aside.

Heat a tablespoon of oil in a frying pan. Beat the eggs together and lightly fry the eggs in the frying pan to make a soft omelette. Season lightly and then tip the omelette onto a plate. Cut into shreds.

Heat the remaining tablespoon of oil in the wok or sauté pan and stir in the rice. Add the chicken mixture, stir for 2 minutes until hot, gently stir in the omelette and sprinkle with sesame oil.

Cook's notes
If you don't have a wok that will sit on the Aga hot plate, a large sauté pan works well. Whatever you use, make sure that it is large enough to continually move the food around the hot pan ensuring that the contents stir-fries rather than stews!

Cup Cakes

Cup cakes have become very fashionable over recent years. I see them in smart boxes in bakeries and supermarkets and marvel at the prices they are charging. After all, a cup cake is simply a sponge bun with fancy icing! Let your imagination run riot when it comes to decorating the cup cakes.

2 eggs
110g/4oz self-raising flour
110g/4oz caster sugar
110g/4oz softened butter
1 teaspoon vanilla essence

12 hole deep muffin tin
12 muffin paper cases

For the icing
225g/8oz icing sugar
110g/4oz soft butter
colouring of choice
sugar dragees or other
   decorations

Makes 12

Line the muffin tin with the paper cake cases.

Put all the ingredients together in a mixing bowl and beat together with a wooden spoon or an electric beater until light and fluffy.

Spoon the mixture into the paper cake cases to fill about half the case.

For a two-oven Aga put the shelf on the floor of the roasting oven and put in the muffin tin. Slide the cold shelf on to the second set of runners from the bottom of the roasting oven and bake for 15–20 minutes until the cakes are risen, golden brown and springy when lightly pressed. Cool on a wire rack.

For a three- or four-oven Aga put the shelf on the bottom set of runners of the baking oven and put in the muffin tin. Bake for 20–25 minutes until the cakes are risen, golden brown and springy when lightly pressed. Cool on a wire rack.

Sieve the icing sugar into a mixing bowl and add the butter. Beat the ingredients together with a wooden spoon or electric beater until light and fluffy. Beat in a little food colouring, if using. Spoon some icing over each cake or, alternatively, put the icing in a piping bag and swirl the icing on the cakes.

Decorate the cakes with dragees, crystallised flowers, etc.

Allow the icing to firm up before serving.

Cook's notes
Make sure the cup cakes are completely cold before trying to decorate. If you haven't overfilled the cake cases there should be plenty of room for the icing.

Roast Swede

Many people roast potatoes regularly but don't often roast other root vegetables. Parsnips and carrots work well, but keep an eye on them as they burn easily because of their high sugar content. The Aga roasts these wonderful winter vegetables beautifully.

1 tablespoon vegetable oil
25g/1oz butter
1 large swede, cut into medium-sized cubes
salt and pepper

Serves 4

The swede is a cross between a turnip and a cabbage, and despite being labelled a root vegetable, it is not strictly a member of this family, as it is the bulbous base of the stem that is eaten as opposed to the actual root of the plant. Its season runs from early autumn through until as late as the end of winter. It adopted its English name in the 18th century when Sweden began exporting a vast amount of its crop. In Scotland, swedes are somewhat confusingly known as turnips or 'neeps'. North of the border, it is often served with haggis and mixes well with heavy meat-based stews. Swede appears in two main varieties: yellow-fleshed and white-fleshed, although the latter is not as common or readily available.

Put the oil and the butter in the small roasting tin and place this on the floor of the roasting oven, until the butter has melted and the oil is hot. Toss in the swede and season. Hang on the top set of runners of the roasting oven for 25–35 minutes, until the swede is tender and golden brown. The cooking time will depend upon the age of the swede. Serve with roast meat or fish.

Cook's notes
Baby turnips or cubes of turnip can be cooked in the same way.

February
9

Slow Roast Pork

Pork is a favourite winter meat for me and this long slow cooking is perfect if you want to cook a traditional roast for a lot of people. The roasting oven will be free to cook the potatoes, parsnips and the like. It also produces meat that is beautifully flavoursome and moist.

Ask your butcher for a large boned leg joint or a meaty boned belly of pork. Have him score the skin well so that you have crispy crackling.

2.25kg/5lb leg of pork
1 onion
1 lemon
gravy
flour
vegetable stock

Serves 8

Peel and slice the onion and lay the slices in the base of a roasting tin where the meat will sit. Place the joint of pork on top of the onions, skin side uppermost. Cut the lemon in half and rub the skin of the pork with the cut side of the lemon, squeezing out the juice as you rub. Hang the tin on the second set of runners from the bottom of the roasting oven for $1^{1}/_{2}$ hours. At the end of this time good crispy crackling should have formed.

Move the joint of pork to the middle of the simmering oven and continue cooking for 6–8 hours.

Remove the pork from the oven and lift the joint onto a warm serving plate. Stand somewhere warm, but do not cover or the crackling will go soft.

Make the gravy. Skim off any excess fat from the base of the tin. You will need about a tablespoon of fat. Sprinkle over about 2 tablespoons of flour and work into the pan with a whisk. Slowly whisk in enough stock to cover the base of the tin. Stand the tin on the simmering plate and bring the gravy to the boil, stirring and adding enough liquid to make a gravy to the consistency you like.

The meat may well fall apart when carved. Serve with roast potatoes, parsnips and apple sauce.

Cook's notes
When making gravy add the flour using a flour shaker – this way you are less likely to get lumpy gravy – whisk together using a balloon whisk.

Almond Crusted Salmon Fillet

The almonds add moisture as well as a crust to this easy-to-make fish dish.

600g/1lb 4oz fillet of salmon, or 4 even portions
juice 1 lemon
50g/2oz butter, softened
1 clove garlic, peeled and crushed
50g/2oz ground almonds
2 tablespoons chopped parsley
1 tablespoon dry sherry
1 tablespoon olive oil
1 tablespoon white wine vinegar
salt and pepper

Serves 4

Use some of the butter to grease a shallow, ovenproof dish.

Wash the salmon fillet and dry with kitchen towel. Cut into 4 even-sized fillets. Lay the salmon, skin side down, in the buttered dish. Sprinkle the salmon with the lemon juice and some salt.

In a basin, mix together the remaining butter, garlic, almonds, parsley and sherry. Use this almond butter to top the salmon fillets.

Hang the shelf on the third set of runners from the top of the roasting oven and slide in the dish of salmon. Bake for 10–15 minutes, until the crust is golden and the salmon is cooked.

Mix together the olive oil and vinegar and sprinkle over the salmon. Dust with pepper and serve immediately.

Cook's notes
This dish can be prepared in advance ready to bake just before serving.

February 11

Butter Digestive Biscuits

With the advent of multi-flavoured 'cookies', my palate sometimes cries out for a plainer biscuit; something that feels more wholesome and perhaps less indulgent. Wholemeal digestive biscuits fit the bill.

75g/3oz plain wholemeal flour
25g/1oz plain flour
pinch salt
1/2 teaspoon baking powder
15g/1/2oz oatmeal
50g/2oz butter
25g/1oz caster sugar
2–3 tablespoons milk

Put all the dry ingredients together in a mixing bowl and mix well. Rub in the butter until you have a consistency of fine breadcrumbs. Stir in enough milk to make a firm dough. Turn the dough out onto a lightly floured work surface and knead to make the dough smooth. Roll out the dough thinly and stamp out rounds with a $6^1/_2$cm/$2^1/_2$-inch cutter.

Place the biscuits on a baking tray lined with Bake-O-Glide. Prick the biscuits well with a fork.

For a two-oven Aga, put the shelf on the floor of the roasting oven and slide on the baking tray. Put the cold shelf on to the third set of runners from the top. Bake the biscuits for 15–18 minutes, until pale golden brown.

For a three- or four-oven Aga, put the shelf on the bottom set of runners of the baking oven and slide in the baking tray (or put directly on the runners if it is an Aga tin). Bake for 15–20 minutes until the biscuits are a pale golden brown.

Move the biscuits to a cooling rack to become firm.

Cook's notes
Only store in an airtight container when completely cold.

February
12

Spice-Crusted Chicken with Rose Harissa

I have served this brilliant chicken dish hot and also cold – it works well both ways. Chicken breasts are very popular but can lack flavour and be rather dry – the marinating overcomes the problem.

6 chicken breast fillets, skinless
2 teaspoons cumin
2 teaspoons coriander
4 tablespoons olive oil

For the dressing
1 teaspoon rose harissa
4 tablespoons vinaigrette dressing,
  mixed with 1 tablespoon
  tomato purée

300g/10^1/$_2$ oz cherry tomatoes,
  halved

To serve
canned flageolet beans, drained
  and rinsed
cooked green beans

Serves 6

Mix together the cumin and coriander. Slice each chicken breast horizontally into 2 thin slices and rub with the spice mixture. Leave to infuse for 1–2 hours.

Lay the chicken slices on a baking tray lined with Bake-O-Glide and brush each one with some olive oil. Hang the tray on the second set of runners from the top of the roasting oven and bake the chicken for 10–12 minutes. Move to the floor for of the oven for 5 minutes, the chicken should be cooked through with any juices running clear.

Meanwhile, pour any remaining olive oil into a shallow pan with the rose harissa and 4 tablespoons of water and the salad dressing. Slowly bring to the boil on the simmering plate and add the tomatoes. Cook for 1–2 minutes.

Slice the chicken and serve on a bed of flageolet and green beans with the tomato sauce spooned over.

Cook's notes
Rose harissa is milder than a standard harissa paste, adding a more gentle flavour.

February
13

Cauliflower Soufflés

Cauliflower has a very distinctive flavour and can be an acquired taste. I must say though that I don't understand how anyone can resist those beautiful creamy florets sitting snugly in their green, leafy coat? If you buy a large cauliflower, use some florets for this recipe and the rest for a crunchy winter salad.

225g/8oz cauliflower florets
salt and pepper
40g/1$\frac{1}{2}$oz butter
40g/1$\frac{1}{2}$oz flour
200ml/7fl oz milk
1 good teaspoon mustard
110g/4oz good Cheddar cheese, grated
4 eggs, separated

Makes 4–8

Butter 8 small or 4 medium ramekins. Stand them on a baking tray.

Put the cauliflower in a saucepan with a pinch of salt. Add enough water to come 2$\frac{1}{2}$cm/1 inch up the sides of the pan. Put the pan to boil and cook the cauliflower for 2 minutes on a fast boil. Drain all the water off and put the pan in the simmering oven for 10 minutes or until the cauliflower is cooked.

Meanwhile put the butter, flour, milk and salt and pepper into a saucepan. Stand on the simmering plate and whisk constantly until a smooth, glossy sauce has been formed. Remove from the heat and add the mustard. Mix the sauce with the well drained cauliflower and blend together in a processor or with a stick blender.

Tip the cauliflower mixture into a bowl and beat in the grated cheese and the egg yolks.

Whisk the egg whites until white and fluffy. Beat 1 tablespoon of egg white into the sauce and then gently fold in the rest of the egg whites. Spoon the mixture into the prepared ramekins.

Wipe the edge of the ramekins to ensure the soufflés can rise.

Hang the tray on the second set of runners from the bottom of the roasting oven and bake for 20–25 minutes until risen, golden and firm to the touch.

Serve immediately.

Cook's notes
If you don't have a food processor or stick blender to hand, you can use a potato masher instead, provided that the cauliflower is well cooked.

Passion Cake

I have had to include this recipe here even though it appears in my
Traditional Aga Cookery Book because it is simply so popular. I now
usually make it in the small roasting tin and then cut it into squares.
I am not sure why it bears the name 'Passion Cake' – perhaps because it
is so moist and luscious and we become passionate for the cake – or the
cook! I do know though that this is the best carrot cake ever, and I
doubt there is a more aptly named sweet to serve on February 14th!

275g/10oz plain flour
1 level teaspoon salt
1 level teaspoon bicarbonate of soda
2 level teaspoon baking powder
175g/6oz soft brown sugar
3 eggs, beaten
2 ripe bananas, peeled and
  mashed
175g/6oz grated carrot

50g/2oz finely chopped walnuts
175ml/6fl oz light corn oil

For the frosting
75g/3oz butter
75g/3oz cream cheese
175g/6oz icing sugar
1/2 teaspoon vanilla essence
walnut halves to decorate

Line the small roasting tin with Bake-O-Glide.

Put the flour, salt, bicarbonate of soda and baking powder into a
mixing bowl. Add the sugar and chopped nuts. Add the eggs, add
mashed bananas and grated carrot. Add the corn oil and beat the
mixture well to make a soft cake batter.

Spoon the mixture into the prepared roasting tin.

For a two-oven Aga, hang the tin on the bottom set of runners of the
roasting oven. Slide the cold shelf on to the third set of runners from
the top of the oven and bake the cake for 25–30 minutes, until risen and
firm to the touch.

For a three- or four-oven Aga, hang the tin on the second set of
runners from the bottom of the baking oven. Bake the cake for
30–35 minutes, until risen and firm to the touch.

Turn the cake onto a cooling rack and cool.

To make the frosting, beat the butter and cheese together until soft.
Beat in the sieved icing sugar and vanilla essence to make a soft and
creamy frosting. Spread the icing over the top of the cake and cut into
squares. Decorate with either whole or chopped walnuts.

Cook's notes

Make sure the cake is completely cold before decorating. As this cake is
moist and has a cheese frosting I like to keep any leftovers in the fridge
or a cold pantry.

February

15

Braised Carrots with Parmesan

This way of cooking carrots adds flavour when you want to serve them with plainly cooked meat or fish.

700g/1¹/₂lbs carrots, peeled
50g/ 2oz butter
salt
pinch sugar
3 tablespoons grated Parmigiano
  Reggiano cheese

Serves 6

Slice the carrots into 1cm/¹/₂-inch discs. Put the carrots in a shallow pan, cover with a minimum of water. Bring the carrots to the boil on the boiling plate, boil for 1 minute and then drain off all the water. Add the butter, a little salt and the pinch of sugar.

Put the pan, uncovered into the simmering oven and cook the carrots until tender. They may look brown and slightly wrinkled, which is as they should be.

Add the grated Parmesan and toss to coat the carrots. Serve immediately.

Cook's notes
This also a good way to serve late-season carrots that may not be so full of flavour.

Venison Casserole with Parsley Dumplings

This recipe has proven to be one of my family's absolute favourites. I like to serve it during the early months of the New Year. With the inclusion of the parsley dumplings there is no need to serve potatoes.

For the parsley dumplings
175g/6oz plain flour
1 teaspoon salt
2 level teaspoons baking powder
1 tablespoon olive oil
2 tablespoons chopped parsley
3 tablespoons snipped chives
100ml/3¹/₂ fl oz milk

1kg/2lb 4oz braising venison, cut into cubes
seasoned flour
2 tablespoons vegetable oil or beef dripping
175g/6oz smoked bacon, diced
2 stalks celery, diced
1 onion, peeled and chopped
2 cloves garlic, peeled and chopped
2 tablespoons redcurrant jelly
300ml/¹/₂ pint red wine

300ml/¹/₂ pint beef or game stock
1 tablespoon tomato purée
1 strip orange rind
2 bay leaves
1 tablespoon Worcestershire sauce
150ml/¹/₄ pint port
12 prunes
50g/2oz dried cherries
50g/2oz dried cranberries
225g/8oz chestnuts
110g/4oz button mushrooms

Serves 6

Toss the venison in the seasoned flour. Heat the oil or dripping in a roomy flameproof casserole and toss the seasoned venison in it. Stir in the bacon, celery, onion and garlic. Mix together the redcurrant jelly, red wine, stock, tomato purée and Worcestershire sauce. Pour over the meat mixture and bury the bay leaf and orange rind in the meat. Cover with a lid and bring to the boil on the simmering plate. After 2–3 minutes boiling move the casserole to the simmering oven for 1 hour.

At this stage the casserole can be cooled and frozen. Thaw overnight in the fridge, return to the casserole dish, bring to the boil and continue as below.

For the dumplings measure the flour, seasoning, baking powder and herbs into a container or bag and freeze with the casserole. When ready to use add the oil and milk and continue as below.

In a bowl mix together the port, prunes, cherries, cranberries, chestnuts and mushrooms. Leave to stand for an hour for the flavours to marry well.

After one hour stir the fruit mixture into the casserole and return the casserole to the simmering oven for a further 30 minutes.

Meanwhile make the dumplings. Place all the flour, a seasoning of salt, baking powder and the chopped herbs in a basin. Mix together and then add the oil and the milk. Mix together to make a firm but slightly sticky dough. Divide the dough into 6 even-sized portions and shape into rounds. Remove the casserole from the simmering oven and place the dumplings on top of the meat mixture, half submerged in the gravy. Put the shelf on the bottom set of runners of the roasting oven and put in the casserole. Cook until the dumplings are risen and cooked through, about 20 minutes.

Cook's notes
Don't add the liquid to the dumplings until you are ready to cook them as the baking powder will start working as soon as any liquid is introduced. To achieve light and fluffy dumplings make sure the dough is slightly sticky and not too dry.

February
17

Smoked Fish Risotto with Poached Egg

A softly poached egg served on top of this risotto really gets my taste buds jumping! Smoked fish and poached egg is the perfect combination.

300ml/¹/₂ pint milk
1 bay leaf
250g/9oz piece smoked cod or
  un-dyed haddock, skinned
50g/2oz butter
1 tablespoon olive oil
1 large leek, trimmed, washed and thinly sliced
2 cloves garlic, peeled and crushed
250g/9oz Arborio rice
150ml/5¹/₂ fl oz white wine
750ml/1¹/₄ pints hot vegetable stock
150g/5¹/₂oz frozen peas
2 tablespoons chopped chives
4 soft-poached eggs to serve

Serves 4

Put the milk, bay leaf and cod in an oven proof dish. Slide into the middle of the roasting oven and cook for 10–15 minutes, until cooked. Reserve the liquid and flake the fish, removing any bones. Set aside.

Heat half the butter and the olive oil in a roomy sauté pan, add the leeks and the garlic and cook for 2–3 minutes and then stir in the rice. Coat the rice well with the butter and, stirring well, add the wine. When the wine has evaporated, add half the stock. Stir until all the stock has been absorbed by the rice and then add the remaining stock. Continue stirring while the risotto is cooking, this will help to give a creamy texture. When all the stock has been absorbed, add the poaching milk, continue to cook for a further 5 minutes. Stir in the fish, peas and half the chopped chives. Cook for 1–2 minutes and then stir in the remaining 25g/1oz butter.

Serve each portion of risotto topped with a poached egg and a few chives on top.

Cook's notes
Take care not to over-season this with salt. The smoked fish and the stock may well be salty, so taste just before serving.

As with any risotto, it is important that the stock is added gradually to the rice, ladle by ladle, and thoroughly absorbed between each addition to avoid it becoming too moist.

Fudge Nut Tranche

My husband is the major nut eater in our family. This has to be one, amongst many, of his favourite puddings. This flan is made in a tranche tin but it can easily be made in a 28cm/11-inch round flan tin.

For the pastry
110g/4oz butter
225g/8oz plain flour
25g/1oz caster sugar
1 egg yolk
2–3 tablespoons water

For the filling
110g/4oz butter
110g/4oz skinned hazelnuts

110g/4oz pecan nuts
75g/3oz soft brown sugar
150ml/5fl oz double cream
rind and juice of 1 lemon
1 egg, beaten
175g/6oz mixed whole nuts (such
    as brazils, walnuts, hazelnuts)
2 tablespoons warm apricot jam

Serves 6–8

For the pastry, rub the butter into the flour until it resembles breadcrumbs. Stir in the sugar. Add the egg yolk and enough water to bind the ingredients together to make a firm but pliable dough. Roll the dough to line a 34 x 11 cm/14 x 4-inch tranche tin. Chill well.

Toast the hazelnuts and pecans until lightly browned on a baking tray towards the top of the roasting oven: watch them carefully. Cool and chop roughly.

Cream the butter and sugar, stir in chopped nuts, the finely grated lemon rind, 2 tablespoons of the lemon juice, and then the beaten egg. Beat in the cream. Pour into the flan case and arrange whole nuts on top.

Bake on the floor of the roasting oven for 25–30 minutes until set.

Brush the flan evenly with warm apricot jam.

Cook's notes

A packet of dessert shortcrust pastry can be used as a substitute to making your own.

Aga *year*

Middle Eastern Shepherd's Pie

This is a really tasty way to eat minced lamb and the inclusion of parsnips makes a pleasing change to the usual potatoes.

2 tablespoons olive oil
1¹/₂ kg/3lbs 5oz minced lamb
2 onions, peeled and chopped
2 sticks celery, chopped
2 carrots, peeled and chopped
4 cloves garlic, peeled and
  crushed
2 teaspoons ground cumin
2 teaspoons mixed spice
2 teaspoons ground cinnamon
2 tablespoons flour
salt and pepper

2 strips dried orange rind
75g raisins
3 tablespoons tomato purée
150ml vegetable or chicken stock

For the parsnip topping
1kg/2lbs 4oz parsnips, peeled
500g/1lb 2oz potatoes, peeled
salt
1 teaspoon ground cinnamon
50g/2oz butter

Serves 6–8

Pour the oil into a large saucepan and stand on the simmering plate. Add the lamb and then move to the boiling plate to brown the meat and break it up. When it is browned, spoon the meat from the pan into a bowl, set aside. Add the onion, celery, carrots and garlic to the pan and cook gently to soften them but not brown them. Return the meat to the pan and add the cumin, mixed spice and cinnamon. Stir the mixture and cook for 3–4 minutes before stirring in the flour and a seasoning of salt and pepper. Add the orange rind, the raisins and the tomato purée. Stir well before adding the stock. Cover with a lid and slowly bring to the boil. When boiling move the pan to the simmering oven and cook the meat for 1–1¹/₂ hours.

Meanwhile, cut the parsnips and potatoes as usual for boiling. Place in a saucepan and pour on enough water to come 2.5cm, up the side of the saucepan. Add a good pinch of salt. Cover and bring to the boil on the boiling plate. Boil well for 2 minutes and then drain off all the water. Put the covered pan of vegetables in the simmering oven for 40–50 minutes, or until the vegetables are soft enough to mash.

When the parsnips and potatoes are cooked drain well. Add the cinnamon and butter to the vegetables and mash well.

Spoon the meat into a shallow ovenproof dish and top with the mashed parsnip mixture.

Hang the shelf on the third set of runners from the top of the roasting oven and put in the Shepherd's pie. Cook until piping hot and golden on the top, about 15–20 minutes.

Cooks notes

If you like pine nuts they go very well with the spiced lamb. Add a handful to the meat before topping with the parsnip.

Dried orange peel is often used to flavour meat dishes from the middle east and Mediterranean. Use a potato peeler to remove the rind thinly from the orange. Put the rind on a baking tray and dry in the simmering oven for 4–5 hours. When cold store in a jar.

Chicken Noodle Soup

Chicken noodle soup is wonderfully healing when you need a bit of cosseting or even when you need some light comfort after too much indulgence.

1¹/₂ litres/3¹/₂ pints chicken or vegetable stock
2 boneless and skinless chicken breasts
2 teaspoons chopped fresh ginger
2 cloves garlic, finely chopped
100g/3¹/₂oz rice noodles
4 tablespoons canned or frozen sweetcorn
4 mushrooms, thinly sliced
4 spring onions, finely sliced
4 teaspoons soy sauce

Serves 4–6

Pour the stock into a saucepan and add the chicken, ginger and garlic. Bring to the boil, cover and move to the simmering oven for 30–40 minutes, until the chicken is tender.

Remove the chicken to a board and shred to bite-sized pieces with a fork.

Return the chicken to the stock and add the noodles, corn, mushrooms and half the spring onions. Stir in the soy sauce and then simmer the soup for 3–4 minutes, until the noodles are tender.

Spoon the soup into serving bowls and scatter over the remaining spring onions.

Cook's notes
To make this soup more economical and possibly more tasty, use chicken on the bone, either breast or thighs. You will need to cook the soup longer in the simmering oven, 50–60 minutes. Try to remove the skin before cooking so that the finished soup is not overly fatty.

Chelsea Buns

These buns remind me of my teacher training days in the 1970s. It was this recipe that was thought perfect for teaching basic skills of yeast cookery and rolling out. Sadly, Chelsea buns are not made in school very often these days, but do try making them at home, they are far superior to the shop variety and quite delicious.

450g/1lb strong plain flour

1 teaspoon salt

50g/2oz caster sugar

15g/$\frac{1}{2}$oz yeast or 1 teaspoon instant dried yeast

225 ml/8fl oz lukewarm milk

1 egg, beaten

50g/2oz butter, melted

For the filling

75g/3oz soft brown sugar

175g/6oz mixed dried fruit

50g/2oz butter, melted

For the glaze

2 tablespoons caster sugar

3 tablespoons milk

Makes 9 buns

Measure the flour, salt and sugar into a mixing bowl. Stir in the dried yeast, if using, or, in a separate bowl, blend the yeast together with a little milk and then add to the flour mixture. Then add the egg, melted butter and the remaining milk. Mix to a dough and then knead until smooth and stretchy. Place in a bowl and cover with a damp tea-towel or oiled clingfilm. Stand on a trivet on top of the Aga and leave to rise until doubled in volume.

Grease and line the base of a 23cm/9-inch square cake tin. Turn the dough out onto a lightly floured worktop. Knock back lightly and then roll to a rectangle, roughly 40 x 22.5cm /16 x 9-inch. In a bowl, mix the filling ingredients together and then spread these evenly over the rolled out dough. Roll the dough tightly, from the longest side, like a Swiss roll. Using a sharp knife, cut into 9 even portions. Lay the portions in the prepared tin, cut side up. Cover with oiled clingfilm and return to the top of the Aga. Allow to rise until the dough fills the tin.

To bake, put the oven shelf on the floor of the roasting oven and slide in the tin of buns. Bake for 25–30 minutes, until the buns are golden brown and slide from the tin easily.

Prepare the glaze: heat the milk and sugar gently on the simmering plate until the sugar has dissolved. Bring to the boil and bubble well for 1 minute. As soon as the buns come out of the oven, brush them with the glaze. Cool on a wire rack.

Cook's notes

If you don't have a square tin to hand, use a 24cm/9$\frac{1}{2}$-inch deep cake tin.

Roquefort Feuilleté

This is a real favourite of mine and a dish that I find very useful as a standby. I prepare it the day before I am out to work. On my return, I simply pop it in the roasting oven, throw together a salad and have supper ready on the table in no time – who needs readymade meals?

225g/8oz onion, peeled and sliced
25g/1oz butter
60ml/4 tablespoons single cream
1 tablespoon chopped rosemary leaves
black pepper
175g/6oz Roquefort cheese
225g/8oz puff pastry
1 egg, to glaze

Serves 6

Melt the butter in a small saucepan and add the onion. Cook the onion until soft and just starting to colour. Drain on kitchen paper and cool.

Pour the cream into a basin and add the rosemary leaves and a grinding of pepper. Crumble in the cheese. Mix well.

Cut the pastry in half. Roll one piece to an oblong about 30.5 x 20.5cm/ 12 x 8-inch. Lay on a baking tray. Spread the onions down the centre of the pastry and spread on the cheese mixture, leaving a border all round.

Roll the second sheet of pastry a little larger than the first piece. Brush the border of the base sheet of pastry with the beaten egg and lay over the second sheet of pastry. Seal and knock up the edges and glaze the feuilleté. Cut 3 small air holes in the top.

Hang the tray on the third set of runners from the top of the roasting oven and bake for 15–20 minutes until evenly golden brown and risen. Then move the tray to the floor of the oven and cook for a further 5–10 minutes to crisp the base.

Cool slightly before cutting. Serve with a green salad.

Cook's notes
Put Bake-O-Glide on the baking tray as a liner to make washing-up easier. It will last for years, providing you don't cut it with a sharp knife.

Oriental 'Paella'

As the name implies this is a real East meets West dish.
Serves 6

500g/1lb 2oz mussels, cleaned, debearded and any damaged ones discarded
350g/12oz hake or pollock fillets, skinned and cut into 5cm/ 2-inch pieces
110g/4oz tiger prawns, cooked
12 shell-on Atlantic prawns, cooked
bunch spring onions, trimmed and sliced
1 clove garlic, peeled and crushed
110g/4oz shitake mushrooms, quartered

2 tablespoons vegetable oil
400g/14oz paella rice
1$^1/_2$ teaspoons turmeric
1 small red chilli, deseeded and chopped
2 tablespoon Thai fish sauce
1 red pepper, deseeded and cut into short strips
4 tablespoons roughly chopped coriander
110g/4oz bean sprouts
2 limes, quartered
salt and pepper

Despite the value traditionally assigned to pollock – 'pollock for the puss/coley for the cat' – the fish has, in recent years, become far more popular and readily available. It is a full, white-fleshed fish and a far more sustainable alternative to cod and haddock, both of which are currently in danger from over-fishing. Other names for the common Pollock include European Pollock, Atlantic Pollack, Lieu Jaune, coalfish and coley. It is a mild, delicate-tasting fish with a slightly coarse texture, and perhaps a little more taste than cod, due in part to its higher oil content.

Put the mussels in a pan with 100ml/3$^1/_2$ fl oz water, cover with a lid and cook on the boiling plate for 5 minutes, shaking the pan from time to time, until the mussels are opened. Discard any unopened mussels. Remove the empty top shells from 12 mussels and the meat from the rest. Set aside. Pour the mussel juice into a measuring jug and make up to 1$^1/_5$ litres /2 pints with boiling water.

Heat a paella dish on the boiling plate and add the oil. Cook the onions, garlic and mushrooms, stirring for about 4 minutes. Stir in the rice, turmeric and chilli. Stir well to mix and then pour on the hot mussel liquid and the Thai fish sauce. Season and bring to the boil. Move to the simmering plate and cook for 15 minutes, stirring frequently. Add the red pepper, the hake or pollock, cook for 2 minutes and then stir in the mussel meat, tiger prawns, coriander and bean sprouts. Cook for 2 minutes. By this time the liquid should have been absorbed by the rice and the rice will be soft but slightly chewy in the middle.

Garnish the paella with the shell-on prawns, the mussels in their shells and the lime wedges.

Cook's notes
Serve the paella as soon as it is cooked. Leaving shellfish and rice somewhere warm is not a good idea!

Almond Marmalade Tart

The tang of the marmalade makes this tart popular with those who don't like their desserts too sweet.

For the pastry
200g/7oz plain flour
1 tablespoon icing sugar
100g/3¹/₂ oz butter, diced
1 egg yolk

For the filling
125g/4¹/₂oz ground almonds
25g/1oz butter, softened
2 eggs
50g/2oz caster sugar

2 tablespoons brandy or orange
  liqueur
75ml/3fl oz single cream
grated rind and juice of 1orange
4 tablespoons fine-cut
  marmalade

For the glaze
1 tablespoon marmalade
1 tablespoon brandy or orange
  liqueur

Serves 8

Make the pastry. Put the flour and icing sugar into a bowl and add the chilled butter. Rub the butter into the flour until the mixture resembles breadcrumbs. Add the egg yolk and enough cold water to bind the mixture together and make a firm dough.

Roll the pastry out to line a 23cm/9-inch shallow flan tin. Chill.

When the pastry case is chilled, spread the base with the marmalade.

Put the almonds, butter, beaten eggs, brandy and the cream in a basin. Grate in the rind of the orange and squeeze in the juice. Beat the mixture together until smooth. Spoon over the marmalade in the pastry case.

Put the tart on the floor of the roasting oven and slide the cold shelf on to the second set of runners from the bottom of the oven. Bake for 20–25 minutes until set and the pastry is golden brown.

Mix the marmalade and brandy for the glaze in a basin and stand at the back of the Aga to warm.

Remove the tart from the tin onto a serving plate and brush over the warm marmalade glaze.

Cook's notes

I find rolling the pastry as soon as it is made easier to do than after chilling. Be sure to give the pastry time to rest and chill before baking. If short of time you can pop the pastry in the freezer briefly.

25

Sultana and Nut Pilaf

Sometimes rice needs some additional flavourings to help it along, especially if it is to be served with plain foods such as fish or grilled meats. If you need colour as well, simply add a few strands of saffron to the water to give the rice both a golden colour and an extra flavour.

2 tablespoons vegetable oil
1 onion, finely chopped
2 sticks celery, finely chopped
225g/8oz long grain rice
600ml/1 pint vegetable stock
175g/6oz sultanas
110g/4oz pistachios
2 spring onions, finely sliced

Serves 4

Heat the oil in a saucepan and sauté the onion and celery until soft but not browning. Add the rice and stir well to coat in the oil. Stir in the sultanas and pistachios and then add the stock. Bring to the boil. Cover and move to the simmering oven for 20 minutes (or 30 minutes if using brown rice).

Check that all the liquid has been absorbed and the rice is cooked. Taste and adjust the seasoning. Stir in the spring onions and serve.

Cook's notes
If there is any pilaf left don't be tempted to re-heat it. Simply pour over a little oil and lemon juice dressing and serve it cold as a salad.

Mascarpone and Gorgonzola Tart with Balsamic Onions

Caramelised onions complement savoury dishes very well and go particularly well with this smooth and creamy tart. Serve the tart warm or cold but in small slices as it is very rich. I have suggested using readymade pastry here, but you could of course make your own.

For the balsamic onions
3 tablespoons olive oil
500g/1lb red onions, peeled and sliced
2 tablespoons soft brown sugar
1–2 tablespoons balsamic vinegar

For the tart
1 pack chilled, readymade shortcrust pastry
4 eggs
500g tub mascarpone
225g/8oz Gorgonzola cheese

Serves 6–8

You should make the balsamic onions a day before they are needed and keep them in the fridge.

Heat the oil in a saucepan and add the onions. Stir well and cover with a lid. Heat for 1 minute on the simmering plate and then move to the simmering oven for 40–50 minutes or until the onions are very soft. Add the sugar and cook, stirring, until slightly caramelised. Stir in the vinegar and cook for a further 5–10 minutes until thick. Cool and then store in the fridge for use the following day.

Roll the pastry out and line a 23cm/ 9-inch flan tin. Chill.

Put the eggs and cheeses in a food processor or blender and whiz until smooth. Season with salt and pepper. Pour into the pastry case.

Put the tart on the floor of the roasting oven and put the cold shelf onto the second set of runners from the bottom. Bake for 25–30 minutes until set and golden.

Cook's notes
Try not to rush the onions caramelising as there is a real danger that they will burn and become bitter. Though there isn't enough vinegar to store the onions safely in a cupboard, they will keep well in the fridge.

February
27

Orange and Vanilla Custard Tart

Custard tart with a twist. My husband is very keen on custard tart and until we had an Aga I always told him they were something I couldn't make without them leaking. Now I make all sorts of tarts with a custard filling and this is one of his favourites!

350g dessert shortcrust pastry
3 eggs
110g/4oz caster sugar
pulp and seeds from 2 vanilla pods
finely grated rind 1 orange
2 rounded tablespoons cornflour
$^{1}/_{2}$ teaspoon freshly grated nutmeg
200ml/7fl oz milk
200ml/7fl oz crème fraîche
3 tablespoons rum

To serve
1 tablespoon sieved icing sugar,
   mixed with a little grated nutmeg

Serves 6–8

Line a 23cm/9-inch shallow flan tin with the pastry. Chill.

Place the eggs, sugar and vanilla in a mixing bowl and whisk until pale and smooth. Whisk in the cornflour, orange rind and nutmeg and then whisk in the milk, crème fraîche and rum. Pour into the pastry case.

Bake on the floor of the roasting oven for 20 minutes, until the pastry is a pale golden colour and the filling set. After 10 minutes, slide the cold shelf onto the second set of runners from the top to prevent the filling browning.

Cool for 5 minutes and then remove from the tin. Serve warm or cold dusted with the icing sugar.

Cook's notes
I am not a great believer in 'low-fat', 'low sugar' products but I do find the low-fat crème fraîche is sometimes easier to mix in, as in this case.

Cheese Ramekins

These little cheese pots are similar to soufflés but easier to make. They won't rise to the same level as soufflés but are very tasty none the less.

50g/2oz Double Gloucester cheese,
  finely grated
50g/2oz Yarg, finely grated
60ml/2 tablespoons single cream
50g/2oz fresh breadcrumbs
3–4 drops Worcestershire sauce
pinch mixed spice
salt and pepper
2 eggs, separated

Serves 4

Butter 4 ramekin dishes and stand on a baking tray.

Put the cheeses in a basin with the cream, breadcrumbs, Worcestershire sauce, mixed spice, a seasoning of salt and pepper and the egg yolks. Beat the mixture well.

Whisk the egg whites until stiff and then fold into the cheese mixture. Divide the mixture between the ramekins.

Hang the baking tray on the third set of runners from the top of the roasting oven and bake for 10–15 minutes until risen and golden.

Serve immediately.

Cook's notes
Remember to remove the nettle leaves from the Yarg! This is a perfect recipe to experiment with different cheeses. Choose a firm cheese or a crumbly cheese, but not something soft.

March

1st Rich Casserole of Hare 2nd Smoked Haddock Vichyssoise 3rd Pot Roast Lamb in Cider 4th Crêpe Caribe 5th Broccoli Quiche 6th Chicken in Sherry Sauce 7th Malthouse Bread 8th Rhubarb and Orange Meringue 9th Leek and Saffron Risotto 10th Grilled Lemon and Pepper Mackerel with Lemon Pilaf 11th Baked Stuffed Mushroom Caps 12th Italian Rhubarb Tart 13th Sugar-Glazed Gammon with Butterbean Mash 14th Monkfish Stir-Fry 15th Cheesey Bubble and Squeak Cakes 16th Spicy Sausage and Tomato Ragu 17th Guinness Cake 18th Braised Chicken and Chicory 19th Onion and Gorgonzola Pizza 20th Pâté Maison 21st Almond and White Chocolate Tart 22nd Chicken with Sparkling Wine 23rd Chocolate Brownies 24th Devon Flats 25th Pot Roast Beef in Red Wine 26th Leek Tart 27th Herb-Crusted Fish 28th Ethel's Shortcake Biscuits 29th Gorgonzola Risotto 30th Ginger Cake 31st Herrings in Oatmeal

Rich Casserole of Hare

As the season draws to an end, this is a great way to make the most of hare – the meat lends itself so well to rich casseroles cooked slowly. Served with creamy, mashed potatoes and simple vegetables, this makes a wonderfully warming dish.

4 hare portions
1 bouquet garni
150ml/5fl oz rich, red wine
2 onions, peeled and sliced
25g/1oz plain flour
50g/2oz butter
1 teaspoon made mustard
50ml/5fl oz beef stock

Put the hare portions into a non-metallic dish. Season with salt and pepper, pour on the wine and bury the bouquet garni in the centre. Cover and leave to marinate for 2–3 hours.

Melt the butter in a frying pan. Cook the onion until softened, but not browned. Transfer to a casserole dish. Toss the drained hare joints in the flour and brown well in the remaining melted butter. Transfer it to the casserole.

Pour the remaining marinade, stock and mustard into the pan juices and, stirring, bring to the boil. Pour the liquid over the meat. Bring the entire casserole to the boil and then transfer to the simmering oven for 2–2$\frac{1}{2}$ hours until the meat is tender.

Place the meat on a plate and keep warm. Boil the juices to reduce to a thick sauce, then pour over the meat and serve immediately.

Cooks notes
You should be able to find prepared portions of hare in supermarkets these days.

Smoked Haddock Vichyssoise

As a nation we don't seem overly fond of fish soups, which is a terrible shame and our loss! Try this warming and delicious fish soup, a meal in itself, accompanied with some good crusty home-baked bread. I have suggested blending the soup in the recipe, but you could also serve it straight from the pan. Either way is good!

50g/2oz butter
1 large onion, peeled and finely chopped
2 small leeks, finely chopped
1 sprig fresh thyme
1 bay leaf
2 pinches best quality curry powder
300g/10$^{1}/_{2}$oz smoked haddock fillet,
    skinned and diced
750ml/1$^{1}/_{4}$ pints fish stock
150ml/5fl oz double cream
parsley, to garnish

Serves 6

Melt the butter in a large saucepan and add the onion, leek, thyme and bay leaf. Cover with a lid and cook until softened but not browned. Add the curry powder and cook for 2–3 minutes before adding the smoked haddock.

Add the fish stock and bring to the boil. Remove from the heat, take out the sprig of thyme and bay leaf. Blend until smooth. Stir in the double cream and check the seasoning.

Serve garnished with parsley.

Cooks notes

The fish takes very little cooking, so beware overcooking, which will make it tough.

Pot Roast Lamb in Cider

Lamb succumbs well to long, slow cooking and, of course, it won't dry out during its 3 to 4 hours in the simmering oven. A more mature piece of lamb works best for this; it would be a waste to use young, new season's lamb.

2.5kg/5$^1/_2$ lb leg of lamb, part-boned
250g/9oz shallots, peeled
500ml/18fl oz cider
300ml/$^1/_2$ pint water
100ml/3$^1/_2$ fl oz cider vinegar
4 sprigs thyme
4 cloves garlic, peeled and halved

Serves 6–8

Shallots are available year round in the UK, and refer to two different species of the same plant. Shallots have a sweeter and milder flavour than regular onions, and are a close relative of the spring onion. They are more expensive than other members of the onion family. Available raw, fresh or pickled, shallots grow in clusters as opposed to the single bulbs of normal onions.

Place the lamb in the small roasting tin and add the shallots. Pour over the cider, water and cider vinegar. Add the thyme and the garlic.

Hang the tin on the bottom set of runners of the roasting oven for 45 minutes and then move to the simmering oven for 3–4 hours, or until the meat is cooked through and very tender.

Lift the lamb onto a plate and keep warm. Spoon the shallots and garlic around the meat. Stand the roasting tin on the simmering plate and boil to reduce the pan juices to a sauce.

Cook's notes
If you don't have any cider to hand you can use white wine to cook this, along with white wine vinegar.

Crêpe Caribe

It's that time of year that pancakes are still on my mind – and these are oh-so-rich! They work best after a light and simple main course.

50g/2oz butter, melted
150g/5oz plain flour
150g/5oz caster sugar
2 large eggs
150ml/5fl oz tepid milk
pinch salt
1 tablespoon dark rum
finely grated rind 2 limes
double cream, rum, lime juice or sugar,
    to serve

Makes 20–30 small pancakes

Place the flour, sugar, eggs and salt in a bowl and mix in the melted butter. Beat in the milk to make the batter to a consistency of double cream. Add the rum and lime rind.

Either wipe the simmering plate with a little oil on a piece of kitchen paper or put a circle of Bake-O-Glide on the plate. Spoon on 1 tablespoon of batter per pancake – it is best to make small pancakes. You should be able to get about 5 or 6 cooked at a time. Turn each pancake over when it will lift easily from the plate and is golden brown. Cook for 2–3 minutes on the second side.

Serve warm and freshly cooked with cream, lime juice, rum or sugar.

Cook's notes

I prefer to make my pancakes directly on the simmering plate. Give the plate a good rub with a wire brush before you start to get rid of any crumbs or carbon.

Broccoli Quiche

I found this recipe helped persuade my children when young, to eat and appreciate green vegetables – I think it was due to the thin layer of tomato ketchup on the base! I still make this recipe for Aga demonstrations and it is eternally popular.

225g/8oz shortcrust pastry
1 head of broccoli florets
2 tablespoons tomato ketchup
3 eggs
300ml/$^1/_2$ pint milk
pepper
110g/4oz Gruyère cheese, grated

Serves 6

Broccoli is a member of the cabbage family – which includes numerous cabbage varieties, cauliflower and Brussels sprouts. Broccoli is at its best between October and April and comes in a variety of colours including green, purple and white.
It is typically boiled or steamed but its tightly-packed florets and pale green stalk can also be eaten raw.

Line a 28cm/10$^1/_2$-inch loose bottomed flan tin with the pastry. Chill.

Break the head of broccoli into florets and boil in a small amount of water until just tender. Drain well and cool.

Spread the ketchup over the base of the pastry case. Break the broccoli into small florets, using the stalks as well, and scatter over the ketchup.

Beat together the eggs, milk and pepper and half the grated cheese. Pour over the broccoli. Sprinkle on the remaining cheese. Bake on the floor of the roasting oven for 30 minutes, until the quiche is golden brown and set.

Cook's notes

A metal flan tin will give a crisper base to the pastry, but porcelain flan dishes also work well as long as the bottom is completely flat.

March
6

Chicken in Sherry Sauce

This is a brilliant variation of chicken in red wine.

4 chicken portions
rind and juice of 1 lemon
150ml/^{1}/$_4$ pint sweet sherry
150ml/^{1}/$_4$ pint light chicken stock
50g/2oz sultanas
2^1/$_2$ cm/1-inch cube ginger, shredded
salt and pepper
1 teaspoon cornflour blended with water
   to thicken

Serves 4

Place the chicken in a non-metallic dish and add the rind and juice of
the lemon, the sherry and stock, the sultanas and ginger, and a
seasoning of salt and pepper. Leave to marinade somewhere cool for at
least 1 hour or preferably overnight.

Place the chicken and marinading ingredients in a flameproof
casserole. Cover and bring to the boil. Move to the simmering oven for
1^1/$_2$–2 hours.

Spoon some of the juices from the casserole onto the slaked cornflour.
Stand the casserole dish on the simmering plate and pour in the cornflour
mixture and bubble to thicken the sauce.

Serve the chicken with green leafy vegetables.

Cook's notes
Lighter raisins or sultanas are best with the sherry in this dish, Lexia
raisins are particularly luscious if you can get them.

Malthouse Bread

Bread is such a homely thing to make. Choosing the flour can be fun and the dough making and kneading can be relaxing and a great stress-buster. As for the smell of freshly baked bread, there is nothing to beat it.

700g/1¹/₂lbs malthouse mixed grain flour
2 teaspoons salt
2 level teaspoons instant dried yeast
50g/2oz butter
425ml/³/₄ pint warm water
butter and flour for the tin

Makes 1 large loaf

Put the flour, salt and yeast into a large mixing bowl. Add the butter and rub it in. Pour in half the water and start stirring the ingredients together to form a dough, adding more water as needed. You need a dough that is firm but with a slight stickiness to allow the dough to absorb water during kneading and rising. When the dough has bound together enough to leave the bowl clean, place the dough on a lightly floured work surface.

Knead the dough until smooth and pliable, about 10 minutes by hand or 5 minutes in a table-top mixer.

Return the dough to the mixing bowl and cover with lightly oiled clingfilm. Stand a trivet or an Aga Chef's Pad on one of the Aga lids and put the dough on top to rise until doubled in size.

Butter a 1kg/2lb loaf tin and dust with flour.

Lightly flour the worktop and tip out the risen dough. Roll to make a smooth round and then pull the two opposite sides together to make an oblong shape. Turn over and drop the dough into the tin with the smooth side on the top. Cover loosely with oiled clingfilm and return to the top of the Aga until the dough is just rising above the top of the tin.

Put the shelf on the bottom set of runners of the roasting oven and put in the loaf. Bake for 20–25 minutes until risen and sounding hollow when tapped. Turn the loaf from the tin and return to the oven for 5 minutes to crisp the crust. Cool on a wire rack.

Cook's notes

This basic bread recipe can be adapted for any type of flour. Source the best quality flour that you can to get the best bread. If you prefer, make 2 smaller loaves, one to eat and one to freeze.

Rhubarb and Orange Meringue

I have been making this recipe for at least 30 years, so you can guess that it must be popular in the Walker household! Orange goes particularly well with rhubarb and indeed reduces the amount of sugar needed to sweeten the meringue. A dish packed full of Vitamin C.

450g/1lb rhubarb, washed and trimmed
1 orange
50g/2oz sugar
25g/1oz cornflour
2 eggs, separated
110g/4oz caster sugar, for the meringue

Serves 6

Cut the rhubarb into short lengths, about $2^1/_2$cm/1 inch long. Put into a shallow ovenproof dish.

Grate the rind from the orange. Squeeze the juice and pour into a measuring jug and top up with water to the 450ml/$^3/_4$ pint mark. Put the orange rind, cornflour and sugar into a small saucepan and slowly stir in the orange juice. Stand on the simmering plate and stir until the sauce thickens. Remove from the heat and cool slightly. Beat in the egg yolks and pour the sauce over the rhubarb.

For a two-oven Aga, put the oven shelf on the floor of the roasting oven and put in the dish of rhubarb. Slide the cold shelf onto the third set of runners from the top of the oven. Bake for 20 minutes.

For a three- or four-oven Aga, put the shelf on the bottom set of runners of the baking oven and put in the rhubarb dish. Bake for 25 minutes.

Make the meringue. Whisk the egg whites until stiff and whisk in the caster sugar one teaspoonful at a time. Pile the meringue onto the rhubarb mixture and return to the oven for 15–20 minutes, until golden brown and the rhubarb is soft.

Cook's notes
If you are using the cold shelf, it may need to be moved higher once the meringue is topping the rhubarb, so allow for some rising space.

Leek and Saffron Risotto

A chill March day will be warmed making a risotto and this fits the bill for something simple but sustaining.

25g/1oz butter
1 tablespoon olive oil
500g/1lb 2oz leeks trimmed, washed
  and finely sliced
2 cloves garlic, peeled and crushed
225g/8oz saffron risotto rice
1 sprig rosemary
1 litre/1³/₄ pints vegetable stock, hot
25g/1oz flaked almonds
2 tablespoons pumpkin seeds
salt and pepper

Serves 4

In a roomy frying pan, heat the oil and the butter. Fry the leeks and the garlic for 3–4 minutes until soft but not brown. Stir in the rice and coat well with the buttery mixture. Add the sprig of rosemary. Stir in the stock, and when the rice has just about absorbed all the liquid, add another ladleful. Continue like this, stirring constantly for 15 minutes or so, or until the rice is cooked but still has a little bite to it.

Put the almonds and the pumpkin seeds on a baking tray in the top of the roasting oven. Toast lightly.

Remove the sprig of rosemary from the risotto and adjust the seasoning. Scatter the toasted almonds and pumpkin seeds over the rice and serve immediately.

Cook's notes
If you can't find saffron risotto rice, then soak some saffron strands in the hot stock.

Grilled Lemon and Pepper Mackerel with Lemon Pilaf

Mackerel is a great British fish that was once hugely popular. I can remember eating and enjoying it frequently as a child. Now you often have to search hard for a fishmonger who has it really fresh – and fresh is very important with mackerel!

2 lemons
1 tablespoon peppercorns, crushed
4 mackerel, filleted
200g/7oz Basmati rice
2 teaspoons vegetable bouillon powder
1 small red onion, peeled and chopped
2 tomatoes, peeled, seeded and chopped
4 tablespoons chopped parsley
1 tablespoon olive oil, plus a little to
    oil the cooking pan
salt

Serves 4

Grate the zest from the lemons. Set aside.

Squeeze the juice from one lemon and pour into a shallow, non-metallic dish. Cut a few slashes through the skin of the mackerel fillets and lay flesh-side down in the dish with the lemon juice. Set aside until ready to cook.

Measure the rice in a measuring jug, add the bouillon powder and put in a saucepan. Measure in $1^1/_2$ times the volume of the rice in water and add to the pan. Cover the pan and bring to the boil and then put the pan in the simmering oven for 12–15 minutes, until the rice is cooked and has absorbed all the water.

Remove the pith from the remaining lemon and chop the flesh. Add the lemon flesh, chopped red onion, prepared tomatoes, parsley and olive oil to the cooked rice and gently stir through. Keep warm at the back of the Aga until the fish is cooked.

Remove the fish from the lemon juice and pat dry. Mix half the lemon zest with the crushed peppercorns. Press the peppercorn mixture onto the fillets of fish. Line a flat baking tray. Place the fish, skin-side up, on the tray. Hang the baking tray on the second set of runners from the top of the roasting oven and cook until the fillets are cooked, 6–10 minutes depending upon the size of the fillets. Spoon some pilaf onto a plate and serve 2 mackerel fillets per portion. Scatter over the remaining lemon zest.

Cook's notes

Don't add any salt to the rice before cooking if you are using a commercial bouillon stock. Taste for seasoning after cooking as these bouillons can be salty.

Grind the peppercorns with a pestle and mortar to ensure that you get nice coarse pieces of black pepper with which to coat the fish.

Baked Stuffed Mushroom Caps

In the Bath Farmer's Market we have a stall selling the most wonderful mushrooms. The smell of the tasters sizzling in butter first thing on Saturday morning really gets the taste buds going. I often succumb, though I fail miserably to persuade the men in my family to join me. So it just means all the more for me!

25g/1oz dried porcini mushrooms
6 tablespoons fresh breadcrumbs
4 tablespoons milk
6 large mushrooms, for stuffing
110g/4oz pancetta
4 anchovy fillets
4 basil leaves, torn into small pieces
1 clove garlic, peeled and finely chopped
1 egg
3 tablespoons chopped parsley
$1/_4$ teaspoon chopped marjoram
salt and pepper
6 tablespoons olive oil

Serves 6

Put the dried mushrooms in 500ml/16 fl oz warm water and leave to soak for 30 minutes.

Put the fresh breadcrumbs and the milk in a basin to soak.

Wipe the fresh mushrooms with damp kitchen paper. Remove the stalks carefully. Reserve. Butter a shallow ovenproof dish large enough to lay the mushrooms in a single layer. Place the mushrooms in the prepared dish.

Line a sieve with kitchen paper and stand over a saucepan. Strain the soaking mushrooms through the sieve. Rinse the reconstituted mushrooms, making sure there is no grit. Add them to the liquid in the pan and place on the boiling plate and cook briskly until the liquid has boiled away.

Finely chop the mushrooms. Chop the reserved stalks, the pancetta and the anchovy fillets. This can be done in a food processor. Add the basil leaves and chopped garlic. Squeeze the milk from the breadcrumbs and add to the remaining ingredients. Finally, add the parsley and marjoram, salt and pepper and the egg. Mix the stuffing well.

Stuff the mushroom caps with the stuffing, making a rounded filling. Drizzle over the olive oil.

Hang the shelf on the second set of runners from the bottom of the roasting oven and put in the dish of mushrooms. Bake for 30 minutes.

Allow to set for a few minutes before serving.

Cook's notes

The dried porcini add depth of flavour to this dish. When you buy them, the packet seems very small but expensive. Don't worry: a little goes a long way.

Italian Rhubarb Tart

Rhubarb is coming into its own in March and this delectable tart shows it off perfectly, aided by a lovely, sugary topping. I suggest baking just before serving, as the rhubarb tends to soften the topping if left to stand for too long.

225g/8oz shortcrust pastry
2 eggs
150g/5$^1/_2$oz caster sugar
grated rind 1 orange
400g/14oz rhubarb, trimmed and sliced
vanilla sugar or icing sugar, to dust

Serves 6–8

Line a 23cm/9-inch flan tin with the pastry. Chill
   Scatter the rhubarb slices over the base of the pastry case.
   Beat together, using an electric mixer, the orange rind, eggs and the caster sugar until pale and fluffy. Pour over the rhubarb.
   Slide the tart onto the floor of the roasting oven and the cold shelf onto the second set of runners from the bottom.
   Bake the tart for 25–30 minutes, until the filling is set.
   Cool and then dust with sugar. Serve while warm.

Cook's notes
Cut older rhubarb into thinner slices than the new season's pink crop.

Sugar-Glazed Gammon with Butterbean Mash

Gammon when cooked in the Aga cannot be beaten! I simply cannot understand why gammon joints are so often neglected – the joint is delicious hot and goes a long way when cold and keeps well in the fridge. If your butcher cures his own hams, check with him to see if the joint needs soaking prior to cooking.

Gammon is available in the UK all year round, and refers to the thigh and rump of a pig. Although ham can be cooked and served fresh, most ham is cured. Ham can either by wet or dry-cured. A dry-cured ham has been rubbed in a mixture containing salt and other ingredients. Following this, the meat is dried and aged. Wet-curing involved immersing the meat in brine for an extended period. This process is also commonly followed by light smoking.

1 kg/1¹/₄lb joint smoked gammon
600ml/1 pint dry cider
2 tablespoons Demerara sugar
¹/₂ teaspoon mustard powder
6 cloves

For the butterbean mash
2 bunches spring onions, trimmed and
   finely chopped
2 x 410g cans butter beans, drained
2 tablespoons olive oil
2 cloves garlic, peeled and crushed
2 tablespoons crème fraîche
salt and pepper

Serves 4–6

Cook's notes
If you are not a great lover of butter beans then you could substitute them for other canned beans such as flageolets.

If you have gammon from a good butcher, the gammon may be traditionally cured, so soak in water overnight. Drain.

Place a trivet or old saucer in the base of a saucepan large enough to hold the joint. Place the meat in the pan and pour over the cider. Cover with a lid and stand on the simmering plate. Allow the liquid to come to the boil and then simmer for 20–30 minutes. Move to the simmering oven and cook for 2 hours.

Remove the gammon from the saucepan and cool slightly. Peel off the skin. Mix together the sugar and mustard to make a paste. Score the fat of the gammon and spread over the paste. Spike the fat with the cloves.

Line a small roasting tin with Bake-O-Glide and stand in the gammon joint. Cover the lean meat with a little foil to stop it drying out.

Hang the tin on the third set of runners from the top of the roasting oven and bake to form a nice golden crust, about 15–20 minutes.

Prepare the butterbean mash. Heat the olive oil in a frying pan and cook the onions and garlic until soft but not brown. Whiz the butter beans in a food processor until smooth and then add the onion mixture. Return to the pan and heat through. Just before serving, stir through the crème fraîche and season to taste.

93

Monkfish Stir-Fry

Monkfish is not only very delicious but is also an extraordinarily useful fish as it has a firm texture and stands up well to the extreme rigours of stir-frying. However, it has become increasingly expensive so cooking it with a lot of flavours and vegetables will help make it go further and ease the pain of the fishmonger's bill! I find monkfish is at its best if you can find time to marinate it for a few hours prior to cooking.

350g/12oz monkfish – or other firm,
*   white fish – skinned and trimmed*
juice 1 lemon
2 tablespoons hot red pepper oil or a few
*   shakes Tabasco and 2 tablespoons olive oil*
1 tablespoon tomato purée
8 spring onions, trimmed and sliced
1 red pepper, de-seeded and finely sliced
225g/8oz baby corn
noodles to serve

Serves 6

Wash the fish and pat dry on kitchen paper. Trim into $2\frac{1}{2}$cm/1-inch cubes. In a bowl mix together the lemon juice, tomato purée and the hot red pepper oil. Toss in the fish, mix well and cover. Leave to marinade for 2–3 hours in the fridge.

Heat a wok or large frying pan. Stir in the lightly drained fish. Stir well and add the onions, pepper and corn. Keep stirring for 1–2 minutes until cooked. Add the remaining marinade and heat through.

Cook's notes
Make sure that the wok is absolutely clean and the surface clear before placing it on the boiling plate to heat through for at least 10 minutes prior to use.

Cheesey Bubble and Squeak Cakes

Bubble and squeak is, of course, the classic British 'leftovers' dish.
I think it comes into its own when using a variety of winter vegetables.
Adding cheese makes these flavour-filled cakes a meal in themselves.

700g/1¹/₂ lbs potatoes
350g/12oz swede
1 large leek, trimmed and shredded
225g/8oz cabbage, finely shredded
1 tablespoon vegetable oil
1 large carrot, peeled and grated
1 egg yolk
175g/6oz Raclette or Gruyère cheese,
  cut into 4 cubes
1 tablespoon flour
4 tablespoons oil, to fry

Serves 4

Peel and dice the potato and swede and place in a saucepan with
2.5cm/1-inch water. Bring to the boil, drain off all the water. Put the
covered pan in the simmering oven for 30 minutes, or until the
vegetables are soft enough to mash. Drain any excess moisture and
roughly mash the potatoes and swedes.

Heat the tablespoon of oil in a large sauté pan and add the leek and
cabbage. Sauté until softening but not browning and then add the carrot
and the mashed potatoes and swede. Remove from the heat and stir in
the egg yolk.

Divide the mixture into 4. Wet your hands and flatten out a portion of
potato mixture. Place a portion of cheese in the middle and mould the
potato mixture round it. Dust each cake with flour.

Heat 2 tablespoons of oil in a frying pan on the floor of the roasting
oven. Fry the four bubble and squeak cakes on one side until brown.
Add more oil to the pan, if needed, and then cook the second side until
golden brown, about 10 minutes in all.

Serve immediately so that the cheese oozes when the Bubble and
Squeak cakes are cut.

Serve with baked tomatoes.

Cook's notes
Gruyère melts wonderfully and has a sumptuously intense flavour,
though you could substitute a good West Country Farmhouse Cheddar.

Spicy Sausage and Tomato Ragu

Using sausages, as in this recipe, is a cheats way of making meatballs. I have found this is a good dish to double up when I'm cooking for a crowd of my sons' rugby playing friends. They usually expect pasta, so the appearance of cannellini beans instead takes them a bit by surprise – but they seem not to mind too much!.

800g/1lb 12oz Toulouse and
*   Merguez sausages (or similar ones)*
4 red onions, peeled and sliced
3 cloves garlic, peeled and chopped
150ml/$^1/_4$ pint red wine
2 x 350g/400g jars spicy pasta sauce
125ml/4fl oz chicken or vegetable stock
1 teaspoon chopped thyme
2 tablespoons chopped parsley
cannellini beans or mashed potatoes, to serve

Serves 6

Skin and cut the sausages into 5cm/2-inch pieces. Brown the sausages in a large sauté pan or casserole, turning for about 5 minutes. They should cook in their own fat. Add the onion and garlic to the pan and continue cooking until the onion is softening well.

Add the wine to the pan and allow to bubble well to reduce the wine and then stir in the pasta sauce, vegetable stock and the thyme. Bring to a bubble and then move the pan to the simmering oven for 15–20 minutes.

Serve with mashed potatoes or cannellini beans, drained and mashed with a little cream and olive oil. Scatter over the chopped parsley when serving.

Cook's notes
You may, of course, like to make your own pasta sauce. Be sure to add a little chilli to it for extra flavour.

Guinness Cake

I like to make this cake for St Patrick's Day after I have sorted through my kitchen cupboards and found a few bottles of Guinness left over from Christmas cakes and puddings. You can, of course, drink any of the Guinness that is left; after all, it is famously supposed to be good for you!

75g/3oz sultanas
75g/3oz currants
75g/3oz raisins
75g/3oz cherries, halved
150ml/¹/₄ pint Guinness
110g/4oz butter
225g/8oz soft brown sugar
3 eggs, beaten
350g/12oz self-raising flour
1 teaspoon mixed spice

Butter and base-line an 18cm /7-inch deep round cake tin.

Place the sultanas, currants, raisins and cherries in a mixing bowl and pour over the Guinness. Stir and cover. Leave to soak overnight.

Cream together the butter and sugar until light and fluffy. Beat in the eggs, one at a time, adding a little flour after each addition. Fold in the flour and the mixed spice. Stir in the mixed fruit. When the fruit is well mixed in, spoon the mixture into the prepared tin. Bake.

If using the cake baker; stand the cake in the trivet, remove the hot cake baker from the oven and put in the cake. Replace the lid. Return the cake baker to the roasting oven and bake the cake for 1–1¹/₂ hours.

For the two-oven Aga, stand the cake in the large roasting tin. Cover loosely with foil from front to back of the tin. Slide the tin onto the bottom set of runners of the roasting oven. Put the cold shelf on the second set of runners from the top of the oven and bake the cake for 50–60 minutes.

For the three- and four-oven Aga, place the shelf on the bottom set of runners of the baking oven and bake the cake for 1–1¹/₂ hours.

The cake, when baked, will be risen, firm to the touch, slightly shrunk from the sides of the tin and a skewer inserted in the middle will come out clean. Cool in the tin.

This cake is best wrapped in foil and kept for 4 or 5 days before eating.

Cook's notes

If you are cooking this in a two-oven Aga without the cake baker do keep an eye on the cake, it may need turning around during baking. Don't worry, it won't sink if you open the oven door and move it.

Braised Chicken and Chicory

Chicory is a much under-appreciated vegetable and yes, it can have a certain bitterness which may explain its lack of supporters. Cooked this way it benefits from a little sugar added. I love it braised and find that it goes particularly well with chicken. In this recipe, the crème fraîche helps makes a creamy yet light sauce.

25g/1oz butter
2 tablespoons vegetable oil
12 chicken thighs
3 heads chicory
2 teaspoons brown sugar
salt and pepper
6 shallots, finely chopped
juice 1¹/₂ lemons
200ml/7fl oz dry white wine
250ml/9fl oz crème fraîche
chopped parsley, to garnish

Serves 6

Heat the butter and oil in a frying pan and brown the chicken thighs. Drain and put in a casserole. Split the chicory heads lengthways and brown in the hot pan. Toss with the sugar and allow to caramelise a little. Add to the chicken and season with salt and pepper.

Sauté the shallots in the frying pan and when softened add the lemon juice and wine. Boil for 1–2 minutes and then whisk in the crème fraîche. Pour over the chicken, cover the casserole and gently bring to the boil on the simmering plate.

Transfer to the simmering oven and cook for 1¹/₂ hours or until the chicken is tender. Check the seasoning, garnish with parsley and serve.

Cook's notes
Ensure you use a full-fat crème fraîche for the sauce as it is far less likely to 'split' during heating than the low-fat variety.

Onion and Gorgonzola Pizza

The dough for homemade pizzas is easy to make. Try it and be amazed!
I have suggested a favourite topping here but you can experiment with
whatever takes your fancy.

For the pizza base
450g/1lb strong white flour
1 teaspoon salt
$1/_2$ teaspoon dried, powdered
  yeast or 15g/$1/_2$oz fresh yeast
2 tablespoons olive oil
200ml/7fl oz warm water

For the onion and gorgonzola
  topping
1 tablespoon olive oil
1 large onion, peeled and sliced
14 anchovies
pepper
75g/3oz Gorgonzola cheese,
  chopped
1 Buffalo Mozzarella, chopped
12 black olives

Makes 4 pizzas

Put the flour and salt into a large mixing bowl. If using dried yeast add
this to the flour. If using fresh yeast blend this in a basin with a little
warm water. Cream this well and add to the flour. Add the olive oil.

Pour half the water into the flour mixture and mix the dough, using
one hand to mix and one to hold the bowl. Add more water as needed
to make a dough that is stretchy but not sticky. There mustn't be any
flour left in the bowl. When the dough leaves the bowl clean turn the
dough out onto a lightly floured worktop and knead until smooth and
stretchy, about 5–10 minutes. Return the dough to a clean bowl and
cover with clingfilm. Stand the bowl on a trivet on one of the Aga lids
and leave the dough to rise until doubled in size. While the dough is
rising, make the topping. Heat the olive oil in a shallow pan and add the
onion and 2 of the anchovies. Cook for 2–3 minutes, then cover and
cook in the simmering oven for 50–60 minutes, until soft. Return to the
simmering plate, remove the lid and cook until all the liquid has
evaporated. Season with pepper.

Divide the dough into 4 portions and roll out each portion to a circle.
At this stage decide how thick you like your pizza bases and roll
accordingly. Place the base on a baking tray lined with Bake-O-Glide.
Scatter the cheeses over the pizza base, top with the cooked onions and
then decorate with the remaining anchovies and olives.

Bake on the third set of runners from the top of the roasting oven for
10 minutes, until the dough is crisp and the topping browning. Put the pizza
tray on the floor of the roasting oven for 5–8 minutes to crisp the base.

Cook's notes
If you are looking for new
ideas for pizza topping then
have a look in the
supermarket or the menu for
a pizza restaurant. You will
find it easy to replicate the
ideas.

Pâté Maison

Pâtés are quick and easy to make, especially if you have a food processor or an electric mincer. They taste much nicer than commercial varieties and are much more economical. This is a coarse pâté, good for picnics and cold lunches with tasty Aga-made bread or toast.

2lb/900g streaky pork rashers
¹/₂lb/225g pig's liver
4oz/100g streaky bacon
1lb/450g minced lamb or veal
2 tablespoons brandy
4 tablespoons white wine
2 cloves garlic, peeled
ground black pepper
4 juniper berries, crushed
1 teaspoon salt

Coarsely mince the pork rashers, liver and bacon. Combine in a mixing bowl all the ingredients and stir well to mix.

Put the mixture into a 2-pint capacity terrine or loaf tin.

For the 2-oven Aga, stand the oven shelf on the floor of the roasting oven, slide in the pâté tin and put the cold shelf one runner above the top of the tin. For the four-oven Aga, put the oven shelf on the third set of runners from the top of the baking oven and then put in the pâté. Cook for about 2 hours, or until the pâté is shrinking from the sides of the tin. Cool and chill before slicing.

Cook's notes
You can line the loaf tin with stretched rashers of streaky bacon before filling with the mixture. This isn't as convenient when it comes to slicing to fill sandwiches, but it does look attractive on a cold meats board.

Almond and White Chocolate Tart

White chocolate adds a richness to this tart that I love, especially accompanied by the fresh pineapple.

350g pack dessert pastry
110g/4oz butter
110g/4oz icing sugar
2 eggs, beaten
110g/4oz ground almonds
1 level tablespoon plain flour
100g/3^1/$_2$oz white chocolate, melted
^{1}/$_2$ teaspoon vanilla essence

For the topping
1 pineapple, peeled and thinly sliced, cut into rings and then quarters
1 orange, peeled and cut into segments
3 tablespoons apricot jam
icing sugar

Serves 6–8

Roll the pastry and line a 23cm/9-inch flan tin. Chill.

Beat together the butter and the icing sugar, gradually beat in the eggs. Stir in the ground almonds, flour, melted chocolate and the vanilla essence. Spoon into the pastry case.

Bake the tart on the floor of the roasting oven, sliding the cold shelf onto the third set of runners from the bottom. Bake for 20–25 minutes until set in the middle. Allow to cool and the filling to become firm.

Freeze at this stage if wanted. Thaw on a serving plate for 2–3 hours and complete as below.

Place the apricot jam in a basin at the back of the Aga to soften. Sieve icing sugar liberally over the pineapple. 'Grill' in a pre-heated frying or ridged pan, until caramelising. Arrange the pineapple and the orange segments on the tart. Glaze with the warmed apricot jam and finish with a sprinkling of icing sugar.

Cook's notes

The pineapple will smoke a little when it is first put onto the hot ridged pan so try and use the floor of the roasting oven to both heat the pan and do the cooking. This way the smells will be dispersed through the flue rather than into the kitchen.

Chicken with Sparkling Wine

The sparkling wine in this recipe makes a delicate and light-flavoured sauce for the chicken. Any leftover wine may be enjoyed by the cook.

2 tablespoons olive oil
25g/1oz butter
1 chicken, cut into 8 pieces
2 shallots, peeled and sliced
350ml/12fl oz sparkling white wine
150ml/$^{1}/_{4}$ pint chicken stock
pinch chilli powder
1 sprig parsley, chopped
1 sprig thyme, chopped
1 sprig rosemary, chopped
100ml/3$^{1}/_{2}$ fl oz double cream
salt and pepper

Serves 4–6 depending upon the size of chicken used

In a large frying pan or shallow casserole, heat the oil and the butter and brown the chicken portions. If you have a suitable frying pan this can be done on the floor of the roasting oven, not only will you reduce any heat loss but any splashes from the frying will be in the oven and not needing to be cleaned from the top of the Aga! When brown, remove to a plate and keep warm. To the pan add the shallots and cook slowly until softening, then return the chicken to the pan.

Pour the wine and stock over the chicken and add the chilli powder, parsley, thyme and rosemary. Cover and bring to the boil. Transfer to the simmering oven for 1–1$^{1}/_{2}$ hours, until the chicken is tender.

Lift the chicken from the pan to a warm serving plate. Bubble the pan juices on the simmering plate to reduce a little and then stir in the cream. Check the seasoning and strain the sauce over the chicken.

Cook's notes
Take care not to allow the butter to burn during the browning process as it will then impart a bitter taste to the delicate sauce.

Aga *year*

Chocolate Brownies

I make no apologies for putting this chocolate brownie recipe in from my *Traditional Aga Book of Breads and Cakes*. It is always fantastically popular whenever I make it and I modestly think it the best brownie recipe I have ever tasted! Try it and see if you agree....

200g/7oz butter
450g/1lb caster sugar
4 level tablespoons cocoa powder
175g/6oz plain flour
pinch salt
4 eggs, beaten
2 teaspoons vanilla extract
100g/3oz chocolate chips

Line the small roasting tin with Bake-O-Glide.

Put the butter in a small basin and stand at the back of the Aga until the butter has melted.

Measure the sugar, cocoa powder, flour and salt into a mixing bowl and stir to mix – I use a balloon whisk for this. Stir in the melted butter and then the eggs and vanilla extract. Try not to overmix the batter. Fold in the chocolate chips. Spoon the mixture into the prepared tin.

For a two-oven Aga, slide the tin onto the bottom set of runners of the roasting oven and the cold shelf onto the third set of runners from the bottom. Bake for 25–30 minutes.

For a three- or four-oven Aga, hang the tin on the bottom set of runners of the baking oven for 40–45 minutes.

The brownies are baked when the top looks crusty and a skewer inserted in the middle comes out clean. Cool in the tin and then cut into squares.

Cook's notes
This recipe is easy to double up for a crowd by baking in the large roasting tin.

March
24

Devon Flats

These biscuits are from a traditional Devon recipe and, as you would expect, use clotted cream instead of milk. They should be eaten with fresh fruit and more clotted cream!

225g/8oz self-raising flour
pinch salt
110g/4oz caster sugar
100ml/4fl oz clotted cream
1 egg, beaten
1 tablespoon milk

Makes about 24

Grease, or line with Bake-O-Glide, the large baking tray.

In a bowl put the flour, salt and caster sugar. Stir in the egg and the cream and enough milk to make a firm dough.

Roll out the biscuit dough on a lightly floured work surface to the thickness of two one-pound coins. Cut out circles using a $7^1/_2$cm/3-inch cutter and place the biscuits on the baking tray.

For a two-oven Aga, hang the tin on the bottom set of runners from the bottom of the roasting oven and slide in the cold shelf on the third set of runners from the top and bake for 8–10 minutes. Bake until a pale golden brown. Cool on a wire rack.

For a three- or four-oven Aga, hang the tray on the bottom set of runners of the baking oven for 10–12 minutes until golden brown.

Cook's notes
Try not to handle the dough too much when cutting out the flats, somehow the first rolling is always the best.

Pot Roast Beef in Red Wine

I suspect that a lot of people buy topside of beef because it looks lean, but I find that it can often be rather disappointing precisely because it is so lean and consequently the meat comes out of the oven overly dry. This is, however, a delicious way to cook topside or silverside – the slow and sealed cooking helps retain any moisture from the meat and vegetables. The vegetables add an extra richness to the meat and contribute to a wonderful sauce. Any cold meat leftover can be thinly sliced to make wonderful sandwiches.

2 tablespoons vegetable oil
1kg/2¹/₄lbs silverside or topside of beef
2 carrots, cut into large dice
2 parsnips, cut into large dice
1 large onion, cut into quarters
2 cloves garlic, crushed
2 tablespoons tomato purée
2 bay leaves
pinch sugar
salt and pepper
¹/₂ bottle red wine

Serves 6

Heat the oil in a flameproof casserole and brown the meat all over. Remove to a plate. Add the prepared vegetables to the casserole and sauté until just beginning to colour. Stir in the tomato purée, bay leaves, sugar, salt and pepper, and wine. Place the meat on top. Cover and slowly bring to the boil on the simmering plate. Simmer for 10 minutes and then move to the simmering oven for 3–4 hours.

The braising vegetables may be served as they are or puréed to make a sauce. Slice the meat into thick slices and pour over any pan juices.

Cook's notes
You will find that the vegetables around the meat will be very soft. I like to purée them with some stock or wine to make a sauce and serve brightly coloured green vegetables to accompany.

Leek Tart

If I have been making bread, I like to use some of the dough to make either a pizza or this Leek Tart recipe ,which makes a great alternative to quiche. This base is rather richer than a usual bread dough. Use the small roasting tin to make an oblong tart.

250g/9oz strong white flour	**For the filling**
1 teaspoon salt	*50g/2oz butter*
75g/3oz butter	*1kg/2lb leeks, sliced*
15g/^{1}/$_2$ oz fresh yeast	*salt and pepper*
150ml/^{1}/$_4$ pint warm milk	*2 eggs, beaten*
2 eggs, beaten	*150ml/^{1}/$_4$ pint double cream*

Serves 6–8

Butter a small Aga baking tray or round pie plate.

Put the flour and salt into a large mixing bowl and roughly rub in the butter. Blend the yeast with a little of the warm milk. Add the yeast, eggs and most of the milk to the flour and knead well, adding more milk as necessary to make a soft, pliable dough. Knead well for 5 minutes, then cover with a damp tea-towel and leave to rise for 20–30 minutes, until doubled in size.

Make the filling: melt the butter in a saucepan and stir in the leeks. Season and, when softening, cover with a lid and move to the simmering oven for 20–25 minutes, until the leeks are soft. Beat together the eggs, cream and salt and pepper.

Turn the dough onto a floured work surface and roll to fit the base and sides of the tin. Line the tin with the dough. Pour in the cream mixture. Remove the leeks from the saucepan using a slotted spoon to remove excess moisture. Add to the tart. Stand the tart on a trivet on the simmering plate lid for 15–20 minutes, until the pastry is puffy and the rim has doubled in size.

Bake on the floor of the roasting oven for 30–40 minutes, until the filling is set and the crust is golden-brown.

Cook's notes

Scatter some grated Gruyère cheese over the top of the filling for added flavour.

Herb-Crusted Fish

Choose a firm white fish for this recipe. Ask your fishmonger for some of the less common species, which are both under appreciated and under fished.

50g/2oz breadcrumbs
grated rind 1 lemon
25g/1oz grated Parmesan
2 tablespoons chopped parsley
salt and pepper
1 tablespoon light olive oil
4 fillets firm white fish (such as
    pollock, hoki, sea bass, John Dory)
50g/2oz butter
juice 1 lemon
225g/8oz baby spinach leaves,
    trimmed and washed

Serves 4

Mix together the breadcrumbs, lemon rind, Parmesan, chopped parsley and a seasoning of salt and pepper.

Place the washed spinach in a saucepan, cover with a lid and place on the simmering plate for 2–3 minutes, until the spinach has collapsed. Keep warm.

Heat the oil in a frying pan, one that will go in the roasting oven. Season the fish fillets and fry in the frying pan for 3 minutes. Turn over and cover with the crumb mixture. Hang the shelf on the second set of runners from the top of the roasting oven, slide in the frying pan and cook the crumbed fish for 4–5 minutes, until golden brown.

Place a pile of spinach on each of four dinner plates. Place a fillet of fish, crumb side uppermost, on top. Melt the butter in the frying pan, add the lemon juice. Mix well and pour round the fish. Serve hot.

Cook's notes
Fish cooks very quickly so be sure to get everything ready before you start cooking.

Ethel's Shortcake Biscuits

This wonderful recipe appeared in my first book, *The Traditional Aga Cookery Book*. The biscuits are named after my mother's friend, Ethel. I have not found a better recipe for delicate shortcakes.

225g/8oz self-raising flour
125g/5oz unsalted butter
75g/3oz icing sugar
2 egg yolks

Rub the butter into the flour until the mixture resembles fine breadcrumbs. Stir in the icing sugar. Add the egg yolks and work in until the mixture binds together well.

If the mixture is sticky wrap and chill the dough. If it isn't too sticky, roll out to 1cm/^{1}/$_4$-inch thickness and then stamp out circles.

Space the biscuits on a baking tray lined with Bake-O-Glide. Chill.

For a two-oven Aga, put the shelf on the floor of the roasting oven and slide in the tray. Put the cold shelf on the third set of runners from the top and bake for 8–12 minutes.

For a three- or four-oven Aga, hang the tray on the bottom set of runners of the baking oven and bake the biscuits for 10–15 minutes.

The biscuits should be a very pale gold and look dry.

Remove from the oven and, after 1–2 minutes, lift carefully onto a cooling rack until cold.

Cook's notes
I sometimes melt some chocolate in a basin at the back of the Aga and dip half the biscuit into it and leave to set on the wire rack. Delicious!

Gorgonzola Risotto

This is a wonderfully rich risotto that goes a long way. The Gorgonzola melts well to give a really creamy texture to the rice.

1.2 litres/2 pints vegetable stock
4 shallots, peeled and finely chopped
50g/2oz butter
salt and pepper
300g/10$^1/_2$ oz risotto rice
150ml/5 fl oz dry white wine
250g/9oz Gorgonzola, cut into small pieces
2 tablespoons chopped parsley

Serves 3 for a main course or 4–6 for a starter

Heat the stock and keep warm at the back of the Aga.

Put the butter and the shallots in a large, wide saucepan. Add a pinch of salt (this prevents the shallots burning so easily). Stand the pan on the simmering plate and cook the shallots until soft and translucent but not browning.

Add the rice to the shallots and stir well to coat with the buttery mixture. Pour over the wine and allow it to bubble away. Gradually add the stock, stirring well between each addition. As the rice absorbs the liquid, add more stock.

Before the rice is fully cooked stir in the Gorgonzola and stir until the cheese has melted. Continue adding the remaining stock, adding water if you run out of stock.

When the rice is al dente season the risotto, taking care not to add too much salt. Transfer to a warm bowl and scatter over the chopped parsley. Serve immediately.

Cook's notes
It is best to use shallots rather than onions for this dish as they have a gentle and mild sweetness. If you haven't got any to hand then use a medium white onion instead.

Ginger Cake

I love ginger cakes and like to try out new recipes when I can – and if they go wrong then they can always be made into a bread and butter pudding! My friend Jane has an outstandingly busy stall at our farmers' market in Bath that sells all her wonderful homemade cakes and biscuits. She has found that round cakes don't sell well where as anything in the shape of a loaf proves very popular! I don't know the reason for this but I thought I would try making this as a loaf cake for a change. You could be very extravagant and serve it sliced and buttered!

225g/8oz plain flour
½ teaspoon bicarbonate of soda
1 tablespoon ground ginger
1 teaspoon ground allspice
110g/4oz treacle
150g/5oz golden syrup

175g/6oz butter
50g/2oz soft brown sugar
150ml/5fl oz milk
2 eggs
110g/4oz crystallised stem
  ginger, chopped

Grease and base-line a 20cm/8-inch square cake tin.

Put the flour, bicarbonate of soda, ginger and allspice in a large mixing bowl.

Put the treacle, syrup, butter, sugar and milk in a saucepan and stand on the simmering plate to gently melt the butter. Stir to mix well. Pour onto the flour and spices and mix well. Beat the eggs together and beat into the cake mixture.

Spoon the mixture into the prepared tin. Scatter the chopped ginger over the top.

For the two-oven Aga, put the shelf on the floor of the roasting oven and put in the cake. Slide the cold shelf onto the third set of runners from the top of the oven and bake for 30–40 minutes.

For the three- and four-oven Aga, put the shelf on the bottom set of runners of the baking oven and put in the cake. Bake for 40–50 minutes.

The cake will be cooked when a skewer inserted in the middle comes out clean.

Cool in the tin for 5 minutes before turning onto a rack. This cake is best made a day or two before eating.

Cook's notes

If you are not crazy about ginger pieces you can leave them out or replace with a handful of sultanas.

Herrings in Oatmeal

These herrings are delicious and, of course, can be cooked in the Aga
without smelling out the whole house. A good fishmonger will remove
most of the bones and the heads from the herrings for you. Serve with
good Aga-baked wholemeal bread.

4 herrings
salt and pepper
fine oatmeal
50g/2oz butter
1 lemon, cut into wedges

Serves 4

Clean the flesh of the fish by rubbing with a little salt and rinse off.
Dry well on kitchen paper. Season the fish with salt and pepper and
coat well with the fine oatmeal, pressing it on well. Put the butter in a
frying pan or the roasting tin.

   Melt the butter in a heavy-bottomed saucepan, add the fish and then
fry until golden brown. Turn it over and do the second side – about
5 minutes per side depending on the thickness of the fish.

   Serve the drained fish with lemon wedges on warm plates.

Cook's notes
If you have time, prepare the fish at least half an hour before cooking to
allow the oatmeal to form a firmer crust.

April

1st Seed and Grain Loaf 2nd Cheese Soufflés 3rd Roast Leg of Lamb with Roasted Peppers and Courgettes 4th Rhubarb and Ginger Crumble 5th Corn and Prawn Cakes with Vietnamese Dipping Sauce 6th Five-Spice Lamb 7th Asparagus, Serrano Ham and Taleggio Tart 8th Indian Chutney 9th Chicken with Watercress Sauce 10th Steamed Lemon and Pistachio Puddings 11th Plaice Baked with Cheese 12th Pork Casserole with Herb Dumplings 13th Celery Soup 14th Gruyère and Watercress Roulade 15th Scones 16th Rabbit in Dijon Mustard 17th Provençal Bean Stew 18th Mustard and Herb-Rubbed Leg of Lamb 19th Chocolate Tea Pots 20th Hot Cross Buns 21st Squid Provençal 22nd Rhubarb Cake 23rd Braised and Spiced Topside of Beef 24th Simnel Cake 25th Easter Biscuits 28th Smoked Haddock au Gratin 27th Spring Lamb Stew 28th Pears in Red Wine 29th Potato Gratin with Leeks 30th Chocolate and Cointreau Soufflés

Seed and Grain Loaf

Homemade bread is so easy to make once you have mastered the basic recipe. It is the one thing that I get asked about time and again. I think most people make two mistakes when making bread. The first is to kill the yeast by using water that is too hot. If in doubt err on the cool side, the Aga will warm the dough. The second is failing to make the dough wet enough. When you have added the water, and before kneading, the dough needs to be slightly sticky. During kneading and rising the flour will absorb the water. If there isn't enough water then the dough won't rise enough and you will be left with a heavy loaf.

700g/1½lbs mixed grain bread flour
1½ tablespoons each sesame and poppy seeds
1 teaspoon or 1 sachet easy-blend yeast
1½ teaspoons salt
400ml/12 fl oz tepid water
3 tablespoons olive oil
1 tablespoon honey

Makes 1 large loaf

Put the flour, seeds, yeast and salt in a large mixing bowl. Stir to mix. Mix the water, oil and honey in a jug and add to the flour. Mix well to make a soft dough.

Knead the dough for 5 minutes until smooth and pliable, adding more flour if the dough is sticky. Rub a little oil round a mixing bowl and put in the dough. Cover with oiled clingfilm and stand on the top of one of the Aga lids, insulated with an Aga Chef's Pad or trivet. Leave until doubled in size.

Butter and flour the inside of a 1 kg/2lb loaf tin. Lightly knock back the dough and shape to a loaf with a smooth top. Put the dough in the tin. Cover with a tea towel or oiled clingfilm. Return the tin to one of the lids of the Aga insulated with an Aga Chef's Pad or trivet. Leave until the bread has risen to the top of the tin. Brush the top of the loaf with water and scatter over poppy and sesame seeds.

To bake, put the shelf on the bottom set of runners of the roasting oven and put in the loaf. Bake for 30–40 minutes until risen, golden and sounding hollow when tapped. Tip out of the tin and, if you like a crusty loaf, return the loaf to the oven without the tin for 5 more minutes. Cool on a wire rack.

Cook's notes
Make sure the tin is well buttered and floured thus allowing the loaf to slip out easily once baked.

Cheese Soufflés

Soufflés are often thought of as difficult to make. They're not! Just think of it as a white sauce with egg whites whisked in! The trick with soufflés is to have everyone at the table at the moment that it emerges from the oven looking spectacular!

75g/3oz butter
75g/3oz plain flour
450ml/³/₄ pint milk
200g/7oz Gruyère cheese, grated
a grating of nutmeg
pepper
6 eggs, separated
melted butter, to grease the soufflé dishes
grated Parmesan cheese, to dust the dishes

Makes 8 individual soufflés

Brush the base and sides of 8 x 200ml/7 fl oz ramekin dishes with melted butter. Sprinkle in a teaspoonful of grated Parmesan cheese and shake round to coat the base and sides. Set aside.

Put the butter, flour and milk in a, preferably, non-stick saucepan. Whisk lightly with a balloon whisk to disperse the flour. Stand the pan on the heat and whisk constantly until a smooth, glossy sauce has formed. Continue whisking while the sauce cooks for one more minute. Remove from the heat. Stir in the grated cheese, nutmeg and pepper. Stir until the cheese has melted and then beat in the egg yolks, one at a time.

Whisk the egg whites until white and fluffy. Spoon one tablespoon of egg white in to the sauce and beat in well. Gently fold the remaining egg white into the sauce taking care not to over-mix the mixture, knocking out the air. The mixture should resemble scrambled eggs.

Divide the mixture between the prepared ramekin dishes. Wipe the rim of the dish to make sure it is free of any mixture as this will prevent rising during cooking.

At this stage the soufflés can be left somewhere cool for up to 3 hours before cooking.

Put the shelf on the third set of runners from the top of the roasting oven, put in the soufflés and bake for 20–25 minutes.

The soufflés will be risen and golden but slightly wobbly when cooked.

Serve immediately.

Cook's notes
Take care not to over mix the soufflé mixture when folding in the egg whites – they are the raising agent. The mixture should look like scrambled egg and you should be able to see some egg white.

Aga *year*

Roast Leg of Lamb with Roasted Peppers and Courgettes

Cooking vegetables below a roast joint helps give the vegetables a lovely flavour. Here the courgettes and peppers add vibrant colour as well as flavour. Serve this lamb with early cropping new potatoes for a taste of the summer soon to come.

2 kg/4$\frac{1}{2}$lb leg of lamb
2 cloves garlic, sliced
1 red onion, peeled and cut into wedges
2 red peppers, quartered and seeds removed
3 courgettes, cut into thick slices
2 tablespoons olive oil

Serves 6–8

Make several slits in the lamb and insert a slice of garlic in each slit.

Stand the rack inside the small roasting tin and place the lamb on it. Hang the tin on the third set of runners from the top of the roasting oven. Calculate the cooking time at 20 minutes per 450g/1 lb plus 20 minutes.

One hour before the end of the cooking time, lift the lamb and rack from the tin and put in the vegetables. Toss in the meat juices and the olive oil. Season with a little salt and replace the lamb on the rack on top of the vegetables. Return to the oven for the remaining cooking time.

Remove the lamb from the oven. Keep the vegetables warm and allow the lamb to rest for 15–20 minutes before carving and serving with the vegetables.

Cook's notes
Any selection of vegetables can be cooked this way and as the year goes on add aubergines and tomatoes as well.

April
4

Rhubarb and Ginger Crumble

Rhubarb and ginger work together so well and are matched perfectly in this scrumptious crumble. You could substitute ginger with the rind and juice of an orange if you wanted a variation.

800g/1lb 12oz rhubarb
3 balls crystallised ginger, finely chopped
225g/8oz plain flour
1 level teaspoon ground ginger
75g/3oz soft brown sugar
110g/4oz butter, chilled and diced

Serves 6–8

The British rhubarb season begins in late winter but continues through until late spring. By May, the rhubarb loses its acidic pink appearance and becomes a darker, almost maroon colour by midsummer. As it becomes darker, the flavour becomes sharper. When used for cooking around April time, the rhubarb will require more sugar to sweeten and make it palatable. When used earlier in the year, rhubarb's brilliant pinkish-red hue makes it ideal for use in a compôte.

Trim the rhubarb and cut into 4cm/1$\frac{1}{2}$-inch lengths. Rinse and place in the base of an ovenproof dish. Scatter over the chopped crystallised ginger. Set aside.

Make the crumble. Put the flour and ginger in a mixing bowl and stir in the soft brown sugar. Rub the butter into the flour mixture until it resembles fine breadcrumbs. Spoon the crumble over the prepared fruit.

For a two-oven Aga, put the shelf on the floor of the roasting oven and put in the crumble. Slide the cold shelf on to the second set of runners from the bottom and cook for 20 minutes. This gives time for the fruit to cook through. Remove the cold shelf and cook the crumble for a further 20 minutes or until the crumble mix is golden brown and the fruit is bubbling round the edges.

For a three- or four-oven Aga, put the shelf on the bottom set of runners of the baking oven and put in the crumble. Cook for 30–40 minutes until the fruit is cooked and the crumble is golden on the top.

Serve with custard or cream.

Cook's notes

Rhubarb does not need to be swamped with sugar. In this dish the sweet crumble will contrast with the rhubarb, the ginger taking the sharpness away.

Corn and Prawn Cakes with Vietnamese Dipping Sauce

These little corn and prawn cakes are very easy to cook on the simmering plate. You can make the mixture an hour or two before cooking and keep chilled in the fridge. Of course, your guests might like to cook their own!

For the dipping sauce
2 large red chillies, stalks
   removed and halved
5 tablespoons Thai fish sauce
9 tablespoons water
5 tablespoons rice vinegar
6 tablespoons caster sugar
juice 1 lemon or 2 limes

For the corn cakes
330g can sweetcorn, drained
150g/5$^1/_2$ oz plain flour
90ml/3 fl oz milk
3 eggs, beaten
50g/2oz butter, melted
salt and pepper
350g/12 oz cooked, shelled
   prawns, roughly chopped
2 spring onions, finely chopped

Serves 6

Make the dipping sauce first.Remove the seeds from the chilli and reserve. Finely chop the flesh and add to the seeds. Set aside.

Into a small saucepan put the Thai fish sauce, water, vinegar and sugar. Bring to the boil on the simmering plate, stirring to allow the sugar to dissolve. Pour into a bowl and allow to cool. Add the chilli flesh and seeds and the juice from the lemon or limes.

For the corn cakes, put the corn, flour, milk, eggs and melted butter in a processor and whiz until smooth. Season with salt and pepper and stir in the prawns and spring onions.

Place a sheet of Bake-O-Glide on the simmering plate and drop spoonfuls of the corn cake mixture on to cook. When set and golden on the underside turn over to cook the second side.

Serve with the dipping sauce.

Cook's notes
Discard the chilli seeds if you don't like a lot of heat. Take care not to rub your eyes after preparing the chillies!

Five-Spice Lamb

Lamb is found in a lot of Middle Eastern cooking and is often spiced. Lamb is a meat that takes a variety of flavours well but try not to use a fatty piece as it will tend to drown out the spices. Allow plenty of time to make this casserole as it really benefits from a long marinade.

700g/1^1/$_2$lbs lamb, cubed
3 cloves garlic, crushed
1 teaspoon finely chopped root ginger
1 teaspoon five-spice powder
5 tablespoons soy sauce
3 tablespoons dry sherry
450ml/^{3}/$_4$ pint beef stock
25g/1oz soft brown sugar
1 tablespoon cornflour
fresh coriander leaves for garnish

Serves 6

Mix all the ingredients together, except the cornflour, and leave to marinade for 4 hours or even overnight. Pour the meat and marinade into a flameproof casserole, stand it on the boiling plate and bring to the boil Transfer to the simmering oven and cook for 1–2 hours.

Blend the cornflour with some water to make a paste. Just before serving, stir the cornflour into the casserole, allow to boil either in the roasting oven or on the simmering plate until a thick sauce is formed. Garnish with coriander.

Serve with rice or couscous.

Cook's notes
Meat taken from the leg will be fairly tender and will cook in an hour while other cuts will benefit from 1^1/$_2$–2 hours cooking.

Asparagus, Serrano Ham and Taleggio Tart

This is good to make during the early asparagus season using good thick stalks to add flavour.

375g/13oz pack ready-rolled puff pastry
225g/8oz shallots, peeled and quartered
2 tablespoons olive oil
1 tablespoon finely chopped basil leaves
500g/1lb 2oz asparagus
75g/3oz Serrano ham
225g/8oz Taleggio cheese

Serves 6

It is hard to find a variety of asparagus that measures up to home-grown British asparagus. The majority of the crops grown in Britain come from Suffolk and the Cotswolds. In the height of the season – late April to mid-June – freshly cut asparagus is hard to beat, and is far superior to that which is sold in supermarkets.

Heat the oil in a sauté pan and cook the shallots gently until soft. This can be done on the floor of the roasting oven.

Trim the asparagus of their thick stalks and plunge into boiling water for about 5 minutes, or until just cooked. Drain. Cool.

Add the basil to the cooked onions and season with salt and pepper.

Unroll the pastry onto a large baking tray. With a sharp knife, mark a border 2cm/³⁄₄-inch in from the edge of the pastry.

Spoon the shallots over the pastry and then arrange the asparagus over the onions. Tear the ham into pieces and scatter over the tart. Trim the rind from the cheese and cut into thin slices. Scatter over the tart.

Slide the tin onto the third set of runners from the top of the roasting oven and cook for 15 minutes, until the tart is bubbling and slightly golden. Move the tin to the floor of the oven for 5 minutes to crisp the base.

Serve scattered with basil leaves.

Cook's notes
To peel the shallots, place them in a basin and cover with boiling water for a minute or two and the skins will slide off easily.

Indian Chutney

This recipe has been a firm favourite in our family for many years. It gives a rich, sweet chutney, lovely with cheese and cold meats.

450g/1lb apples, peeled, cored and chopped
450g/1lb onions, peeled and chopped
450g/1lb/ ripe tomatoes
450g/1lb raisins
450g/1lb sultanas
450g/1lb brown sugar
1 teaspoon ground ginger
1 teaspoon cayenne pepper
$1^1/_2$ teaspoons fresh curry powder
50g/2oz salt
450ml/$^3/_4$ pint malt vinegar

Makes about $2^3/_4$kg/6lb

Mix the spices with some of the vinegar. Put all the ingredients in a large pan, stand on the simmering plate and heat, stirring, until the sugar is dissolved and the mixture is boiling. Transfer to the simmering oven and cook until the vegetables are soft – about 1–$1^1/_2$ hours. Return to the simmering plate and boil slowly until the mixture is thick and brown. Pour into warm, sterilised jars.

Cook's notes
Store in a cool dark place for about 4 weeks before eating to allow time for the flavours to mature.

Chicken with Watercress Sauce

Chicken and eggs were always associated with Easter. Now chicken is with us all the time and it is easy to feel we eat too much of it. This peppery watercress sauce gives the chicken a lively spring flavour and a gorgeous green colour. Needless to say, I recommend buying free-range chicken, not just for the chickens' welfare but because the meat will have a superior texture and flavour.

6 chicken breasts, preferably on the bone, with skin on
2 spring onions, chopped
50g/2oz butter
1 tablespoon olive oil
300ml/$^1/_2$ pint chicken stock
150ml/$^1/_4$ pint double cream
1 large bunch watercress, thick stalks removed
salt and pepper

Serves 6

Spring onions, also known as scallions, green onions and salad onions, belong to the same family as the common onion, but have a more subtle flavour and bright green stalks which can also be used along with the small bulb in cooking. Popular in both western and South East Asian cuisines, the spring onion can be eaten raw, steamed or grilled, and can be added to salads and many other savoury dishes.

Heat the butter and oil in a frying pan and fry the chicken, skin side down, in the pan until the skin is crispy and brown. Remove from the pan and put in a casserole. You will probably have to do this in two batches. Add the chopped onions to the pan and stir round until golden. Pour in the stock, bring to the boil and pour the pan contents into the casserole. Stand the casserole on the simmering plate, season and bring to the boil, covered. Move the casserole to the simmering oven for between 45 minutes and 1 hour, until the chicken is tender.

Remove the casserole from the oven and move the chicken to a warm plate and keep warm. Add the cream to the pan, boil and then stir in the watercress. Remove from the heat and then blend the pan contents until smooth. Check the seasoning.

Spoon a little sauce with the chicken and serve the rest separately.

Cook's notes
As the sauce is boiled, use only double cream or full-fat crème fraîche. Lower fat content creams will 'split'.

Steamed Lemon and Pistachio Puddings

Making individual steamed puddings isn't a lot of extra work but they do look smart when served and, of course, cook quickly. The pistachios in this pudding add a lovely crunch but also pretty specks of colour.

For the syrup
3 lemons
10 cardamom pods
150g/5^1/$_2$oz caster sugar
1 teaspoon arrowroot

For the puddings
100g/3^1/$_2$oz unsalted pistachios
150g/5^1/$_2$oz butter, softened
150g/5^1/$_2$oz caster sugar
finely grated rind of 2 lemons
2 eggs
150g/5^1/$_2$oz self-raising flour

Serves 6

Prepare the syrup. Pare the rind from 1 lemon, taking care not to remove the pith. Shred the rind into fine strips. Reserve for garnish.

Grate the zest finely from the other 2 lemons and set aside. Squeeze the juice of the 3 lemons.

Lightly crush the cardamom pods and remove the seeds. Place the seeds in a saucepan along with the sugar and 150ml/^{1}/$_4$ pint water. Stand on the simmering plate and stir until the sugar has dissolved. Strain through a sieve and return to the saucepan. Add the grated lemon zest and juice and boil for 5 minutes. Blend the arrowroot with a little water and pour into the syrup, stirring. Cook for 2–3 minutes and remove from the heat.

For the puddings butter 6 x 150ml/^{1}/$_4$ pint pudding basins. Reserve 12 pistachios and set aside. Chop the rest. Put the butter, sugar, lemon zest, eggs and self-raising flour in a mixing bowl and beat well until smooth. Stir in the chopped pistachios.

Put a scant tablespoon of syrup in each pudding basin and gently swirl around. Divide the sponge mixture between the basins. Cover each basin with buttered foil and stand in the small roasting tin. Pour boiling water around the puddings to come one third of the way up the side of each basin.

Put the roasting tin on the bottom set of runners of the roasting oven and slide the cold shelf onto the third set of runners from the top. 'Steam' the puddings for 30–40 minutes. Check that the puddings are cooked by inserting a skewer into the middle of one pudding. If the skewer comes out clean, the puddings are cooked.

Put the reserved lemon rind in a saucepan, cover with water and bring to the boil. Drain, refresh with cold water and then dry on kitchen paper. Dust with caster sugar. Roughly chop the reserved pistachios.

Turn out the puddings onto a serving plate, spoon over the syrup and decorate with lemon rind and nuts.

Cook's notes
Make sure you use unsalted pistachios for this recipe. If you have problems finding them unsalted then give the salted variety a thoroughly good wash before using.

April
11

Plaice Baked with Cheese

Plaice is a delicate fish and should be cooked quickly but gently. This oven method is perfect. Use a finely grated mature cheese such as Parmesan for the best taste and appearance. The plaice can easily be replaced with lemon or Dover sole; whichever is used it needs to be in thin fillets.

4 large fillets of plaice
15g/¹⁄₂oz butter
3 tablespoons dry white wine
juice ¹⁄₂ lemon
3oz/75g grated Parmesan cheese
black pepper

Serves 4

Butter a large, shallow ovenproof dish. Wash and pat dry the fish. Season it on both sides with the pepper and lay it out in the dish.

Pour the wine and lemon juice round the fish and sprinkle with the finely grated cheese.

Have the oven shelf on the floor of the roasting oven, slide in the dish and bake for 15–20 minutes until the fish is cooked and a light golden brown.

Cook's notes
Prepare the fish for the oven and pop in at the last minute so there is no danger of overcooking the fish.

April
12

Pork Casserole with Herb Dumplings

At the time of writing there is much concern about the British pig industry and how it can survive. We need to ask more questions about our food production and realise that the reason British pork is sometimes more expensive than imported products is because our farmers pay more attention to the welfare of their pigs. The result is, of course, far better quality meat. Make sure you buy best quality British pork, and not just for the Sunday roast! Here is a recipe for cheaper cuts from the pig.

1kg/2¼lbs pork shoulder steaks
2 tablespoons seasoned flour
2 tablespoons vegetable oil
2 onions, peeled and sliced
2 large carrots, sliced
4 celery stalks, chopped
600ml/1 pint chicken or vegetable stock
1 bouquet garni
salt and pepper

For the dumplings
110g/4oz self-raising flour
110g/4oz fresh breadcrumbs
110g/4 oz shredded suet
salt and pepper
1 tablespoon chopped fresh mixed herbs

Serves 6

Toss the pork in the seasoned flour. Heat the oil a frying pan and brown the meat on all sides. Transfer to a casserole dish. Add the onion, celery and carrot to the frying pan and sauté until softening. Pour in the stock and bring to the boil. Pour the mixture over the meat and add the bouquet garni and a seasoning of salt and pepper. Cover and bring to the boil. Transfer to the simmering oven for about 2–3 hours .

Prepare the dumplings. In a mixing bowl, mix together the flour, breadcrumbs, suet, salt, pepper and herbs. Bind together with enough cold water to make a stiff dough. Shape into 12 dumplings. Place the dumplings on the top of the meat, so that the base is sitting in the gravy. Transfer the casserole to the bottom set of runners of the roasting oven and cook for a further 20–30 minutes.

Cook's notes
Add the liquid to the dumplings no more that 30 minutes before putting into the casserole.

Celery Soup

Celery seems to have gone out of fashion, which is a great shame. It is such a versatile vegetable, both raw and cooked. Make sure that you look out for traditionally grown celery for the very best flavour.

1 head of celery, cleaned and sliced
1 onion, chopped
25g/1oz butter
25g/1oz flour
450ml/³/₄ pint chicken or vegetable stock
1 blade mace
salt and pepper
300ml/¹/₂ pint milk
cream, for serving

Makes enough for 6 small or 4 large portions

Melt the butter in a pan on the simmering plate, stir in the chopped celery and onion, and cook until it is soft but not coloured.

Add the flour and stir well, cooking gently for 1 minute. Gradually add the stock, mace and a little salt and pepper.

Bring to the boil, cover and place in the simmering oven for 30 minutes.

Remove the pan from the oven and take out the blade of mace. Discard. Blend the soup. Rinse the pan, return the soup to the pan and add the milk. Heat through until piping hot. Taste and season.

Serve in warm bowls with a swirl of cream.

Cook's notes
Blade mace is not as easy to get hold of nowadays so use a pinch of ground mace instead, but not too much – even a light grating of nutmeg will help lift the flavour.

April
14

Gruyère and Watercress Roulade

The fresh peppery flavour of watercress is a spring flavour that goes brilliantly with the Gruyère. It's an expensive cheese but the intensity of flavour and its ability to melt so well makes it perfect for cooking.

175g/6oz Gruyère, finely grated
50g/2oz soft curd cheese
5 eggs, separated
150ml/¼ pint single cream
50g/2oz Parmesan, grated
pepper

For the filling
250ml/9 floz low-fat crème fraîche
1 bunch watercress, trimmed, washed and dried

Serves 6 as a main course

Grown in Britain since the 1800s, the dominant British season for watercress is from October through to May. Watercress takes its name from the fact that it grows in clear running water, and has long being reputed for its health benefits. It is rich in vitamins and minerals, particularly iron, and is a proven antibiotic; the reason perhaps for Hippocrates' sighting of the first hospital by a stream in order to have it close to hand.

Line a large baking tray with a sheet of Bake-O-Glide.

Put the Gruyère, curd cheese, egg yolks, cream and a grinding of pepper in a bowl and mix together well.

Whisk the egg whites until light and fluffy. Add 1 tablespoon of egg white to the cheese mixture and beat in. Gently fold the remaining egg white into the cheese mixture until it resembles scrambled eggs.

Spoon the mixture into the prepared tin and lightly level out.

Put the shelf on the floor of the roasting oven and slide in the tray. Bake for 15–20 minutes until evenly golden brown and firm to the touch. Remove from the oven and sprinkle over the grated Parmesan. Cool.

When cold, turn the roulade onto a plain sheet of Bake-O-Glide. Spread over the crème fraîche, right to the edges, and then scatter over the washed watercress.

Have the short edge nearest you and tightly roll the roulade. Place onto a plate and leave with the furthest edge underneath to stop it rolling off the plate. Leave to set before slicing.

Cook's notes
If you don't have Bake-O-Glide use baking parchment to line the tin.
If you don't have an Aga baking tray use the large roasting tin.

Scones

Nothing beats a freshly baked scone, especially one served with homemade jam and thick clotted cream.

225g/8oz self-raising flour
25g/1oz butter
pinch salt
25g/1oz caster sugar
150–200ml/5–7fl oz milk

Line a small baking tray with Bake-O-Glide.

Put the flour in a mixing bowl and add the butter and the salt. Rub the butter in to the flour, using your fingertips, until the mixture resembles breadcrumbs. Stir in the sugar.

Using a table knife stir, in the milk, a little at a time, until a firm but slightly sticky dough is formed. Lightly knead together.

Put the dough onto a lightly floured worktop and press the dough out until it is the thickness of your hand. Stamp out scones using a sharp 6cm cutter. Place the scones on the baking tray and brush the tops with a little milk.

Hang the baking tray on the third set of runners from the top of the roasting oven and bake for 15–20 minutes until risen and golden brown. They should be just firm when squeezed round the middle.

Cool on a wire rack and eat warm.

Cook's notes
If you want scones rather than biscuits, be sure not to let a rolling pin near the mixture! You will almost certainly be tempted to make them too thin and to handle them too much!

Rabbit in Dijon Mustard

In recent years wild rabbit has become much more readily available in butchers' shops. If you don't see it on the counter, ask your butcher if he can get it for you. It is an excellent and economical meat, shown off to its best in this classic recipe.

1 tablespoon olive oil
25g/1oz butter
1 kg/2lb 4oz rabbit joints
2 small onions, finely chopped
225g/8oz mushrooms, sliced
2 tablespoons brandy
150ml/5fl oz chicken stock
150ml/5fl oz double cream
4–6 tablespoons Dijon mustard
salt and pepper
chopped parsley, to garnish

Heat the oil and butter in a frying pan and brown the rabbit joints all over. Remove from the pan. You will probably need to do this in several batches. Soften the onions and fry the mushrooms in the hot pan. Pour on the brandy, heat through and then ignite the brandy to drive off the alcohol. When the flames have died down, pour in the chicken stock and then the double cream. Leave the sauce to simmer very gently while smearing the mustard over the rabbit pieces.

Put the rabbit joints in a casserole dish and pour over the pan juices. Season with salt and pepper. Stand the casserole on the simmering plate and allow to come to the boil. Cover the casserole and then move to the simmering oven for $1^1/_2$ hours.

Remove from the oven. The rabbit should be tender. Check the seasoning.

Serve sprinkled with chopped parsley.

Cook's notes
You can use English mustard if you prefer but it does have a slightly sharper taste.

Provençal Bean Stew

Years ago I used to cook dried beans in the Aga. Now I tend to buy the beans in cans, partly to save time but also because I consider them a good buy – convenient and well cooked. This recipe was originally in my *Traditional Aga Book of Slow Cooking* but has been 'modernised'. It is a meal in itself.

2 tablespoon olive oil
1 onion, peeled and sliced
1 red pepper, de-seeded and cut into strips
1 green pepper, de-seeded and cut into strips
2 cloves garlic, crushed
1 x 400g can chopped tomatoes
2 tablespoons tomato purée
salt and pepper
2 x 410g cans haricot beans,
    drained and rinsed
12 black olives, pitted
10 basil leaves, shredded

Serves 4–6

In a flameproof casserole or saucepan, heat the oil on the simmering plate and add the onion. Cook until soft but not brown, then add the peppers and garlic. Cook until softening and then stir in the tomatoes and tomato purée and a seasoning of salt and pepper. Stir in the beans and bring slowly to the boil. Cover and move to the simmering oven for 1 hour.

Stir in the olives and sprinkle over the basil. Serve.

Cook's notes
Be sure to tip the beans into a colander and rinse well before using to remove all the canning salts.

April
18

Mustard and Herb-Rubbed Leg of Lamb

Lamb is such a versatile meat. Here, the lamb is cooked with the potatoes and carrots all in one roasting tin.

$1^1/_4$–$1^1/_2$ kg/2lb 12oz–3lb 5oz leg of lamb
4 tablespoons wholegrain mustard
4 tablespoons English mustard
2 cloves garlic, peeled and finely chopped
4 sprigs rosemary, chopped
6 sprigs thyme, leaves chopped
2 tablespoons olive oil
1kg/$2^1/_4$ lbs potatoes, peeled
3 large carrots, peeled

Serves 6

Rosemary is a perennial herb and one of the hardiest and easiest to grow. Worth growing for its appearance alone, it can withstand all types of weather and drought. Its 'pine-needle' leaves impart flavour to a variety of dishes and stuffings, and it is the herb perhaps most readily associated with roast meats, ably partnering chicken, turkey and pork, but especially, most gloriously, lamb.

Using a sharp knife, cut deep incisions all over the lamb. Mix together the mustards and the garlic, chopped rosemary and the thyme. Spread this mixture over the lamb. If time allows, leave the joint to absorb the flavours.

Place the meat in a roasting tin and drizzle over the olive oil. Hang the tin on the third set of runners from the top of the roasting oven and roast the lamb for 30 minutes.

Roughly chop the potatoes and cut the carrots into chunky lengths. Add to the roasting tin and toss in the lamb juices.

Roast the lamb for a further 60 minutes, or until the lamb is cooked through. Allow to sit in a warm place for 15–20 minutes before carving.

Cook's notes

A shoulder of lamb can be cooked this way for a cheaper roast but you may want to put it in the simmering oven for 1 hour extra at the end of the time listed above.

Chocolate Tea Pots

Serve these in pretty coffee cups or espresso cups. They are very rich so only a little is needed!

125g/ 4¹/₂ oz dark chocolate,
*   at least 70% cocoa content*
400ml/14fl oz single cream
1 tablespoon Earl Grey tea
1 teaspoon orange flower water

Serves 8

Finely chop the chocolate and put in a heatproof bowl. Scald the cream by bringing it to the boil. Add the tea to the cream and leave it to infuse for 2 minutes. Strain.

Pour the cream gently onto the chocolate, stirring to make a smooth emulsion. If the chocolate is not melting, stand the bowl at the back of the Aga just long enough to soften the chocolate. Add the orange flower water.

Pour into small coffee cups and chill for 2 hours.

Cook's notes

Take care not to let the cream burn. Once the chocolate is added don't put the pan back on the heat. If you make this in a large measuring jug with a fine spout it will be easy to pour into the little espresso cups.

Hot Cross Buns

Make these and you won't ever want to buy hot cross buns again!

Makes 24 buns

1kg/2lbs 4oz strong white flour	instant dried yeast
1 teaspoon salt	450ml/³/₄ pint warm milk
4 teaspoons ground mixed spice	
1 teaspoon grated nutmeg	**For the crosses**
110g/4oz caster sugar	4 tablespoons plain flour
110g/4oz butter	water
250g/8oz currants, sultanas or	
mixed peel or a selection	**For the glaze**
2 eggs, beaten	4 tablespoons caster sugar
50g/2oz fresh yeast or 2 teaspoons	4 tablespoons milk

Line 2 large baking trays with Bake-O-Glide or butter and flour well.

If using fresh yeast, blend with a little warm milk and then add a teaspoon of caster sugar. Stand on a warm (not hot) spot on the Aga and allow to froth while preparing the remaining ingredients.

Into a large mixing bowl measure the flour, salt, mixed spice, nutmeg and sugar. Rub in the butter. Make a well in the middle of the flour and add the currants, the eggs, the yeast mixture and most of the milk. Beat together to make a soft dough, adding milk as needed – it is easiest to use your hand for this. Turn onto a lightly floured work surface. Knead for about 5 minutes until the dough is smooth and elastic. Put the dough into a clean bowl and cover with oiled clingfilm. Stand on a trivet or an Aga Chef's Pad on top of one of the lids of the Aga. Leave until doubled in size.

Return the dough to a floured worktop, gently knock back and divide the dough into 24 equal portions. Shape each into a roll and place on a baking tray. Return to the lid of the Aga, covered again with oiled clingfilm or a damp tea towel. Leave until doubled in size. Make the crosses. Put the flour into a basin and gradually add enough water to make a smooth paste a little thicker than double cream. Spoon the paste into a plastic bag and tie the opening securely. When ready to make the crosses, snip a tiny corner from the bottom of the bag and use this to pipe crosses on to the buns. Bake on the bottom set of runners of the roasting oven for about 20–25 minutes until golden brown and sounding hollow when tapped on the bottom. Make the glaze while the buns are baking. Put the sugar and milk in a small saucepan and bring to the boil. Brush over the buns to form a sticky glaze as soon as they are taken from the oven. Cool the buns on a wire rack. Serve slit and buttered.

Cook's notes

If you want to make the dough in a mixer, such as a Kitchen Aid, then add the dried fruit after the first rising otherwise the fruit will be chopped.

Squid Provençal

It seems to me that a lot of people think they don't like squid because they have eaten it overcooked and rubbery. If you have a good fishmonger with a good turnover, the chances are that the squid will be fresh and need little cooking. This is a quick and easy recipe to try.

1 tablespoon olive oil
1 onion, chopped
450g/1lb squid, cleaned and sliced
1 clove of garlic, crushed
1 courgette, quartered and diced
$1/_2$ red pepper, seeded and chopped
2 tomatoes, peeled and chopped
salt and pepper
1 tablespoon chopped parsley, to serve

Serves 2

Heat the olive oil in a frying pan and add the onion. Cook until softening but not browning. Add the squid and garlic, stir well and then add the courgette and pepper. Cook for 1–2 minutes before stirring in the tomatoes. Cook until the tomatoes are beginning to 'fall'. Season with salt and pepper and sprinkle in the parsley.

Serve immediately

Cook's notes
If you don't fancy cleaning the squid, ask the fishmonger to do it for you.

Rhubarb Cake

I am often told how popular my 'German Apple Cake' is that appears in *The Traditional Aga Cookery Book*. So here is a springtime variation. I added ginger because I think it goes so well with rhubarb, but it can be left out if you prefer. If you have a glut of rhubarb this recipe freezes very well after baking.

110g/4oz self-raising flour
50g/2oz soft brown sugar
50g/2oz ground almonds
75g/3oz butter, chopped into cubes
1 egg, beaten

For the filling
450g/1lb rhubarb, cut into
    2$\frac{1}{2}$cm/1-inch lengths

2 pieces crystallised ginger,
    finely chopped

For the topping
110g/4oz self-raising flour
50g/2oz soft brown sugar
$\frac{1}{2}$ teaspoon ground ginger
50g/2oz butter, chopped into cubes

Cuts into 8–10 slices

Butter a 23cm/9-inch spring-release cake tin.

Make the base first. Put the self-raising flour, brown sugar and ground almonds in a mixing bowl. Add the butter and rub in until the mixture resembles breadcrumbs. Bind together using the egg. Press the mixture lightly into the base of the tin. Cover the base with the rhubarb and scatter over the ginger.

Make the topping: place the self-raising flour, sugar and ginger in a mixing bowl and rub in the butter until the mixture resembles breadcrumbs. Scatter over the rhubarb.

For a two-oven Aga, place the oven shelf on the floor of the roasting oven. Put in the cake and slide the cold shelf on the second set of runners from the top of the oven. Bake for 1 hour until the topping is golden-brown and the rhubarb is cooked.

For a three- or four-oven Aga, place the oven shelf on the second set of runners from the bottom of the baking oven. Put in the cake and bake for about 1 hour until the topping is golden-brown and the rhubarb is cooked.

Serve warm as a pudding or cold as a cake.

Cook's notes
If you have a lot of rhubarb you may like to add more to the filling.

Braised and Spiced
Topside of Beef

Here is a perfect recipe for Sunday lunch. The meat is delicious and tender to serve hot, and when cold its lightly spiced flavour makes wonderful sandwiches. This recipe is not a last minute option as the meat needs marinating for 2–3 days before cooking.

2 kg/4½ lbs topside of beef, boned
   and rolled
2 teaspoons salt
1 teaspoon ground allspice
3 teaspoons ground ginger
450ml/¾ pint cider
1 cinnamon stick
6 cloves
1 tablespoon black peppercorns,
   lightly crushed
2 blades mace
2 tablespoons olive oil
2 onions, peeled and sliced
1 large carrot, peeled and sliced

Serves 6–8

Wipe the beef and rub with the allspice and ginger. Put the cider in a saucepan and add the cinnamon stick, cloves, peppercorns and mace. Bring to the boil. Stand the meat in a non-metallic dish and pour over the cider mixture. Cool and then cover. Leave to marinate for 48 hours in a cool place, turning the meat periodically.

Remove the meat from its marinade and pat the joint dry with kitchen paper. Heat the oil in a frying pan and brown the meat all over. When brown, put the meat in the small roasting tin. Add the onions and carrots to the pan and sauté until just softening. Pour over the marinade and bring to the boil. Pour the pan contents over the meat.

Hang the roasting tin on to the bottom set of runners of the roasting oven and cook the meat for 40–50 minutes, then move the pan to the simmering oven. Cook the meat for 3–4 hours, the shorter time for slightly rarer or thinner joints.

Serve hot or cold, but leave to stand for 20–30 minutes before carving.

Cook's notes
Ask your butcher for a joint that is a nice even shape so that it will cook evenly.

Simnel Cake

This cake is now usually made as an Easter cake. I have made it here as a tray bake to cut into slices but you can, of course, make it as a round cake if you wish.

175g/6oz plain flour
50g/2oz ground almonds
1/2 level teaspoon baking powder
1/2 level teaspoon grated nutmeg
1/2 level teaspoon mixed spice
grated rind 1 lemon
175g/6oz caster sugar
175g/6oz soft butter
3 eggs, beaten
200g/7oz sultanas

200g/7oz raisins
50g/2oz glacé cherries, halved
  and washed
500g/1lb 2oz marzipan

For the decoration
250g/9oz sieved icing sugar
juice 1 lemon
sugared eggs

Line the small roasting tin with Bake-O-Glide.

Put the flour in a bowl and add the ground almonds, baking powder, nutmeg and mixed spice. Add the grated lemon rind and stir to blend together.

Put the butter and sugar in a bowl and beat together using a wooden spoon or an electric mixer, until light and fluffy. Add half the beaten egg along with 1 tablespoon flour mixture and beat well. Repeat with the remaining egg. Fold in the remaining flour mixture followed by the dried fruits and cherries.

Spoon half the cake mix into the lined tin and level the surface. Roll the marzipan to an oblong just smaller than the roasting tin. Lay the marzipan over the cake mixture and then spoon over the remaining cake mixture and level the surface.

For a two-oven Aga, hang the tin on the bottom set of runners of the roasting oven and slide the cold shelf onto the second set of runners from the bottom of the oven. Bake the cake for 40–45 minutes until golden brown on the top and a skewer inserted in the middle comes out clean.

For a three- or four-oven Aga, hang the tin on the second set of runners from the bottom of the baking oven and bake for 50–55 minutes until golden brown and a skewer inserted in the middle comes out clean.

Cool the cake in the tin.

When the cake is cold, make the icing. Sieve the icing sugar into a basin and slowly add the lemon juice, beating as you go. Add boiled water or more lemon juice to make the icing smooth and just thin enough to spread. Pour the icing over the cake and smooth over the top. Decorate with sugared eggs.

Cook's notes

If making well in advance of serving add sugared eggs when the icing has dried otherwise the moisture in the icing makes the sugar coating go 'frilly'.
This cake keeps well for a week.

Easter Biscuits

Easter Biscuits add to the tea table on Easter Sunday. Currants used to be much prized and were used for special occasions. Sometimes these biscuits were given to children after church on Easter morning, though nowadays I think they prefer chocolate eggs!

110g/4oz butter, softened
110g/4oz caster sugar
2 egg yolks or 1 whole egg
225g/8oz plain flour
$\frac{1}{2}$ teaspoon ground cinnamon
50g/2oz currants
caster sugar, to dust when baked

Place the butter and sugar in a bowl and cream together until light and fluffy. Beat in the egg yolks with 1 teaspoon of flour. Add the flour, cinnamon and currants and fold into the butter mixture. Flour the work surface lightly and roll the biscuit dough to the thickness of a 50p piece. Cut out rounds and place on a baking tray lined with Bake-O-Glide or lightly buttered.

For a two-oven Aga, put the shelf on the floor of the roasting oven and slide in the tray of biscuits. Put the cold shelf on the second set of runners from the bottom of the oven and bake the biscuits for 10–15 minutes until a pale golden brown.

For a three- or four-oven Aga, put the tray or shelf on the bottom set of runners of the baking oven and bake the biscuits for 12–15 minutes until pale golden brown.

Immediately dust with caster sugar and then move the biscuits gently to a cooling rack to become firm.

Cook's notes

If the biscuit dough is too sticky to handle then chill for a short time in the fridge or freezer or cut the biscuits out and then chill on the tray. Firm dough will hold a better shape during baking.

Smoked Haddock au Gratin

This classic early Spring dish is easy to make in large quantities in the roasting tin if cooking for a crowd. Serve with new or mashed potatoes and a green vegetable.

1 kg/2¼ lbs un-dyed smoked haddock fillet
300ml/½ pint milk
25g/1oz butter
4 large tomatoes, sliced
150ml/5fl oz single cream
110g/4oz mature Cheddar or
    Gruyère cheese, grated
black pepper

Serves 6

Place the fish in the small roasting tin. Pour on the milk. Slide the tin onto the bottom set of runners of the roasting oven and cook for 15–20 minutes until just flaking. Drain the fish, skin and break into large chunks. Place in a shallow ovenproof dish. Season with pepper. Pour over the cream, lay on the tomatoes and sprinkle with the grated cheese. Return to the oven with the shelf on the bottom set of runners of the roasting oven and bake for 20 minutes until golden brown.

Cook's notes
Try to buy un-dyed smoked haddock as it has a better, less salty flavour. For this dish choose thick, chunky fillets if possible.

Spring Lamb Stew

It seems strange to have a stew made from tender young spring lamb but the butcher will always have cheaper cuts to dispose of and young lamb shouldn't be fatty.

1kg/2.2 lbs boneless lamb, cubed
2 bay leaves
4 sprigs fresh thyme
1 onion, peeled and quartered
1 leek, roughly chopped
3 cloves garlic, peeled and
   crushed
salt and pepper
600ml/1 pint cold water

To finish
200g/7oz baby carrots, scraped
   or washed

200g/7oz baby turnips, scraped
   and quartered
200g/7oz baby onions or shallots,
   peeled
200g/7oz baby leeks, trimmed
200ml/7 fl oz white wine
100ml/3 fl oz lamb or vegetable
   stock
200g/7oz french beans, trimmed
200g/7oz frozen petit pois
chopped parsley, to garnish

Serves 6

Put the lamb, bay leaves, thyme, onion, leek, garlic, a seasoning of salt and pepper and the water in a flameproof dish. Place on the simmering plate and slowly bring to the boil. Cover and move to the simmering oven for $1\frac{1}{2}$–2 hours.

Remove the dish from the oven and discard all the vegetables, leaving the lamb and the stock in the dish. Stand on the simmering plate and add the carrots, turnips, onions, leeks, white wine and stock. Bring to the boil and then move to the simmering oven for 20–30 minutes. Return to the simmering plate and add the beans and the petit pois. Simmer for 2–3 minutes.

Garnish with chopped parsley and serve with crusty bread.

Cook's notes
The first stage can be cooked the day before serving. All those lovely spring vegetables need a fairly short time cooking and should be served immediately.

April 28

Pears in Red Wine

Pears in red wine is a great Aga dish, one which I love to cook in the winter when pears are flourishing, but one which I can't resist bringing out again when the pear season is coming to its end. It is so easy to make using the simmering oven. A wide shallow pan is best for this so that the pears become evenly pink and evenly flavoured. I think a fairly robust but not too expensive red wine is best for this method of cooking. Rich double cream, or good ice cream, served to accompany makes a simple dish special.

300ml/½ pint red wine
225g/8oz sugar
2 cloves or 1 cinnamon stick
1kg/2¼lbs pears, peeled, halved and cored
flaked almonds, to decorate

Serves 6–8

Pour the wine into a saucepan, add the sugar and the cloves or cinnamon. Dissolve the sugar over gentle heat, bring to the boil and then add the prepared pears. Cover and transfer to the simmering oven for 1½–2 hours. Sprinkle with almonds and serve warm with cream.

Cook's notes
The cooking time depends upon the ripeness of the fruit. If they are juicy, cut the time down to 1 hour. Spoon out into a serving dish carefully with a slotted spoon.

Potato Gratin with Leeks

Potatoes and leeks are a perfect combination. Use a floury variety of potato, if possible. The gratin will cook well in the bottom of the roasting oven while a joint of pork or ham is roasting above – or it can even be cooked for a couple of hours in the simmering oven while a casserole is cooking.

50g/2oz butter
2 leeks, sliced
salt and pepper
grated nutmeg
700g/1¹/₂ lb potatoes (such as
*   King Edward), thinly sliced*
1 tablespoon chopped parsley
225ml/8fl oz hot chicken or
*   vegetable stock*
150ml/¹/₄ pint single cream

Serves 4–6

Potatoes are the world's fourth largest produced crop after wheat, rice and maize, and are available all year round in the UK. Not introduced to Europe until the early 18th century, potatoes are today one of the most important food staples throughout the world.

Use a little of the butter to grease a shallow ovenproof dish.

Melt half the remaining butter in a saucepan and fry the leeks with salt, pepper and nutmeg. Cover and cook slowly for 5 minutes.

Layer half the potatoes in the buttered dish with the leeks, parsley and more salt and pepper. Put a final layer of potatoes on top. Pour on enough hot stock to come almost to the top of the potatoes. Dot with the remaining butter. Put the oven shelf on the floor of the roasting oven and bake the gratin for about 50 minutes, until the potatoes are tender.

Pour the cream over the potatoes, shake the dish slightly and then transfer to the simmering oven for 15 minutes.

Cook's notes

If you want to cook this slowly, give the dish 20–25 minutes in the bottom of the roasting oven to get some heat into the potatoes and then move to the simmering oven for 2 hours or until the potatoes are cooked when pierced with a sharp knife.

Chocolate and Cointreau Soufflés

Prepare these soufflés ahead of time if you are entertaining. They are simple to make and don't require any special ingredients except the Cointreau and if you don't have that use brandy or Tia Maria – anything that goes with chocolate, really.

50g/2oz butter, soft for greasing
100g/3¹/₂oz caster sugar
10 tablespoons cocoa powder
3 tablespoons Cointreau
80ml/3fl oz milk
5 eggs, separated

Serves 6

Butter 6 ramekin or soufflé dishes and sprinkle with a little caster sugar. Stand on a baking tray and set aside.

In a large mixing bowl, mix together the remaining sugar, cocoa and Cointreau. Warm the milk slightly and add to the cocoa mixture. Beat the egg yolks together and beat into the cocoa mixture.

Whisk the egg whites until forming peaks. Whisk 1 tablespoon of egg white into the cocoa mixture and then fold in the remaining egg white gently.

Spoon the mixture into the prepared ramekins. Chill until needed, up to 24 hours before baking.

When ready to bake, hang the baking tray on the first set of runners from the bottom of the roasting oven. Bake for 15–20 minutes, until risen and puffed up.

Serve immediately, dusted with icing sugar.

Cook's notes
Remove from the fridge 20 minutes or so before baking, especially of your soufflé dishes are delicate.

May

1st Crema Catalana 2nd Garlic and Mint Stir-Fried Noodles
3rd Roast Sea Bass with Fennel with Confit de Tomates
4th Herby Chicken with Lemon and Herb Butter
5th Butterbean Vinaigrette 6th Lemon and Almond Tart
7th Lamb Tagine with Minted Couscous 8th Cheese and
Asparagus Tart 9th Trout Baked in Red Wine 10th Mint Sauce
11th Spring Chicken with Lemon Rice 12th Asparagus Soup
13th Salmon en Croûte with Watercress and Lemon Butter
14th Grilled Tuna with Aubergine 15th Chocolate Bread
16th Braised Five-Spice Pork with Pak Choi 17th Baby Leaf
Risotto with Lemon 18th Salmon with Grilled Asparagus
19th Hot Banana Brioche 20th Fougasse Farci
21st Steamed Jam Sponge 22nd Slow Cooked Lamb
with Puy Lentils 23rd Aubergine and Asparagus Bruschetta
24th Herb Pancakes with Smoked Salmon
25th Pan-Fried Lamb's Liver with Caramelised Onion Sauce
26th Pea and Spinach Soup 27th Almond Swiss Roll
28th Aubergine and Goat's Cheese Rounds 29th Wild Garlic
Soup 30th Taglioni in a Lemon Cream Sauce 31st Fruit Flan

Crema Catalana

The weather in May can catch us out with the odd very warm and bright day. These little desserts are perfect for those warm days, served with some fresh fruits. I like to serve these in coffee cups, alternatively you can use ramekin dishes. Just take care when caramelising the sugar that the cups don't shatter if they are delicate.

600ml/1 pint milk
zest from $^1/_2$ lemon
1 cinnamon stick
4 egg yolks
$1^1/_2$ tablespoons cornflour
7 tablespoons caster sugar

Serves 4

Place the milk, lemon peel and cinnamon stick in a saucepan. Heat the milk gently to boiling point and then remove from the heat. Leave to stand for 30 minutes to allow the lemon and cinnamon flavours to infuse the milk.

In a mixing bowl, place the egg yolks and 3 tablespoons of sugar. Whisk until a pale lemon colour. Beat in the cornflour. Strain the milk into the egg mixture, a little at a time, whisking as you go. Rinse out the saucepan and pour in the egg mixture. Stand the pan on the simmering plate and whisk until smooth and thickened. Remove from the heat and spoon into 4 serving cups. Cool and then chill.

Sprinkle the remaining sugar over the custards and heat gently with a cook's blow torch to caramelise the sugar and make a crunchy topping.

Cooks notes
This is a perfect dessert to make if you have egg yolks leftover from recent meringue making.

May
2

Garlic and Mint
Stir-Fried Noodles

Sometimes it is easy to get in a rut when cooking vegetables. This is an interesting way to serve cabbage or other seasonal green, leafy vegetables.

2 tablespoons sesame oil
3 cloves garlic, peeled and finely sliced
6 stalks mint, leaves removed
250g egg noodles, cooked according
  to the packet
400g/14oz pak choi or cabbage, shredded

Serves 8

Mint is available both fresh and dried and is an easy herb to grow at home. Mint has a sweet, cool and flavoursome leaf which can be used in a variety of sweet and savoury dishes, including teas, desserts and lamb dishes. The essential oil from the plant is also frequently used in toothpastes, chewing gum and breath fresheners.

Heat the wok on the boiling plate for 10 minutes.

Add the sesame oil and fry the garlic, taking care not to let the garlic burn. Stir in the mint leaves and cook until the garlic is golden.

Stir in the cooked noodles and stir-fry for 1–2 minutes before adding the shredded greens. Add 3–4 tablespoons water and cook until the greens are wilting. Allow any liquid to evaporate and serve immediately.

Cook's notes
Noodles can easily be reconstituted by covering with boiling water, covering and standing on the back of the Aga for 10 minutes. Drain well and they are then ready to serve.

Aga *year*

Roast Sea Bass with Fennel with Confit de Tomates

This is a very Mediterranean way of serving fish, especially now that line-caught sea bass is so readily available. The wonderful flavours of the confit complement the fish so well, and it's a perfect way to use up any tomatoes which are nearly past their best.

For the confit de tomates
6 large, very ripe tomatoes
4 tablespoons extra virgin olive
*   oil, plus extra to cover*
1 large sprig thyme, leaves
*   removed from the stalk*
salt and pepper
a little caster sugar

4 medium fillets sea bass or
*   1 whole sea bass about 1kg*
2 large fennel bulbs
16 cloves garlic, blanched in
*   boiling*
*   water and then skinned*
12 strips dried orange zest
100ml/3½fl oz olive oil
salt and pepper
1 lemon, cut into wedges, to serve

Serves 4

Fennel can be enjoyed raw in salads and lightly dressed on its own as an accompaniment to fish and chicken dishes. However, its aniseed flavour is more potent when eaten raw than when cooked, where brief boiling makes it ideal for soups, or slower braising for sweeter, more tender dishes.

First make the confit. Blanch the tomatoes in boiling water and remove their skins. Cut each tomato in half, discard the seeds and then place in a mixing bowl. Pour over 4 tablespoons of the olive oil, the thyme, a pinch of sugar and season with salt and pepper. Turn the tomatoes over to coat them well.

Line a large roasting tin or baking tray with Bake-O-Glide and stand it on the roasting rack. Spread the tomatoes on the rack. Hang the tin in the middle of the simmering oven and allow the tomatoes to dry for 8 hours or overnight. The tomatoes should be shrunk to about half their original size and be slightly chewy. Allow to cool completely. Set aside half for the sea bass and then place the other half into a jar and cover with olive oil – it will keep for up to 2 weeks in a cool place.

Trim the fennel bulbs and cut each bulb into 6 lengthways. Blanch in boiling water for about 10 minutes, until just soft. Drain well and then scatter over the base of an oven proof dish. Add the tomatoes, garlic and orange zest.

Lay the sea bass on the vegetables, skin side uppermost and pour over the olive oil. Sprinkle with salt and pepper.

Hang the shelf on the bottom set of runners of the roasting oven and put in the fish. Bake for 15–20 minutes, basting with the olive oil mixture 2 or 3 times. If cooking the whole fish, remove it from the oven when a knife inserted near the head comes out hot. Leave to stand for 10 minutes in a warm place before filleting.

Serve with the confit de tomates, the fennel, the pan juices spooned over and wedges of lemon.

Cook's notes
If you don't have the confit to hand, you can serve semi-dried tomatoes or tomatoes in oil.

Herby Chicken with Lemon and Herb Butter

Bring variety to a simple chicken breast by using freshly picked herbs for added flavour.

1 small bunch chives, finely chopped
1 teaspoon finely chopped lemon thyme
1 small bunch flat leaf parsley,
  finely chopped
1 teaspoon finely chopped tarragon
finely grated rind and juice 1 lemon
50g/2oz unsalted butter, softened
salt and pepper
4 tablespoons extra virgin olive oil
6 chicken breast fillets, skinned
lemon wedges to garnish

Tarragon, also known as dragon's-wort is a perennial herb related to wormwood. Two popular varieties of tarragon that are commonly used in cooking are French and Russian Tarragon, the latter producing more robust leaves that can even be used as a substitute to asparagus in the early spring. Tarragon is a fantastic herb to pair with chicken and lemon dishes.

Mix together the chopped herbs and the lemon zest and then divide into two bowls. To one bowl, add 1 teaspoon lemon juice, the butter and a seasoning of salt and pepper. Beat well with a wooden spoon until well mixed. Lay a sheet of clingfilm on the work top. Spoon on the herb butter, loosely wrap with the clingfilm and roll into a sausage shape. Wrap completely and chill.

To the second bowl of herbs, add the remaining lemon juice, the olive oil and a seasoning of pepper to make the herb marinade.

Trim the chicken breasts removing any fat, tendons or bloody pieces. Remove any fillets and set aside. Place the chicken breasts between layers of clingfilm and gently flatten with a rolling pin to make a thin escalope. Lay all the chicken in a shallow dish and smear over the herb marinade. Cover and chill for at least 30 minutes.

To cook, pre-heat a griddle pan on the floor of the roasting oven and cook the chicken portions in the hot pan for 4 minutes on each side. Alternatively, lay the portions on a baking tray lined with Bake-O-Glide and place the tray on the floor of the roasting oven and bake the chicken for 5 minutes, then turn over the chicken and cook the second side for 4–5 minutes.

Serve the chicken portions with a slice of herb butter on the top and a lemon wedge. Serve with new potatoes and green beans or a green salad.

Cook's notes
The chicken can easily be prepared in the morning and cooked in the evening.

5

Butterbean Vinaigrette

I have chosen butterbeans for this recipe, but the same method can be used for other beans or even a mixture of beans. Check the beans after one hour as they may be cooked – remember, all Aga simmering ovens vary slightly!

225g/8oz butter beans, soaked overnight
3 tablespoons olive oil
1 tablespoons white wine vinegar
salt and pepper
4 spring onions, finely chopped
1 clove garlic, crushed
chopped parsley, to garnish

Serves 4–6

Rinse the beans and place in a flameproof casserole. Cover with water and bring to the boil. Cover and place in the simmering oven for $1\frac{1}{2}$ hours until the beans are cooked, but not mushy. Drain and transfer to a serving dish.

Place the oil, vinegar, salt and pepper in a clean jam jar. Shake well and pour over the warm beans. Add the onions and garlic and mix well, taking care not to break up the beans. Leave until cold, then sprinkle with chopped parsley to serve.

Cook's notes
Don't put any salt in with the butterbeans when cooking, it will toughen the skins. Add the seasoning to the vinaigrette.

Lemon and Almond Tart

Lemon tart is eternally popular in restaurants. I don't know why because so many of them have a dull flavour with poor pastry. As usual, homemade is usually best and this twist with almonds is one that I love.

375g/13oz packet dessert pastry

For the filling
3 eggs
140g/5oz caster sugar
finely grated rind and juice
 2 lemons
125g/4¹/₂oz butter, softened
100g/3¹/₂oz ground almonds
25g/1oz peeled almonds, halved
slices lemon to decorate

Serves 8

Roll the pastry to fit a shallow 28cm/11-inch flan tin. Line the flan tin with the pastry and chill.

In a bowl, beat together the eggs and the sugar until light and fluffy. Add the lemon rind and juice, the softened butter and the ground almonds. Mix well until smooth and then pour into the pastry case. Arrange the sliced almonds on top.

Bake the tart on the floor of the roasting oven for 20–25 minutes until the filling is firm and the pastry golden brown. When cool, decorate with lemon slices.

Cook's notes
You shouldn't need the cold shelf for this tart but if it is browning too quickly, and you don't want much colour, slide the cold shelf on to the third set of runners from the top of the oven after 15 minutes.

Lamb Tagine with Minted Couscous

Cinnamon, orange and honey is redolent of Morocco and other north African countries. The light spicing works so well with lamb and dried fruits. Couscous is easy to prepare and serve – it is the perfect accompaniment to this dish. The meat can be cooked the day before serving to allow the flavours to develop.

1¹/₄kg/2lb 12oz lamb, diced
1 tablespoon olive oil
10g/¹/₂oz butter
2 x 400g cans chopped tomatoes
1 tablespoon honey
grated rind and juice 1 orange
2 pinches chilli flakes
1 stick cinnamon
250g/9oz pitted, ready-to-eat prunes
flaked almonds, to serve

For the marinade
2 onions, peeled and finely chopped

2 cloves garlic, peeled and chopped
3 tablespoons olive oil
1 teaspoon paprika
1 teaspoon ground ginger
salt and pepper

For the minted couscous
500g/1lb 2oz couscous
3 tablespoons finely chopped mint
squeeze lemon
¹/₂ cucumber, finely diced
4 tomatoes, seeded and chopped

Serves 6

Mix all the marinade ingredients together in a non-metallic bowl and add the lamb. Stir to coat well, cover and leave to marinade for 4 hours or overnight.

Put the oil and the butter into a casserole dish and heat through. Add the lamb mixture and stir well. Add the tomatoes, honey, orange rind and juice, the chilli flakes and the cinnamon stick. Stir well and bring to the boil. Cover and move the pan to the simmering oven for 2–3 hours.

Just before serving, stir the prunes into the lamb and return to the oven to heat through.

Prepare the couscous. Put the couscous into a heatproof bowl. Pour over enough boiling water to cover the couscous well. Cover with a plate and leave to stand for 5 minutes at the back of the Aga. Fork through and stir in the mint, lemon juice, cucumber and tomatoes.

Serve the couscous and lamb together, scattered with flaked almonds.

Cook's notes
Buy the best couscous you can find for the best flavour and texture.

Cheese and Asparagus Tart

A spring-like tart that uses a little of the early season asparagus. Cook the tart gently to get a silky smooth filling to contrast with the crisp pastry. I love to eat this with a light salad in the garden on a warm late spring day.

For the pastry
175g/6oz plain flour
pinch salt
75g/3oz butter, chilled
75g/3oz finely grated mature
  Cheddar cheese
1 teaspoon mustard

For the filling
450g/1lb asparagus
3 large eggs
salt and pepper
450ml/ ³/₄ pint single cream
a little grated nutmeg

Prepare the cheese pastry. Put the flour and salt in a mixing bowl . Dice the butter and add to the flour. Rub the butter into the flour until the mixture resembles fine breadcrumbs. Stir in the grated cheese and add the mustard. Bind the dough together with cold water. Start with 4 tablespoons of water and add more as needed to bind the pastry to a dough.

Roll the pastry on a lightly floured work surface to a circle and use to line a 22cm/9-inch shallow flan tin. Chill well.

Trim the asparagus and then cook in the minimum of water until just cooked. Drain and plunge into cold water to keep the colour. Rinse and dry. Lay the prepared asparagus neatly in the pastry case.

Beat together the eggs, a seasoning of salt and pepper, a grating of nutmeg and the cream. Pour the filling over the asparagus.

Carefully lift the tart onto the floor of the roasting oven and slide the cold shelf onto the third set of runners from the top.

Bake for 20–25 minutes until the pastry is golden and the filling is set. Serve warm or cold.

Cook's notes
Keep the asparagus water and any trimmings to go into a soup.

Trout Baked in Red Wine

Trout seems to be the sad relation to salmon these days, but I feel it is an under-used fish and a very good buy.

4 trout, cleaned
salt and pepper
1 small carrot, peeled and
  chopped
2 shallots, peeled and chopped
1 stick celery, chopped
1 clove garlic, peeled
2 bay leaves
3–4 stalks parsley

4 sage leaves
sprig thyme
2 tablespoons olive oil
300ml/10 fl oz red wine
25g/1oz butter mixed together
  with 1 tablespoon flour
6 anchovy fillets, drained and
  chopped

Serves 4

Wash and dry the trout and season inside and out with salt and pepper. Lightly oil the base of a shallow baking dish and place the trout in it.

Place the carrots, shallots, celery, garlic, bay leaves, parsley, sage and thyme in a saucepan. Add the olive oil and 2 tablespoons of water and a pinch of salt. Cook gently on the simmering plate until boiling and then add the wine. Bring to the boil and move to the simmering oven for 20 minutes.

Put the oven shelf on the second set of runners from the bottom of the roasting oven and put in the trout for 5 minutes. Spoon over the red wine sauce and bake the fish in the sauce for 10 minutes. Keep the fish warm in the simmering oven.

Strain the sauce into a saucepan and stand on the simmering plate. When the sauce boils, whisk in small pieces of the butter and flour paste and the finely chopped anchovy fillets. Check the seasoning and spoon the sauce over the trout.

Serve immediately.

Cook's notes
Use a red wine that is not too full bodied for this dish so as not overwhelm the fish with the sauce.

Aga *year*

May 10

Mint Sauce

I can remember making mint sauce for Sunday lunch from a very early age. To safely chop the mint my mother put it in a jug and I snipped away with a pair of scissors. It worked well and I sometimes do it that way now. Oh, and the sublime smell of the mint brings back such fond memories of sunny spring days! The perfect mint sauce must accompany the perfect roast lamb – try it with Roast Leg of Lamb, page 119, and some new potatoes.

a good bunch of mint
2 teaspoons caster sugar
1 tablespoon boiling water
3 tablespoons wine vinegar

Snip the leaves off the stems of mint. Chop the leaves finely. Place in a small jug or basin. Add the sugar and then the boiling water – this retains the colour of the mint as well as dissolving the sugar. Add the vinegar and stir well. Do not prepare too long in advance because the mint tends to turn brown.

Cook's notes
If you have a lot of mint in the garden try making mint jelly for the winter – it is by far the the best way to preserve it.

Spring Chicken
with Lemon Rice

Finding tasty ways of using chicken breast isn't always easy, as it can have a tendency to dryness. Cooked like this, in the simmering oven, keeps the chicken moist. If you prefer, you could also make this recipe with chicken legs, but allow 10 minutes longer cooking time.

6 tablespoons olive oil
4 chicken breast fillets, skinless
1 large onion, finely chopped
4 cloves garlic, crushed
200ml white wine
1 tablespoon chopped oregano
400g can chopped tomatoes

4–6 black olives, pitted and sliced
salt and pepper
300g long-grain or Basmati rice
4 tablespoon chopped parsley
2 tablespoons chopped mint
grated zest and juice 1 lemon

Serves 4

Heat 1 tablespoon oil in a frying pan and brown the chicken. Remove from the pan and put to one side.

Add 1 more tablespoon of oil to the pan and cook the onion and garlic until softening but not brown. Add the wine and bring to the boil. Stir in the oregano, tomatoes and olives and then the reserved chicken. Season and then, when bubbling, move the pan to the simmering oven for 25–30 minutes, until the chicken is cooked through.

Measure the rice into a measuring jug and pour into a saucepan. Add $1^1/_2$ times the volume of the rice in water. Season the rice and bring to the boil. Cover and transfer to the simmering oven for 15 minutes.

Meanwhile, make the dressing. Measure the remaining 4 tablespoons olive oil into a basin and whisk in half the parsley, the mint and the zest and juice of the lemon. Season with salt and pepper.

Fork through the rice, draining if needed, and then pour over the dressing. Fork through and divide among 4 plates. Slice the chicken fillets and lay on the rice. Spoon over the onion mixture and garnish with the remaining chopped parsley.

Cook's notes
Test the chicken to see if it is cooked by inserting the point of a sharp knife into one portion to see if the juices run out clear.

Asparagus Soup

That short time in May and June when home-grown asparagus is available needs to be made the most of. If you have asparagus no longer in peak perfection then this is the recipe you need!

25g/1oz butter
1 onion, peeled and chopped
225g/8oz asparagus
450ml/³/₄ pint vegetable stock
150ml/¹/₄ pint single cream
salt and pepper

Serves 4

Melt the butter in a saucepan and add the onion. Sauté until softening. Meanwhile, trim the asparagus and wash well. Cut a few of the spears off and reserve for garnish. Chop the rest of the asparagus and add to the onion. Toss in the butter and pour on the stock. Cover and bring to the boil and then move the pan to the simmering oven for 20–30 minutes, until the asparagus is cooked.

Cook the spears in a little water or steam until just tender.

Blend the soup and adjust the seasoning. Stir in the cream and heat through gently.

Ladle the soup into warm bowls and put a few asparagus spears on top.

Cook's notes

If you have been cooking asparagus for other dishes then keep the water and use as stock in this recipe.

Salmon en Croûte with Watercress and Lemon Butter

Salmon is very good value for money and very versatile. In this recipe I make individual portions and flavour them with watercress, which I consider a much under-used leaf.

4 salmon fillets, about 175g/6oz each,
*   skinned*
125g/5oz butter, softened
25g/1oz watercress
finely grated zest $^1/_2$ lemon
1 tablespoon lemon juice
$1^1/_2$ teaspoons chopped chives
salt
375g/13oz pack ready-rolled puff pastry
1 egg, beaten for glazing

Serves 4

Season the salmon and set aside.

Put the butter, watercress, lemon zest, lemon juice and chives in a processor or blender and whiz to make a paste. Divide into two and put one portion to chill.

Unroll the pastry and place on a large sheet of Bake-O-Glide in a tin. Roll lightly to make a little larger and then cut into 4 equal portions. Lay a salmon fillet to one side of each pastry rectangle. Divide the unchilled watercress butter into 4 portions and put a portion on each salmon fillet. Spread over the top of the salmon. Brush the edges of the pastry with a little beaten egg and then fold the pastry over the salmon. Seal the edges with a fork and make three slits through the pastry top with a sharp knife. Brush with beaten egg.

Hang the tin on the third set of runners from the top of the roasting oven and bake for 20 minutes and then move to the floor of the roasting oven for 10 minutes, until the pastry is crisp and golden. Serve with a portion of watercress butter on the vegetables that you are serving with the salmon.

Cook's notes
Make these in advance and chill well before baking for the best results.

Grilled Tuna with Aubergine

Tuna does have a tendency to dryness, even if just slightly overcooked. The aubergine mixture here is beautifully moist and also makes a very good dip as an appetiser.

1 aubergine
1 clove garlic, peeled
1 tablespoon pitted black olives
150ml/¼ pint olive oil
2 tablespoons chopped coriander
2 x 150g/5oz tuna steaks
handful rocket leaves
1 lemon

Serves 2

Place the aubergine on a baking tray and hang on the bottom set of runners of the roasting oven and roast for 45 minutes to 1 hour, until soft. The aubergine will look charred and deflated. Cool.

Scoop the flesh from the aubergine into a blender or processor. Add the garlic and olives and whiz to make a paste. Keep the blender going and slowly pour in most of the olive oil to make a smooth emulsion. Stir in the coriander.

Brush the tuna steaks with a little olive oil. Heat the ridged pan for 10 minutes on the floor of the roasting oven until hot. When nearly ready to serve, season the tuna and place in the hot pan. Cook for 2–3 minutes on each side, depending upon the thickness of the steaks and how well you like them cooked. Remove the tuna from the pan onto warmed plates.

Top each tuna steak with some aubergine mixture and some rocket leaves. Squeeze over a little lemon juice and serve with lemon wedges.

Cook's notes
The aubergine can be cooked and blended several hours before using with the tuna. Keep covered in the fridge.

Chocolate Bread

This chocolate loaf will appeal to young and old alike. I like to dunk my slices in coffee, or even eat it for breakfast.

25g/1oz fresh yeast
1 teaspoon caster sugar
about 300ml/$^1/_2$ pint warm water
450g/1lb strong plain flour
25g/1oz cocoa powder
1 teaspoon salt
100g/4oz chocolate chips
2 tablespoon soft brown sugar
25g/1oz butter, melted

Blend the yeast and caster sugar together in a basin with a little of the warm water. Place on the Aga for 1–2 minutes, until frothing.

In a large bowl, mix together the flour, cocoa powder, salt, chocolate chips and brown sugar. Stir in the yeast, melted butter and most of the remaining water. Mix to a manageable but moist dough, adding all the water, if necessary. Turn onto a floured surface and knead until the dough is smooth and elastic. Return the dough to the bowl, cover with oiled clingfilm and stand on a trivet or an Aga Chef's Pad on the Aga until doubled in size.

Grease and flour 2 x 450g/1lb loaf tins. Gently knock back the dough and divide in half. Shape and fit each half into a tin. Return to the top of the Aga and cover again with the oiled clingfilm and leave until risen to just above the top of the tin.

Put the oven shelf on the bottom set of runners of the roasting oven and slide in the loaf tins. Bake for 25 minutes or until the loaves have risen and sound hollow when tapped underneath.

Turn out and cool on a wire rack.

Cook's notes

If you like, this bread can be sliced and toasted, but be sure to put a sheet of Bake-O-Glide on the simmering plate before toasting otherwise the chocolate chips will melt and burn on the hot plate.

16

Braised Five-Spice Pork with Pak Choi

Pork tenderloin is a useful cut of meat but it can so often be rather dry to eat. Braised as it is in this recipe, it is moist and tender. Pak choi is one of those vegetables, newly grown in this country, that can be used in a variety of ways. I like to use the white fleshy stalk in salads and I also enjoy it braised. The green leafy part of the vegetable goes well in all stir-fries. In this recipe I have used the whole vegetable.

1 cm/$^1/_2$-inch piece fresh ginger, peeled and thinly sliced
200ml /7 fl oz good chicken stock
2 tablespoons soy sauce
100ml/3$^1/_2$fl oz Chinese cooking wine or dry sherry
1 tablespoon sugar
1 teaspoon Chinese five-spice powder
3 large strips orange zest

2 teaspoons vegetable oil
200g/7oz piece pork tenderloin
1 red pepper, deseeded and cut into chunks
200g/7oz pak choi, cut into quarters lengthways
150g/5$^1/_2$oz straight-to-wok noodles
2 salad onions, finely shredded

Serves 2

Place the ginger, stock, wine or sherry in a saucepan with 300ml/$^1/_2$ pint water. Add the sugar, five-spice and orange zest. Bring to the boil and simmer for 5 minutes.

Heat the oil in a shallow pan and brown the pork fillet. When browned all over, pour on the liquid from the saucepan. Cover the pork with a lid and transfer the pan to the simmering oven for 30 minutes or until there is no pink meat. Transfer the meat to a board and allow to stand for 5 minutes before cutting into thin slices.

Discard the orange zest and then add the pepper chunks to the sauce. Simmer for 2–3 minutes and then add the pak choi and pork slices. Cook for a further 2–3 minutes until the pak choi is wilted.

Divide the noodles between 2 serving bowls and spoon the pork, vegetables and sauce on top. Sprinkle over the salad onions and serve immediately.

Cook's notes
Straight-to-wok noodles are very convenient and time saving and should be looked out for in your local supermarket or delicatessen.

Baby Leaf Risotto with Lemon

This is one of my favourite late spring dishes. It is soothing to make and an excellent way to serve green leaf vegetables. I sometimes serve it topped with a fillet of fish.

25g/1oz butter
1 large onion, peeled and finely chopped
250g/9oz Arborio or risotto rice
1 litre/1$^3/_4$ pints vegetable stock, hot
300g/10$^1/_2$oz baby leaf greens, finely shredded
50g/2oz Parmesan, finely grated
grated rind and juice 1 lemon
salt and pepper
50g/2oz Parmesan cheese shaved, for garnish

Serves 4 as a light lunch or supper dish

Heat the butter in a large, roomy pan, taking care not to let it brown. Add the onion and cook until just softening. Stir in the rice and coat with the buttery mixture.

Gradually add the stock, a ladleful at a time, and stirring between each addition, until most of the stock has been absorbed and the rice is just tender.

Stir in the shredded greens, cover and cook for a further 2–3 minutes. Remove from the heat and stir in the lemon rind and juice and the grated Parmesan cheese. Season.

Serve immediately with the shavings of Parmesan as garnish.

Cook's notes
Stirring the risotto frequently during cooking helps ensure a lovely creamy finish to the dish.

Salmon with Grilled Asparagus

Salmon and asparagus seem to go together like a horse and carriage –
two fairly gentle flavours that make a lovely light meal on a spring day.
Serve with baby new potatoes.

2 bunches of asparagus,
*   about 36–40 stalks*
25g/1oz butter
juice $^1/_2$ lemon
salt and pepper
pinch sugar
250ml/9 floz full-fat crème fraîche
4 salmon fillets, skin on

Serves 4

If the asparagus stalks are a little woody, then peel them lightly with a
potato peeler. Bring a large pan of water to the boil and add the butter,
lemon juice, pinch of salt and a pinch of sugar. Add the asparagus and
cook until tender. Drain well and trim off the tips from 12 stalks. Set
aside. Purée the asparagus stalks and then pass through a sieve.

   Mix the sieved asparagus with the crème fraîche and a seasoning of
salt and pepper. Chill.

   Heat a ridged pan on the floor of the roasting oven for 15–20 minutes.
When the pan is hot, put the salmon, skin side down, in the ridged pan
for 4–5 minutes. When the fish moves easily from the pan, carefully turn
over to cook the salmon through, for 2–3 minutes, depending on the
thickness of the fillet.

   When the salmon is cooked, put onto a plate and spoon a little sauce
beside the fish. Garnish with the reserved asparagus spears.

Cook's notes
Try cooking the fish in the oven so the smell doesn't invade the house.

Hot Banana Brioche

I have to produce a pudding more or less every day for my husband –
he doesn't feel satisfied with fruit or yoghurt! So this recipe was devised
out of desperation one day, using what came to hand!

4 slices brioche, about 1cm/$^1/_2$-inch thick
4 ripe bananas, peeled
juice $^1/_2$ orange
Greek yoghurt to serve

Serves 4

Line a small baking tray with Bake-O-Glide.
  Lay the slices of brioche on a baking tray.
  Slice the bananas to about the thickness of a one pound coin. Lay them,
slightly overlapping, on the brioche. Dribble over the orange juice.
  Hang the baking tray on the second set of runners from the top of the
roasting oven and bake until the bananas are turning a golden brown,
about 5–7 minutes.
  Serve hot with yoghurt.

Cook's notes
Brioche contains a fair amount of sugar so take care that the edges
don't get too dark when being toasted.

Fougasse Farci

These filled rolls are a meal in themselves and, served warm, go very well with cheese and salad.

500g/1lb 2oz strong white flour
1 tablespoon salt
25g/1oz fresh yeast
300ml/$^{1}/_{2}$ pint warm water
3 tablespoons extra virgin olive oil

For the filling
6 preserved artichoke hearts, sliced
9 dried tomatoes
9 anchovy fillets
1 tablespoon olive oil

Make 3 loaves

Artichokes are available all year round in the UK, but need to be protected from harsh winter frosts. The peak period of harvesting artichokes is the spring, but they can continue to be harvested throughout the summer and even into early autumn.

Put the flour in a mixing bowl and stir in the salt.

Blend the yeast with a little of the warm water and add to the flour. Add the olive oil. Pour half the remaining water into the flour and start to mix the dough, adding more water, as needed, to make a slightly sticky dough. Knead well for about five minutes, until the dough is smooth. Return the dough to the bowl and cover with a damp tea towel and stand somewhere warm or on the simmering plate lid. Leave until doubled in size.

Line a large baking tray with Bake-O-Glide.

Turn the risen dough onto a lightly floured worktop and divide the dough into 3 equal portions. Roll each portion into slightly oblong circles. Divide the filling into three equal portions and lay down the middle of each 'circle'. Fold the dough over and seal the edges well. Turn each loaf over and lay on the baking tray with the join underneath. Slice three lines through the dough to expose the filling. Brush with the olive oil.

Hang the tray on the bottom set of runners of the roasting oven and bake for 20–25 minutes until golden brown and sounding hollow when tapped. Cool on a wire rack.

Cook's notes
You will probably find good artichokes and anchovies on the delicatessen counter of the supermarket or at your local delicatessen.

Steamed Jam Sponge

At this time of the year, just before the first fresh soft fruits of June come around, you might be at a loss when it comes to finding a fruit pudding. I turn to jars of homemade jam from last summer – perfect for using up something special from the storecupboard and especially when there is a lull in fresh produce. Almost every Aga owner I know has cooked a steamed pudding at one time or another – I am pleased they are coming back into favour.

200g/7oz jam
3 eggs
175g/6oz self-raising flour
175g/6oz caster sugar
175g/6oz soft butter
1 teaspoon vanilla extract

Serves 6–8

Spoon the jam into the bottom of a 1 litre/2 pint pudding basin.

Put all the remaining ingredients into a mixing bowl and mix well until light and fluffy. Spoon the sponge mixture carefully over the jam.

Cover the top of the basin – either with a lid, if using a boilable plastic basin, or a buttered sheet of foil. Fold a long strip of foil under the basin and over the top to form a lifting handle.

Put either a trivet, a wad of kitchen paper or an old saucer into the base of a large saucepan. Stand the pudding basin on top. Add enough water to come 3cm/1^1/$_2$ inches up the side of the saucepan. Cover with a lid.

Stand the saucepan on the simmering plate and simmer the pudding for 20–25 minutes. Move the pudding to the simmering oven for 1^1/$_2$–2 hours until risen and cooked.

Remove the pan from the oven and allow to stand for 3–4 minutes before turning the pudding onto a serving plate. This standing helps the pudding to shrink slightly and turn out of the basin more easily.

Serve with custard or cream.

Cook's notes
The pudding will be happy in the simmering oven for up to 4 hours and the saucepan will not dry out.

Slow-Cooked Lamb with Puy Lentils

The gentle cooking of this lamb is a good way to prepare a cheaper cut of meat, producing a sweet tender meat that marries perfectly with moist Puy lentils.

1¹/₂ kg/3lb 5oz shoulder of lamb
1 onion, sliced
3 cloves garlic, peeled and sliced
1 teaspoon dried oregano
juice 1 lemon
2 tablespoons olive oil
300ml/¹/₂ pint white wine
175g/6oz Puy lentils
50g/2oz semi-dried tomatoes
3 sprigs mint

Serves 4

Put the onion slices in a flameproof casserole large enough to hold the lamb. Season the lamb with salt and pepper and place on top of the onions. Scatter over the garlic. Pour over the lemon juice, olive oil and the wine. Cover the casserole with a well fitting lid. Stand the casserole on the simmering plate and leave until the mixture comes to the boil. After 2–3 minutes of boiling, move the pan to the simmering oven for about 4 hours.

Remove the pan from the simmering oven to the simmering plate. Stir the Puy lentils, tomatoes and mint into the lamb. Cover and allow to come to the boil. Return to the simmering oven for 1 hour.

To serve, remove the lamb to a plate and pull the meat from the bone using a spoon and fork. Serve the meat surrounded by the lentil mixture.

Cook's notes
If you don't have a casserole large enough to take the shoulder of lamb, you can use the small roasting tin and a sheet of foil as a lid to tightly seal the tin.

May
23

Aubergine and Asparagus Bruschetta

Early summer lunch in the garden? The crispy bread is a great foil for the soft aubergines and the tender asparagus. When asparagus is in season, I try to find every possible way of eating it.

1 aubergine
6 spears of asparagus, trimmed
juice 1 lemon
3 tablespoons olive oil
6 slices sour-dough bread
6 tablespoons black olive tapenade

Serves 6

Wipe the aubergine and trim the ends. Slice into 12 slices and place in a bowl of water for 10 minutes. Drain and dry on kitchen paper.

Trim the asparagus spears in lightly salted water until just tender. Drain well.

Brush the dried aubergines with olive oil and lay on a baking tray lined with Bake-O-Glide. Slide the tin onto the second set of runners from the top of the roasting oven and cook until the aubergine is soft and browning round the edges, about 15–20 minutes.

Lightly toast the bread slices on the simmering plate and then spread on the tapenade.

Lay 2 slices of aubergine on each slice of bread and then an asparagus spear. Mix together the lemon juice and the remaining tablespoon of olive oil and drizzle the dressing over the bruschettas.

Cook's notes
If you are making a lot of bruschetta, you can toast the bread on a baking tray at the top of the roasting oven. For just a few slices, toast directly on the simmering plate.

Herb Pancakes with Smoked Salmon

I have so often looked at blinis in the supermarket and thought how expensive they are and, having tried some, how dry and tasteless they are, so when I first made these little pancakes on the Aga they came as a revelation. They look and taste delicious.

110g/4oz self-raising flour
pinch salt
1 tablespoon chopped dill
1 egg
150ml/¼ pint milk
vegetable oil to grease the
    simmering plate

For the topping
crème fraîche
smoked salmon
caviar
a few dill fronds

Put the flour in a mixing bowl and add the salt and the chopped dill. Add the egg and gradually whisk in the milk until a batter the thickness of double cream has formed.

Brush any crumbs from the surface of the simmering plate and lightly oil. Drop dessert-spoonfuls of batter onto the oiled plate. When the surface is covered in bubbles, flip the pancakes over and cook the second side for 1–2 minutes. Remove from the plate and cool. Continue to use all the batter.

The size you make the pancakes will be according to how you wish to serve them, very small ones are good for canapés, larger ones for starters.

At this stage the pancakes can be layered with clingfilm and frozen. To thaw out, put on a baking tray and refresh in the simmering oven for 10–15 minutes.

Spoon a little crème fraîche on each pancake and top with a little smoked salmon, caviar, if using, and a tiny piece of dill.

Cook's notes
Allow the pancakes to cool completely before adding the crème fraîche, as otherwise the topping will slide off down your guest's front!

Pan-Fried Lamb's Liver with Caramelised Onion Sauce

I have always loved liver and onions and I am delighted that it is becoming popular again. Lamb's liver has a gentler flavour than pig's liver and is ideal to serve to novice liver eaters.

2 tablespoons vegetable oil
15g/^{1}/$_2$oz butter
2 onions, peeled and thinly sliced
1 teaspoon ground cumin
2 tablespoons flour
1 tablespoon Demerara sugar
150ml/^{1}/$_4$ pint red wine
300ml/^{1}/$_2$ pint meat stock
salt and pepper
50g/2oz butter
450g/1lb lamb's liver, sliced
seasoned flour

Serves 4

Heat the oil and a small amount of butter in a frying pan. Add the onions and stir well to coat in the oil. Place the pan on the floor of the roasting oven for about 10 minutes, until the onions are softening. Stir in the cumin, cook for 2–3 minutes and then stir in the sugar. Return the pan to the oven and allow the onions to caramelise. Move the pan to the simmering plate and add the wine and stock. Bring the contents to the boil and then move the pan to the simmering oven for 20–30 minutes.

Coat the liver lightly in seasoned flour. Melt the butter in another frying pan and fry the liver for 2–3 minutes on each side, depending upon thickness.

Serve the liver with creamy mashed potatoes and the caramelised onion sauce.

Cooks notes
Liver becomes dry and unpleasant to eat if overcooked so take care with your timings!

Pea and Spinach Soup

This is a quick and easy soup to make. If you like really smooth soups, you can pass it through a sieve after it has been blended.

50g/2oz butter
1 large potato, peeled and diced
2 sticks celery, scrubbed and chopped
125ml/$^1/_4$ pint white wine
1 litre/$1^3/_4$ pints vegetable stock
500g /1lb 2oz frozen peas
100g/4oz spinach, well washed, stalks removed
pinch of sugar
1 tablespoon chopped parsley or mint
salt and pepper

Serves 6

Heat the butter in a large saucepan, add the diced potato and celery and toss them in the butter. Cover with a lid and cook for 4–5 minutes until the vegetables are softening but not browning.

Pour the wine into the saucepan and bubble the mixture until the wine has reduced by half. Pour in the vegetable stock and then add the peas and the spinach leaves. Bring to the boil, replace the lid and put into the simmering oven for 30 minutes. Remove the pan from the oven and stir in the sugar and chopped herbs.

Whiz the soup in a blender. Rinse the pan out and pour the puréed soup back into the pan. Adjust the seasoning, heat through and serve either with a little cream or crunchy croûtons.

Cook's notes
To make croûtons, cut some bread into small cubes. Put into a plastic bag and pour in some olive oil and chopped herbs. Shake the bag well and pour the bread cubes onto a baking tray. Hang the tray on the second set of runners from the top of the roasting oven for 10–15 minutes until crisp and golden. When cold, store in an airtight container.

May
27

Almond Swiss Roll

Swiss rolls are quick to make in the Aga but they don't keep well beyond 24 hours. However, I needed one for an event and I knew that it would be impossible to make a cake 'on the day'. So I tried adding ground almonds to keep the cake moist. It worked, this Swiss roll keeps well for a couple of days.

4 eggs
110g/4oz caster sugar
50g/2oz self-raising flour
50g/2oz ground almonds

For the filling
75g/3oz plain chocolate
25g/1oz butter
4 tablespoons soft apricot jam

For the topping
50g/2oz chocolate
1 tablespoon icing sugar

Line the large Aga baking tray or roasting tin with Bake-O-Glide.

Place the eggs and caster sugar in a mixing bowl. Whisk well until light and fluffy and the mixture holds a trail. Gently fold in the flour and the ground almonds. Pour the mixture into the lined tin and gently level the surface.

Hang the tin on the bottom set of runners of the roasting oven. Bake the Swiss roll for 7–8 minutes until risen, pale gold and firm to the touch.

Place a plain sheet of Bake-O-Glide on the worktop and tip out the Swiss roll. Peel off the lining sheet and roll, from a short side, into a Swiss roll, keeping the Bake-O-Glide inside as you roll. Cool.

Put the filling chocolate and the butter in a basin and stand at the back of the Aga to melt. Put the topping chocolate in a small jug and stand on the Aga to melt.

When the cake is cold, carefully unroll the cake and spread the chocolate and butter mixture over the cake. Spoon on the apricot jam and spread over the cake. Roll the Swiss roll and place on a serving plate.

Drizzle over the melted chocolate and dust with icing sugar.

Cooks notes
If the cake cracks slightly when being unrolled, don't worry, it can easily be covered with chocolate drizzles and no-one will notice. It will still taste very good.

Aubergine and Goat's Cheese Rounds

It seems to me that aubergines are either loved or loathed. Some people don't like the slightly slimy texture they can have when cooked in a lot of oil. To avoid the sliminess, cook them in a ridged pan or blanch them in boiling water. The combination of aubergine and goat's cheese in this recipe works wonderfully well.

1 large aubergine, cut into 8 slices
olive oil
3 tablespoons of pesto
8 round slices goat's cheese
4 tomatoes, skinned, seeded and the flesh diced
salt and pepper

Serves 4

Heat a ridged pan on the boiling plate for 5–7 minutes. Brush the aubergine slices with olive oil on both sides. When the pan is hot, 'grill' the aubergines for 3–4 minutes on either side. Remove from the heat and spread the slices with pesto. Place a round of cheese on top of the pesto and then tomato pieces. Season with salt and pepper.

Place the aubergine rounds on a baking tray and carefully slide onto the third set of runners from the top of the roasting oven and cook until the cheese is bubbling, about 5–8 minutes

Serve hot with crusty bread.

Cook's notes
Aubergines are grown so quickly these days that there is really no need to salt them prior to cooking.

Wild Garlic Soup

In spring, wild garlic grows in great profusion in the grounds of Prior Park in Bath. The star shaped white flowers are so delicate and pretty, though the green leaves give off a stridently pungent smell when crushed. However, the leaves are excellent when picked to make soup or for inclusion in a salad. The soup should be a really vibrant green.

1 tablespoon olive oil
1 large onion, chopped
50g/2oz long-grain rice
225g/8oz wild garlic leaves, stalks
  removed and washed
225g/8oz spinach, stalks removed
  and washed
900ml/1½ pints chicken or vegetable stock
salt and pepper
a little cream to swirl over the top
  when serving

Serves 6

A member of the allium family which also includes chives, onions, garlic and leeks, wild garlic can be harvested from late winter through until the end of spring. It is most often found growing in woodland areas, in, near or among bluebells, however it is easy to cultivate in most soils. Unlike domestic garlic, wild garlic is harvested for its leaves and flowers, however, all parts of the plant are edible and can be used in anything from salads to soups. Once cooked wild garlic will lose some of its pungency, but the flavour is beautifully mild.

Heat the oil in a large saucepan and sauté the onion until soft but not browned. Stir in the rice and toss well in the oil. Cook for 1–2 minutes before adding the wild garlic and the spinach leaves. Heat with the lid on for 1 minute while the leaves wilt. Add the stock and salt and pepper and bring to the boil. Cover and transfer to the simmering oven for about 20 minutes, until the rice is tender and the leaves are soft. Remove from the simmering oven and whiz through a blender.

Return to the rinsed pan, adjust the seasoning and re-heat. Serve immediately with swirls of cream.

Cook's notes
Make sure the wild garlic is very fresh for this soup. If you don't have spinach, then use all wild garlic leaves, but be warned, it will have a very full-on flavour!

Taglioni in a Lemon Cream Sauce

Pasta dishes come in handy when in a hurry to get a meal on the table, though the ubiquitous tomato sauce can get boring after a while. Try this deliciously creamy and lemony recipe for a change.

3 egg yolks
200ml /7fl oz crème fraîche
salt and pepper
grated zest and juice 1 lemon
250g/9oz taglioni pasta
170g/7oz frozen petit pois
25g/1oz butter
100g/4oz grated Parmesan cheese

Serves 6

Beat together the egg yolks and 4 tablespoons of crème fraîche. Season and set aside.

Place the remaining crème fraîche in a saucepan with the lemon zest and warm through. Allow to cook gently for 5 minutes to allow the lemon flavour to develop. Set aside at the back of the Aga.

Bring a large pan of water to the boil and cook the pasta for the time suggested on the packet. 2–3 minutes before the end of the cooking time, add the petit pois to the pasta. Drain.

Return the drained pasta to the pan and stir in the beaten egg yolks, the butter, the lemon juice and the warm crème fraîche. Mix in the grated Parmesan and serve immediately with shavings of Parmesan on top.

Cook's notes
If your lemons are small or a little past their best, use an extra lemon – the lemon flavour needs to be fairly pronounced in this dish.

Fruit Flan

This fruit flan has a smooth, creamy filling. Chill well before topping
with fruit and glazing.

225g/8oz dessert shortcrust pastry,
  homemade or a packet of chilled
50g/2oz shelled hazelnuts
2 whole eggs and 2 egg yolks
250 g/9oz crème fraîche
150ml/5 fl oz single cream
3 tablespoons icing sugar
selection of seasonal fruits
redcurrant jelly, to glaze

*Redcurrants belong to the
gooseberry family and are
at the height of their season
in mid-summer. Slightly
more tart that blackcurrants,
redcurrants are typically
combined with sugar to
counteract their sourness.
Despite their seasonality,
redcurrants are often
associated with Christmas
dishes, and other autumnal
and winter dishes, such as
game.*

Use the pastry to line a 22cm/9-inch loose-based flan tin. Chill.

Put the hazelnuts on a baking tray and toast for 2–3 minutes at the
top of the roasting oven. Grind in a processor.

In a mixing bowl, whisk together the nuts, eggs, egg yolks, crème
fraîche, single cream and icing sugar. Pour into the pastry case.

Bake on the floor of the roasting oven with the cold shelf on the
second set of runners from the bottom. Bake for about 30 minutes until
the filling is just set and the pastry case golden brown. Cool.

Put the redcurrant jelly at the back of the Aga or in the simmering
oven to melt.

Remove the flan from the tin and stand on a serving plate. Decorate
with seasonal fruit. Brush with the redcurrant jelly to glaze the fruit.

Cook's notes
A few new season's summer fruits can be made to go a long way with
this fruit flan, and it really does look something quite special.

June

1st Grilled Fennel with Feta 2nd Tomato and Courgette Salsa 3rd Broad Bean and Bacon Soup 4th Lemon and Seed Drizzle Cake 5th Smoked Salmon and Goats Cheese Roulade 6th Pecan Tarts 7th Gnocchi with Sun-Dried Tomatoes, Rocket and Lemon 8th Aromatic Asian Pesto with Chicken 9th Elderflower Fritters with Elderflower Mousse 10th West Indian Fish Curry in Coconut Cream Sauce 11th Quail in Bacon 12th Apricot and Walnut Biscotti 13th Crumbed Tomatoes 14th Paella 15th Fried Scallops with Pak Choi and Peanut Sauce 16th Chicken and Apricot Koresh 17th Cherry and Marzipan Cake 18th Lettuce and Watercress Soup 19th Harissa Prawns 20th Courgette Tart 21st Raspberry Cheesecake 22nd Couscous-crusted Fish Fingers with Mint Peas 23rd Lemon Roulade with Passionfruit Cream 24th Seafood and Leek Tart 25th Thai-style Red Lamb Curry 26th Strawberry Meringue Roulade 27th Spinach Soup 28th Gooseberry and Raspberry Crumble 29th Pork Fillet with Puy Lentils 30th Rosemary and Raspberry Pavlovas

Grilled Fennel with Feta

I love to serve this fennel recipe as a starter or as a salad to accompany cold meats and cheeses.

3 fennel bulbs
a little olive oil, for brushing
4 tablespoons olive oil
2 tablespoons lemon juice
salt and pepper
150g/5oz Feta cheese
a few black olives

Serves 6

Trim the feathery leaves from the top of the fennel. Trim the root end. Remove any outer layers that look bruised or tough. Bring a pan of water to the boil and add the fennel bulbs. Simmer for 5 minutes, drain and then plunge into cold water to cool. Drain. Cut each bulb into quarters from the top to the root. Brush with olive oil and lay on a baking tray. Hang on the second set of runners from the top of the roasting oven and grill for 10 minutes, until starting to brown.

Whisk together the olive oil, lemon juice and salt and pepper. Put the grilled fennel in a serving dish and pour over the dressing. Break the Feta over the fennel and add the olives. Serve warm or chilled.

Cook's notes
Use any trimmings from the outside of the bulbs for soup or flavouring in a fish stock.

Tomato and Courgette Salsa

Try this recipe with grilled or barbecued chicken or quickly seared tuna steaks. Assemble the salsa about an hour before serving to allow the courgettes to soften and the flavours to develop.

2 medium sized courgettes, finely diced
450g/1lb ripe but firm tomatoes,
    deseeded and finely diced
1 shallot, peeled and finely chopped
2 cloves garlic, peeled and finely chopped
finely grated rind and juice 2 limes
2 red chillies, deseeded and finely chopped
2 tablespoons chopped parsley or coriander
small pinch sugar
salt and pepper

Serves 8

Put the diced courgettes in a mixing bowl. Add the tomatoes, the shallot and the garlic. Stir gently to mix. Add the remaining ingredients, seasoning with salt and pepper to taste.

Spoon the salsa into a serving dish and cover with clingfilm. Set aside at room temperature for 30–60 minutes.

Stir and check the seasoning before serving.

Cook's notes
To grill fish or meat successfully in a ridged pan, place the empty frying pan on the floor of the roasting oven for 20 minutes.

June
3

Broad Bean and Bacon Soup

When I was growing up, my father grew all our vegetables. Before we had a freezer, my brother and I used to joke about 'broad beans for breakfast, lunch and tea'. It was some years after leaving home before I could bring myself to face a broad bean! Now I love them all over again. Their season of June to August is short, so make the most of it. Try to use small beans that haven't yet developed a tough skin.

225g/8oz broad beans, shelled weight
225g/8oz peas, shelled weight
1 large onion, chopped
450ml/³/₄ pint milk
300ml/¹/₂ pint vegetable stock
salt and pepper
2 rashers of bacon, rinds removed

Serves 4

Place the beans, peas, onion, milk and stock in a saucepan. Stand on the simmering plate and slowly bring to the boil. Cover and move to the simmering oven for 30 minutes. Remove from the oven and pureé half the soup. Mix with the remaining soup and adjust the seasoning.

Place the bacon on a baking tray at the top of the roasting oven for 8–10 minutes until the bacon is cooked and very crispy.

Warm the soup through, ladle into soup bowls. Crumble the bacon on top.

Cook's notes
For older and drier broad beans, remove their outer skin prior to cooking.

Lemon and Seed Drizzle Cake

Lemon drizzle cakes are eternally popular. I have found that most cakes made in fan ovens have a rather dry texture, so the drizzle helps to moisten them, which could partly explain their popularity. This, of course, is not a problem with cakes made in the Aga! Still, the lemon drizzle does intensify the lemon flavour. Will you be able to resist spooning out the dregs from the condensed milk tin? I know I can't!

225g/8oz butter, softened
4 large eggs, beaten
397g can condensed milk
50g/2oz ground almonds
finely grated rind and juice 1 lemon
225g/8oz self-raising flour
1 level teaspoon baking powder
1 tablespoon poppy seeds

For the syrup
juice 3 lemons
75g/3oz icing sugar

For the icing
2 tablespoons lemon juice
110g/4oz icing sugar

Butter and base-line a 20cm/8-inch spring-release cake tin.

Put all the cake ingredients together in a bowl and beat well until light and fluffy. Spoon into the prepared tin and level off.

For a two-oven Aga stand the cake tin inside the large roasting tin. Cover loosely with foil and slide the roasting tin onto the bottom set of runners of the roasting oven. Then put the cold shelf on the third set of runners from the top. Bake for 45–50 minutes. If your Aga cooks more on the left hand side, turn the roasting tin round half way through baking.

For a three- and four-oven Aga, put the shelf on the floor of the baking oven and put in the cake. Bake for 50–60 minutes.

The cake is cooked when it looks golden brown, is firm to the touch and a skewer inserted in the middle comes out clean.

Make the syrup while the cake is baking. Put the lemon juice and the icing sugar in a saucepan and stir over a gentle heat until the sugar has dissolved. Then increase the heat and allow the liquid to bubble until a syrup has formed. Keep warm.

When the cake has just come from the oven, prick the top all over with a skewer. Spoon over the lemon syrup. Cool the cake in the tin.

When the cake is cold, sieve the icing sugar into a jug and stir in enough lemon juice to make a soft, pouring icing. Drizzle the icing over the cake.

Cook's notes

If you wish, you can replace the ground almonds with more flour, though be aware that this will reduce the keeping quality of the cake.

Smoked Salmon and Goat's Cheese Roulade

No apologies for this recipe appearing here, even though it is in my *Traditional Aga Christmas* book. I find it such a useful recipe – not just at Christmas time but also in the summer, serving it either for buffet lunches or made into small roulades for canapés.

50g /2oz butter	***For the filling***
300ml/¼ pint milk	*110g/4oz cream cheese*
50g/2oz flour	*1 tablespoon chopped dill*
110g/4oz goat's cheese	*50g/2oz smoked salmon pieces*
50g /2oz grated Parmesan cheese	*salt and pepper*
4 eggs, separated	

Line the large baking tray with a sheet of Bake-O-Glide.

Place the milk, flour, butter and a seasoning of salt and pepper in a saucepan. Whisk over a medium heat until the sauce is thick, smooth and shiny. Remove from the heat. Stir in the goat's cheese and half the Parmesan. Mix in the egg yolks. Set aside.

Whisk the egg whites until they are forming stiff peaks. Fold one spoonful of the egg whites into the sauce. When well combined fold in the remaining egg whites until they are just folded in and the mixture looks like scrambled eggs. Spread the mixture into the prepared tin.

Hang the tin on the bottom set of runners of the roasting oven and bake for 15-20 minutes, until pale gold and firm to the touch. Remove the roulade from the oven and scatter over the remaining Parmesan. Set aside to cool.

Place the cream cheese in a basin and stir in the chopped dill and a seasoning of salt and pepper.

Turn the roulade out onto a plain sheet of Bake-O-Glide, cheese side down. Remove the lining sheet of Bake-O-Glide and spread over the cream cheese. Scatter over the smoked salmon pieces.

Roll the roulade from the long side and roll onto a serving plate.

Cook's notes

If you want to make canapés from this roulade, simply cut the large base in half and then fill and roll as above – this will give you a smaller roulade that can easily be cut into thin whirls. Try to give the roulade time to set before slicing to help prevent the whirls from falling apart.

Pecan Tarts

I find the combination of chocolate and nuts irresistible. This recipe
will make one large $22^1/_2$ cm/9-inch tart or six individual tarts. You could
also use muffin tins which give deep tarts with plenty of filling.

175g/6oz plain white flour
110g/4oz butter
25g/1oz icing sugar
1 egg yolk
175g/6oz plain chocolate
50g/2oz butter
4 eggs
175g/6oz maple syrup
a few drops vanilla extract
225g/8oz shelled pecan nuts
icing sugar

Serves 8-12

Sieve the icing sugar and flour together into a large bowl. Cut the butter
into cubes and rub into the flour until the mixture resembles fine
breadcrumbs. Bind together with the beaten egg yolk and enough water
to make a firm, smooth dough. Roll the pastry out to fit either a
$22^1/_2$ cm/9-inch tart tin or 12 muffin tins. Chill.

Put the broken chocolate and butter in a basin and stand in a warm
spot at the back of the Aga until melted. Whisk together the eggs, maple
syrup and vanilla essence. Whisk in the chocolate mixture. Reserve
12 whole pecans. Roughly chop the remaining nuts and stir into the
egg mixture. Pour into the pastry cases and top with the whole pecans.

Put the pecan tart directly on the floor of the roasting oven for
20 minutes for the small tarts and 30 minutes for the large tart, or
until just set in the middle and the pastry is golden around the edges.
Serve warm or cold, dusted with icing sugar.

Cook's notes
Leave the tarts to cool before easing out of the muffin tins. Pecans have
a distinctive flavour and texture and are expensive, so walnuts can be
substituted, if preferred.

Gnocchi with Sun-Dried Tomatoes, Rocket and Lemon

We all have days when we need a quick supper dish. This wonderful Italian inspired recipe be made in an instant. I find that the gnocchi sold in the chilled counters to be better than the long-life variety.

1kg/2lb 2oz gnocchi (2 packets)
12 pieces semi-dried tomatoes, finely chopped
1 large bag rocket, washed
juice $^1/_2$ lemon
300ml/$^1/_2$ pint double cream
salt and pepper

Serves 6

Cook the gnocchi in plenty of boiling water according to the packet instructions. Drain well.

While the gnocchi is cooking put the tomatoes, rocket, lemon juice and cream in a saucepan and heat through on the simmering plate for 1–2 minutes until the rocket is wilted.

Return the drained gnocchi to the saucepan and pour over the rocket sauce.

Serve immediately.

Cook's notes
Semi-dried tomatoes have a lovely intense flavour. You may have some that you have dried in the Aga which would be perfect for this dish.
I like to snip them with kitchen scissors for speed.

Aromatic Asian
Pesto with Chicken

Pesto originated in Genoa in Italy and we usually think of it as a basil based sauce. However, a variety of herbs and nut combinations can be used and, in this case, I have matched coriander with peanuts to give a more Asian flavour to the chicken. Keep the Oriental theme and serve the chicken with noodles.

4 chicken breast fillets, skinless
olive oil to brush the chicken
150g/5¹/₂oz noodles

For the pesto
large handful basil leaves
large bunch coriander leaves
finely grated rind 1 lemon
finely grated rind and juice 1 lime

50g/2oz peanuts
2 red chillies, seeded and
  chopped
2¹/₂cm/1-inch piece fresh ginger
1 stalk lemongrass, chopped
1 teaspoon sesame oil
6 tablespoons groundnut or
  sunflower oil

Serves 4

Place all the ingredients for the pesto except the oils, in a blender and whiz to a paste. Set the machine running and gradually pour in the oils. Put into a bowl and adjust seasoning.

Heat a ridged pan on the floor of the roasting oven for 15–20 minutes. Brush the chicken with olive oil. Add the chicken to the hot pan and cook for 6–7 minutes on each side.

Cook the noodles as recommended on the packet. Drain.
Add 4 tablespoons pesto and toss well. Put the noodles on 4 serving plates, slice the chicken breasts and serve on the noodles with a little extra pesto on top.

Cook's notes
The pesto needs to be freshly made, though it will keep in the fridge for 2 days – any longer and it will need freezing.

Aga *year*

June
9

Elderflower Fritters with Elderflower Mousse

Over the last few years elderflower cordial has become a very popular non-alcoholic drink, encouraging many of us to look at other interesting culinary ways of using these beautiful wayside flowers. These fritters are temptingly light to eat and easy to make. Choose flower heads that have plenty of open flowers, and use them as soon as possible. Pick them in an area away from heavy traffic fumes and do not wash before cooking, just shake to remove any insects.

For the fritters
110g/4oz plain flour
salt
2 tablespoons light vegetable oil
150ml/¹/₄ pint water or lager
1 egg white
oil, for frying
8–12 elderflower heads
icing sugar, for dusting

For the elderflower mousse
250g/9oz Mascarpone cheese
2 tablespoons elderflower cordial
150ml/¹/₄ pint double cream,
  lightly whipped
2 egg whites
1 tablespoon icing sugar, to taste

Serves 6–8

Previously thought to be a member of the honeysuckle family, elderflower is a common flowering plant in the UK, appearing from the end of May and flowering throughout June, July and into August. Elderflowers are highly versatile and both their flowers and berries can be used to produce wine, jelly, chutneys, ice creams, sorbets and compôtes, as well as herbal tea and cordial.

Place the flour, and salt in a roomy bowl and whisk in the oil and water or lager. Beat to a smooth batter and then cover and leave to stand in a cool place for 1 hour.

Meanwhile, make the mousse: place the Mascarpone cheese in a bowl and beat in the cordial. Fold in the cream. Whisk the egg white until stiff but not dry and gently fold into the mousse. Taste and add the icing sugar, if needed. Chill well.

Whisk the egg white until stiff and fold into the batter. Heat the oil to a depth of 2cm/ ³/₄-inch in a large frying pan on the boiling plate. When the oil is hot, holding the stalk, dip each flower head into the batter and drop into the hot oil. Fry until golden-brown and then drain on kitchen paper. Sprinkle with icing sugar and serve on a plate with a scoop of elderflower mousse.

Cook's notes
Use a light flavourless oil for frying the elderflower heads such as corn or sunflower oil.

199

West Indian Fish Curry in Coconut Cream Sauce

Use any firm white fish for this recipe – such as monkfish, haddock, cod or pollock – but be sure to choose the best and freshest available.

110 ml/4 fl oz olive oil
1 teaspoon ground coriander
1 teaspoon mustard seeds
pinch cayenne pepper
6 fennel seeds, ground
6 white peppercorns, ground
black pepper, ground
1 cardamom pod, ground
1 teaspoon curry powder,
    strength to taste
400g can tomatoes
1 large tomato, chopped

1 onion, peeled and chopped
1 clove garlic, peeled
25g/1oz coconut cream
2 teaspoons stock powder or
    1 beef stock cube
2 bay leaves
fish stock or water, as needed
1cm/^{1}/$_2$-inch cube fresh ginger
4 fish steaks

Serves 4

In a frying pan, heat the oil and fry the spices for about 10 minutes, or until the mustard seeds pop. In a blender, blend the canned tomatoes, chopped fresh tomato, onion, garlic and ginger. Add this tomato mixture to the spices along with the bay leaves. Bring to a bubble on the simmering plate and then move to the simmering oven for 30 minutes. Stir the coconut cream and the stock powder, or cube, into the sauce and reheat. Move to the simmering oven for a further 30 minutes. If the sauce is thickening too much, add some fish stock.

Add the fish to the pan and simmer on the simmering plate or on the floor of the roasting oven for 10–15 minutes. Adjust the seasoning.

Serve with plain rice.

Cook's notes
Keep an eye on the spices frying in the pan - you don't want them to burn and become bitter - if they do, then throw them away and start again!

June
11

Quail in Bacon

Quail have a deliciously mild, slightly gamey flavour. Serve one as a starter or two as a main course. Everything is cooked in the oven so, if cooking for a crowd, prepare the bread rounds in advance and then reheat and crisp just before serving.

4 quail
salt and pepper
4 rashers streaky bacon with rinds
    trimmed off
4 slices white bread
25g/1oz butter
1 tablespoon vegetable oil
watercress to garnish

Serves 2 for a main course or 4 as a starter

Stretch the streaky bacon with the back of a table knife. Wrap one rasher of bacon round each quail. Place in the small roasting tin and hang on the second set of runners from the top of the roasting oven. Roast for 25–30 minutes until crisp, golden brown and cooked through.

Meanwhile prepare the bread. Cut each slice into a circle, use a pastry cutter if you have a large one. Put the butter and oil in a frying pan and heat on the floor of the roasting oven. When hot, fry the bread, turn over and fry the second side. When crisp and golden brown, put the toast on a warm serving plate, place a cooked quail on top, garnish with watercress and serve.

Cook's notes
To ensure the best possible roasting results, be sure not to have the quail fitting too snugly in their roasting dish.

The term quail refers to a number of species in the pheasant family which are usually medium-sized. Alongside the tender meat of the bird, quail eggs are also a popular ingredient in starters or appetisers for their rich, gamey flavour and high fat content. Due to their size and palatability once cooked, the bones of quail are also commonly consumed with the meat of the bird.

Aga *year*

June
12

Apricot and Walnut Biscotti

Making the biscotti with wholemeal flour means they are more substantial than the more traditional variety. I like to serve these crisp beauties with a cup of coffee for breakfast.

100g/3^1/$_2$oz walnuts
125g/4^1/$_2$oz wholemeal flour
125g/4^1/$_2$oz plain flour
50g/1^3/$_4$oz caster sugar
1 level teaspoon baking powder
1 level teaspoon salt
pinch black pepper
75g/2^3/$_4$oz dried apricots, finely chopped
3 eggs, beaten
50ml/2fl oz water

Put the walnuts on a baking tray and hang on the second set of runners from the top of the roasting oven. Toast the nuts for 2–3 minutes, but watch that they don't burn! Cool and then roughly chop.

Put the flours, sugar, baking powder, salt and pepper in a mixing bowl. Stir in the apricots and cooled chopped nuts. Add the eggs to the flour mixture and add enough water to bind the dough together. Remove the dough from the bowl and put onto a lightly floured worktop. Lightly knead the dough and divide it into four equal portions. Shape each portion into a long roll about 2^1/$_2$cm /1-inch thick, 25cm/ 10-inch long. Place the rolls on a baking tray lined with a sheet of Bake-O-Glide. Space the rolls out to allow room to spread.

For a two-oven Aga, hang the baking tray on the bottom set of runners of the roasting oven and the cold shelf on the third set of runners from the top of the oven. Bake for 20 minutes.

For a three- or four-oven Aga, hang the tray on the second set of runners of the baking oven and bake for 25–30 minutes.

Remove the biscotti from the oven when they are golden brown and firm to the touch.

Allow the biscotti to cool a little and then place on a chopping board. Use a sharp knife to cut the rolls at an angle, about 2cm/^{3}/$_4$-inch thick. Lay the slices on the baking tray and return to the oven for 10–12 minutes until dry and crisp. Cool on a wire rack.

Cook's notes
It really is worth toasting the nuts to really enhance their flavour. Leave the oven door open so that you can keep an eye on them.

Crumbed Tomatoes

If you are cooking a simple piece of grilled meat or fish, then this is the perfect vegetable dish to accompany. Ideal for when that frustrating lull appears before the rush of high summer vegetables begins.

2 medium onions
50g/2oz butter
2 x 400g cans tomatoes
175g/6oz fresh breadcrumbs
1 tablespoon parsley, chopped
finely grated rind of $^{1}/_{2}$ a lemon
salt and pepper

Serves 4–6

Today, there is increasing demand for organic and heirloom tomatoes for their flavour and texture which far exceeds that of the commercially, mass-produced tomato which can often be bland and watery instead of juicy and rich. Many commercially produced tomatoes are picked whilst still green and immature, and are then artificially ripened. These tomatoes are typically inferior to those that have been allowed to ripen naturally.

Peel and finely slice the onions. Melt 25g/1oz butter in a pan and add the onions. Cook slowly until pale golden brown. Spoon into a shallow, ovenproof dish.

Halve the tomatoes and add to the onions, along with the tomato juice.

Mix the breadcrumbs with the parsley, lemon rind, salt and pepper and scatter over the tomatoes. Dot with shavings of the remaining butter.

Put the shelf on the bottom set of runners of the roasting oven and put in the dish of tomatoes. Bake for 30 minutes until bubbling hot and crisp on top.

Cook's notes
Make sure that you try to remember to make some breadcrumbs when you have spare bread to hand. They can be placed in the freezer and scooped out as and when needed.

June
14

Paella

This simple summer dish is perfect for eating in the garden, served straight from the cooking dish. Fresh seafood can be added according to what you can find on the day. If the seafood is already cooked, add it right at the end of the cooking to allow to heat through.

1kg/2lb 4oz chicken, cut into manageable portions
225g/8oz lean pork, diced
salt and pepper
2 tablespoons olive oil
1 onion, chopped
2 cloves of garlic, crushed
4 tomatoes, chopped
$^1/_2$ red pepper, seeded and diced
$^1/_2$ green pepper, seeded and diced

110g/4oz green beans, cut into 5cm/2-inch lengths
$1^1/_5$ litres/2 pints chicken stock
2 teaspoons paprika
good pinch of saffron
12 prawns, mussels or whatever mixture of shellfish takes your fancy
225g/8oz risotto or arborio rice
110g/4oz peas

Serves 4

Season the chicken and pork. Heat the oil in a paella pan or very large frying pan and fry the chicken until brown. Add the pork and cook until brown. Now add the onion, garlic, tomatoes, peppers and beans. Cook for 2-3 minutes and then add the stock, paprika and saffron. Stir in the rice and bring to the boil. Move to the simmering oven for 15 minutes. Add the seafood, if raw, and stir on the simmering plate for 5 minutes, adding more liquid if needed. Add the peas and any cooked seafood, check the seasoning and heat through.

Cook's notes
If you choose to use frozen seafood, make sure it is thoroughly thawed and drained as otherwise it will make the paella weak and watery.

Fried Scallops with Pak Choi and Peanut Sauce

Scallops are increasingly popular and can now even be found in the freezer compartment in the supermarket! This dish works equally well with scallops that are not straight from the sea onto the plate!

12–16 scallops
sesame oil
salt and pepper
1 tablespoon sunflower oil
800g/2lbs pak choi, finely shredded
2 tablespoons fish sauce diluted
  with 2 tablespoons water

For the sauce
110g/4oz unsalted, roasted peanuts

1 clove garlic, peeled
1 tablespoon grated fresh ginger
1 green chilli, deseeded and
  chopped
1 tablespoon brown sugar
150–200ml/5–7fl oz coconut milk
small bunch coriander leaves,
  chopped
lemon wedges

Serves 4

Trim and clean the scallops and dry on kitchen paper. Sprinkle over a little sesame oil. Set aside while making the sauce.

Put the peanuts, garlic, ginger, chilli and brown sugar in a blender or processor and whiz to make a pesto. Gradually stir the pesto into the coconut milk.

Heat the empty wok on the boiling plate for 10 minutes and then cook the scallops for 1 minute on each side. Remove from the wok and keep warm.

Reheat the wok and then add the sunflower oil. Stir-fry the pak choi until cooked and crisp and then stir in the fish sauce. Add the peanut sauce and stir, bringing to the boil. Add the scallops and briefly heat through.

Serve the stir-fry immediately, garnished with the chopped coriander and lemon wedges.

Lemon flavoured rice is a good accompaniment.

Cook's notes
As with all stir-fries, be careful to ensure that all ingredients are prepared before starting to cook.

Chicken and Apricot Koresh

Apricots have a short season so I like to make the most of them. This recipe is ideal if the apricots you buy are too firm to be eaten raw.

3 onions, peeled and chopped
2 tablespoons olive oil
750g/1lb 10oz chicken breast fillets, cubed
³/₄ teaspoon turmeric
³/₄ teaspoon ground cinnamon
³/₄ teaspoon ground ginger
300ml/ ½ pint chicken or vegetable stock
salt and pepper
18 fresh apricots, halved and stoned
juice 1 lemon
4 tablespoons chopped parsley or coriander

Serves 6

Heat the oil in a flameproof casserole and sauté the onions until soft. Add the chicken pieces and cook until just browning. Stir in the spices and toss the chicken so that it becomes coated with the spice. Add the stock and season. Cover with a lid, bring to the boil and after 2–3 minutes move the casserole dish to the simmering oven. Cook for 40 minutes and then return to the simmering plate. Stir in the halved apricots, cover and return to the boil. Move to the simmering oven and cook for another 15–20 minutes.

Adjust the seasoning, stir in the lemon juice and parsley or coriander. Serve with rice or couscous.

Cook's notes
Mix the spices together in a basin before adding to the chicken to ensure an even blend of flavours.

Cherry and Marzipan Cake

I discovered this recipe when an Aga customer came to me for advice. She was having difficulty getting the cake to cook through to the middle. After several attempts, I discovered the best solution was to bake it in a loaf tin. The freshly cut slices look so pretty and irresistible that you may be well advised to make two!

225g/8oz softened butter
225g/8oz caster sugar
4 eggs, beaten
225g/8oz self-raising flour
110g/4oz ground almonds
225g/8oz glacé cherries, halved and washed
$1/_2$ teaspoon almond essence
250g/9oz marzipan

Cherries are of the same family as plums, apricots and peaches, and have a sharp, berry flavour. Originating in Persia, cherries are available in the UK from June until September but enjoy a peak in mid July, but persist until late summer. Cherries range in colour from bright orange-red to deep maroon.

Grease and line the base of a 1kg/2lb loaf tin.

Place the butter, sugar, eggs and flour in a bowl and mix until smooth. Stir in the glacé cherries and the almond essence. Spoon half the mixture into the prepared tin. Roll the marzipan to a strip just a little smaller than the length and width of the tin. Place the marzipan on top of the cake mix and then top with the remaining mixture and level off.

For the two-oven Aga, stand the tin in the large roasting tin and cover the top of the loaf tin loosely with a sheet of foil. Hang the roasting tin on the bottom set of runners of the oven and slide the cold shelf on to the second set of runners from the top of the roasting oven. Bake for 50–55 minutes until risen and golden and a skewer inserted in the middle comes out clean.

For a three- or four-oven Aga, hang the shelf on the bottom set of runners of the baking oven. Put the cake in to bake for $1-1^1/_4$ hours until risen and golden and a skewer inserted in the middle comes out clean.

Cool in the tin for 10 minutes and then turn out and cool on a wire rack. Dust with icing sugar.

Cook's notes

If the eggs are on the large side then the cake mix can become very soft and the cherries will sink. So if the mix is sloppy, just stir in an extra spoonful of flour.

Lettuce and Watercress Soup

A great way to use those surplus lettuces from the garden. Although this is primarily a soup to serve chilled, I have served it hot when the weather has been on the chilly side.

25g/1oz butter
1 onion, peeled and finely chopped
1 medium potato, peeled and finely chopped
1 litre/1³/₄ pints vegetable stock
1 round lettuce, washed
1 bunch watercress, washed, thick stalks removed
salt and pepper
150ml/¹/₄ pint single cream
chives, chopped to garnish

Serves 6

Melt the butter in a roomy saucepan and sauté the onion until soft but not coloured. Add the potatoes and toss them in the butter and then pour in the stock. Bring to the boil and cover with a lid.

Move to the simmering oven and cook for 15–20 minutes. When the potato is cooked, move the pan to the simmering plate and add the lettuce, torn into pieces, and the watercress. Bring to the boil and remove from the heat.

Blend the soup and pour into a bowl to chill. Adjust seasoning. Just before serving, stir in the cream and garnish with chopped chives.

Cook's notes
If you have them to hand, a few fresh peas added along with the potatoes gives extra flavour and texture.

Harissa Prawns

These spicy prawns can be served as canapés or as a starter. They take minutes to cook, so serve immediately.

48 large, raw peeled prawns, fresh
  or thawed from frozen
1 tablespoon olive oil
2 tablespoons rose harissa paste
1 small pickled lemon, finely diced
1 tablespoon chopped coriander or parsley
10 strands saffron
6 tablespoon mayonnaise

Serves 6 as a starter

Put the saffron strands in a small bowl and add 2-3 teaspoons boiling water. Leave to stand until cold. When cold mix the saffron liquid into the mayonnaise. This will make a dip for the prawns.

Put the prawns into a bowl and add the harissa paste and the pickled lemon. Mix very well to coat the prawns.

Pour the oil into a wide saucepan that has a lid. Stand the pan on the simmering plate and heat for 1–2 minutes and then tip in the prawns. Shake the pan so that the prawns are evenly distributed in the pan and then cover with a lid. The prawns will now steam. Cook for 3–4 minutes until the prawns are coral pink.

Serve the prawns with the saffron mayonnaise for dipping and salad leaves, if serving as a starter.

Cook's notes
The prawns can be left to marinate in the harissa paste mixture for 1–2 hours before cooking. Cook just before serving.

Courgette Tart

I like this flan in the summer when there are always courgettes to be eaten up. Take some time to arrange the courgette slices prettily on the top.

225g/8oz shortcrust pastry
1 onion, finely chopped
2 tablespoons olive oil
4–6 small courgettes, finely sliced
pinch black pepper
4 eggs
300ml/¹/₂ pint single cream
150ml/¹/₄ pint milk
freshly grated nutmeg
110g/4oz Gruyère, grated

Serves 6

Roll out the pastry to line a 23cm/ 9-inch flan dish. Chill.

Put the olive oil in a frying pan and gently cook the onion until soft but not brown. Remove with a slotted spoon and put in to the pastry case.

Fry the courgette slices until golden brown. Remove from the pan and put half the slices in the pastry case.

Beat the eggs and add the milk, cream, pepper and the nutmeg. Pour this mixture over the courgettes and sprinkle over the grated Gruyère. Arrange the remaining courgette slices on the top.

Bake on the floor of the roasting oven for about 30 minutes until the tart is set in the middle and golden brown.

Cook's notes
Use a good, tasty cheese for this tart as courgettes are not exactly packed with flavour.

Raspberry Cheesecake

For some reason, cheesecakes have dropped a little out of fashion
– I really don't know why and nor, I suspect, will you, if you try this
wonderful recipe. Make the day before to allow it to chill. Top with a
good layer of fresh fruits prior to serving.

1 box of trifle sponges, slit in half
450g/1lb low-fat curd cheese, such as Quark
50g/2oz caster sugar
2 tablespoons cornflour
salt
2 eggs, beaten
1 egg yolk
finely grated rind of 1 lemon
300ml/$^1/_2$ pint double cream
110g/4oz frozen raspberries
fresh fruit, to serve

Cuts into 8–10 slices

Butter the base and side of a 23cm /9-inch spring-release cake tin. Line
the base with the trifle sponges, making sure there are no gaps.

Mix together the cheese, sugar, cornflour, salt, eggs, egg yolk, lemon
rind and cream. When well mixed, gently fold in the frozen fruit. Pour
the cheese mixture carefully over the sponge base and level the surface.

For a two-oven Aga, put the shelf on the floor of the roasting oven,
put in the cheesecake and slide the cold shelf one runner above the top
of the tin.

For a three- and four-oven Aga, put the oven shelf on the bottom set
of runners from the bottom of the baking oven and put in the cheesecake.

Bake for 40–50 minutes, until set. After 30 minutes check to see if the
top is becoming brown; if it is, place a sheet of foil loosely over the top,
to prevent browning.

Cool completely in the tin then chill well before serving. Decorate
with fresh fruit.

Cook's notes
I like to use the fruit frozen as then it won't squash whilst being folded
into the cheesecake mixture and leach colour.

June
22

Couscous-Crusted
Fish Fingers with Mint Peas

These are adult fish fingers that can be eaten by all. I have used salmon but any firm fish can be used. Chips are often eaten with fish fingers so go the whole way and make home made 'oven chips'.

For the crust
75g/3oz couscous
salt and pepper
finely grated zest $^1/_2$ lemon
5ml/1 teaspoon paprika
5ml/1 teaspoon ground cumin
5ml/1 teaspoon ground coriander
5ml/1 teaspoon ground ginger

4 skinless salmon fillets, about
  150g/5$^1/_2$oz each
1 tablespoon seasoned flour,
  on a plate
1 egg, lightly beaten on a plate
1 tablespoon olive oil
400g/14oz frozen peas
a few mint leaves
small bunch chives
1 tablespoon wholegrain mustard

Serves 4

Prepare the crust. Measure the couscous into a basin and pour over enough boiling water to cover it. Leave to stand for 5 minutes and then fork through. Tip the couscous onto a plate and allow to cool. When cool, return to the basin and stir in the lemon zest and spices. Return to the plate.

Cut each salmon fillet in half lengthways to make 8 fish fingers. Dip the salmon fillets in the seasoned flour, shake off any excess and then dip into the beaten egg. Finally dip the salmon into the couscous mixture to coat evenly.

At this stage the salmon can be put on a plate, covered with clingfilm and chilled for several hours until needed.

To cook the salmon, put the oil into a frying pan and heat for 2 minutes. Gently fry the salmon either on the simmering plate or on the floor of the roasting oven, for 2–3 minutes on each side.

While the salmon is cooking cook the peas in a little salted water. Drain and return to the saucepan. Toss the peas with the mint, snipped chives and mustard.

Serve two fingers on a plate with a portion of peas.

Homemade oven chips should be served!

Cook's notes

If you like a finer crumb on the fish use a coarse semolina instead of the couscous. Homemade chips are just potatoes scrubbed, sliced into chip shapes, tossed in oil and 'fried' on a baking tray in the roasting oven.

June
23

Lemon Roulade with Passionfruit Cream

Roulades always look impressive and are so easy to make. This is one of my favourites and just seems to celebrate the summer sun.

For the roulade
5 eggs, separated
150g/5$^1/_2$oz caster sugar
3 tablespoons self-raising flour
finely grated zest 3 lemons

For the filling
4 passionfruit
274ml/$^1/_2$ pint double cream
150g/5$^1/_2$oz lemon curd
icing sugar, to dust

Serves 6–8

Line a large baking tray with a sheet of Bake-O-Glide.

Place the egg whites in a large bowl and whisk until firm peaks have formed. Set aside. Put the egg yolks and sugar together in a bowl and whisk until thick and pale in colour. Fold in the flour and the lemon zest. Beat 1 tablespoonful of the egg white into the yolk mixture to slacken it and then gently fold in the remaining egg white. Do not over mix the mixture – it should look like scrambled egg at this stage. Gently spoon the mixture into the lined baking tray and level the surface.

Hang the tray on the bottom set of runners of the roasting oven and bake for 12-15 minutes, until evenly golden brown and springy when gently pressed. Lift the roulade on the Bake-O-Glide onto a cooling rack and leave to cool.

When ready to roll, lay a plain sheet of Bake-O-Glide on the work top. Invert the cooled roulade onto the sheet and peel off the lining sheet of Bake-O-Glide. Spread the lemon curd over the sponge. Lightly whisk the cream until it forms soft peaks and spread over the lemon curd. Halve the passion-fruit and scoop out the flesh and the seeds. Spoon over the cream.

Roll the roulade along its long edge and roll onto a serving plate. Chill well if time allows, this will make cutting easier. Sieve over icing sugar before serving .

Cook's notes
If you are using homemade lemon curd and it is too stiff to spread on the roulade, just gently fold in the whipped cream which in turn will slacken the curd thus making it easier to spread.

Seafood and Leek Tart

Any sort of tart is so easy to make in the Aga as there is no baking blind involved and less chance of leakage. This recipe is a change from the usual cheese-based tart and uses seafood instead.

For the pastry
175g/6oz plain flour
pinch salt
pinch paprika
75g/3oz butter
25g/1oz grated Parmesan

For the filling
400g packet frozen seafood

cocktail, thawed and drained
2 medium leeks, cleaned and
    finely sliced
25g/1oz butter
2 tablespoons dry vermouth
2 eggs and 1 egg yolk
200ml/7 fl oz crème fraîche
2 tablespoons milk
salt and pepper

Prepare the short crust pastry. Mix the flour, salt and paprika together in a bowl. Stir in the cheese and rub in the butter until the mixture looks like breadcrumbs. Add enough cold water to make a firm dough. Roll out the pastry to fit a 23cm/9-inch flan tin. Chill.

Melt the butter in a saucepan and add the leeks. Toss them in the melted butter, cover with a lid and cook gently until just softening. Stir in the vermouth and bubble to evaporate all the liquid. Set aside to cool.

Mix the drained seafood with the leeks and spread over the base of the pastry case. Beat together the eggs, crème fraîche, milk and a seasoning of salt and pepper. Pour over the seafood mixture.

Slide the tart onto the floor of the roasting oven and cook for 20–25 minutes, until the filling is just firm in the middle. Leave to stand for 10–15 minutes before serving.

Cook's notes
Make sure the seafood is well thawed and drained before putting in the tart otherwise it will make for a very watery filling.

Thai-style Red Lamb Curry

I love this very rich curry, with its magical combination of cashew nuts
and coconut milk, especially when cooking for a crowd – the potatoes
replace the usual rice and everything is served from one pot.

1 tablespoon sunflower oil
8 teaspoons ($^1/_2$ jar) red Thai curry paste
1 kg/2$^1/_4$ lbs leg lamb meat, diced
100g/3$^1/_2$oz cashew nuts, ground
400ml can coconut milk
2 tablespoons tomato purée
4 dry Thai lime leaves, crushed
500g/1 lb 2oz baby new potatoes
2 tablespoons Thai fish sauce
1 tablespoon Demerara sugar
lime wedges, to serve

Serves 8

Heat the oil in a roomy shallow pan with a lid. Add the curry paste and
fry for 1 minute. Add the lamb and stir-fry until the lamb is coated in the
curry paste. Add the ground cashew nuts, the coconut milk and the
tomato purée. Sprinkle over the crushed lime leaves, stir well and
cover. Allow the mixture to come to the boil and after 1–2 minutes
move the pan to the simmering oven and cook for 1$^1/_2$–2 hours.

Meanwhile, cut the potatoes in half and cook in the usual way for
25 minutes, until cooked but still firm.

Add the potatoes to the curry and stir in the fish sauce and Demerara
sugar. Return to the oven for 15 minutes, until heated through.

Serve with lime wedges to squeeze over.

Cook's notes
Ask your butcher to dice the lamb for you, but make sure it is not fatty
as the nuts in the curry will produce some oiliness. Use a pestle and
mortar to grind the nuts roughly for a crunchy texture.

Aga *year*

Strawberry Meringue Roulade

Roulades always look, and taste, spectacular. You could always make a jar of lemon curd with the egg yolks to fill the roulade instead of the strawberries!

For the meringue
5 large egg whites
280g/10oz caster sugar

For the filling
250-300g/9–10oz strawberries
300ml/ $^1/_2$ pint double cream

a little icing sugar to dust

Serves 6–8

Line the large baking tray with a sheet of Bake-O-Glide.

Place the egg whites in the bowl of an electric beater and whisk until stiff white peaks. Continue running the machine at full speed and, very slowly, whisk in the caster sugar, one teaspoon at a time. When all the sugar has been added, spoon the meringue onto the lined baking tray and spread evenly.

Put the shelf on the floor of the roasting oven and slide on the meringue tray. Bake for 7-8 minutes until a pale golden colour and firm to the touch. Move the tray to the middle set of runners of the simmering oven and bake for a further 20 minutes.

Remove from the oven. Slide the meringue, on the Bake-O-Glide, onto a cooling rack and leave until cold.

Turn the meringue over onto a plain sheet of Bake-O-Glide. Whip the cream to soft peaks and spread all over the meringue. Slice the strawberries thinly and scatter over the cream.

Have a serving plate ready and roll up the roulade from the longest side. Roll onto a plate and dust with icing sugar. Chill before serving.

Cook's notes
Very fresh eggs do not make the best meringues, so if you have a lot of eggs nearing the end of their shelf life, make a batch of meringues to keep and some jars of lemon or orange curd.

Spinach Soup

Since writing my first recipe for spinach soup the tasty green leaves have become very popular and are to be found all the year round in supermarkets. Spinach is easy to grow and the young, tender leaves are excellent in salads. Slightly more mature leaves cook in minutes, just in their washing water, and add a wonderful flavour to cheese and fish dishes.

25g/1oz butter
1 large onion, chopped
1 large potato, peeled and chopped
225g/8oz spinach, thick stalks removed
600ml/1 pint chicken stock
salt and pepper
150ml/$^1/_4$ pint single cream
freshly grated nutmeg

Serves 4

Melt the butter in a saucepan and sauté the onion until soft but not brown. Stir in the potato and the spinach. Allow the leaves of the spinach to wilt and then add the stock and salt and pepper, cover and bring to the boil. When boiling, move to the simmering oven for 30–40 minutes. Purée the spinach mixture and return to the rinsed pan. Check the seasoning, heat through and then ladle into soup bowls. Pour on a little cream and grate on a little nutmeg.

Cook's notes
The flavour of nutmeg diminishes very quickly, so always try to grate freshly.

Gooseberry and Raspberry Crumble

Gooseberries are in many ways the forgotten British fruit, maybe because they generally need cooking. Raspberries and gooseberries come into season at about the same time and I often combine them, as in this recipe, for a perfect summer crumble.

450g/1lb gooseberries, topped and tailed
225g/8oz raspberries
1 teaspoon cornflour
sugar, to taste
225g/8oz plain flour
salt
75g/3oz caster sugar
110g/4oz butter, chilled and diced

Serves 4–6

Gooseberries, along with juniper and blackberries are among the quintessential British hedgerow fruits, and are at their best through June and July. Indigenous to Europe and western parts of Asia, gooseberries have sharp thorns and are pale green or red in colour with translucent skin. Also known as a 'grozet' in northern parts of Scotland, the gooseberry responds well to cooler climates such as those in Britain. Commonly used in desserts and puddings, gooseberries have a strong, sour flavour which can be balanced with sugar for use in coulis, compôtes or jams.

Place the fruit in an ovenproof dish. Stir together the cornflour and sugar. The amount of sugar depends upon the ripeness of the fruit and your personal taste. Mix the sugar mixture into the fruit.

Place the flour, salt and sugar into a mixing bowl and add the butter. Rub in the butter until the mixture looks like breadcrumbs. Scatter the crumble mixture over the fruit.

Put the shelf on the bottom set of runners of the roasting oven and slide in the crumble. Bake for 25–30 minutes, until the crumble is golden-brown and the fruit is just cooked.

Serve with fresh cream.

Cook's notes
I use cornflour to slightly thicken the juices, so mixing with the sugar in this way will help prevent lumps of cornflour forming.

Pork Fillet with Puy Lentils

Pork fillet gently cooked in the oven will be moist and juicy. This makes an easy one-pot meal. Accompany the pork very simply with some fresh seasonal greens briefly cooked and tossed in butter.

1 tablespoon olive oil
500g/1lb 2oz pork fillet
4 tablespoons grainy mustard
400g/14oz Puy lentils
2 medium potatoes, peeled and cut into chunks
3 red onions, peeled and quartered
8 pieces sun-dried tomatoes
3–4 sprigs thyme
1.2 litres/2 pints vegetable stock
2 tablespoons chopped parsley
salt and pepper

Serves 4

Spread 2 tablespoons mustard over the pork fillets. Heat the oil in a frying pan and brown the meat (this can be done on the floor of the roasting oven). Remove the pork from the pan and set aside.

To the pan add the potatoes, onions, sun-dried tomatoes and the thyme sprigs. Mix the stock with the remaining 2 tablespoons of mustard and pour over the lentil mixture. Bring to the boil, cover and move to the simmering oven for 15 minutes. Place the pork fillet on top of the vegetables, return to the boil and then move to the simmering oven for a further 15–20 minutes.

Allow the meat to rest for 5 minutes before slicing.

Spoon the lentil mixture onto warm plates and top with slices of pork and a scattering of parsley.

Cook's notes
I find a deep sauté pan with a lid, that will go both in the oven (with a detachable handle) and on the hob, invaluable for this and other recipes.

Rosemary and Raspberry Pavlovas

Raspberry pavlova is the quintessential summer dessert, ideal for a buffet party and can easily made into individual portions for all shapes and sizes.

3 egg whites
175g/6oz caster sugar
2 teaspoons cornflour
$^1/_2$ tablespoon finely chopped
   rosemary
1 teaspoon white wine vinegar

For the topping
285ml carton extra-thick double
   cream
200g/7oz raspberries
200g/7oz white grapes, halved
   and seeded

To decorate
icing sugar
a few sprigs rosemary

Serves 6

Line a baking tray with Bake-O-Glide.

Whisk the egg whites in a clean, grease-free bowl until stiff peaks form. Gradually whisk in the sugar one teaspoonful at a time. Whisk the cornflour into the egg whites with the last two teaspoon of sugar. Fold in the rosemary and the vinegar.

Spoon the meringue onto the baking tray in 6 evenly-sized blobs. Spread each into a circle about 9cm/$3^1/_2$-inch in diameter.

Hang the tray in the middle of the simmering oven and bake for 1–1$^1/_2$ hours. The meringues should be crisp on the outside and marshmallowy in the middle. Cool.

Just before serving, spoon the cream onto the meringues. Mix together the raspberries and grapes and spoon on top of the cream. Dust with icing sugar and decorate with a sprig of rosemary.

Cook's notes
Rosemary has a very strong flavour so take care not to be heavy handed with it.

July

1st Tian of Aubergines 2nd Pork Tenderloin Roast with
Pineapple 3rd Hazelnut and Chocolate Chunk Cookies
4th Pea Soup 5th Bread with Olives and Tomatoes
6th Cous Cous, Tomato and Haloumi Salad
7th Coconut Lamb 8th Pistachio and Chocolate Torte
with Summer Fruits 9th Chilled Lemon Chicken
10th Fennel Gratin 11th Potato and Courgettes with Pistou
12th Blueberry Butter Cake 13th Thai-Spiced Scallop and
Prawn Salad 14th Salmon Filo Tart 15th Chocolate
Meringue 16th Three Tomato Risotto 17th Braised Peppers
with Olives 18th Sweetcorn Relish 19th Cheese, Basil and
Pine Nut Triangles 20th New Potato, Chorizo and Roast
Pepper Salad 21st Compôte de Tomates 22nd Pineapple
Upside-Down Puddings 23rd Aga-Dried Tomatoes
24th Goat's Cheese and Rocket Slice 25th Summer Fruit
Torte 26th Roast Tomatoes with Ricotta Pesto
27th Exotic Fruit Salad 28th Seared Tuna Niçoise
29th Aga Lemon Curd 30th Falafel and Tomato Salsa
31st Caramelised Pineapple with Raspberries

Tian of Aubergines

Aubergines seem to be a vegetable you either love or loathe – I fall into the former camp. Make this dish at the height of summer to give a Provençal feel to your meal.

3 aubergines, cut into large dice
8 tablespoons olive oil
1 red onion, peeled and chopped
2 cloves garlic, peeled and chopped
800g/1lb 12oz plum tomatoes, peeled and chopped
4 or 5 basil leaves
salt and pepper

Serves 6 as a side dish

Heat half the olive oil in a frying pan and sauté half the aubergines until browning. Remove them and then drain on kitchen paper. Repeat with the remaining oil and aubergines.

Using any oil remaining in the pan, cook the chopped onion until soft and then add the garlic. Cook for 2–3 minutes and then add the tomatoes and the basil leaves. Season with salt and pepper. When the sauce is bubbling, move to the simmering oven and allow to cook and thicken, without a lid, for 30–40 minutes.

Butter a shallow ovenproof dish and pour in the tomato sauce. Stir in the drained aubergines. Put the shelf onto the bottom set of runners of the roasting oven and slide in the aubergine dish. Bake for 20 minutes, and, if the aubergines are not cooked, transfer to the simmering oven for a further 30 minutes.

Cook's notes
Aubergines do not need salting before cooking, as they used to years ago – they are grown so quickly nowadays that they don't have time to become bitter.

Pork Tenderloin Roast with Pineapple

Pork and pineapple complement each other very well and in this recipe they are roasted together to great effect! It is all too easy to overcook tenderloin and make it dry – roasting on a bed of pineapple and onion helps keep the meat moist.

$1/_2$ small pineapple, peeled, cored and eyes removed
50g/2oz butter
2 red onions, peeled and thickly sliced
a few small leaves from a sprig of rosemary, chopped
3 good tablespoons Dijon mustard
2 pork tenderloins, about 900g/2 lbs
200ml/7fl oz dry white wine

Serves 6

Stand a colander in a bowl. Chop the pineapple into bite-sized pieces and put in the colander to drain for 15 minutes.

Melt 25g/1oz butter in a small roasting tin or ovenproof frying pan and stir in the onions. Put the pan on the floor of the roasting oven and cook the onions, stirring occasionally. When the onions are cooked stir in the pineapple.

Mix 2 tablespoons mustard and the rosemary into the pineapple juice. Season the tenderloins and smear the mustard mixture over. Place the tenderloins on top of the onion and pineapple mixture.

Put the oven shelf on the third set of runners from the top of the roasting oven and slide in the pan of tenderloins. Roast for 20 minutes and then turn the tenderloins over and cook for a further 15–20 minutes, until cooked through.

Remove the pan from the oven and allow the meat to rest for 5–10 minutes. When the meat has rested, slice the tenderloins and arrange on a warmed plate. Use a slotted spoon to lift the onion and pineapple mixture onto the serving plate. Put the roasting pan on the simmering plate and add the wine. Whisk in the remaining 25g/1oz butter and 1 tablespoon mustard and allow to come to the boil. Spoon a little sauce over the meat and serve the rest separately.

Cook's notes
Remove any skin from the tenderloin before cooking to prevent it curling up during roasting.

Hazelnut and Chocolate Chunk Cookies

A wonderful recipe from my friend Jean. The combination of nuts and chocolate is always popular and very moreish.

225g/8oz butter, softened
225g/8oz caster sugar
170g tube condensed milk
350g/12oz self-raising flour
110g/4oz chocolate chunks
110g/4oz hazelnuts, roasted and roughly chopped

Put the butter and the sugar together in a mixing bowl and beat until light and fluffy. Stir in the condensed milk. Mix in the flour and then the chocolate and the nuts.

Divide the mixture in half. Place each half on a square of foil or clingfilm and roll the dough into a sausage shape. Wrap in the foil or clingfilm and chill well or freeze until needed.

When ready to bake line a large baking tray with a sheet of Bake-O-Glide. Peel off the wrapping and cut thick slices of biscuit mix. Lay the circles on the baking tray with a gap in case the biscuit spreads a little.

For a two-oven Aga, put the shelf on the floor of the roasting oven and slide in the baking tray. Hang the cold shelf on the third set of runners from the top of the roasting oven. Bake for 12–15 minutes.

For a three- or four-oven Aga, hang the baking tray on the bottom set of runners of the baking oven and bake for 15–18 minutes.

Bake until the biscuits are a pale golden brown but a little soft to touch. Cool on a wire rack.

Cook's notes
This cookie dough is very handy to keep in the fridge or freezer so that you can bake biscuits freshly as and when needed. Make the roll of biscuit dough to the size that you like to serve your cookies. Remove the dough rolls from the freezer and leave to stand at room temperature for half an hour before cutting and baking.

Pea Soup

This is a quick, easy and delicious soup to make and goes well with some homemade bread for a simple lunch. The soup will retain a fantastic colour as long as you don't cook the peas for too long. In the event of a lack of fresh peas then frozen will work very well instead.

1 medium onion, peeled and chopped
25g/1oz butter
150ml/$^1/_4$ pint white wine
1 litre/1$^3/_4$ pints vegetable stock
907g packet frozen peas
small carton single cream
salt and pepper

Serves 8–10

Although we commonly treat the garden pea as a vegetable, it is, botanically, a fruit. Harvested for their tender sweet pods, peas have been cultivated for thousands of years and are a common vegetable in European cuisine. At their best through the summer season, peas are fantastic on their own, simply blanched and served with a little melted butter. They are also a common ingredient in the traditional English roast dinner and a classic addition to soups, stews and mashed vegetables. Older peas tend to be less tender than young ones, and are therefore best used for soups or purées.

Put the butter and onion into a roomy saucepan and sauté the onion until soft but not brown. Add the wine, bubble for 2–3 minutes and then add the stock. Bring to the boil and then add the peas. Bring to the boil again, cover and move to the simmering oven for 15–20 minutes, until the peas are cooked.

Blend the soup until smooth. Return to the rinsed out pan and stir in the cream. Check the seasoning. Heat through and serve.

Cook's notes
If you don't like bits in your soup then simply pass it through a sieve after blending. A little fresh mint can be blended with the soup for an extra herby kick.

Bread with Olives and Tomatoes

Two Mediterranean ingredients are added to this bread to make the perfect summer loaf! Of course, it can be made at any time of the year to eat with cheese and cold meats.

700g/1 $^1/_2$ lbs strong white flour
2 teaspoon salt
2 level teaspoon dried fast-action yeast
2 tablespoons olive oil
300ml/ $^1/_2$ pint warm water
100g/3 $^1/_2$ oz semi-dried tomatoes
  or sun-dried tomatoes in oil
100g 3 $^1/_2$ oz black olives, without
  stones
1–2 tablespoons olive oil, to brush
  the loaves with

Makes 2 small loaves

Put the flour in a large mixing bowl and stir in the salt and the yeast. Add the olive oil and gradually add the water. The amount of water needed will depend upon the flour so be careful not to add too much at the beginning. Mix to make a dough that is slightly sticky. Knead well. When the dough is smooth, cover with oiled clingfilm and stand on a trivet on top of the Aga and leave until doubled in size.

Drain the tomatoes from their oil if using the ones in oil. Finely chop the tomatoes and the olives and knead into the dough. Divide the dough into two halves and shape each one into an oval loaf. Put the loaves on a baking tray lined with Bake-O-Glide and brush each loaf with olive oil. Cover with clingfilm and stand on top of the Aga, on a trivet, until doubled in size. Brush again with olive oil.

Hang the tin on the bottom set of runners of the roasting oven and bake the bread for 25–30 minutes, until golden brown and sounding hollow when tapped on the bottom.

Cook's notes
If you make your bread by hand, the tomatoes and olives can be mixed into the dough at the beginning. A mixer tends to break them up too finely during the kneading process.

July
6

Cous Cous, Tomato and Haloumi Salad

Haloumi is a strange cheese that tastes of little when cold but has a wonderful flavour when fried or grilled and served warm. Serve this salad with the cheese freshly cooked as a main course salad.

225g/8oz couscous
3 tablespoons olive oil
salt and pepper
600ml/1 pint boiling water
1 red onion, peeled and thinly sliced
250g/9oz Haloumi
12 baby plum tomatoes, halved
2 cloves garlic, peeled and sliced
75g/3oz olives, a mixture of green and black
1 tablespoon parsley, chopped
parsley, sprigs to garnish
lemon wedges

Serves 4

Place the couscous and 1 tablespoon of olive oil in a bowl, season with salt and pepper. Pour over the boiling water. Stand at the back of the Aga until the water has been absorbed, about 10 minutes, then fluff up with a fork.

Heat another tablespoon of the oil in a frying pan and fry the onion until softening. Remove to a plate and keep warm. Pour the remaining tablespoon of olive oil in the pan and fry the slices of haloumi for 2–3 minutes on each side. Add the tomato halves and garlic slices and toss in the pan juices for 1–2 minutes, just to coat but not to cook the tomatoes as they need to keep their shape. Add the olives and the reserved onions and season with salt and pepper.

Stir chopped parsley into the couscous and divide out onto plates. Top with Haloumi slices and the pan contents. Serve with lemon wedges.

Cook's notes
Everything can be prepared ahead of serving with just the frying of the cheese to do at the last minute.

Coconut Lamb

Coconut makes a rich and creamy sauce. Ensure the lamb that you use isn't fatty so as to avoid the finished dish being overly oily.

4 red chillies, seeded
6 tablespoons chopped coriander leaves
4 cloves garlic, peeled
5cm/2-inch piece fresh ginger
1 teaspoon salt
450ml/³/₄ pint thick coconut cream
1kg/2¹/₄ lbs boned leg of lamb, cubed

75g/3oz unsalted butter
¹/₂ fresh coconut, grated
1 tablespoon white poppy seeds
1 tablespoon cumin seeds
1 tablespoon black peppercorns
1 teaspoon turmeric
¹/₂ teaspoon grated nutmeg
2 onions, peeled and chopped
450g/1 lb potatoes, peeled and cubed

Serves 6

In a blender whiz together the chillies, coriander, garlic, ginger and salt with 2–3 tablespoons coconut cream to make a smooth paste. In a non-metallic bowl place the lamb and stir in the blended sauce. Cover and leave in the fridge for about 6 hours for the flavours to infuse the meat.

Melt 25g/1oz butter in a frying pan and add the grated coconut, cumin seeds, poppy seeds, peppercorns, turmeric and nutmeg. Fry lightly for 4–5 minutes. Blend this mixture with 110 ml/4 floz coconut cream until smooth.

Melt the remaining butter in a large pan and fry the onions until soft and brown and then add the coconut and spice mixture. Add the lamb and the remaining coconut cream. Cover and bring to simmering point before moving to the simmering oven for 1 hour. Stir in the potatoes and adjust the seasoning. Bring to a gentle bubble on the simmering plate and return to the simmering oven without the lid. Cook until the potatoes are cooked and the sauce thickened, about 30–40 minutes.

Serve with rice and chopped coriander.

Cook's notes
Cook the onions gently so that they turn a golden colour but do not brown, otherwise they will impart a burnt flavour to the lamb.

Pistachio and Chocolate Torte with Summer Fruits

The pistachios give an attractive green fleck to this torte.

100g/3¹/₂oz unsalted pistachios
50g/2oz plain chocolate, finely chopped
5 egg whites
200g/7oz caster sugar
25g/1oz plain flour
2x284ml cartons extra thick cream
250g/9oz strawberries
125g/5oz raspberries
125g/5oz blueberries
icing sugar to dust

Butter a 23cm/9-inch deep spring-release cake tin and base-line.

Put the chocolate and the nuts in a food processor and whiz briefly. Mix with the chocolate.

Whisk the egg whites until forming stiff peaks. Whisk in the sugar, a teaspoon at a time. Fold in the pistachios and the chocolate mixture followed by the sieved flour.

Spoon into the prepared tin. Level the top.

For the two-oven Aga, put the oven shelf on the floor of the roasting oven and slide in the cake tin. Put the cold shelf on the third set of runners from the top. Bake for 30–40 minutes, until firm to the touch and a pale golden brown.

For the three- and four-oven Aga, put the shelf on the second set of runners from the floor of the baking oven and slide in the cake tin. Bake for 40–45 minutes, until firm to the touch and pale golden brown.

Cool in the tin for 5 minutes and then carefully remove from the tin and allow to completely cool.

To serve, place the torte on a serving plate. Spoon the cream over the top and slice over the strawberries. Scatter over the raspberries and blueberries. Dust with icing sugar. Do not do this more than an hour before serving otherwise the torte will go soft.

The torte may be made 2–3 days before it is needed. Wrap in foil and chill. Add the cream and fruit just before serving.

Cook's notes
Sometimes, the torte seems to collapse a little when cooling. It doesn't matter as it will be topped with cream and fruit.

Chilled Lemon Chicken

I love the delicate flavour of this lemon chicken which I serve for a cold buffet dish as an alternative to the seemingly ever present Coronation Chicken. The recipe is enough for six, but larger chickens can be used, or even two or three chickens cooked at a time, if catering for a crowd. Serve with fragrant Thai rice and a colourful salad.

1.5 kg/3 lb 5oz chicken
1 onion, peeled
2–3 bay leaves
salt and pepper

For the sauce
25g/1oz butter
25g/1oz flour
300ml/$^1/_2$ pint chicken liquor
salt and pepper
1 lemon, finely grated rind and juice
2 egg yolks
300ml/$^1/_2$ pint single cream

Serves 6

Place the chicken in a large saucepan. Put in the peeled whole onion, the bay leaves and some salt and pepper. Cover with cold water. Put on the lid and stand the pan on the simmering plate. Bring slowly to the boil. When boiling, move to the simmering oven and cook for a further 1–1$^1/_2$ hours, depending on the size of the chicken. Remove from the oven and allow the chicken to cool in the liquor. When cool, remove the chicken. Discard the skin and bones and chop the flesh into even-sized chunks.

To prepare the lemon sauce, skim the fat from the liquor and measure it into a saucepan. Add the butter and flour and stand it over a medium heat and whisk all the time until a thickened sauce is made. Simmer for 1–2 minutes. Add the lemon juice and rind. In a basin mix the egg yolks and cream, add to the hot sauce and whisk well. Cook gently on the simmering plate, whisking all the time for 1–2 minutes. Do not allow to boil. Remove from the heat, check seasoning, then pour into a bowl and allow to cool. When cold, fold in the prepared chicken. Chill and allow the flavours to mingle.

Cook's notes
If you like a good, strong lemon flavour then add the rind and some juice from a second lemon – remember cold dishes often need more flavouring!

Aga *year*

Fennel Gratin

I am frequently asked for suggestions for how to cook fennel. This is a very tasty way to accompany plain meat or fish or as a stand alone vegetarian dish.

2 large fennel bulbs
4 eggs
200ml crème fraîche
6 generous tablespoons grated Parmesan cheese
salt and pepper

Serves 6 as a side dish

Trim the root end of the fennel and remove any damaged outer leaves. Cut each bulb into quarters and remove the hard core. Grate the fennel coarsely.

Beat the eggs in a mixing bowl and stir in the grated fennel and 4 tablespoons of Parmesan. Season with salt and pepper.

Butter a shallow, ovenproof dish. Pour in the fennel mixture and sprinkle over the remaining 4 tablespoons of Parmesan cheese.

Hang the shelf on the bottom set of runners of the roasting oven and put in the fennel gratin. Bake for 25–30 minutes until golden brown.

Cook's notes
If you have a food processor, use the grating blade to prepare the fennel – you will find it a lot easier than by hand.

Blueberry Butter Cake

Blueberries have taken over from blackcurrants as the ultimate 'super food'. This is a delicious way of serving them, either as a pudding or as a cake.

For the topping
200g/7oz soft brown sugar
50g/2oz plain flour
75g/3oz chilled butter

For the cake
225g/8oz plain flour
2 teaspoons Baking Powder

pinch salt
110g/4oz soft butter
225g/8oz caster sugar
3 eggs
142ml carton soured cream
250g/9oz blueberries, washed

Butter and base-line a 23cm/9-inch deep spring-release cake tin.

Prepare the topping. Place the sugar and flour in a mixing bowl and add the butter. Rub in the butter until the texture resembles fine breadcrumbs. Set aside.

Place the flour, baking powder, salt, butter, caster sugar, eggs and soured cream in a mixing bowl and stir until smooth. Pour the cake mix into the prepared tin. Scatter over the blueberries and then the topping mix.

For the two-oven Aga, put the shelf on the floor of the roasting oven, slide in the cake and put the cold shelf on the third set of runners from the top. Bake for 40 minutes. If the top of the cake is browning, but a skewer inserted in the middle come out sticky, then cover the top of the cake with a sheet of foil and cook for a further 10 minutes.

For the three- and four-oven Aga, put the shelf on the bottom set of runners of the baking oven. Slide in the cake and bake for 55–60 minutes. It is baked when the top is bubbling and dark on the top, a skewer inserted in the centre comes out clean.

Allow the cake to set for 5 minutes and then release the side. Allow to cool.

Serve warm as a pudding or cold as a cake.

Cook's notes
If you can't get soured cream you can use plain yoghurt or crème fraîche or just 'sour' some single cream with a little lemon juice. The soured cream helps lighten the sponge.

Aga *year*

Thai-Spiced Scallop and Prawn Salad

When I am travelling for work I try to seek out suppliers of the freshest ingredients possible. One place I always aim to get to is the Fish Hut in Sidmouth – their scallops and other spankingly fresh fish are well worth making a detour for, armed with a good-sized cool bag. On the way home I think of making something like this summer salad for supper!

For the dressing
2 tablespoons Thai fish sauce
2 tablespoons light soy sauce
2 tablespoons sunflower oil
juice 2 limes
2 teaspoons sugar
2 teaspoons hot chilli paste
2 teaspoons fresh ginger, grated
2 teaspoons fresh crushed garlic

For the scallop and prawn salad
2 tablespoons sunflower oil
2 bunches spring onions, trimmed and chopped
500g/1 lb 2oz scallops, cleaned
200g/7oz uncooked prawns
2 bags or a selection prepared salad leaves
1 large mango, peeled, stoned and diced
1 tablespoon roughly chopped coriander leaves

Serves 8

Put all the dressing ingredients together in a jam jar and shake well to combine.

Heat the wok on the boiling plate for 10 minutes and then move to the simmering plate. Pour in the sunflower oil and quickly add the spring onions. Stir well and then add the scallops and prawns. Return the wok to the boiling plate and stir-fry the onions, scallops and prawns until the prawns are pink, take care not to overcook them. Tip the wok contents into a bowl and chill.

Put the salad leaves in a bowl and toss them in half the salad dressing. Top with the seafood and onion mixture and scatter the diced mango over the top. Drizzle over the remaining salad dressing and scatter over the chopped coriander.

Cook's notes
I find mangoes can be a bit disappointing to prepare. At the end of all the effort put in you often end up with just a mushy pile. An Aga shop customer told me that it is the one fruit she buys ready prepared – I now agree with her. For me, it often turns out to be better value for money.

Salmon Filo Tart

I first wrote this recipe for my *Traditional Aga Cookery Book* and I still use it often as a way of using up leftover salmon. The filling in this rises like a soufflé and looks stunning. Serve with new potatoes and baby vegetables for a delightful lunch or supper.

50g/2oz butter, melted
110g/4oz filo pastry

For the filling
225g/8oz salmon
300ml/½ pint milk
50g/2oz butter

1 bay leaf
35g/1½oz plain flour
4 eggs, separated
2 tablespoons chopped fresh dill
1 tablespoon chopped chives
75g/3oz grated Gruyère
salt and pepper

Serves 6

Chives are available in the UK all year round but are at their best in the late winter and early spring. The smallest plant in the allium family, chives are a very close relative of the onion and glean their name from the French word cive, *which derives from the Latin term for onion,* cepa. *The chive is a sturdy herb that is often grown at home for its insect-repelling qualities as well as for its versatility across a range of dishes and its subtle flavour. They are also rich in vitamins A and C.*

Brush the base and sides of 23–25cm/9–10-inch flan dish with melted butter. Lay the pastry out on the worktop and brush the top sheet with melted butter. Lay a sheet of buttered pastry over the base of the flan dish. Continue in this way until the dish is lined. Cover with clingfilm. Chill.

Put the salmon in a small roasting tin. Pour on the milk, add the bay leaf. Put the tin in the centre of the roasting oven and cook the salmon for 15–20 minutes. Drain, reserving the milk.

Skin the salmon, remove the bones and flake the flesh.

Put the butter and the flour and reserved milk in a saucepan on the simmering plate and whisk. Bring to the boil and simmer until thick and smooth. Off the heat, beat in the egg yolks, herbs, cheese and seasoning.

Whisk the egg whites until softly stiff. Fold one tablespoon of egg white into the sauce to slacken the mixture and then gently fold in the remaining egg white. Fold in the salmon. Take the clingfilm off the pastry case and fill it with the sauce.

Place the flan dish on the floor of the roasting oven and bake for 25–30 minutes, until the filling is risen and golden. Serve immediately.

Cook's notes
This tart can be made up to 3 hours ahead of baking and kept somewhere cool. Bake and serve immediately.

Chocolate Meringue

Anything with chocolate or meringue is unfailingly popular, so I have combined the two! If you prefer, the meringue can be made into individual 'blobs' and sandwiched together with whipped cream. I have used raspberries here but other summer soft fruits work just as well.

3¹/₂oz/100g plain chocolate
3 egg whites
175g/6oz caster sugar
1 teaspoon white wine vinegar
*   and 1 teaspoon cornflour, blended*
300ml/3¹/₂oz double or whipping cream
225g/8oz fresh strawberries

Serves 6

Break up the chocolate and put to melt on the back of the Aga.

Line the cold shelf with Bake-O-Glide or non-stick baking parchment.

Whisk the egg whites in a clean, dry and grease-free bowl until white and fluffy. Continue to whisk while adding the sugar, 1 teaspoon at a time. Adding the sugar too quickly will cause the meringue to leak. Lightly fold in the cornflour mixture.

Pour the melted chocolate over the meringue mixture and stir through with a large metal spoon once or twice, to give a swirled effect.

Spoon the meringue mix onto the prepared baking sheet. To make a 'basket' spoon the meringue round the sides of the circle and slightly hollow in the middle.

Bake in the simmering oven for 2 hours until well set. Remove from the baking sheet and turn upside-down onto the sheet. Return to the oven, leaving the door slightly ajar, unless your oven is very cool. Continue to dry for 4–6 hours. Remove from the oven and allow to cool before wrapping and storing or filling. When ready to fill, whip the cream until it forms soft peaks. Fold half the raspberries into the cream. Pile the mixture into the meringue shell. Decorate with raspberries. Because this method dries out the meringue shell, the meringues can be filled 1–1¹/₂ hours before eating.

Cook's notes
If the meringue is for immediate consumption, it may only need 3 hours in the oven. It will then be more like a pavlova with a moist inner.

Three Tomato Risotto

I like to serve this risotto with something very summery such as grilled fresh sardines. The colours of the tomatoes and parsley look lovely against the white rice.

450g/1lb vine tomatoes
1 onion, peeled and chopped
1 clove garlic, crushed
2 tablespoons olive oil
350g/12oz arborio rice
120ml/ 4 fl oz white wine or vermouth
1 litre/ 1^1/$_4$ pints hot chicken or vegetable stock
25g/1oz semi-dried tomatoes, cut into pieces
2 tablespoons chopped parsley
150g/5^1/$_2$oz cherry tomatoes, halved
50g/2oz Parmesan cheese, grated
salt and pepper

Serves 6

Peel the vine tomatoes and cut into quarters. Remove the seeds if you like.

Heat the oil in a large frying pan and cook the onion until soft but not brown. Add the garlic and rice and stir to coat in oil. Add the wine and stir until absorbed. Gradually add the stock, stirring, until all the liquid has been absorbed. Add the quartered tomatoes, dried tomatoes and the herbs. Stir well. Season to taste and check that the rice is cooked, adding a little more water and cooking a little longer if needed.

Stir in half the Parmesan and the halved cherry tomatoes. Cover with a lid for 3–4 minutes to heat through.

Serve with the remaining cheese.

Cook's notes
I specified 'vine tomatoes' for this recipe, really meaning a flavoursome tomato, not the large tasteless ones we import.

July
17

Braised Peppers with Olives

Raw peppers are usually used in salads but I think they have a much better and cleaner flavour when cooked. This recipe needs to be prepared ahead of time to allow the peppers to cool.

2 red peppers
2 yellow peppers
salt and cayenne pepper
4 cloves garlic, peeled
100ml/3^1/$_2$fl oz olive oil
50ml/2 fl oz red wine vinegar
50g/2oz anchovy fillets
16 black olives, pitted
small bunch flat-leafed parsley

Serves 4 as a starter

Cut each pepper in half lengthways and remove the seeds. Cut in half again. Lay the peppers skin side up in a shallow ovenproof dish. Season. Lightly crush the garlic cloves and add to the peppers. Pour over the olive oil and vinegar and cover the dish with foil.

Put the shelf on the floor of the roasting oven and put in the peppers. Cook for 25–30 minutes, until the peppers are completely soft. Set aside and leave to cool, covered.

When cool, peel the skin from the peppers.

Remove the garlic from the dish. Place in a bowl and lightly crush. Whisk in the cooking juices, season with salt and cayenne pepper.

Lay the peppers in a serving dish and top with the olives, anchovies and the leaves from the bunch of parsley. Pour over the dressing.

Cook's notes
Serve with good buffalo Mozzarella and freshly baked bread to make a deliciously light lunch.

243

Sweetcorn Relish

I have loved corn relish ever since I visited Canada in the early 1970s. It goes well with barbecue-style food and is excellent in sandwiches.

500g/1lb 2oz sweetcorn kernels
1 red pepper, seeded and very finely diced
1 green pepper, seeded and very finely diced
110g/4oz granulated sugar
2 teaspoons salt
2 teaspoons dry mustard powder
600ml/1 pint cider vinegar or white wine vinegar

Bring a pan of water to the boil and plunge in the corn and the diced peppers for 2 minutes. Drain and plunge into cold water. This helps retain their colour.

In a jug, blend together the sugar, salt, mustard powder and vinegar. Put the vegetables and vinegar mixture in to a saucepan and stand on the simmering plate and bring to the boil, stirring occasionally.

When boiling, move to the simmering oven, uncovered for $1^{1}/_{2}$–2 hours. Pour into warm sterilised jars and, when cold, seal and label.

Store in a cool dark place for at least 2 weeks before eating.

Cook's notes
Stand the cob on its end and strip the kernels away by slicing down the length of the cob with a sharp knife.

Cheese, Basil and
Pine Nut Triangles

Serve these as part of a selection of nibbles or for a summer drinks party instead of as a formal starter. As with all pastry, it is best to serve these freshly baked from the oven. They can easily be prepared in advance and the baking tray popped into the oven when needed. Don't forget to put the timer on – filo pastry burns easily!

110g/4oz butter
110g/4oz Feta cheese
110g/4oz Ricotta cheese
2 tablespoons freshly chopped basil leaves
3 tablespoons pine nuts, toasted
1 egg, beaten
salt and pepper
14 sheets filo pastry (the quantity will vary
    according to the type you buy – they all
    come in varying sizes!)

Makes about 28

Place the butter in a basin and stand at the back of the Aga to melt.

Put the cheeses, basil, pine nuts and the egg in a basin. Season to taste. Mix very well.

Lay a sheet of filo pastry on the worktop and brush with melted butter. Lay a second sheet of filo pastry on top and cut the pastry into four long strips. Each strip will make one triangle.

Place two teaspoons of the cheese mixture at the base of one strip and fold the pastry over diagonally to form a triangle. Continue folding the pastry up the length of each strip of pastry enclosing the filling. Place on a buttered or Bake-O-Glide lined baking tray and continue until all the filling and the pastry have been used.

Brush the triangles with the remaining melted butter and bake on the third set of runners from the top of the roasting oven for 15 minutes, until crisp and golden brown. Serve hot.

Cook's notes
A great variation is to sauté a small, finely chopped onion with a crushed clove of garlic in 1 tablespoon of olive oil until soft. Add two finely chopped red chillies. Cook for 1 minute. Drain a 400g can of kidney beans and mash them. Add the onion mixture and 1 tablespoon of readymade tomato salsa. Use this mixture to fill the filo pastry and continue as above. You can let your imagination run riot when it comes to fillings once you know what the consistency should be like.

New Potato, Chorizo and Roast Pepper Salad

If you don't usually cook potatoes in the simmering oven then give this recipe a try. I meet so many Aga owners who cook all their root vegetables on the top of the Aga and thus waste a lot of heat. As we are now becoming so aware of how to save fuel, both for the planet and for our pockets, it really is worth learning to use the Aga ovens economically.

600g/ 1lb 4oz new potatoes, scrubbed
4 red peppers, quartered and seeded
3 tablespoons white wine vinegar
1 tablespoon Dijon mustard
good handful chives, chopped
10 tablespoons extra-virgin olive oil
salt and pepper
350g/12oz chorizo sausage
50g/2oz wild rocket, washed

Serves 6

Put the prepared potatoes in a saucepan, add enough water to come 2.5cm/1-inch up the side of the saucepan, cover and bring to the boil. Drain off the water, re-cover and put the pan of potatoes in the simmering oven for 40–50 minutes or until the potatoes are cooked. Drain off any moisture left in the pan.

Lay the peppers skin side up, on a baking tray lined with Bake-O-Glide, hang the tray on the second set of runners from the top of the roasting oven and cook for 15–20 minutes, until the peppers are cooked and slightly blackened. Remove from the oven and cool. When cool enough remove as much skin that will peel easily. Cut each quarter into broad strips.

Whisk together the vinegar, mustard, chives and olive oil in a bowl. Season to taste. Add the potatoes and peppers and toss gently.

Slice the chorizo into thick slices and lay in a frying pan. Put the pan on the floor of the roasting oven and fry the sausage until crisp, turning during cooking. Drain on kitchen paper and mix in with the potato mixture. Mix in the rocket leaves just before serving.

Cook's notes
If chorizo is unavailable, use spicy sausages from your butcher or a spicy cured meat found in the local delicatessen – cut into chunks, not thin slices.

247

Compôte de Tomates

Take a break from grilled or baked tomatoes and serve this brilliant dish as a vegetable accompaniment to meat or fish or even as a simple pasta sauce.

1 large onion, peeled and finely chopped
4 cloves garlic, peeled and finely chopped
4 tablespoons olive oil
4 large ripe tomatoes, chopped and cored
1 tablespoon tomato paste
2 tablespoons balsamic vinegar
2 strips dried orange zest
salt and pepper

Serves 4

Heat the oil in a saucepan and cook the onion and garlic until softened but not brown. Add the tomatoes, tomato paste, balsamic vinegar and orange zest. Add 100ml/3½ fl oz water. Stir well and allow to bubble. Transfer to the simmering oven for 30 minutes, uncovered. Most of the liquid should have evaporated. Adjust the seasoning.

Cook's notes
Some tomatoes are rather more watery than others and will make for a thinner sauce. So, either cook longer in the simmering oven or give them a quick boil on the simmering plate to evaporate the water.

Pineapple Upside-Down Puddings

I can remember making these puddings in the 1960s when upside-down puddings were quite the thing. Traditional puddings have had a resurgence, pleasing many, not least my ever-hungry husband!

For the topping	For the pudding
110g/4oz butter	*50g/2oz unsweetened desiccated*
110g/4oz soft brown sugar	*coconut*
2 tablespoons rum	*110g/4oz butter*
432g can pineapple rings in	*175g/6oz caster sugar*
juice, drained	*3 eggs*
6 glacé cherries	*175g/6oz self-raising flour*
	1 teaspoon vanilla extract
	2 tablespoons milk

Serves 6

Butter well six 200ml/7fl oz ramekin dishes.

Put the butter, sugar and rum in a small saucepan. Allow the butter to melt and then bubble for 1 minute. Pour the sauce into the ramekin dishes. Then place a pineapple slice and a cherry in the base of each ramekin dish.

Make the pudding by placing all the ingredients together in a bowl and beating well together until light and fluffy. Divide the mixture between the ramekins. Stand the ramekins on a baking tray.

For a two-oven Aga, hang the tray on the bottom set of runners of the roasting oven and slide the cold shelf on the second set of runners from the top of the oven. Bake the puddings for about 20 minutes.

For a three- or four-oven Aga, hang the tray on the second set of runners from the bottom of the baking oven and bake for 20–25 minutes.

The sponges will be well risen and firm to the touch when cooked.

Turn out onto plates and serve with cream or custard.

Cook's notes
This can also be made as a single pudding in a 23cm/ 9-inch cake tin.

Aga-Dried Tomatoes

Should you be lucky enough to have a glut of tomatoes, or find some cheaply in the market, there are many ways of preserving them for later in the year. Sun-dried or semi-dried tomatoes have become very popular in recent years, adding an intensity and a real tomato 'hit' to dishes.

tomatoes, any size will do but preferably
   not the huge beefsteak variety.
salt flakes
herbs, optional
olive oil

Sterile jam jars and lids

Line a large baking tray with Bake-O-Glide.
   Cut the tomatoes in half and lay cut side up on the baking tray. Sprinkle over a little salt and some chopped herbs if you like.
   Slide the tray into the middle of the simmering oven and leave the tomatoes until dry and wrinkly. This timing will depend upon your Aga, how large and watery the tomatoes are and how dry you want them. If you plan to leave them overnight this will work well if you know that your simmering oven isn't too hot and won't blacken them. If it is your first time doing these tomatoes then dry them during the day when you can keep and eye on them. I prefer to dry mine to the semi-dried state so that they are not too chewy.
   Remove them from the oven and allow to go completely cold. Pack the cold tomatoes into a jam jar and cover with olive oil. Put on a lid and label. Store somewhere dark and cool but not in the fridge.

Cook's notes
Only dry one tray at a time as the Aga oven becomes too moist with too many tomatoes in at one time.

Goat's Cheese and Rocket Slice

It may seem unusual to cook rocket in this way but I first got the idea in a pizza restaurant and I think it works really well. You can, of course, use different types of pesto.

375g/13oz packet ready-rolled puff pastry
1 jar roasted aubergine pesto
200g/7oz goat's cheese, in rounds
a large handful of rocket leaves
olive oil

Serves 6

Line the large baking tray with a sheet of Bake-O-Glide.

Unroll the pastry onto the baking tray. Spread over the roasted aubergine pesto, leaving a border of about 1.5cm/ $^3/_4$-inch.

Cut the goat's cheese into 8 rounds and lay over the pesto. Scatter over the rocket and drizzle lightly with olive oil.

Hang the baking tray on the third set of runners from the top of the roasting oven and bake for 15 minutes. Move the tray to the floor of the oven for a further 5 minutes.

Serve hot.

Cook's notes
As long as you leave a border around the edge of the pastry it will puff up during cooking and hold the filling in place.

Summer Fruit Torte

A summer fruit torte is an ideal recipe for when you have a supply of soft summer fruits to hand. It also helps a little fruit to go a long way.

300g /10^1/$_2$oz plain flour
salt
150g/5oz butter, chilled and diced
50g/2oz caster sugar
1 egg, beaten
cold water

For the filling
450g/1lb soft summer fruits, e.g. raspberries, strawberries,
*   blackcurrants*
icing sugar, for dusting

Serves 6

Enjoying a peak period from April through July, British strawberries are a common ingredient in many British desserts. They are ideal for use in cakes, puddings and compôtes and are fantastic for jam due to their high pectin content, which helps the fruit preserve to set. With cream at Wimbledon or as jam to accompany scones and clotted cream for high tea – strawberries are now a quintessentially British fruit. Popular etymology suggests that the term 'strawberry' was coined after gardeners' practice of mulching the strawberries with straw to protect the growing fruit from rot.

Place the flour, salt, butter and sugar in a bowl and rub in until the mixture resembles fine breadcrumbs. Take out 3 tablespoons of crumble mixture and set aside. Add the egg and enough cold water to bind the mixture together to form a dough. Roll out to fit a shallow 23cm /9-inch flan tin. Chill.

Scatter the summer fruits over the pastry case. Sprinkle over the reserved crumble mixture.

Bake on the floor of the roasting oven for 20–25 minutes, until golden-brown and the fruit is soft. Dust with icing sugar.

Cook's notes
The crumble topping helps to absorb any juices from the fruit. Don't add any extra liquid, and if you have washed the fruit, dry it well before putting in the pastry case.

July 26

Roast Tomatoes with Ricotta Pesto

A simple lunch dish to eat on a long, hot summer's day. Just looking at the ingredients list makes me think of lunch in the garden during late July and early August!

leaves from a small bunch basil
1 clove garlic, peeled and crushed
3 tablespoons pine nuts or walnut kernels
225g/8oz Ricotta
6 tablespoons olive oil
9 large vine tomatoes

Serves 6

First make the pesto. Place the basil leaves, garlic, nuts, Ricotta and 4 tablespoons olive oil in a food processor or blender. Whiz until mixed and then check seasoning.

Cut the tomatoes in half and scoop out the seeds. Season with salt. Line a baking tray with Bake-O-Glide and place the tomatoes, cut side up, on the baking tray. Sprinkle over the remaining 2 tablespoons of olive oil.

Hang the tin on the second set of runners from the top of the roasting oven and roast for 10–15 minutes, until soft but not scorched. Cool for 5 minutes.

Place 3 tomato halves on each serving plate and spoon over a little pesto. Scatter with a few basil leaves.

Cook's notes
It really is worth making your own pesto, so try growing lots of basil at home. I find mine grows very well on the windowsill in the kitchen if the weather outside is too cold.

Exotic Fruit Salad

Summer is the time for fruit salads. I sometimes get carried away at the selection of fresh fruits when I am shopping, so a mixed salad is often on offer at the end of a meal. Think about a contrast of colour and texture when choosing fruits.

110g/4oz white sugar
300ml/¹/₂ pint water
pared rind and juice of 1 lemon
a selection of fruits such as pineapple,
    star fruit, raspberries, strawberries,
    lychees, kumquats

Choose a selection of fruits available in season. Consider colours, textures and size. Have about 4 different fruits. Place the sugar and water in a saucepan, stand it on the simmering plate and stir while the sugar dissolves. Add the lemon rind and bring to the boil. Remove from the heat and add the lemon juice. Allow to cool. Pour into a serving dish. Prepare the fruit according to type. Toss in the syrup. Chill and serve.

Cook's notes
The syrup can be made and kept for a day or two in the fridge, but don't put the fruit in for too long as it tends to go mushy if left.

Seared Tuna Niçoise

A Nicoise salad is perfect on a mid-summer's day using fresh vegetables heady with the aromas of the Mediterranean. Use new seasons potatoes and relish their flavour. This is a salad topped with hot fish. Tuna steaks vary in size and the flesh is very filling, so consider everyone's appetite before you buy.

100g/4oz small new potatoes
100g/4oz French beans
1 red onion, finely chopped
3 plum tomatoes, quartered
12 black olives, pitted
6 anchovy fillets

4 tablespoons balsamic vinegar
150ml/¹/₄ pint olive oil
salt and pepper
2 eggs, hard-boiled and quartered
4 tuna steaks
1 tablespoon chopped chives

Serves 4

Cook the potatoes. Put the potatoes in a saucepan and add enough water to come 2.5cm/1-inch up the side of the pan. Bring to the boil and boil for 1 minute. Drain all the water from the pan and place the pan, covered, in the simmering oven for about 20 minutes or until the potatoes are cooked but not too soft. Leave to cool then slice into a roomy bowl. Plunge the beans into a pan of boiling water and cook until just tender but still crisp. Drain and then leave in cold water. When cold, dry and cut into 7.5cm/3 inch lengths.

Add the beans, onion, tomatoes, olives and anchovies to the potatoes.

Put the olive oil and the vinegar in a screw-top jar, season with salt and pepper and put on the lid. Shake well to make a dressing. Moisten the vegetables in the bowl with some of the dressing and then divide the vegetables between 4 serving plates. Arrange the egg portions on the salads.

Heat a cast-iron ridged pan on the boiling plate or on the floor of the roasting oven for 5 minutes, until really hot. Sear the tuna steaks for about 2 minutes on each side, depending on how you like your fish to be cooked and the thickness of the steaks. Too much cooking will make the fish dry. Place a steak onto each salad and pour over a little more dressing. Sprinkle over the chives.

Cook's notes
Should you over-cook the fish, break it into chunks, toss it in the remaining dressing and then spoon on top of the salad. Not as pretty, but it neatly avoids a disaster!

Aga *year*

Aga Lemon Curd

This method of making lemon curd in the Aga is taken from Richard Maggs' excellent primer, *The Complete Book of Aga Know-How*, (Absolute Press). It is the perfect way to use up egg yolks and will make a very welcome gift for friends.

50g/2oz unsalted butter
175g/6oz caster sugar
finely grated rind and juice 2 small lemons
3 egg yolks
1 whole egg

Makes 2 x 350g/12oz jars

Put the sugar and butter in a large measuring jug (I use a large Pyrex jug), and put the jug in the simmering oven. Time for 30 minutes. After 30 minutes whisk the butter and sugar together and stir in the lemon rind and juice. The sugar may not be completely dissolved at this stage, it doesn't matter. Return the jug to the simmering oven for a further 30 minutes.

Whisk together the egg yolks and the whole egg. After the second 30 minutes whisk the eggs into the lemon mixture and cover the jug with a plate. Return to the simmering oven for 45–50 minutes.

The lemon curd should be thickened – if it is not the thickness of pouring cream then return to the oven for 15–20 minutes longer.

Pour the lemon curd into 2 warm, sterile jam jars. Either seal immediately or wait until cold before sealing.

Cook's notes
This recipe works well with oranges, Seville oranges or clementines. Make sure the fruit has been warmed before using to extract the maximum juice.

Falafel and Tomato Salsa

These popular chickpea balls can be eaten hot or cold. It is essential to chill them well before frying to help form a good shape, so be sure to allow plenty of time for the preparation. I like to use the wok for the deep-frying.

400g/14oz chickpeas, soaked for 4 hours or overnight.
1 small onion, peeled and finely chopped
2 cloves garlic, peeled and crushed
2 tablespoons parsley, chopped
1 tablespoons coriander, chopped
2 teaspoons ground cumin
1 tablespoon water
$^1/_2$ teaspoon baking powder
vegetable oil for frying

Serves 4

Drain the soaked chickpeas and place in a food processor. Blend until the chickpeas are finely ground. Add the onion, garlic, parsley, coriander, cumin, water and baking powder. Whiz to make a rough paste. Turn into a bowl and cover. Leave to stand for 30 minutes.

Take tablespoons of the mixture and squeeze out any excess water. Roll into balls. Chill.

Heat enough oil in a pan to be half the depth of each falafel ball. To test if the oil is the right temperature, drop a cube of bread into the oil and if it floats quickly to the top and turns golden brown then it is hot enough to fry the falafel.

Fry the falafel balls, turning in the oil, until brown all round. Remove with a slotted spoon and drain on kitchen paper.

Serve hot or cold with tomato salsa.

Cook's notes
I don't often deep fry. Most things can be cooked in the Aga but I have found no alternative to deep-frying for these tasty morsels. Take care to have a cover handy in case you overheat the oil, and somewhere safe to put the pan to cool down.

July
31

Caramelised Pineapple with Raspberries

This recipe makes the most of raspberries as they near the end of their season. They pair so well with fresh pineapple – the flavours marry in such sweet perfection.

1 pineapple
2 tablespoons icing sugar
175g/6oz raspberries

Serves 4

There are many species of raspberry, although the main variety available in Britain is the common red raspberry, and, occasionally, the black raspberry. These two varieties have also been crossed to produce purple raspberries. Raspberries appear both in the summer and autumn seasons; the former appearing in June and lasting until the end of July, with autumn raspberries appearing in August and running as late as October. The autumn fruit are larger and not quite as tart as the summer fruit.

Put a ridged pan to heat on the floor of the roasting oven.

Remove the skin of the pineapple with a sharp knife and cut the fruit into 8 slices. Remove the core – I do this with a cocktail cutter.

Dust the pineapple with icing sugar on one side and place in the pan, sugared side down. Cook for 2–3 minutes until the sugar has caramelised into stripes. Dust the upper side with sugar and turn over. Cook for 2–3 minutes, depending upon the ripeness of the pineapple. The pineapple should just be a little softened by the heat.

Serve the pineapple garnished with the raspberries

Cook's notes
This is another use for your faithful, heavy-based ridged Aga pan – remember, no oil needed!

August

1st Thai Fishcakes with Cucumber Relish 2nd Roasted Pepper Tartlets 3rd Mediterranean Chicken with Lemon and Olives 4th Penne with Aubergine and Pine Nuts 5th Amaretti Meringues with Raspberry Coulis 6th Lemon and Lamb Meatballs 7th Fruity Glazed Chicken 8th Haddock, Sweetcorn and Coconut Chowder 9th Baked Tomatoes on Brioche 10th Breakfast Bars 11th Cous Cous with Roast Summer Vegetables and Goat's Cheese 12th Coconut Rice Pudding with Papaya 13th Pigeon and Peach Salad with Hazelnut Dressing 14th Chicken and Mango Stir-Fry 15th Apricot and Cherry Crumble 16th Seared Tuna with Chickpea and Pepper Salad 17th Queen of Puddings 18th Marinated Courgettes 19th Spanish Quiche 20th Sweet and Sour Pork 21st Seared Salmon with Ginger and Lime Dressing 22nd Fruit Yakitori 23rd Strawberry Crumble Cake 24th Stuffed Peppers 25th Warm Chicken Salad 26th Strawberries and Lemon Curd with Filo Pastry 27th Summer Vegetable Flan 28th Plum and Almond Puddings with Bay-Scented Custard 29th Blueberry Muffins 30th Roast Salmon with Courgettes and Pine Nuts 31st Roast Garlic Bread

August
1

Thai Fishcakes with Cucumber Relish

Canapés for parties are so often made with pastry or bread, so it is good sometimes to vary things a little – these fish cakes are an excellent alternative and can easily be made in large quantities for hungry guests.

For the cucumber relish
150 ml/5 fl oz rice vinegar
50g/2oz caster sugar
¼ cucumber
¼ red onion
1 small red chilli

For the fishcakes
500g/1 lb 2oz firm white fish, roughly chopped

1 tablespoon sugar
50ml/2 fl oz fish sauce
1 tablespoon Thai red curry paste
¼ red pepper, very finely chopped
¼ green pepper, very finely chopped
oil to grease tins

Makes 36 mini fish cakes

Cucumbers are in season between May and August. The cucumber is a member of the squash family. It grows as a creeping vine which roots into the ground and grows in tendrils. Cucumbers are typically served and eaten raw and have a light, watery melon flavour. However, cucumbers can also be pickled to increase flavour and shelf life. Cucumbers should be firm with a smooth, brightly coloured dark green skin.

For the relish, put the vinegar and sugar in a saucepan. Stand on the simmering plate and heat to allow the sugar to dissolve. Bring to the boil and remove from the heat. Cool. Remove the seeds from the cucumber and chop into very small dice. Peel and finely chop the onion. Remove the seeds and finely chop the chilli. Place the prepared vegetables in a serving dish and pour over the cooled rice vinegar syrup.

Line a baking tray with Bake-O-Glide.

Put the fish, sugar and fish sauce in a food processor and whiz until a smooth purée. Add the curry paste and whiz to combine. Mix in the chopped peppers.

Shape a teaspoonful of mixture into a ball and place on the baking tray. Flatten slightly.

Hang the tray on the bottom set of runners of the roasting oven and put in the fishcakes. Bake for 12–15 minutes, until lightly browned.

Remove from the tin and serve with the cucumber relish to dip into.

Cook's notes
Make the fish cakes in advance but serve them freshly cooked.
The cucumber relish can be made up to 24 hours ahead of serving.

Roasted Pepper Tartlets

If you are serving these wonderful little tarts as a main course then some Feta cheese sprinkled over before cooking is a nice addition.

2 red peppers, cored and seeded
2 green peppers, cored and
  seeded
salt and pepper
3 tablespoons olive oil
375g/13oz pack ready-rolled puff
  pastry
2 tablespoons grainy mustard
2 tablespoons tomato purée
8 cherry tomatoes

Makes 8

Cut the peppers into strips and place on a shallow baking tray. Drizzle over the olive oil and season with salt and pepper. Hang the tin on the second set of runners from the top of the roasting oven and roast the peppers for 25–30 minutes, until softened.

Unroll the pastry onto a large baking tray and cut into eight rectangles.

Mix together the mustard and the tomato purée. Spread this mixture over the middle of each rectangle, leaving a border.

Quarter the cherry tomatoes and divide these between the pastry rectangles along with the roast peppers.

Hang the tray on the second set of runners from the top of the roasting oven for 10–15 minutes, until the pastry has risen and become golden brown. Move the tray to the floor of the roasting oven for 5 minutes to crisp the base of the pastry.

Serve hot.

Cook's notes
These little tartlets can be made to any size, from nibbles to starters to main course.

Mediterranean Chicken with Lemon and Olives

You can prepare this wonderful dish well in advance and have it ready to pop into the oven as family or guests arrive. For a dish like this I don't see the point in frying the meat to brown it.

12 chicken thighs
2 tablespoons olive oil
2 cloves garlic, peeled and
  crushed
2 tablespoons chopped mixed
  herbs
1 teaspoon dried oregano
salt and pepper
1 lemon, sliced
1 teaspoon sugar
1 x 400g can chopped tomatoes
150g /5$\frac{1}{2}$oz kalamata olives,

pitted and chopped
1 tablespoon capers, optional
75g/3oz currants
50g/1$\frac{3}{4}$oz almonds

For the couscous
450g/1lb couscous
1 litre/1$\frac{3}{4}$ pints hot chicken or
  vegetable stock
1 tablespoon olive oil
2 tablespoons chopped parsley

Serves 6

The skin can be left on or removed from the thighs. Place the chicken in a shallow, ovenproof dish.

Mix together the oil, garlic and herbs in a small bowl and spread over the chicken.

Combine the lemon slices, sugar, tomatoes, chopped olives, capers and currants. Spread over the chicken. Sprinkle the almonds over.

Hang the shelf on the second set of runners from the bottom of the roasting oven. Put in the chicken dish and cook for 30–35 minutes, until the chicken is tender. If there are a lot of juices pour them off into a saucepan, keeping the chicken warm in the simmering oven, and bubble well to reduce the sauce.

About 10 minutes before the chicken is cooked put the couscous in a heatproof serving dish. Pour on the oil and the hot stock. Cover with a lid or plate, and place at the back of the Aga until the couscous is fluffy and all the liquid has been absorbed, about 10 minutes. Stir in the parsley before serving.

Cook's notes
If the lemon is browning too quickly on top of the chicken, slide a sheet of foil loosely over the dish to prevent any burning.

Penne with Aubergine and Pine Nuts

Like a lot of families we don't eat meat and fish every day. This is one of those vegetable dishes I love for its variety of textures and flavours.

400g/ 14oz penne pasta
2 large aubergines
4 mild chillies, deseeded and chopped
8 cloves garlic, peeled
1 teaspoon allspice
6 tablespoons olive oil
100g/4oz pine nuts
400g/14oz crème fraîche
handful parsley, roughly chopped
salt and pepper

Serves 4

Aubergines crave heat, so there are a limited amount grown successfully in the UK. Those that are appear from around mid-July to early September. There are many varieties, though the fat, pear-shaped, near-black and glossy-skinned ones are the ones we recognise best. When buying, look for unblemished, firm, lustrous skin with a bright green stem. Aubergines can be stuffed and roasted and they are also fantastic when made into chutneys or pickles.

Trim the ends from the aubergines and cut into chunks. Put onto a baking tray, lined with Bake-O-Glide. Scatter over the chillies, garlic and allspice. Drizzle over the olive oil.

Hang the baking tray on the second set of runners from the top of the roasting oven and roast for 15 minutes. Add the pine nuts and return the tray to the oven for a further 10–15 minutes, or until the aubergine is soft and beginning to brown.

Meanwhile, cook the pasta in a pan of boiling water for the time recommended on the packet. Drain well. Return to the saucepan.

Spoon the contents of the baking tray into the pasta saucepan, add the crème fraîche, parsley and a seasoning of salt and pepper.

Serve immediately.

Cook's notes
Make sure the pine nuts don't catch and burn while the aubergine is softening.

Amaretti Meringues
with Raspberry Coulis

Amaretti biscuits are a favourite in the Walker household and these are a popular recent addition to my collection of meringue recipes. The biscuits add a lovely flavour and make a slightly special meringue for summer raspberries.

3 egg whites
175g/6oz caster sugar
110g/4oz amaretti biscuits,
  crushed

For the coulis
450g/1lb raspberries

75g/3oz caster sugar
2 tablespoons elderflower cordial

To serve
150ml/¼ pint double cream
mint sprigs

Serves 6

Line the large baking tray with Bake-O-Glide.

Whisk the egg whites until stiff but not dry. Start whisking in the sugar a teaspoon at a time. When all the sugar has been whisked in and the meringue is stiff and shiny, fold in the crushed amaretti.

Lightly oil a pastry cutter and place on the baking tray. Fill the cutter with the meringue mixture and level off the top. Repeat until all the meringue has been used up, leaving some space between each meringue.

Hang the tray in the middle of the simmering oven and bake for $1\frac{1}{2}$ to 2 hours until dry and easy to lift off the baking tray. Cool.

To make the coulis, reserve about 24 raspberries and put the remainder in a saucepan with the sugar and 125ml/¼ pint water. Place on the simmering plate and gently bring to the boil, stirring to dissolve the sugar. Cook until the raspberries are soft. Purée the raspberry mixture and then push through a sieve. Add the elderflower cordial and check the sweetness. Whip the cream until just forming peaks.

To serve, place the meringues on individual plates, put a generous spoonful of cream on each meringue, arrange the reserved raspberries and the sprig of mint on top of the cream. Pour the coulis around the meringue and serve the remainder of the coulis separately.

Cook's notes
Avoid putting the coulis round the meringue until just ready to serve, as otherwise the meringue will turn pink and soft.

Aga *year*

Lemon and Lamb Meatballs

Lemon imparts a fresh taste to lamb cutting through any hint of fattiness. I like to serve this dish with tagliatelle.

450g/1lb minced lamb
1 onion, grated
1 potato, peeled and grated
2 lemons, grated rind and juice
1 egg, beaten
salt and pepper
1 tablespoon chopped parsley
25g/1oz flour
25g/1oz butter
150ml/¹/₄ pint light stock
2 teaspoons cornflour blended
  with a little water

Serves 4

Put the lamb, onion, potato, rind and juice of 1 lemon, egg, salt and pepper and parsley in a bowl and mix well. Take tablespoons of the mixture and form into balls. Roll in flour and chill in the fridge for about half an hour.

Melt the butter in a flameproof casserole on the simmering plate. Fry the meatballs until browned. Pour in the stock, lemon juice and rind. Cover and bring to the boil. Transfer to the simmering oven and cook for about 1 hour.

Return the casserole to the simmering plate. Stir in the slaked cornflower, bring to the boil, stirring to thicken the sauce.

Taste, adjust seasoning and serve.

Cook's notes
The meatballs will hold together best if well chilled before cooking.

Fruity Glazed Chicken

Marinating the chicken gives it a great flavour and allows the dried fruit to plump up. This has to be one of the easiest chicken dishes ever!

200ml/7fl oz orange juice
2 cloves garlic, peeled and crushed
2 tablespoons chopped oregano
150g/5oz dried ready-to-eat apricots
150g/5oz dried ready-to-eat prunes
50g/2oz semi-dried tomatoes
50g/2oz olives
4 chicken breast fillets
150ml/5fl oz dry white wine
1 tablespoon soft brown sugar

Serves 4

Into a large non-metallic bowl place the chicken breasts. Add all the other ingredients except the wine and the sugar. Cover with clingfilm and put in the fridge for 4 hours or overnight.

Pour the wine over the chicken mixture and stir well. Place the chicken in a shallow ovenproof dish and spoon round the remaining marinade ingredients. Sprinkle over the sugar.

Put the oven shelf on the bottom set of runners of the roasting oven and put in the dish of chicken. Cook for 30–35 minutes, until the chicken is well cooked. Test by piercing the thickest part of the chicken with a sharp knife – the juices should run clear.

Serve with boiled baby potatoes.

Cook's notes
The fruit in this dish has a tendency to 'catch' and get too brown during cooking. Check after 20 minutes and, if browning too much, slide a sheet of foil loosely over the top.

Haddock, Sweetcorn and Coconut Chowder

I can remember enjoying bowls of chowder of different styles when I travelled across America many moons ago. I loved the meal-in-a-dish chunkiness of the soup both then and now. This slightly oriental chowder is quick and easy to make.

250g/9oz fresh haddock, skinned and cut into chunks
400g can sweetcorn kernels
400ml can coconut milk
2 shallots, peeled and finely chopped
1 tablespoon light vegetable oil
2.5cm/1-inch piece fresh ginger, peeled and grated
1 hot red chilli, deseeded and finely chopped
1 stalk lemongrass
300ml/$^{1}/_{2}$ pint light vegetable or fish stock
3 tablespoons chopped coriander leaves

Serves 4

Heat the oil in a roomy saucepan and add the shallots, cook until softened but not brown. Add the ginger, lemon grass (whole) and chilli and cook, stirring for 2–3 minutes.

Add the drained sweetcorn, the can of coconut milk and the stock. Bring to the boil. Reduce the heat and carefully add the fish. Simmer for 4–5 minutes, until the fish is opaque. Remove the lemongrass stalk.

Add the coriander and serve in warm, deep bowls.

Cook's notes
Try to buy a thick piece of fish that will cut into chunky pieces thus helping to ensure that the fish remains moist.

August
9

Baked Tomatoes on Brioche

I am always looking for starters that are easy to make and can largely be prepared in advance of guests' arrival. My kitchen is downstairs from the sitting room, where guests gather for drink, so I try to avoid being isolated all the time. This recipe requires little last-minute preparation. And, yes, the melting Mozzarella is not always elegant to eat but is undeniably delicious with the tomatoes.

12 medium vine tomatoes
salt and pepper
6 fresh sage leaves
1 tablespoon chopped parsley
3 chives
12 small Mozzarella balls
a little olive oil
6 slices brioche, toasted and lightly buttered

Serves 6

Line a plate with kitchen paper. Cut a slice from the stalk end of each tomato. Using a teaspoon, remove the pulp and the seeds (a grapefruit knife is sometimes helpful). Try not to break the 'shells'. Sprinkle the insides with a little salt and turn upside-down on the kitchen paper.

Chop all the herbs and lay on a plate. Season with pepper. Roll each ball of Mozzarella in the herbs. Place a ball in each tomato. Stand the tomatoes in a buttered ovenproof dish. Hang the oven shelf on the third set of runners from the top of the roasting oven. Put in the tomatoes and bake until the cheese is starting to melt, 15–20 minutes.

Serve the tomatoes on the toasted brioche slices.

Cook's notes
Choose a dish into which the tomatoes will fit snugly so that they support each other during cooking.

271

August 10

Breakfast Bars

For those who don't much care for breakfast, or are in too much of a hurry, these little bars are perfect. Wrap each bar individually or put in a little box and take with you.

150g/5¹/₂oz butter
75g/3oz soft brown sugar
3 tablespoons honey
350g /12oz porridge oats
50g/2oz hazelnuts (or nuts of your
*   choice), chopped*
¹/₂ teaspoon baking powder
2 medium bananas

A common plant in the UK, the hazel is native to Europe and some parts of western Asia and was a significant plant in making up the hedgerows of England. A wonderful late-summer nut, the hazelnut can be eaten raw or roasted, or ground into a paste and is also a common addition to desserts.

Line the small roasting tin with Bake-O-Glide.

Put the butter, sugar and honey in a large saucepan and melt together over a gentle heat. Stir in the oats, nuts and baking powder and mix well.

Mash the bananas on a plate and stir into the mixture. Spoon into the prepared tin.

For a two-oven Aga, hang the tin on the bottom set of runners of the roasting oven. Slide in the cold shelf onto the third set of runners from the top.

For a three- or four-oven Aga, hang the tin on the second set of runners from the bottom of the baking oven.

Bake for 25–30 minutes, until golden. Mark into bars while warm. Cool in the tin and then cut into bars.

Cook's notes
It really is worth lining the tin with Bake-O-Glide when making these Breakfast Bars as they tend to be quite sticky when cooked. Take care not to pierce the lining when cutting the bars.

Cous Cous with Roast Summer Vegetables and Goat's Cheese

Many different vegetables can be used for this dish, such as aubergines and courgettes. If you end up cooking too many vegetables, reserve the extras, toss in salad dressing and serve cold as a starter, or even mix with Feta cheese for a light lunch dish.

8 plum tomatoes, halved
1 red onion, quartered
2 red peppers, seeded and cut into chunks
1 red chilli, seeded and halved
4 cloves of garlic, peeled
2–3 sprigs of thyme
3 tablespoons olive oil
1 tablespoon balsamic vinegar
salt and pepper
300g/10oz couscous
600ml/1 pint hot vegetable stock
2 tablespoons herbs, finely chopped
100g/ 3$^1/_2$oz soft goat's cheese to crumble
  or a firm one diced

Serves 4

Line the small roasting tin with Bake-O-Glide. Put the tomatoes, onion, peppers, chilli, garlic and thyme into the tin. Season with salt and pepper and drizzle over the oil and vinegar. Hang on the second set of runners from the top of the roasting oven for 25–30 minutes, until the vegetables are tender but not mushy. They may tinge with colour in this time. If your Aga cooks quickly, keep an eye on the vegetables to make sure the onions don't blacken.

Place the couscous in a heatproof bowl and pour on the hot vegetable stock. Cover with a lid or a plate and stand at the back of the Aga for about 20 minutes, until the stock has been absorbed.

Place half the vegetables in a food processor, process and then pass through a sieve if you don't like 'bits'. Taste and adjust the seasoning.

Stir the herbs into the couscous and pile onto a large serving plate. Pour over the sauce and pile on the remaining roast vegetables. Scatter over the goat's cheese.

Cook's notes
You can vary this dish very easily by using a variety of different grains such as brown rice or quinoa.

August

12

Coconut Rice Pudding with Papaya

Coconut rice pudding is seriously rich, but undeniably delicious. Any fruit such as pineapple or mango will also go well.

For the rice pudding
150g/5¹/₂ oz short grain rice
700ml/24 fl oz coconut milk
300ml/¹/₂ pint whole milk
finely grated rind 1 orange
150g/5¹/₂ oz caster sugar
300ml/¹/₂ pint single cream

2–3 papayas, seeded and roughly diced
juice 1 lime, squeezed over the papaya

Serves 6–8

Place the rice, coconut milk, milk, orange rind and sugar in a saucepan. Stir together and stand on the simmering plate. Stir while the mixture comes to the boil. When boiling, cover with a lid and move to the simmering oven for 1 hour.

The rice should be cooked and the pudding thick. Pour into a bowl and cover. Cool. When cool stir in the cream.

Serve warm or cold topped with the lime squeezed papaya.

Cook's notes
Take care when bringing this to the boil in order to avoid the base burning. Use a heavy-based pan if you have one.

August
13

Pigeon and Peach Salad with Hazelnut Dressing

Pigeons are the smallest and cheapest of all the game birds, and are at their best between May and October, so summer peaches make a good accompaniment. Pigeon breasts are now so popular that you may have to order them from your butcher. If you buy whole birds you will need one bird per person.

8 pigeon breasts, skinned
salt and pepper
1 tablespoon hazelnut oil
4 peaches
salad leaves
50g/2oz hazelnuts, roasted and roughly chopped

For the dressing
2 tablespoons hazelnut oil
2 tablespoons sunflower oil
2 tablespoons wine vinegar
pinch sugar
salt and pepper

Serves 4

Make the dressing: put the oils, vinegar, sugar and salt and pepper into a screw-top jar and put on the lid. Shake well.

Heat a heavy, large frying pan until really hot. Season the pigeon breasts. Add the oil to the hot pan and then fry the pigeon breasts for about 2 minutes on each side until brown on the outside but pink in the middle. Remove from the pan and allow to cool.

Put the salad leaves on serving plates. Cut each peach into 8 slices and place on the salad leaves. Slice the cooked pigeon and add to the salad leaves. Scatter over the hazelnuts and pour on the vinaigrette dressing.

Cook's notes
Cook the pigeon breasts in a frying pan and not a ridged pan as they need to absorb the flavour from the hazelnut oil. You can use walnuts and walnut oil if hazelnut oil is difficult to find.

August
14

Chicken and Mango Stir-Fry

The contrast of the crunchy vegetables with the juicy mango works really well in this stir-fry. If I am buying ready-prepared vegetables for this dish I often buy a pack of ready-prepared mango as well. I find getting mangoes just right quite difficult so I tend to save myself the stress if I am in a hurry!

*1 bunch spring onions, trimmed and
    sliced diagonally
cube of ginger, trimmed and grated
1 clove garlic, peeled and chopped
1 ripe mango, peeled and the flesh cubed
450g/1lb boneless chicken breast, sliced
    for stir-frying
4 tablespoons vegetable oil
350g/12oz pack ready-prepared stir-fry
    vegetables
3 tablespoons soy sauce
1 tablespoon sweet chilli sauce*

Serves 4

Place the wok on the boiling plate to heat through for at least 10 minutes.

Toss the chicken strips in 2 tablespoons of oil and add to the wok. Stir-fry for 4–5 minutes until lightly coloured and cooked through. Remove from the wok onto a plate and keep warm.

Pour the remaining 2 tablespoons of oil into the wok and add the onions, ginger and garlic. Stir round well and add the mango and the prepared vegetables. Stir well for 1–2 minutes and then return the chicken to the wok. Pour over the soy sauce and the chilli sauce, stir well to mix in and then cook for a further 2 minutes until the chicken is piping hot and the vegetables are softening.

Serve hot.

Cook's notes
A variety of finely sliced vegetables can be used instead of the ready-prepared pack.

August
15

Apricot and Cherry Crumble

There is something wonderfully comforting about a crumble on those cool, damp days of summer when we are saying to ourselves 'thank goodness I haven't turned off the Aga'! With British cherry producers and British cherry varieties under threat, we should do all we can to support the great sweet, juicy British cherry.

450g/1lb apricots, quartered and stones removed
450g/1lb cherries, stones removed
1 tablespoon ground rice or semolina
1 tablespoon sugar

For the crumble
110g/4oz plain flour
50g/2oz butter, chilled and cubed
25g/1oz caster sugar
salt

Serves 6

The apricot is in season between May and September. Whilst commonly believed to be a 'subtropical' fruit, the apricot tree can actually withstand very cold temperatures. They can be eaten fresh or dried and it is not only the fruit that can be used in cooking – apricot kernels are very sweet and can be used as a substitute for nuts, or pressed, to produce a cooking oil. The most popular, and certianly one of the best English apricots, is Moor Park.

Put the apricots and cherries in a mixing bowl. Mix together the ground rice and sugar and then stir into the fruit. Tip into an ovenproof baking dish or fill 6 ramekin dishes.

Make the crumble: place the flour, butter, caster sugar and a pinch of salt in a mixing bowl and rub in the butter to resemble fine breadcrumbs. Scatter the crumble mixture over the fruit. Bake on the second set of runners from the bottom of the roasting oven for 20–25 minutes, until the fruit is just soft and the crumble is golden brown.

Cook's notes
The use of ground rice or semolina helps to thicken the fruit juices. If you like a really moist crumble, then simply omit the thickeners.

August
16

Seared Tuna with Chickpea and Pepper Salad

Tuna steaks are always popular, but are so often served dry and overcooked. Get everything ready before you start cooking the fish and have the pan searingly hot.

1 tablespoon olive oil
1 red onion, diced
1 clove garlic, peeled and finely chopped
2 x 400g cans chickpeas, drained and
    rinsed
350g jar marinated peppers
1 tablespoon balsamic vinegar
6 tuna steaks
1 tablespoon olive oil to brush the
    tuna steaks

Serves 6

If using a cast iron ridged pan put this to heat on the floor of the roasting oven.

Put the olive oil in a saucepan and add the onion and garlic. Stand on the simmering plate and cook until the onions are cooked but not brown. Add the drained chickpeas and the marinated peppers with their juices and the balsamic vinegar. Stir to mix and heat through gently. Keep warm while the tuna is being cooked.

Brush the tuna steaks with the olive oil and cook in the hot pan, either on the floor of the oven or on the simmering plate. Cook for 1–2 minutes on each side, depending upon the thickness of the steaks and how well you like them cooked.

Divide the chickpea salad between six serving plates and top each with a tuna steak.

Cook's notes
For this recipe I have used a jar of peppers, a very useful store cupboard standby, but if I have time I prefer the flavour of a few freshly roasted peppers.

August
17

Queen of Puddings

Queen of Puddings is one of those traditional puddings made from simple, possibly leftover, ingredients that looks good on the table and tastes absolutely delicious.

175g/6oz fresh white breadcrumbs
50g/2oz caster sugar
finely grated rind 1 lemon
600ml/1 pint milk
50g/2oz butter
3 egg yolks

3 tablespoons strawberry jam, warmed on the back of the Aga

For the meringue topping
3 egg whites
175g/6oz caster sugar

Serves 6

In a bowl mix together the breadcrumbs, caster sugar and lemon rind. Pour the milk into a saucepan and add the butter. Heat gently on the simmering plate until the butter has melted. Pour the milk onto the breadcrumbs and stir well. Beat in the egg yolks.

Pour the mixture into a buttered round 1.2 litre/2 pint ovenproof dish.

For a two-oven Aga, stand the pudding dish in a small roasting tin and pour round 2.5cm/1-inch boiling water. Hang the tin on the bottom set of runners of the roasting oven and slide the cold shelf onto the second set of runners from the top of the oven. Bake for 25–30 minutes. Remove the cold shelf to cool along with the pudding, you will need it cold again!

For a three- or four-oven Aga, hang the shelf on the bottom set of runners of the baking oven and put in the pudding. Bake for 30–40 minutes.

The filling will be firm and set when ready.

Spread the jam over the pudding.

Make the meringue. Whisk the egg whites in a clean and dry bowl until you get stiff white peaks. Continue whisking and add the sugar, 1 teaspoon at a time, until all the sugar has been used and the meringue is thick and fluffy.

Spoon the meringue over the jam, covering completely. Fork the meringue into peaks.

When ready to serve return the Queen of Puddings to the oven.

For a two-oven Aga, put the shelf on the floor of the roasting oven and put in the pudding. Put the cold shelf on the second set of runners from the top.

For a three- or four-oven Aga, keep the shelf on the bottom set of runners and put in the pudding.

The meringue is cooked when it is a very pale golden colour, about 20–25 minutes. Serve straight from the oven.

Cook's notes
Always try to keep some breadcrumbs in the freezer in order to make a quick pudding like this.

Aga *year*

August
18

Marinated Courgettes

How many of us have a glut of courgettes in the garden during the summer months? Well, this is a really attractive and tasty way to eat courgettes, which so often tend to have a rather bland flavour.

4 courgettes, trimmed and thickly sliced diagonally
2 tablespoons olive oil
juice 2 lemons
1 tablespoon roughly chopped mint
1 tablespoon roughly chopped basil leaves
1 clove garlic, crushed
salt and pepper

Serves 4–6

Heat a ridged pan for 5–10 minutes, either on the boiling plate or the floor of the roasting oven.

Brush the courgette slices with a little olive oil and place in the hot ridged pan. Cook for 2–3 minutes on each side. Place the cooked courgettes on a plate.

Mix the remaining oil in a basin with all the other ingredients. Stir well to blend and then spoon the marinade over the warm courgettes.

Leave to marinate for at least 20 minutes.

This can be made the day before serving and kept in the fridge. Serve at room temperature.

Cook's notes
Have the ridged pan really hot so that the courgettes will sear well and get attractive stripes. Don't be tempted to use too much oil on the courgettes, only a smear is needed.

August
19

Spinach Quiche

Spinach seems to be a very undervalued vegetable, despite all the exertions and efforts of Popeye! Baby leaves make a delicious salad with crisp bacon, though this recipe uses larger leaves.

For the pastry
175g/6oz plain flour
pinch salt
75g/butter, chilled and diced

For the filling
450g/1 lb fresh spinach leaves
4 rashers of streaky bacon,
  rinds removed
25g/1oz pine nuts
3 eggs
150ml/¹/₄ pint milk
150ml/¹/₄ pint single cream
grated nutmeg
salt

Serves 4–6

Put the flour and salt into a bowl and add the butter. Rub together until the mixture resembles breadcrumbs. Add sufficient cold water to bind to a firm dough. Turn the dough onto a lightly floured work top and knead lightly. Make into a ball and roll to fit a 23cm/9-inch flan dish. Chill.

Wash the spinach leaves well and remove any thick stalks. Place in a pan with just the washing water clinging to the leaves. Cover with a lid and place on the simmering plate for 8–10 minutes, until the leaves have collapsed. Drain off any excess moisture and chop well.

Place the rashers of bacon on a baking tray and put towards the top of the roasting oven for 10–15 minutes, until crisp. Leave until cool enough to handle, then crumble the bacon and set aside.

Spread the chopped spinach over the base of the pastry case. Scatter on the pine nuts. Beat together the eggs, milk, cream, nutmeg and salt. Pour onto the spinach and sprinkle with the crumbled bacon.

Place the quiche on the floor of the roasting oven for 20–25 minutes, until the filling is set.

Cook's notes
Watch the spinach carefully to ensure that it doesn't burn as it dries out in the pan.

20

Sweet and Sour Pork

I love the flavours of sweet and sour pork, but I am not overly keen on deep-fat frying, so I prefer to casserole the meat and then add crispy vegetables towards the end of the cooking time. Serve with plain rice.

For the marinade
1lb/450g lean pork, cut into
  cubes
1 tablespoon dry sherry
1 tablespoon light soy sauce

For the sauce
$^{1}/_{4}$ pint/150ml chicken stock
1 tablespoon oil
1 tablespoon soy sauce
$1^{1}/_{2}$ tablespoon cider or white

wine vinegar
1 tablespoon sugar
1 tablespoon tomato purée
$^{1}/_{2}$ green pepper, finely sliced
$^{1}/_{2}$ red pepper, finely sliced
2 carrots, sliced
4 spring onions, chopped
1 small bag bean shoots
1 teaspoon cornflour, blended
  with a little water

Serves 4

Toss the meat in the sherry and the 1 tablespoon of soy sauce. Marinate for at least half an hour to tenderise the meat and add flavour.

Heat the oil in a flameproof casserole and brown the meat. Stir in the chicken stock, soy sauce, vinegar, sugar, tomato purée and carrots. Bring to the boil, put in the bottom of the simmering oven for 45–60 minutes.

Return to the simmering plate, stir in the peppers and spring onions and simmer for 10 minutes. Stir in the cornflour paste and the bean shoots. Stir well until heated through.

Cook's notes
Ask the butcher for lean pork for this dish and cook a little longer to tenderise it if needed.

August
21

Seared Salmon with Ginger and Lime Dressing

Although this is called 'seared' salmon I find if the fish is thinly sliced, that it is easiest to cook it on a baking tray on the floor of the roasting oven. You can, of course, cut the slices thicker and sear them in a hot, ridged pan. This dish makes a good starter without the rice.

For the dressing
3.5cm/1^1/$_2$- inch piece ginger,
    peeled and diced
6 tablespoons soy sauce
1^1/$_2$ tablespoons caster sugar
finely grated zest and juice
    3 limes
4 tablespoons sesame oil
3 tablespoons fresh coriander

For the fish
1 kg/2lb 4oz skinless salmon
    fillet in one piece
salt and pepper

For the relish
1 cucumber, peeled
salt
1^1/$_2$ tablespoons sugar
1^1/$_2$ tablespoons white wine
    vinegar

Serves 6

Coriander and coriander seeds are widely available in the UK. Both have a citrus flavour, however the ground seeds are much woodier with a deeper, spicier flavour than the fresh herb which has a lemony bite. Cooking the herb rapidly diminishes its flavour, so coriander is often added to dishes at the last minute, or used as a garnish. Coriander seeds are often used in spice mixes to achieve warm, rich blends, and are even used to produce certain styles of beer.

Make the relish. Slice the cucumber into slices and then into quarters. Sprinkle with salt and set aside for 15 minutes. Then mix in the sugar and vinegar. Set aside until the salmon is ready.

Place the ginger in a saucepan with the soy sauce and the sugar. Slowly bring to the boil. Simmer for 1 minute and then remove from the heat. Add the lime zest and leave to infuse. When cold, whisk in 2 tablespoons of lime juice and then the sesame oil. Add the coriander and set aside.

Using a long sharp knife slice the salmon into thin, angled slices to form salmon escalopes. Lay the salmon slices in a single layer, on to a baking tray lined with Bake-O-Glide.

Put the baking tray on the floor of the roasting oven and cook the fish for 5–8 minutes.

Pile some cooked basmati rice on a plate, top with salmon slices and spoon over the sauce. Serve a little cucumber relish alongside.

Cook's notes
To slice the salmon you will need a long and very sharp knife. You can always ask your friendly butcher to give your knives a professional sharpen, but do take them along on a quiet day!

August
22

Fruit Yakitori

These fruit skewers are lovely to serve after a heavy or rich meal and make a delightful change from fruit salad!

100ml/3$^{1}/_{2}$ fl oz water
110g/4oz white sugar
2 limes
1 small or $^{1}/_{2}$ large pineapple, cut into chunks
2 firm bananas, peeled and cut into chunks
3 kiwi fruit, peeled and quartered
1 tablespoon icing sugar
6 bamboo skewers, soaked in cold water

Serves 6

Make the syrup. Put the water and sugar in a small saucepan. Thinly peel the rind from the limes and add to the saucepan along with the juice of the limes. Place on the simmering plate and allow the sugar to dissolve and then bubble to form a thick syrup. Cool.

Thread the fruit chunks on to the skewers and dust with icing sugar. Heat a griddle pan on the floor of the roasting oven. When hot place the fruit skewers, about 3 at a time, on the hot pan. Turn over after 1 minute and cook until the fruit is just softening.

Spoon over a little syrup and serve.

Cook's notes
The soaking of the bamboo skewers prevents them from burning, but take care, they still get very hot! These are also excellent when grilled on a barbecue.

Strawberry Crumble Cake

This is a good way to make a few strawberries that are not in perfect condition go a long way, especially on those days when you want something a little more substantial than strawberries and cream.

100g/3¹/₂oz soft butter
100g/3¹/₂oz caster sugar
2 eggs
100g/3¹/₂oz self-raising flour
pinch salt
450g/1 lb strawberries

For the topping
75g/ 2³/₄oz butter
100g/3¹/₂oz plain flour
25g/1oz caster sugar

Grease and base-line a 20cm/8-inch spring-release cake tin.

In a bowl cream together the butter and sugar and when light and fluffy beat in the eggs and fold in the flour and a pinch of salt. Spoon the mixture into the prepared tin and level the surface.

Slice the strawberries and lay over the sponge mixture.

Make the topping. Rub the butter into the flour until it resembles breadcrumbs. Stir in the sugar and then sprinkle the crumble mixture over the strawberries. Bake.

For a two-oven Aga, put the shelf on the floor of the roasting oven. Put in the cake and put the cold shelf on the second set of runners from the bottom. Bake the cake for 40–50 minutes.

For a three- or four-oven Aga, put the shelf on the bottom set of runners of the baking oven and bake the cake for 50–60 minutes.

The cake is cooked when it is golden and crisp on the top and has slightly shrunk from the sides of the tin.

Ease the sides of the tin and allow to set for 5–10 minutes before serving warm with cream as a dessert or cold as a cake.

Cook's notes
This is best served warm rather than hot from the oven and will be easier to cut.

Stuffed Peppers

Peppers lend themselves to a variety of fillings and when roasted in the Aga taste and look fantastic. They are part of my weekly shopping list so I am always hunting out new ways to serve them. They can either be served on their own or with simply cooked meat or fish.

3 large red or yellow peppers
300g/10^1/$_2$ oz fresh breadcrumbs
1 tablespoon salted capers, soaked
  in water and drained
1 tablespoon finely chopped black
  olives
3 large tomatoes, peeled, deseeded
  and finely chopped
1 clove garlic, peeled and finely
  chopped
2 tablespoons chopped parsley
4 anchovy fillets, finely chopped
125ml/5 fl oz olive oil
salt and pepper

Makes 6

Cut the peppers in half through the stalk and remove the seeds. Lay in a shallow ovenproof dish or baking tray.

Put the breadcrumbs in a basin and soak with water to cover and then squeeze out the excess liquid. Mix the bread, capers, olives, tomatoes, garlic, parsley, anchovies and half the olive oil together. Season with salt and pepper – but remember you have some salty ingredients!

Fill the pepper halves with the stuffing and sprinkle over the remaining olive oil.

Hang the shelf on the bottom set of runners of the roasting oven and bake the peppers for 25–30 minutes, until the peppers are soft and starting to char a little.

Serve hot or cold.

Cook's notes
The same stuffing can be used successfully for aubergines and courgettes.

Warm Chicken Salad

A quick and simple lunch or supper dish for lazy, late summer days when you don't want to slave over a hot Aga. The salad dressing makes a good sauce for the chicken. Have everything prepared in advance and cook the chicken at the last minute.

4 boneless and skinless chicken portions, shredded as for a stir-fry
4 spring onions, chopped
1 tablespoon olive oil
50g/2oz flaked almonds
mixed salad leaves, to serve

For the dressing
2 tablespoons balsamic vinegar
3 tablespoons olive oil
2 tablespoons single cream
1 teaspoon mustard
pinch of sugar
salt and pepper

Serves 4

Make the dressing: place all the ingredients in a screw-top jar, put on the lid and shake well. Set aside.

Divide the salad leaves among 4 plates.

Heat the oil in a large frying pan or wok and stir in the chicken and the spring onions. Cook, stirring most of the time, until the onions are soft but not brown and the chicken strips are cooked through. Pour over the dressing and remove from the heat. Scatter over the flaked almonds and divide the chicken among the plates of salad.

Serve immediately.

Cook's notes
You can ring the changes with this dish by using different salad dressings.

Strawberries and Lemon Curd with Filo Pastry

Strawberries go surprisingly well with lemon curd. The filo pastry adds a nice modern touch as well as creating a welcome crunch.

8 sheets filo pastry
50g/2oz unsalted butter, melted
icing sugar for dusting

lemon
50g/2oz icing sugar
50g/2oz unsalted butter

For the lemon curd
1 egg
1 egg yolk
finely grated rind and juice 1

For the strawberries
450g/1 lb strawberries, hulled
110g/4oz icing sugar, sieved

Put 2 sheets of filo pastry together and cut into 3 rectangles. Repeat with the remaining filo sheets so that you have 6 rectangles. Lay the rectangles of filo on a baking tray lined with Bake-O-Glide and brush them well with the melted butter. Dredge well with icing sugar.

Hang the tray on the bottom set of runners of the roasting oven and bake for 6–8 minutes, until golden brown and caramelised on the top. Cool and then store in a dry place.

Make the lemon curd. Put the eggs and sugar in a saucepan and beat in the lemon rind and juice and the butter. Whisk over a medium heat until the curd has thickened to the texture of thick custard. If you like you can heat the mixture on the simmering plate until the butter has melted and then move the pan to the simmering oven, covered, whisking every 10–15 minutes. When the curd is thick pour it into a basin and cover with clingfilm to prevent a skin forming. Cool. This can be made two days in advance of using.

Cut 150g/5$\frac{1}{2}$ oz strawberries into small pieces and place in a saucepan with the icing sugar and 2 tablespoons of water. Heat gently until the sugar has dissolved and then bubble fast until a thick sauce has been made. Cool the sauce and then halve the remaining strawberries and stir into the sauce.

Make the individual millefeuille. Spoon some lemon curd onto a plate, place a filo sheet on top, more lemon curd and some strawberries then another filo rectangle. Repeat and finish with the filo on the top.

Assemble just before serving.

Cook's notes
Filo pastry comes in all different sizes so it is difficult to say what size to cut the pastry. Unroll a sheet and make a judgement on appetites and the size of the plates on which you want to serve.

27

Summer Vegetable Flan

This flan is perfect when all the summer vegetables are in the garden –
it can be made with vegetable thinnings from the main crops.

175g/6oz plain flour
75g/3oz butter, chilled and diced
salt and pepper
50g/2oz walnuts, toasted and
*   coarsely ground*

For the filling
25g/1oz butter
175g/6oz courgettes, cut into
*   sticks*
1 clove of garlic, crushed
175g/6oz thin asparagus
175g/6oz carrots, cut into sticks
50g/2oz shelled peas
1 egg yolk
4 tomatoes, peeled and finely

*   chopped*
110g/4oz cream cheese
150ml/$^{1}/_{4}$ pint single cream
2 eggs, beaten
2 tablespoons chopped mixed
*   herbs*
salt and pepper
50g/2oz Gruyère or mature
*   Cheddar cheese, finely grated*

Serves 6

*Carrots are grown in
Britain throughout the
year, but the summer baby
carrots are sweeter and
more subtle than the more
mature winter carrots and
require very little cooking.
The old wives' tale that
eating carrots will result in
better eyesight may in fact
have some validity as
carrots contain carotene,
which converts to vitamin
A when consumed – an
essential vitamin for the
wellbeing of eyesight.*

Put the flour and salt in a bowl. Add the butter and rub into the flour
until the mixture resembles breadcrumbs. Stir in the ground walnuts.
Bind to a firm dough with cold water. Roll out to fit a 23cm/9-inch flan
tin. Chill.

Make the filling: heat the butter in a frying pan and fry the courgettes
until softening and then add the garlic. Fry until just colouring. Drain from
the pan. Blanch the asparagus, carrot sticks and peas in boiling water
for 2 minutes. Drain and plunge into cold water. Drain and dry.

Brush the pastry case with egg yolk and then scatter over the
tomatoes.

Lay the prepared vegetables on top. Beat together any remaining
egg yolk, the eggs, cream cheese, cream, herbs and salt and pepper.
Pour over the vegetables. Sprinkle over the grated cheese.

Bake on the floor of the roasting oven for 25–30 minutes, until the
filling is set and golden-brown on the top.

Cook's notes
The walnuts will make the pastry more difficult to roll, so try not to
have the dough too dry - it will dry and firm up once rolled and whilst
chilling.

Plum and Almond Puddings with Bay-Scented Custard

I have two bay trees in my garden that really flourish. In late summer I have to prune them hard, so I always have a good supply of bay leaves for cooking. Usually the leaves flavour savoury dishes but they do also add a lovely delicate accent to custards, as in this favourite recipe of mine.

4 plums, halved, stone removed
  and roughly chopped
110g/4oz caster sugar
1 cinnamon stick
110g/4oz butter, softened
2 eggs, beaten
75g/3oz self-raising flour
$1/_2$ teaspoon baking powder
50g/2oz ground almonds

For the custard
284ml/$^1/_2$ pint double cream
3 bay leaves
3 egg yolks
2 tablespoons caster sugar
1 teaspoon cornflour

Serves 6

Butter 6 individual pudding basins. Cut a circle of baking parchment to fit the base and place in each basin.

Put the plums in a small saucepan with 1 tablespoon of the caster sugar, the cinnamon stick and 2 tablespoons of water. Stand on the simmering plate, allow the sugar to dissolve and bubble until the mixture is jammy. Remove the cinnamon stick and divide the plums between the basins.

Put the remaining caster sugar, eggs, self-raising flour, baking powder and the ground almonds in a bowl and beat well until mixed and light and fluffy. Divide between the pudding basins.

Stand the basins on a baking tray and bake.

For a two-oven Aga, hang the baking tray on the bottom set of runners of the roasting oven. Put the cold shelf on the third set of runners from the top of the oven and bake for 20 minutes.

For a three- or four-oven Aga, hang the tray on the bottom set of runners of the baking oven and bake the puddings for 20–25 minutes.

When baked the puddings will be risen and golden brown.

For the custard, pour the cream into a saucepan and add the bay leaves. Heat on the simmering plate until almost boiling. Remove from the heat and allow the flavours to infuse for a couple of minutes.

In a basin beat together the egg yolks, sugar and cornflour. Pour on the infused cream and mix well. Return to the pan and heat gently, stirring constantly, until the custard has thickened. Remove the bay leaves.

Turn out the puddings onto a plate and pour over a little custard.

Cook's notes
Heat the custard very carefully once the eggs have been added. The cornflour will help to prevent the custard 'splitting'.

Blueberry Muffins

Muffins are very quick to make and the Aga is ideal for baking them.

450g/1lb pain flour
175g/6oz caster sugar
pinch salt
4 teaspoons baking powder
2 eggs, beaten
100ml/4 fl oz light vegetable oil
225ml/8 fl oz milk
225g/8oz blueberries

Makes 12

Line 12 deep muffin tins with paper cases or butter the tins.

Mix together the flour, sugar, salt and baking powder. Mix together the eggs, vegetable oil and milk. Add the egg mixture to the flour and mix lightly. Stir in the blueberries, gently.

Spoon the mixture into the prepared muffin tins.

Hang the shelf on the third set of runners from the top of the roasting oven. Slide in the muffin tray and bake for 15–20 minutes, until risen and firm to the touch. Cool on a wire rack and eat warm.

Cook's notes
For the best texture, mix the ingredients as briefly as possible.
Like scones, muffins are best made quickly and handled little.

Roast Salmon with Courgettes and Pine Nuts

Salmon can be dry and tasteless. We eat so much of it these days that it needs to be made slightly more exciting. In this recipe the orange and coriander add flavour while the pine nuts add crunch. This is also a very useful way of cooking courgettes.

2 x 800g /1lb12oz fillets of salmon, with skin on
2 oranges
4 tablespoons olive oil
2 teaspoons ground coriander
4 tablespoons pine nuts
4 medium courgettes

Serves 6

Grate the rind and squeeze the juice from one orange. Mix in a basin with 2 tablespoons of olive oil and 1 teaspoon of coriander. Season with salt and pepper. Brush this mixture over the salmon fillets. Set aside.

Heat 1 tablespoon of olive oil in a frying pan and stir in the remaining 1 teaspoon of coriander and the pine nuts. Stir-fry until the nuts are golden. Remove from the heat.

Trim the ends from the courgettes and slice thinly using a potato peeler.

Line a roasting tin or baking tray with Bake-O-Glide. Spoon in 1 tablespoon of olive oil and lay in the courgette ribbons. Season and scatter over the pine nuts. Lay on the salmon fillets, side by side, skin side up.

Hang the tin on the second set of runners from the top of the roasting oven and roast for 15–18 minutes, until just cooked through. Stand in a warm spot for 5 minutes before serving.

Cut the remaining orange into 6 wedges and serve with each portion of salmon, courgettes and pine nuts.

Cook's notes
The salmon skin should crisp and brown during cooking. It holds the fish together and adds flavour to it. You can remove it before serving, if you prefer.

Roast Garlic Bread

Bread making is becoming ever more popular, not only because of the rising cost of wheat but also because we are concerned to know exactly what is in the food we are eating. Once you have mastered basic bread making it is easy to progress to flavoured breads. This bread is lovely with a simple pasta dish or salad. If you want to roast the garlic in advance of making the bread, it will keep for a day or two in the fridge.

1 large head of garlic
1 tablespoon olive oil for roasting
350g/12oz strong white flour
1 teaspoon salt
1 tablespoon olive oil
15g/³/₄ oz fresh yeast

250ml/8fl oz water
beaten egg, to glaze
2 tablespoons semolina

Makes one large garlic loaf

Place the whole bulb of garlic on a small baking tray and drizzle over the oil. Hang the shelf on the bottom set of runners of the roasting oven and put in the garlic. Roast for 15–20 minutes, until the garlic bulbs are soft but not brown. Remove from the oven and allow to cool.

Place the flour, salt and olive oil in a large mixing bowl. Blend the yeast with a little water to make a runny paste and add to the flour. Add most of the remaining water and mix the dough until soft and pliable, adding more water as necessary. Knead the dough until smooth and elastic. Place the kneaded dough in a mixing bowl and cover either with a damp tea-towel or oiled clingfilm. Stand the bowl on a trivet on top of the Aga and leave the dough to rise until doubled in volume.

While the dough is rising, break off the bulbs of garlic, snip the top off each clove with a pair of scissors and squeeze out the flesh into a bowl. Lightly mash the cloves together.

Turn the risen dough out onto a lightly floured surface and roll out to a rectangle, roughly 30¹/₂ x 20.5cm /12 x 8-inch. Spread the dough with the mashed garlic – it may be patchy but it doesn't matter. Roll up the dough like a Swiss roll and flatten with your hands.

Grease and flour or line with Bake-O-Glide, a large baking tray. Place the garlic loaf i
n the tin and pinch together the open ends. Brush with either beaten egg or with water and dust with the semolina.

Stand the tray on a trivet on top of the Aga, cover the bread with a damp tea-towel or oiled clingfilm. Allow the dough to rise until doubled in size.

Hang the tray or shelf on the bottom set of runners of the roasting oven and bake the loaf for 20–25 minutes, until golden brown and sounding hollow when tapped. Cool on a wire rack.

Like onions and chives, garlic is a member of the lilly family. Garlic is a bulb vegetable that varies in pungency, skin colour and size. Early spring garlic is also often harvested and looks a lot like a leek with a swollen base. The green shoot of the garlic that extends upwards from the bulb is edible too and can be treated in much the same way as a spring onion. Garlic can be used grated, raw in dressings or roasted as individual cloves and chopped in a variety of dishes. Garlic can be pickled and can also be used to gently infuse olive oils.

Cook's notes
You can adapt this recipe by using cheese or olives in the place of the garlic.

September

1st Cheese and Walnut Loaf 2nd Individual White Pizzas
3rd Roast Gammon with Plums and Recurrant Glaze
4th Fig and Blueberry Clafoutis 5th Plum and Apple Chutney
6th Oriental Aubergines 7th Spiced Crusted Leg of Lamb
with Chickpeas 8th Cider Cake 9th Smoked Cod Pasta Bake
10th Beef Stroganoff Pies 11th Sweet Picked Damsons
12th Honeyed Duck and Vegetable Stir-Fry
13th Pear Upside-Down Cake 14th Stuffed Peppers with
Brie 15th Quick Seafood Linguine 16th Curried Sweet
Potato Soup 17th Apple Crumble Tart 18th Pear, Prune and
Walnut Chutney 19th Salmon Pie 20th Twice-Cooked Red
Pepper Soufflés 21st Fudge and Pistachio Baked Apples
22nd Duck Breast with Blackberry Sauce
23rd Blackcurrant Slump 24th Honeyed Fig Kebabs with
Lemon Tzatziki 25th Apple Strudel 26th Thyme Yorkshire
Puddings 27th Baked Pears with Cassis
28th Turkish Ratatouille 29th Marinated Sea Bass Fillets
30th Spiced Fruit with Mascarpone Cream

September 1

Cheese and Walnut Loaf

I love to bake a loaf of bread to go with soup for an economical and warming winter lunch. As the Aga is always warm it is simple to rise a yeast dough, so making your own bread is very easy - and homemade loaves beat most commercial breads hands down for flavour and texture.

15g/$^1/_2$ oz yeast
300ml/$^1/_2$ pint lukewarm water
450g/1lb wholemeal flour
1 teaspoon salt
$^1/_2$ teaspoon paprika
1$^1/_2$ teaspoons mustard powder
175g/6oz Cheddar cheese, grated
110g/4oz walnuts, finely chopped
3 tablespoons freshly chopped herbs

Makes 1 large loaf

Butter and flour a 1kg/2lb loaf tin.
Put the yeast in a basin and blend with a little warm water.
Put the flour, salt, paprika, mustard powder, 110g/4oz of the grated Cheddar, walnuts and herbs in a large mixing bowl. Stir to mix and then add the yeast liquid. Add most of the remaining liquid and mix to a smooth dough. Add more water as needed to make the dough slightly sticky but manageable. Knead for 5–10 minutes until the dough is smooth and pliable. If kneaded on the worktop return to the bowl. Cover the bowl either with a damp tea towel or oiled clingfilm. Stand on a trivet or Aga Chef's Pad on top of the Aga and leave to rise until doubled in volume.
Turn the dough out onto a lightly floured work top and shape into a loaf. Butter and flour a 1kg/2lb loaf tin. Place the dough in the tin. Scatter over the remaining Cheddar and put covered, to rise again on the Aga. When the loaf is risen just above the lip of the tin, put to bake.
Put the shelf on the bottom set of runners of the roasting oven. Slide in the loaf tin and bake for 35–40 minutes. If the loaf is browning too much after 20 minutes then slide in the cold shelf on the second set of runners from the top and add an extra 5 minutes to the baking time.
When cooked the loaf should sound hollow when tapped and slide out of the tin. Cool on a wire rack.

Cook's notes
The cheese on top of this loaf has a tendency to brown very quickly, which is why I suggest the use of the cold shelf, so keep a watchful eye on it.

September
2

Individual White Pizzas

These aren't really pizzas but little flat tarts made with pastry rather than a pizza dough. You can, of course, use the topping on a pizza dough base.

300g/10^1/$_2$oz puff pastry
75g/3oz crème fraîche
1 clove garlic, peeled and crushed
2 teaspoons chopped rosemary
salt and pepper
1 x 400g can artichoke hearts, well drained
125g/ 5oz Gorgonzola
a few basil leaves

Serves 6 as a starter or 3 as a main course

Roll out the pastry to about 3mm thick. Cut out six 12cm circles. Lay on a baking tray lined with Bake-O-Glide.

In a basin, mix together the crème fraîche, garlic, rosemary and a seasoning of salt and pepper. Spread this mixture over the pastry bases, leaving a small border.

Cut the artichoke hearts into quarters and divide between the pizzas. Cut the Gorgonzola into cubes and scatter over the artichokes.

Hang the baking tray on the third set of runners from the top of the roasting oven and bake for 10 minutes, until the pizzas are puffed and golden. Scatter over the basil leaves and serve hot.

Cook's notes
Don't overload the topping on the pastry base - if the topping spreads to the margins of the pizza then the pastry won't puff round the edge to form a border.

September
3

Roast Gammon with Plums and Redcurrant Glaze

Gammon is easy to cook and leftovers can be eaten in so many ways. My husband likes a gammon joint not only for the flavour but because it is easy to carve! This recipe works well with autumn plums. Serve with roast or mashed potatoes.

1 gammon joint, about 1.25kg/3lb
2 tablespoons redcurrant jelly
1 tablespoon mustard
2 tablespoons golden syrup
$1/_4$ teaspoon allspice
pepper
8 plums, halved and stones removed

Serves 8

Place the gammon in the small roasting tin and cover loosely with foil. Slide onto the bottom set of runners of the roasting oven for 30 minutes per 450g/1lb plus 30 minutes extra.

In a small basin, place the redcurrant jelly, mustard, golden syrup, allspice and a grinding of pepper. Stand the basin on the back of the Aga and leave the mixture to melt while the gammon is roasting. Stir to mix when melted to make the glaze.

Thirty minutes before the end of the cooking time, remove the foil from the meat. With a sharp knife, cut the skin from the gammon. Spoon over the glaze and arrange the plums around the base of the joint. Return to the oven and cook for the remaining 30 minutes.

Slice the gammon and serve with the plums.

Cook's notes
Ask your butcher if the gammon joint needs soaking prior to cooking – most supermarket joints don't.

Plums are thought to have originally developed from the sloe and vary in size and colour ranging from dark purple through to yellow-gold. The most popular British variety is the Victoria plum. They can range in taste from tart to very sweet, and are a good source of potassium, fibre and both vitamins A and C. You should pick ones which are plump, smooth and well coloured and a ripe plum should give a little when you press it. The best plums for cooking are those that are just a little bit firmer than ripe ones.

September
4

Fig and Blueberry Clafoutis

A clafoutis is a rich batter cooked with seasonal fruits, a combination that makes the most delicious pudding. Traditionally cherries are used for this dessert but other fruits work well, as here with blueberries and figs. The tang of the fruits contrast perfectly with the smooth batter as as they pop juicily in your mouth.

6 figs, halved
450g/1lb blueberries
25g/1oz butter
75g/3oz caster sugar
1 small carton double cream (150ml/¹/₄ pint)
5 eggs, beaten
75g/3oz plain flour
finely grated zest 2 lemons
75g/3oz butter, melted
crème fraiche, to serve

Serves 6

Blueberries are at their best from May through until October with their peak in mid-July. Blueberries are widely reputed as 'superfoods' for their rich nutrients, antioxidants and phytochemicals, and are renowned for their sweetness and bright colour.

Put the 25g/1oz butter in a shallow, ovenproof dish, just large enough to hold the fruit in a single layer. Put the dish on the floor of the roasting oven until the butter has melted. Add the figs and toss in the butter. Return to the oven for 2 or 3 minutes and then stir in the blueberries. Return to the oven until the juices are just beginning to flow. Remove from the oven and make the batter.

Put the flour in a mixing bowl. Whisk in the cream and eggs. Add the lemon zest and the melted butter and beat well together to make a smooth batter. Pour over the hot figs and blueberries. Hang the shelf on the bottom set of runners of the roasting oven and put in the clafoutis to bake. Bake for 20–25 minutes until the outer edge is set and the middle just trembling when shaken.

Dust with caster sugar and serve warm with a helping of crème fraîche, to taste.

Cook's notes
This clafoutis is best served freshly cooked.

September
5

Plum and Apple Chutney

This recipe is for a small amount of 'fresh' chutney, just enough for one meal. It is easy to increase the quantities but don't make too much as it doesn't have as long a shelf life as traditional chutney. Store either somewhere cool or in the fridge.

6 plums, stoned and diced
2 eating apples, cored and diced
300ml/^{1}/$_2$ pint cider
3 tablespoons soft brown sugar
^{1}/$_4$ teaspoon cinnamon

Serves 8

Place all the ingredients in a saucepan. Place on the simmering plate and, stirring, heat until mixed and bring to the boil. Place the uncovered pan in the simmering oven for 1 hour, until the fruit is softened and most of the cider has evaporated.

Serve with roast lamb.

Cook's notes
Try to make the chutney a few days before eating, if time allows, to let the flavours mingle.

Oriental Aubergines

Aubergines are quite 'meaty' vegetables and make a good main ingredient for a non-meat day.

2 aubergines
1¹/₂ tablespoons sesame oil
1 tablespoon dark soft brown sugar
1 tablespoon brown rice miso paste
2 tablespoons soy sauce
1 tablespoon rice vinegar
1 tablespoon chopped ginger
1 teaspoon crushed garlic
1 pinch crushed chilli
chopped mint, to serve
toasted sesame seeds, to serve
hot egg noodles, to accompany

Serves 2

Cut the aubergines into 6 large chunks each. Brush the flesh of the aubergines with the sesame oil. Put all the remaining ingredients together in a bowl.

Heat a wok or large sauté pan on the boiling plate. When hot add the aubergines and cook for 2 minutes, turning to brown on all sides. Pour over the ingredients mixed in the bowl and immediately move the pan to the simmering plate. Toss the aubergines in the glaze, cover with a lid and move to the simmering oven for 20–30 minutes.

Remove the pan from the oven and leave to stand for 5 minutes. Sprinkle over the mint and the seeds and serve with hot egg noodles.

Cook's notes
If you don't have a lid for the wok then use a baking tray, but remember it will be hot when it comes out of the simmering oven!

September
7

Spice-Crusted Leg of Lamb with Chickpeas

Being a fairly lazy cook I approve of any way of cooking meat and accompaniments together. The chick peas are good lightly crushed and make a good alternative to serving potatoes.

3 red onions, peeled and thickly sliced
2 tablespoons olive oil
1½–2kg/3lb 5oz–4½ lbs leg of lamb
2 teaspoons cumin seeds
2 teaspoons coriander seeds
2 teaspoons paprika
½ teaspoon salt
500ml/18 fl oz vegetable stock
1 tablespoon runny honey
juice 2 lemons
410g can chickpeas, drained
2 tablespoons chopped parsley or coriander

Serves 6

Toss the onions in 1 tablespoon of olive oil and lay over the base of the small roasting tin. Sit the lamb on top of the onions and brush it all over with the remaining olive oil.

Crush the cumin and coriander seeds in a pestle and mortar, add the paprika and the salt. Sprinkle over the lamb.

Hang the roasting tin on the third set of runners from the top of the roasting oven and roast for 45–55 minutes.

Mix the stock, honey and lemon juice together in a basin and pour round the lamb and return to the oven for a further 30 minutes.

Add the chickpeas to the roasting tin and add a little water if the mixture is very dry. Roast for a further 15 minutes. Remove the lamb from the oven and put on a warmed plate. Leave to stand for 15–20 minutes before carving.

Scatter the chopped coriander or parsley over the chickpeas. Serve with new potatoes and green beans.

Cook's notes
If you think your spices are a little stale, pop them on a baking tray into the roasting oven to heat through and slightly toast before crushing. That will intensify the flavour, but watch them, they burn easily!

September 8

Cider Cake

Cider is a blessing from the Somerset orchards that I like to cook with as well as drink. Not all Somerset cider is 'scrumpy' in style – we also produce very high quality single apple cider. Enjoy the leftover cider from this recipe in the peace of your kitchen!

150ml/¼ pint dry cider
225g/8oz sultanas
110g/4oz butter
110g/4oz soft brown sugar
2 eggs, beaten
225g/8oz plain flour
5ml/1 teaspoon bicarbonate of soda

Makes 16 squares

Place the cider and sultanas in a basin and leave to soak for 12 hours or overnight.

Grease and base-line an 18cm/7-inch square cake tin.

Put the butter, sugar, eggs, flour and baking powder in a mixing bowl and stir round with a wooden spoon until smooth. Slowly stir in the sultanas and cider.

Spoon the mixture into the prepared tin and smooth the top. Bake.

For the two-oven Aga, put the shelf on the floor of the roasting oven, put in the cake and slide the cold shelf onto the third set of runners from the top. Bake for 40–45 minutes until a skewer inserted in the middle comes out clean.

For a three- or four-oven Aga, put the shelf on the bottom set of runners of the baking oven. Put in the cake and bake for 55–60 minutes, or until a skewer inserted in the middle comes out clean.

Cool on a wire rack. When cool cut into squares.

Cook's notes
If you don't have a square tin this can be made in a deep 19cm/7½-inch round cake tin.

September
9

Smoked Cod Pasta Bake

When time is tight but I want to serve fish I find this to be a good speedy dish to make. Smoked cod is slightly milder than haddock. It really is worth looking out for when shopping.

300g/10$\frac{1}{2}$oz dried pasta (penne is good)
400g /14oz smoked cod, skinned and
  cut into 3–4cm cubes
350g jar tomato and chilli pasta sauce
125g/ 5oz Mozzarella cheese

Serves 4

Bring a large pan of water to boil on the boiling plate and add the pasta. Return to the boil and move the pan to the simmering oven for 12 minutes, or follow the cooking time stated on the packet. When the pasta is cooked to al dente, drain well.

Return the well drained pasta to the saucepan and stir in the smoked cod and the tomato sauce.

Slice the Mozzarella cheese and scatter over the top of the pasta.

Put the oven shelf on the bottom set of runners of the roasting oven and put in the pasta dish. Bake for 20–25 minutes, until the cod is just cooked.

Serve with lightly cooked broccoli or a salad.

Cook's notes
The short cut pastas can all be cooked in the simmering oven, which eliminates the possibility of water boiling over and the kitchen filling with steam.

September
10

Beef Stroganoff Pies

Beef stroganoff is quickly cooked so you need to buy good quality meat. Though in these individual pies a little goes a long way so cost shouldn't be an issue. Serve with fresh, bright and lightly cooked green vegetables in season.

2 tablespoons olive oil
800g/2lbs rump steak cut into thin strips
25g/1oz butter
2 cloves garlic, peeled and finely chopped
1 red onion, peeled, quartered and sliced
500g/1lb 2oz button mushrooms, sliced
2 teaspoons chopped thyme
2 tablespoons tomato purée
2 tablespoons mustard
1 tablespoon chopped parsley
200ml/ 7 fl oz crème fraîche
375g/13oz ready-rolled puff pastry
1 egg for glazing

Serves 4

Heat a frying pan on the boiling plate, add the oil and then brown all the beef strips in batches. Drain and set aside on a plate.

Add the butter to the hot pan, which you have transferred to the simmering plate, and add the onion and garlic and cook until soft. Stir in the mushrooms and the thyme. Cook for a few minutes and then add the tomato purée, mustard and season.

Return the steak to the pan, add the parsley and remove the pan from the heat. Stir in the crème fraîche.

Divide the mixture between four ovenproof bowls (about 250ml/ 7fl oz size).

Unroll the pastry and cut circles for the top of the bowls. Cut them large enough to hang over the side of the dishes. Put the pastry on the top and drape over the side of the dish. Brush with egg glaze and cut a slit in the top.

Stand the dishes on a baking tray. Hang the tray on the second set of runners from the bottom of the roasting oven and bake for 20–25 minutes, until the pastry is puffed and golden.

Cook's notes
If you cook these pies from cold they may need a little longer in the oven to ensure the filling is piping hot. If you find that the pastry is browning too quickly, slide in the cold shelf.

Sweet Pickled Damsons

Sweet pickled damsons have been an autumn/winter pudding standby for as long as I can remember. Serve a spoonful with rice pudding or custard, or sieve some to make a wonderful sauce for ice cream. The damsons keep well in a cold place, even after opening.

450g/1lb damsons
225g/8oz Demerara sugar
1 tablespoon vinegar

Damsons are a small oval-shaped variety of plum with dark blue or purple colour to their skin and a deep yellow flesh. Their season is very short – just August and September. Eaten raw, they are quite sour, so are best when cooked as they take on a sweetened tangy flavour. Damsons are a highly versatile fruit with a high pectin content which makes them ideal for making jams, jellies and chutneys. They are also used in cheeses, in sloe gin making, pie fillings and in sauces served over fattier meats such as pork, lamb and duck.

Mix the fruit and the sugar and pack into sterilised jars. Add the vinegar. Place a lid on the jar but do not screw the lids down. Stand the jars on newspaper laid on the bottom of the roasting tin. Slide the tin onto the bottom set of runners of the simmering oven and leave for 1–2 hours, until the fruit has cracked but not boiled.

Remove from the oven and seal down the lids immediately. Allow to become completely cold before storing.

Cook's notes
Take care when eating damsons, as they will still contain their stones.

September
12

Honeyed Duck and Vegetable Stir-Fry

Duck makes a delicious stir-fry but take care to remove the fatty layer first and then take further care not to overcook it.

3 tablespoons clear honey
6 tablespoons dark soy sauce
4 skinless duck breasts
2 carrots
bunch spring onions
1 small head Chinese leaf
1 tablespoon vegetable oil
2 teacups rice to serve

Serves 4

In a bowl mix together the honey and the soy sauce.

Slice the duck breasts into strips and toss in the marinade. Set aside.

Peel and cut the carrots into thin strips. Trim the onions and cut into strips. Shred the Chinese leaf finely.

Cook the rice. Measure the rice into a saucepan with a good pinch of salt. Add the water, 3 cups of water to 2 cups rice. Cover with a lid and stand the saucepan on the boiling plate and bring the rice to the boil. As soon as it boils move the pan to the simmering oven. The rice will be cooked in 15 minutes but it will be quite happy in the simmering oven until the stir-fry is cooked.

Heat the wok or large frying pan on the boiling plate. The Aga wok will need 10 minutes to heat through without anything in it.

Add the oil to the hot wok and quickly add the duck, drained from the marinade. Stir-fry the duck for 2 minutes, until browned all over. Remove from the pan and set aside to keep warm.

Add the carrot to the pan and stir-fry for a minute before stirring in the onions and then the Chinese leaf. Add the duck and stir-fry for 2–3 minutes, the duck should still be slightly pink. Pour over the marinade, heat through and serve with rice.

Cook's notes
The wok should be very hot prior to cooking as the Aga cannot compensate quickly for any heat loss. Make sure the food is at room temperature before starting to cook and have warm plates to hand to put the cooked food on.

September 13

Pear Upside-Down Cake

I can clearly remember making upside-down puddings when I was at college training to be a home economics teacher. The children I taught, once I had qualified, used to make Upside-Down cakes in my lesson and would then proudly took them home for the whole family to enjoy. That type of teaching has gone now, sadly, though ironically the fashion for this type of pudding is coming round once again.

411g can pear halves in juice,
drained and dried
generous smearing of butter
for the tin base and side
1 tablespoon caster sugar
3 eggs
175g/6oz softened butter
or margarine
175g/6oz caster sugar
175g/6oz self-raising flour
1 teaspoon vanilla extract

Serves 6–8

Many varieties of pear are available year-round in the UK despite Britain's pear orchards having become much smaller in recent years. Worldwide, more than 3,000 varieties of pear are grown, although only around 100 are grown commercially. The majority of pear varieties are at their best during autumn and winter when they are plump, ripe and juicy.

Butter the inside of a 30cm/12-inch shallow cake tin. Sprinkle over the caster sugar. Lay the dried pears over the base of the tin, cut side down.

Place the eggs, butter, sugar, flour and vanilla in a mixing bowl and beat well until smooth and fluffy. Spoon the mixture gently over the pears.

Put the tin directly on the floor of the roasting oven and hang the cold shelf on the second set of runners from the bottom of the roasting oven. Bake for 20–25 minutes, until the sponge is risen, golden brown and firm to the touch.

Leave to set for 2–3 minutes in the tin then loosen the sides with a table knife and invert onto a plate.

Cook's notes

If you want to add some colour to the cake put a glacé cherry into the core hole of each pear once the pudding has been turned upside-down.

Aga *year*

September 14

Stuffed Peppers with Brie

I often seem to have Brie (Somerset or Cornish) left over after a supper party. This recipe came from one such time. The cheese will melt deliciously when cooked and contrast well with the roast peppers.

4 red peppers
8 teaspoons olive tapenade
150g/5^1/$_2$oz cherry tomatoes, cut in half
25g/1oz black olives, halved and pitted
2–3 basil leaves, torn
225g /8oz Brie, sliced
2 tablespoons olive oil

Serves 4

Halve the peppers through the stalk and remove the seeds. Spread each pepper half with a teaspoon of tapenade. Divide the cherry tomato halves and the black olives between the peppers and scatter over the torn basil leaves.

Stand the peppers in a shallow ovenproof dish and top with slices of Brie. Drizzle over the olive oil.

Hang the shelf on the bottom set of runners of the roasting oven and put in the peppers. Bake for 25–30 minutes, until the peppers are tender.

Serve with crusty bread and salad.

Cook's notes
The peppers look more attractive if you can leave the stalks on. Use a dish that the peppers just fit in snugly, which will help them hold each other in place.

September
15

Quick Seafood Linguine

Oh so quick to make! This pasta dish for those in a hurry makes a change from the usual tomato sauce type pasta and seems perfect for those precious Indian Summer days in the garden.

400g/14oz dried linguine pasta
2 tablespoons olive oil
2 cloves garlic, peeled and finely sliced
600g/1lb 6oz fresh seafood cocktail
4 tablespoons sherry
2 tablespoons chopped parsley
finely grated rind and juice 1 lemon
4 tablespoons crème fraîche ('low-fat'
*   mixes in more easily)*

Serves 4

Cook the pasta according to packet instructions.
    Stand a frying pan on the simmering plate and add the olive oil. Cook the garlic until softening but not brown. Move the pan to the boiling plate and stir in the seafood and the sherry. Stir-fry for 2–3 minutes, until the liquid is reduced. Remove from the heat.
    Drain the pasta well and return to the pan. Add the seafood mixture, half the parsley, the rind and juice of the lemon and the crème fraîche. Season. Toss together and tip onto a serving plate. Scatter over the remaining parsley.
    Serve immediately.

Cook's notes
You can choose a variety of seafood combinations to suit your preference based on what is available at the fishmonger.

September
16

Curried Sweet Potato Soup

The combination of potatoes, banana and spices gives this recipe a Caribbean flavour and warmth. If you don't like banana, and amazingly some people don't, it can be omitted, but it does add a subtle taste to the soup and lifts the overall flavour very well.

1 tablespoon vegetable oil
1 onion, peeled and chopped
2 cloves garlic, peeled and crushed
2 tablespoon curry paste
2 large sweet potatoes, peeled and chopped
1 large courgette, chopped
4 tomatoes, chopped
1 litre/1³/₄ pints vegetable stock
1 banana, peeled and chopped
2 large naan breads

Serves 4–6

Sweet potatoes, also known as kumaras, have starchy white or orange flesh which has a naturally sweet flavour and creamy texture. They are at their best from autumn through to early spring. The green leaves and shoots of the plant can also be eaten, simply by blanching or wilting them in the same way that you would spinach. Despite not actually being a potato, sweet potatoes are used in many similar ways and taste fantastic boiled, mashed, roasted or baked.

You will need a large saucepan to make this soup.

Heat the oil in the saucepan and add the onion. Cook gently until the onion is soft but not coloured. Add the garlic and cook for 1–2 minutes and then stir in the curry paste. Keep stirring and cook for another 1–2 minutes. Add the sweet potatoes, courgettes and tomatoes to the paste mixture and turn until well coated.

Pour over the stock, stir well and bring to the boil. Cover with a lid and transfer to the simmering oven for 30–40 minutes, until the sweet potatoes are soft. Add the chopped banana and cook for a further 5–10 minutes.

Blend the soup and adjust the seasoning.

Toast the naan breads on the simmering plate for 1–2 minutes on each side and then cut into slices to serve with the soup.

Cook's notes
Put the simmering plate lid down on top of the naan breads for a minute and they should puff up nicely.

Apple Crumble Tart

Two popular puddings in one, apple crumble and apple tart. Although this pudding has various assembly stages it really is worth the effort, though I usually find it is eaten far too quickly.

For the pastry
175g/6oz plain flour
100g/ 3 1/2 oz butter
25g/1oz caster sugar
1 egg yolk

1/4 teaspoon ground cinnamon
75g/3oz butter
50g/2oz ground almonds
50g/2oz soft brown sugar
50g/2oz butter, melted

For the filling
1 1/2 kg/3lb 5oz eating apples
finely grated rind and juice 1
  small lemon
50g/2oz caster sugar
110g/4oz plain flour

Serves 8

Make the pastry. Put the flour in a mixing bowl and add the cold butter cut into cubes. Rub the butter into the flour to resemble breadcrumbs. Stir in the sugar and bind the mixture to a firm dough with the egg yolk and enough cold water to bind all the ingredients together.

Roll out the pastry and use to line a 23cm/9-inch flan tin. Chill well.

Peel, core and slice half of the apples and place in a saucepan with the lemon rind and juice. Place on the simmering plate, cover with a lid and cook until the apples are soft and can be mashed. Take care not to let the apples burn. Mash the apples and beat in the caster sugar. Set aside to allow the the apples to cool.

Prepare the crumble. Mix together the flour and cinnamon. Rub in the butter until the mixture is like breadcrumbs. Stir in the ground almonds and the soft brown sugar.

Fill the pastry case with the cold apple purée. Core and slice the remaining apples and lay these over the purée mixture. Brush the apple slices with the melted butter and then scatter over the crumble mix.

Put the tart on the floor of the roasting oven and bake for 30–35 minutes, until the pastry is golden brown and the topping is brown and crunchy.

Cook's notes
I have used eating apples in this recipe, but if you have a glut of cooking apples you can use them for the purée filling, adding sugar if needed.

September
18

Pear, Prune and Walnut Chutney

The flavour of this chutney is delicious and sweet but the colour is rather dark. The juicy pears contrast really well with the crunchy walnuts which will be beautifully moist after the gentle cooking.

4 large onions, peeled and chopped
1kg/2$^{1}/_{4}$ lbs pears, peeled, cored and chopped
250g/9oz prunes, pitted and quartered
6cm/2-inch cube fresh ginger, peeled
   and finely chopped
250g/9oz dark muscovado sugar
400ml/12 fl oz cider vinegar
150g/5$^{1}/_{2}$ oz walnut pieces

Makes about 6 x 450g/1 lb jars

Put all the ingredients in a heavy-based pan, stir well and stand on the simmering plate. Stir until the sugar has dissolved. Bring to the boil and move to the simmering oven, uncovered, for 1$^{1}/_{2}$–2 hours, until the chutney has reduced and is thick.

Pot the chutney into sterile jars. When cold, cover with vinegar-proof lids. Label.

Cook's notes
Store the chutney somewhere cool, not the fridge, for several weeks before trying it. The vinegar needs time to mellow and blend into the other ingredients.

Salmon Pie

Fish pie is ever popular and this one is liked by the many people who tell me they don't like fish. Try it out on a fish sceptic and marvel at the response!

50g/2oz butter
1 medium onion, peeled and chopped
50g/2oz flour
425ml/15 fl oz fish stock
150ml/5 fl oz white wine
900g/2 lbs salmon fillet, skinned and cut into chunks
225g/8oz queen scallops
110g/4oz Gruyère cheese, grated
salt and pepper

For the topping
700g/1¹/₂lbs potatoes, peeled and cut to boil
50g/2oz butter
125ml/¹/₄ pint milk
1 tablespoon chopped parsley

Serves 6

Prepare the potatoes in the usual way for mashing. When cooked, mash with the butter and milk and stir in the parsley. Season with salt and pepper.

Melt the butter in a saucepan, add the onion and cook until softened but not brown. Add the flour, stir and cook for 1–2 minutes and then gradually add the fish stock and the wine. Cook for 2–3 minutes and remove from the heat. Gently stir the salmon, scallops and cheese into the sauce. Season with pepper. Spoon the fish into a pie dish.

Top the fish with the mashed potato and roughen the top.

Hang the shelf on the bottom set of runners of the roasting oven and put in the pie. Bake until browning on the top and the filling is piping hot.

Cook's notes
Hard boiled eggs can be added to the pie if you like. Bury them in the sauce amongst the fish before topping with the potato.

Twice-Cooked Red Pepper Soufflés

Red pepper soufflés have the colour of a hot, early autumn day. In this recipe the soufflés are baked twice, which gives them a beautiful crust.

Serves 4

For the pepper chutney

2 red peppers, seeded and sliced into strips

3 tablespoons olive oil

50ml/2 fl oz water

30ml/ 1 fl oz red wine vinegar

1 tablespoon honey

1 large red pepper, deseeded

1 tablespoon olive oil

salt and cayenne pepper

50g/2oz butter

2 tablespoons flour

100ml /3$^1/_2$ fl oz milk

1 egg yolk

3 egg whites

4 tablespoons herby breadcrumbs

4 teaspoons pesto

Coat the pepper in the oil and season with salt and cayenne pepper. Roast towards the top of the roasting oven for about 20 minutes until soft but not blackened. Put the pepper in a blender and blend until fine. If the blended pepper is watery put in a small saucepan and heat until reduced and thick, taking care not to burn the mixture.

Butter 4 ramekins generously and dust with breadcrumbs.

Put the remaining butter in a saucepan to melt and then stir in the flour. Add the milk and continue to stir well while bringing to the boil. The mixture will be very thick. Beat in the pepper purée. Beat in the egg yolk and season with salt and cayenne pepper.

Whisk the egg whites until forming stiff peaks. Beat one third of the whites into the pepper mixture and then gently fold in the remaining egg whites.

Divide the mixture between the prepared ramekin dishes. Put a teaspoon of the pistou in the middle of each soufflé.

Stand the ramekin dishes in a small roasting tin and pour round enough hot water to come half way up the sides or the dishes. Hang the tin on the second set of runners from the bottom of the roasting oven and bake the soufflés for 8–10 minutes, until risen but slightly soft in the centre. Remove from the oven. At this stage the soufflés can be left for 12 hours (not in the fridge).

Make the chutney. Mix all the ingredients together in a saucepan, heat on the simmering plate, cover and move to the simmering oven for 30 minutes, until the peppers are soft. Remove the lid and bubble on the simmering plate to bubble away most of the liquid. Season with salt and cayenne pepper.

To serve the soufflés hot stand the soufflés on a baking tray and hang the tray on the third set of runners from the top of the roasting oven and bake for 5–6 minutes, until puffed and crusty.

Serve with the pepper chutney.

Cook's notes

I sometimes serve these soufflés after the first cooking when they will be softer and without the crust – just cook them for a minute or two longer.

September 21

Fudge and Pistachio Baked Apples

Most people only bake cooking apples, which I find too large. Shake things up a bit by using all the lovely home grown apples we have available in the autumn. Each variety will cook differently, so keep an eye on them during cooking.

3 tablespoons unsalted, shelled pistachios
120g soft fudge, roughly chopped
2 tablespoons Mascarpone
6 large Egremont Russet or Cox's apples

Serves 6

Put the pistachios on a baking tray and hang at the top of the roasting oven. Toast them for 2–3 minutes. Cool and then roughly chop.

Put the fudge, 1 tablespoon mascarpone and the pistachios in a small saucepan and stand at the back of the Aga to start softening.

Meanwhile core the apples and slit the skin round the middle, stand them in a shallow ovenproof dish.

Stand the saucepan with the fudge mixture on the simmering plate and stir until the fudge has melted, taking care not to let the mixture burn.

Use half the fudge mixture to fill the cavities in the apples. Stir the remaining 1 tablespoon Mascarpone into the fudge to make a sauce to pour over the apples when cooked. Set aside.

Bake the apples. Put the shelf on the bottom set of runners of the roasting oven and slide in the dish of apples. Bake for 25–35 minutes until the apples are soft when pierced, but not collapsed.

Gently re-heat the sauce and pour over the apples when serving.

Cook's notes
Remember to slit the skin round the middle of the apple, otherwise it may burst during cooking.

September 22

Duck Breast with Blackberry Sauce

I am fortunate to live in the beautiful city of Bath and am surrounded by fields belonging to the National Trust. I love picking blackberries along the lane nearby, right on the edge of fields looking down on the city. I used to have the children for company and it seemed such an idyllic way to spend a warm September afternoon, gathering food for free and catching up on family life. The problem with taking the children was that they tended to eat most of the berries they picked, so now I have more berries but less chat – except to the dog!

4 duck breasts
2 tablespoons honey
salt and pepper
225g/8oz blackberries
4 tablespoons water
1 tablespoons lemon juice
2 teaspoons sugar, or to taste
1 teaspoon cornflour, blended with a little water

Serves 4

Blackberries, also known as bramble raspberries, are available in the UK from late July through until early October. A relative of the rose, blackberries are a common hedgerow fruit throughout Europe. Legend has it that blackberries should not be picked after September as the devil urinates on the fruit, turning them bad! As October heralds the beginning of the wetter season, blackberries quickly develop moulds, and this could well account for such popular superstitions.

Score the skin of the duck breasts by making 4–5 diagonal cuts. Place on a rack in the small roasting tin, skin side uppermost. Mix the honey and salt and pepper together and brush over the duck breasts. Slide the tin onto the second set of runners from the top of the roasting oven and grill the duck for 20–25 minutes.

Reserve a few blackberries for garnishing and place the remaining berries, the water, lemon juice and sugar in a saucepan and bring slowly to the boil. Simmer for about 5 minutes, crushing the fruit to release the juices. Pass the sauce through a sieve and return to the rinsed saucepan. Stir in the slaked cornflour and bring to the boil to thicken the sauce.

Slice the duck breasts and lay on serving plates. Add the blackberry sauce and a few blackberries to garnish.

Cook's notes

If the honey you have is thick, stand the jar on the back of the Aga for a little while to soften it enough to spread on to the duck.

September

23

Blackcurrant Slump

Blackcurrants have a wonderful intense flavour and perfume. As a child we had far too many blackcurrants and I got fed up with them. Now I adore their rich, slightly tangy flavour.

'Slump' seems a funny name for a pudding, but it is really no more than a cobbler that has gone wrong! The filling should be fairly soft in order to allow the scone topping to collapse into it – hence the 'slump'. I have adapted my mother's recipe to use Mascarpone cheese instead of thick double cream, but do use whichever you prefer.

700g/1$\frac{1}{2}$lbs blackcurrants, off the stalk
3 tablespoons water
sugar to taste
1 tablespoon cornflour, blended with a little water
250g/9oz Mascarpone

For the scone topping
175g/6oz self-raising flour
1 teaspoon baking powder
pinch of salt
50g/2oz sugar
50g/2oz butter, chopped into cubes
75ml/3fl oz milk

Serves 6

Place the fruit in a saucepan with the water, and sugar to taste. Bring to the boil and add the slaked cornflour. Stir well and cook for 2–3 minutes, until the fruit is cooked but not mushy. Pour into an ovenproof dish that has enough room for the scone mix on top. Place spoonfuls of Mascarpone on top of the fruit, but do not stir in.

Make the scone topping: place the flour, baking powder, salt, sugar and butter in a mixing bowl and rub in the butter. Bind together with the milk, adding more if necessary to form a soft dough. Place spoonfuls of the dough on top of the fruit.

Put the oven shelf on the bottom set of runners of the roasting oven and bake the slump for 25–30 minutes, until the scone is risen and golden-brown and the fruit is bubbling.

Cook's notes
Other soft fruits can be used for this recipe but you may not need much sugar added to them. I have made this with frozen blackcurrants in the winter and it works very well.

Honeyed Fig Kebabs
with Lemon Tsatziki

Fresh figs have such a short season and I love to make the most of them. The lemon will cut through the extreme sweetness of the figs and the honey.

4 bamboo kebab sticks, soaked in water
2 lemons
4 fresh figs, quartered
12 small bay leaves, torn in half
4 tablespoons clear honey
200g tub Greek sheep's milk yoghurt

Serves 4

Cut 1 lemon into 12 pieces.

Grate the rind and squeeze the juice from the other lemon.

Thread the figs onto the kebab sticks, alternating with a piece of lemon and a bay leaf. Start and finish with a piece of fig.

Put the honey and the lemon juice in a small saucepan and stand on the simmering plate. Warm the honey, stir well and then allow to bubble to reduce the mixture by about half.

Line a small baking tray with Bake-O-Glide. Put the kebabs on the tray and brush them with the honey mixture.

Make the tzatziki. Mix the yoghurt with the grated lemon rind. Chill.

Hang the tin on the third set of runners from the top of the roasting oven and 'grill' the kebabs. After 3–4 minutes, when the fruit should be caramelising, turn the kebabs and brush with the honey mixture. Cook for 3 more minutes.

Serve the kebabs brushed with any remaining honey mixture and a spoonful of lemon tzatziki.

Cook's notes
For this recipe it is best to use firm figs as the softer ones will fall off the skewers!

September
25

Apple Strudel

Homemade strudels are easy to make now that filo pastry is so readily available. I can remember trying to make my own pastry for this recipe and running out of space in my tiny kitchen trying to pull the pastry thin enough! Those were the days when I made everything from scratch....

1 packet filo pastry
75g/3oz butter, melted
65g /2¹/₂oz fresh breadcrumbs
1 kg/2 lbs 4oz apples
110g/4oz soft brown sugar
65g/2¹/₂oz sultanas, optional
65g/2¹/₂oz chopped nuts, optional
1 teaspoon ground cinnamon
2–3 teaspoons icing sugar

Makes 8–10

Line a large baking tray with Bake-O-Glide.

The amount of filo pastry you need will depend upon the size of the pastry sheets and the size of the strudel you wish to make. Unroll the filo pastry and brush each sheet with melted butter. Lay enough pastry to cover the baking tray, overlapping some of the sheets as they are usually small.

Sprinkle the breadcrumbs over the pastry.

Peel, core and thinly slice the apples. Place in a mixing bowl and mix together with the sugar, sultanas and nuts (if using) and cinnamon. Spoon onto the pastry sheet leaving a good 15 cm/6-inch border all round. Fold in the short ends and carefully roll the strudel up so that the join is at the bottom.

Brush with any remaining melted butter. Bake on the bottom set of runners in the roasting oven for 20 minutes until brown and crisp and the apples are cooked. Move the tray to the floor of the oven for 5–10 minutes to crisp the base. Sprinkle over the icing sugar and return to the second set of runners from the top of the roasting oven for 5 minutes until golden brown and glazed.

Cook's notes
Individual strudels can be made, if preferred, but be sure to chop the apple finely so that pastry rolling is made easy.

September
26

Thyme Yorkshire Puddings

I have yet to meet anyone who doesn't like Yorkshire puddings. We all have different ideas as to how they should be made. When I was growing up, a Yorkshire pudding was always made in one dish, not as individual ones as I prefer. And Yorkshire friends of the family would have the Yorkshire pudding and gravy before the meat and vegetables. The addition of thyme to these Yorkshire puddings adds an extra flavour that makes them particularly good with roast chicken, not traditional but very popular with family and friends. And the proof of the pudding is in the eating!

vegetable oil, dripping or goose fat for the tin.
225g/8oz plain flour
1 tablespoon chopped thyme leaves
2 eggs
pinch salt
approximately 300ml/¹/₂ pint milk

Makes 12 individual Yorkshire puddings

Put a teaspoonful of oil or fat into each section of a 12 hole muffin tin. Put the tin on the floor of the roasting oven to heat.

While the tin is heating make the batter.

Put the flour and salt in a roomy jug and stir in the chopped thyme leaves. Break in the eggs and about a quarter of the milk. Whisk the ingredients together with a balloon whisk, gradually adding more milk to make the batter the thickness of pouring cream.

When the batter is ready remove the smoking pan from the oven and pour the batter in to the hot tin. Return immediately to the oven. Put the oven shelf on the third set of runners from the top of the roasting oven and put in the Yorkshire puddings.

Bake for 25–30 minutes until the puddings are risen and golden brown. Remove from the oven. Eat immediately or set aside to cool.

When cold the puddings can be put into a bag and frozen.

Re-heat for 5–10 minutes in a hot oven just before serving.

Cook's notes
Make these before cooking the roast meat so that the oven is hot enough to get a good lift to the puddings. You may need to turn the tin round during cooking if your oven has a 'hot spot'.

September
27

Baked Pears with Cassis

Pears are often served poached in red wine but this is slightly different. Here they are lightly roasted and the cassis adds the most wonderful colour.

4 large pears
50g/2oz caster sugar
1 tablespoon lemon juice
50g/2oz butter, melted
2 tablespoons Crème de Cassis
1 vanilla pod

Serves 4

Peel and core the pears and cut them into quarters. Lay them in an ovenproof dish and sprinkle over the sugar. Drizzle over the lemon juice and the melted butter, then the Cassis. Tuck in the vanilla pod.

Put the shelf on the floor of the roasting oven and put in the pear dish. Bake for 10 minutes and then baste the pears with the juices. Repeat after another 10 minutes. Bake for a further 10 minutes or until the pears are tender.

Serve warm with vanilla ice cream.

Cook's notes
Use firm pears for this recipe so they hold their shape during cooking.

Aga *year*

Turkish Ratatouille

Roasting vegetables in the Aga is a fabulous way to cook them. Somehow their flavour intensifies and so little oil is used it is a healthy way as well. A whole variety of vegetables can be cooked this way, not just the ones I have specified below.

3 courgettes, trimmed and sliced
1 aubergine, cut into long wedges
1 onion, roughly chopped
3 cloves garlic, peeled and sliced
2 green peppers, halved, seeded
  and sliced
3 carrots, peeled and cut into
  slices
2 small turnips, cut into wedges
2 potatoes, peeled and cut into
  medium cubes

3 tablespoons olive oil
¹/₂ teaspoon ground allspice
2 teaspoons coriander seeds
¹/₂ 400g can chickpeas, drained
150ml/6fl oz passata
handful flat leafed parsley,
  roughly chopped
handful coriander leaves,
  roughly chopped
salt and pepper

Serves 4–6

Put the courgettes to one side on a plate.

Into a large mixing bowl put the aubergines, onion, garlic, peppers, carrots, turnips and potatoes with the olive oil, allspice and coriander and coriander seeds. Season with salt and pepper and toss together.

Line a large baking tray with Bake-O-Glide. Spoon the vegetables onto the tray. Hang the baking tray on the second set of runners from the top of the roasting oven for 25–30 minutes. Add the courgettes and then return to the oven on the third set of runners from the top of the oven for 15 minutes.

In a saucepan, heat together the passata and chickpeas. Pour this mixture over the cooked vegetables . Season with salt and pepper. Spoon the vegetables into a serving dish and stir in the herbs.

Serves 4–6 as a vegetarian dish with salad or as a side dish to accompany grilled meat or fish.

Cook's notes
If serving this as a vegetarian dish you may like to add some Feta cheese cubes or grated Cheddar on the top.

Marinated Sea Bass Fillets

Try to buy wild rather than farmed sea bass whenever possible as the fish will have a far better flavour and texture. This is a simple but very tasty way to serve the finest sea bass fillet you can find.

4 sea bass fillets

For the marinade
$^1/_4$ teaspoon ground coriander
$^1/_4$ teaspoon ground cumin
$^1/_4$ teaspoon hot chilli powder (optional)
2.5cm/1-inch piece fresh root ginger
   peeled and finely grated
1 tablespoon runny honey
juice $^1/_2$ lemon
2 tablespoons olive oil
salt and pepper

Serves 2

Rinse and dry the fish fillets. Place the marinade ingredients in a shallow dish and mix together. Add the fish and rub over the marinade. Cover and leave in the fridge for at least 30 minutes.

Grease a large sheet of foil with a little olive oil and place on a baking tray. Lay on the fish fillets and the marinade. Fold over the foil and seal to make a puffed-up envelope. Hang the tray on the third set of runners from the top of the roasting oven and bake for 10 minutes. Remove from the oven and leave to stand for 3–5 minutes.

Spoon a portion of creamy mashed potato on to a serving plate and top with two sea bass fillets. Pour over the cooking juices and garnish with a few rocket leaves.

Cook's notes
If you are not too confident about filleting the fish yourself ask your kindly fishmonger to do it for you – he will be more than happy to oblige!

September 30

Spiced Fruit with Mascarpone Cream

At the end of summer, nectarines sold in this country can be firm but don't seem to ripen. They are perfect for baking, and adding new season firm figs really gives this dish a wonderful feast of autumn flavours.

8 nectarines, washed, quartered and stoned
2 figs, washed and quartered
1 cinnamon stick
125g/4oz vanilla sugar
$^1/_2$ teaspoon mixed spice

For the Mascarpone cream
250g tub Mascarpone
1 tablespoon vanilla sugar

Serves 4–6

Nectarines are a subspecies of peach with smooth as opposed to velvety skin. Their season runs from July to September. They are typically tangier and more astringent than peaches and can be either 'cling-stone' or 'free-stone' fruits, (with flesh that clings to or is free from the stone of the fruit). Like peaches, nectarines can be either white or yellow-fleshed, and despite their obvious differences, regular peach trees occasionally produce nectarines and vice-versa.

Place the prepared fruit, cut side up, in a shallow ovenproof dish. Bury the cinnamon stick in the fruit. Mix the sugar and mixed spice together and scatter over the fruit.

Put the shelf on the floor of the roasting oven and slide in the dish of fruit.

Bake the fruit for 15–20 minutes, or until the fruit is just soft, depending on the ripeness of the fruit.

Beat the Mascarpone together with the vanilla sugar.

Serve the warm fruit with a spoonful of the cream.

Cook's notes
Any leftover vanilla pods can be stored in a jar of caster sugar for use whenever the fancy, or a recipe, takes you!

October

1st Roast Rack of Pork with Roast Apples
2nd Corn, Crab and Prawn Chowder
3rd Pigeon with Raisins 4th Plum and Oatmeal
Madeira Cake 5th Chorizo, Pepper and Tomato
Macaroni 6th Figs on Brioche 7th Artichoke and
Wild Mushroom Pie 8th French Onion Soup
9th Braised Chicken Legs in Red Wine
10th Oven-Roasted Vegatable Moussaka
11th Potato and Horseradish Gratin 12th Salmon and
Leek Filo Pie 13th Warm Spiced Duck Salad
14th Tomato and Pepper Soup 15th Apple Custard
Tart 16th Pheasant with Button Mushrooms
17th Beetroot and Red Wine Risotto 18th Coffee Cake
19th Kedgeree 20th Chicken Tikka Skewers
21st Mango Chutney 22nd Sea Bass en Papillote
23rd Roast Beetroot with Goat's Cheese 24th Lamb in
Ale and Chedder Croûtes 25th Italian Beef Burgers
26th Classic Quiche Lorraine 27th Blueberry Pancakes
28th Onion and Cream Tart 29th Venison, Beef
and Cranberry Pie 30th Savoury Fish Crumble
31st Pumpkin Pie

October
1

Roast Rack of Pork with Roast Apples

This dish uses a whole loin of pork, now often called a rack. Have the butcher prepare the meat so that carving is easy. The chine bone is best removed and the skin scored well by the butcher.

3 kg/6$^1/_2$ lbs loin or rack of pork
1 lemon
1 eating apple per person. cored and halved
1 teaspoon cornflour
300ml/$^1/_2$ pint apple juice
300ml/$^1/_2$ pint light stock

Serves 8–10

Twist pieces of foil round any exposed bones to prevent burning. Cut the lemon in half and rub the skin all over very well with the lemon juice, squeezing as you go.

Stand the pork in the large roasting tin and hang on the third set of runners from the top of the roasting oven. Calculate the cooking time which will be as follows – 30 minutes per 450g/1 lb plus 30 minutes

30 minutes before the end of the cooking time lay the apple halves around the meat. Baste with any fat in the pan. If the crackling is very brown move the pan down to the bottom set of runners or slide a piece of foil lossely over the top. Cook for the remaining 20–30 minutes.

Remove the meat to a carving board and the roast apples to a warm dish. Keep warm while making the gravy. If you cover the meat or put it in the simmering or plate-warming oven the crackling will go soft.

Blend the cornflour with a little of the apple juice. Skim any excess fat from the roasting tin leaving all the crusty bits. Pour the apple juice, cornflour mix and stock into the tin and whisk well, scraping all the bits from the tin. Stand on the simmering plate, whisking until a gravy has been made. Pour into a warm jug.

Carve the meat, cutting between each pair of ribs. Serve with the roast apples and apple gravy.

Cook's notes
Red skinned apples look particularly attractive for this dish. Choose crisp apples that won't 'fall' during cooking.

October
2

Corn, Crab and Prawn Chowder

Chowders should be thick and creamy with a gentle flavour. This is a perfect example!

418g can corn, creamed
170g can crab meat, drained
125g/4$^1/_2$ oz cooked tiger prawns
1 small onion, peeled and finely chopped
1 clove garlic, peeled and finely chopped
1 tablespoon sunflower oil
1 large tomato, skinned, seeded and finely chopped
284ml carton/$^1/_2$ pint single cream
200ml/7 fl oz milk
salt and pepper
a few parsley leaves, to garnish
prawn crackers, to serve

Serves 4

In a medium saucepan heat the oil and cook the onion and garlic until soft but not brown. Add the corn, tomato, cream and milk to the pan and bring almost to the boil. Simmer for 2–3 minutes.

Stir in the crab and prawns and heat through for 2 minutes. Adjust the seasoning .

Ladle into warm bowls, scatter over the parsley and serve with the prawn crackers.

Cook's notes
Sometimes it is difficult to find 'creamed corn'. To give a creamier soup, whiz the can contents in a blender briefly until the corn is starting to break.

Pigeon with Raisins

Whole pigeons need long, slow cooking to tenderise their meat – unless you know it is a young pigeon, in which case it can be roasted. Most recipes these days remove the breast meat and use the remaining meat and bones to make a stock. This recipe uses the whole bird, one per person.

50g/2oz butter
3 tablespoons olive oil
4 pigeons
100g/3$^1/_2$oz raisins, soaked in warm water for 30 minutes
4 large onions, thinly sliced
$^1/_2$ teaspoon paprika
salt and pepper

Serves 4

Heat the butter and oil in a frying pan and brown the pigeons well all over. Transfer to a casserole dish. Cook the onions in the hot fat until soft and golden brown. Season with salt, pepper and paprika and add to the pigeons along with the drained raisins. Cover with a well fitting lid or a sheet of foil. Heat gently on the simmering plate for a few minutes before transferring to the simmering oven for about 2 hours.

Cook's notes
Place a tight lid on the casserole or alternatively use foil to cover well – but remember, foil may snag on the runners.

Several species of pigeon and dove are used in cooking due to the strong breast muscles which make delicious and tender meat. Often, the muscles of the pigeon are removed and the rest of the carcass is used for making game stock. In Europe, the variety of pigeon most commonly shot and used in cooking is the wood pigeon, and is available from April through to December. Rock Pigeons were originally domesticated as a food species and were one of many breeds developed for the quality of their meat.

October
4

Plum and Oatmeal Madeira Cake

This moist plum cake recipe was developed for those who have a glut of plums from their garden and need new ideas. Serve this warm as a pudding or cold as a cake.

250g/9oz plums
110g/4oz butter, softened
finely grated zest 1 orange
110g/4oz caster sugar
2 eggs, beaten
125g/5oz self-raising flour
$^1/_2$ teaspoon baking powder
50g/2oz oatmeal or rolled oats
110g/4oz icing sugar
3–4 tablespoons orange juice

Grease and base-line a 500g/ 1 lb loaf tin.

Halve and stone the plums and cut into chunky pieces.

Put the butter, orange zest and the caster sugar in a bowl and beat until light and fluffy. Gradually beat in the eggs with a little flour. Add the baking powder to the remaining flour and fold into the creamed mixture. Stir in the oats or oatmeal. Fold two thirds of the plums into the mixture and then spoon the mixture into the prepared tin. Level the top and scatter the remaining plums over the surface.

Bake the cake.

For a two-oven Aga, stand the loaf tin in the small roasting tin. Hang the tin on the bottom set of runners of the roasting oven and put the cold shelf on the second set of runners from the top of the oven. Bake for 50–60 minutes.

For a three- or four-oven Aga, put the shelf on the bottom set of runners of the baking oven and put in the loaf tin. Bake for 1 hour and 10–20 minutes. When the cake is cooked it will be risen, slightly shrunk from the sides of the tin and a skewer inserted in the middle will come out clean.

Leave in the tin for 15–20 minutes and then cool on a wire rack.

Sieve the icing sugar into a basin and add enough orange juice to make a smooth paste. Drizzle over the top of the cake and leave to set.

Cook's notes

The cake mixture will rise around the plums that you put on the top of the cake, so don't press them down into the mixture prior to baking.

Chorizo, Pepper and Tomato Macaroni

If you can't find an uncooked Chorizo sausage then hunt out something like a pepperoni sausage instead.

400g/14oz macaroni
1 tablespoon olive oil
4 chorizo sausages, sliced
1 medium onion, peeled and chopped
2 cloves garlic, peeled and chopped
2 red peppers, deseeded and chopped
2 x 400g cans chopped tomatoes
2 tablespoons balsamic vinegar
a few torn basil leaves
salt and pepper

Serves 4

Cook the macaroni in a pan of boiling salted water until al dente. Drain. Return to the saucepan and cover and keep warm.

While the pasta is cooking heat the oil in a frying pan and fry the sausage slices, until crisp. Remove from the pan and keep warm. Add the onion, garlic and pepper to the pan and cook until the vegetables are softening. Add the tomatoes and vinegar, stirring occasionally, until the sauce is thickened. Season with salt and pepper. Toss the macaroni into the sauce and then add the chorizo.

Serve immediately scattered with the torn basil leaves.

Cook's notes
Pasta can be cooked in the simmering oven. Plunge the pasta into the boiling water, return to the boil and move the pan to the simmering oven. Cook for the usual time.

October
6

Figs on Brioche

This part French, part Italian inspired recipe has the great advantage of making the precious fig go a long way.

8 figs
4 slices brioche
200g/7oz Mascarpone
a little runny honey
icing sugar to dust

Serves 4

Available from September to October, figs are one of the autumn season's most beautiful riches. Fresh figs typically have a deep purple outer skin and a bright pinkish-red seedy pulp. Whilst we often think of figs as fruits, they are in fact, technically the flower of the tree. What makes it appear like a fruit is its inversion, where the exterior surface of the flower appears like the skin of the fruit, and the flower is only seen once the fig is cut open.

Lay a circle of Bake-O-Glide on the simmering plate.

Cut the figs in half through the stalk and lay cut side down on the simmering plate. 'Cook' the figs until the cut side is just browning and the figs softening. Remove the figs gently to a plate.

Wipe the sheet of Bake-O-Glide and return to the simmering plate. Lay on the slices of brioche and toast on each side. When toasted, place each slice of brioche on a serving plate.

Beat the Mascarpone in a basin to slacken, and then divide it between the slices of brioche. Cut each fig in half again through the stalk and lay on the top of the Mascarpone.

Drizzle over a little honey and dust with icing sugar.

Cook's notes
The brioche toasts very quickly, so keep a watchful eye on it and don't get distracted!

October

7

Artichoke and Wild Mushroom Pie

This is a dish for mushroom lovers! With wild mushrooms plentiful at this time of year, a gentle walk through the countryside, armed with a trusty field guide, should reap fine funghi rewards.

2 tablespoons olive oil
2 onions, peeled and sliced
300g/10oz char-grilled artichoke
*   hearts*
300g/10oz mixed mushrooms
1 clove garlic, peeled and crushed
1 teaspoon chopped thyme leaves
500g packet short crust pastry
1 egg, beaten with a pinch of salt
*   and a tablespoon water, to glaze*
1 tablespoon roughly chopped
*   parsley leaves*
serve with crème fraîche or soured
*   cream and some tangy tomato relish*

Serves 6–8

Heat the oil in a large sauté pan and add the onions. Cook until softened but not brown. Spoon into a large bowl and mix with the artichokes. Season.

Add the mushrooms to the pan and cook for 2–3 minutes and then add the garlic and thyme. Cook for 1 more minute and remove from the heat. Season. Cool.

Roll out the pastry to a large circle and lay on a large sheet of Bake-O-Glide and then onto a large baking tray. Spoon the onion and artichoke mixture onto the middle of the pastry circle and spread out leaving a 10cm/4-inch border round the edge. Spoon the mushrooms over the top.

Bring the pastry edges up over the filling to form a border. Brush the exposed pastry with the egg glaze.

Slide the baking tray onto the floor of the roasting oven and bake the pie for 20–25 minutes, until the pastry is crisp and golden brown.

Scatter over the chopped parsley and serve with the soured cream and tangy tomato relish.

Cook's notes
Individual pies can be made, but be wary of making them too large as the mushroom and artichoke mixture is very filling.

Aga year

French Onion Soup

French onion soup has been a classic for so long. It is very easy to make successfully in the simmering oven, where the gentle heat avoids the risk of burning the onions. You can always double up on the quantity of bread and cheese and serve some as an extra to eat with the soup.

25g/1oz butter
450g/ 1 lb onions, sliced
1.2litres/2 pints light stock
$^1/_2$ teaspoon salt
25g/1oz flour mixed with 150ml//$^1/_4$ pint water
4–6 slices baguette
50g/2oz Gruyère cheese

Serves 4–6

Melt the butter in a large saucepan and stir in the onion. Cover and when the onions are piping hot, transfer to the simmering oven for 1 hour. Add the stock and salt, and bring back to the boil. Return to the simmering oven for a further hour. Stir in the flour mixture and boil for 2–3 minutes.

Place the French bread on a baking sheet, sprinkle on the grated Gruyère and toast for a few minutes at the top of the roasting oven. Place one piece in each soup dish and pour round the soup.

Cook's notes
Take care when eating French onion soup, it retains its heat remarkably well.

PINK GIN PROSECCO

YOU'LL NEED:

- ·ICE
- ·FRESH STRAWBERRIES (CHOPPED)
- ·PINK GIN
- ·LEMONADE
- ·PROSECCO OF YOUR CHOICE

MAKE IT:

First, add ice and a fresh and fruity handful of strawberries to your Ava & I goblets. Pour one part of pink gin into each glass to give your drink pretty colour and mix in two parts of refreshing lemonade. Now add the bubbles! Top off your fabulous cocktails with your choice of prosecco and watch as the tiny bubbles dance and pop. Give the drinks a gentle stir to mix in all the flavours.

CLINK AND ENJOY!

PINK GIN PROSECCO

ava & i™

Creative Tops. A division of Lifetime Brands Europe Ltd, NN17 4DU. www.creative-tops.com

October
9

Braised Chicken Legs in Red Wine

Preparing this dish may seem a little fiddly but the flavour of the gently cooked chicken is really worth the effort.

8 chicken legs divided into legs
    and thighs
1 bottle full-bodied red wine,
    boiled and reduced by half
salt and pepper
2 tablespoons vegetable oil
50g/2oz butter
8 cloves garlic, peeled
24 shallots, peeled
2 tomatoes, roughly chopped
2 tablespoons plain flour
30g/1$^1/_2$oz dried ceps

1 bouquet garni
2 strips dried orange zest
pinch sugar
cornflour to thicken, if needed

To finish
finely grated rind 1 orange
2 large ripe tomatoes, seeded and
    diced
12 large black olives, pitted
a few fresh thyme leaves

Serves 4

Put the chicken in a dish and pour over the reduced wine. Leave to marinate for 30 minutes. Remove the chicken pieces and then dry them.

Heat the oil in a large frying pan and brown the chicken well. Wipe out the pan and add the butter. When hot, return the chicken to the pan and caramelise the portions. Transfer the chicken to a casserole dish.

Put the garlic and shallots into the frying pan, cook for a few minutes and then add the chopped tomato. Cook for 2–3 minutes and then add the flour to the pan, stir well and then add the dried ceps, followed by the reserved wine. Pour over the chicken and bury the bouquet garni and the orange zest in the dish. Cover the casserole and bring to the boil. Move the casserole to the simmering oven for 2–3 hours.

Check that the chicken is tender, it should ideally be soft enough to eat with a spoon. Lift the chicken from the casserole and keep warm. Bring the remaining casserole ingredients to the boil and reduce to a rich, dark sauce.

Adjust the seasoning with salt, pepper and a pinch of sugar.

If you like a really thick sauce you may want to thicken it with a little cornflour.

Put the chicken in a serving dish, pour over the sauce and garnish with the orange rind, chopped tomatoes, olives and thyme leaves.

Serve with pasta. This dish can be made up to 3 days ahead of serving.

Cook's notes
You can make this dish up to 3 days in advance of serving.

Oven-Roasted Vegetable Moussaka

The idea of aubergines topped with a sauce has been kept in this vegetarian version of the Greek classic but the base is vegetables instead of meat. I love it!

1 medium onion, peeled and sliced
1 sweet potato, peeled and diced
2 red peppers, seeded and roughly chopped
1 aubergine, sliced
350g/12oz potato, peeled and sliced
5 cloves garlic, peeled
5 tablespoons olive oil

1 x 400g can chopped tomatoes
4 pieces sun-dried tomatoes, snipped into strips
225g/8oz cottage cheese
3 large eggs
150g/6oz grated Cheddar cheese
3 tablespoons plain yoghurt
salt and pepper

Serves 6

Line the large roasting tin with Bake-O-Glide. Put all the prepared vegetables in the lined tin. Season with salt and toss in the olive oil. Hang the tin on the top set of runners of the roasting oven and roast for 45–50 minutes, until the vegetables are cooked. Pour over the can of chopped tomatoes and the snipped sun-dried tomatoes. Mix well and return to the oven for a further 10 minutes.

In a bowl mix together the cottage cheese, eggs, Cheddar cheese and the yoghurt. Season with salt and pepper.

Spoon the roast vegetables into a shallow ovenproof dish and pour over the cheese mixture.

Bake the moussaka on the third set of runners from the top of the roasting oven for 15–20 minutes, until bubbling hot and golden brown. Alternatively, if you have a three- or four-oven Aga, cook in the baking oven with the shelf on the second set of runners from the bottom for 20–30 minutes.

Cook's notes
This recipe is so useful because it can be frozen before the final baking. Thaw overnight in the fridge and follow the cooking instructions.

October

11

Potato and Horseradish Gratin

Adding the horseradish and the soured cream to these potatoes gives added flavour to a dish which is perfect to accompany beef or chicken. The creamed horseradish has a milder flavour than a traditional horseradish sauce – if you like the intense flavour of horseradish, use the traditional sauce.

1 kg/2lb 4oz main crop potatoes, peeled
425ml/³/₄ pint double cream
140ml/¹/₄ pint soured cream
85ml/3 floz milk
salt and pepper
6 tablespoons creamed horseradish

Serves 6

Horseradish, belonging to the same family as wasabi, mustard and cabbage, is a perennial plant cultivated for its fiery flavour and tapered root. The main root of the plant is typically harvested after the first frosts of autumn. Horseradish can be eaten and treated as a root vegetable, but is most popular as a cream or sauce, where it is coarsely grated before being combined with vinegar to form a hot paste.

Finely slice the potatoes.

Put the cream, soured cream and milk into a saucepan and bring to just below boiling point. Season with salt and pepper.

Butter a shallow ovenproof dish and put in a layer of sliced potatoes. Spread over half the creamed horseradish and some of the cream mixture. Repeat with another layer of potatoes and the remaining horseradish. Top with a final layer of potatoes and pour over any remaining cream.

For a two-oven Aga, put the shelf on the floor of the roasting oven and put in the gratin dish. After 30 minutes slide in the cold shelf and continue to cook for 40–50 minutes, until the potatoes are cooked.

For a three- or four–oven Aga, put the shelf on the bottom set of runners of the baking oven and put in the gratin dish. Bake for 1–1¹/₂ hours until the potatoes are tender and the gratin golden on top.

Serve with roast beef or roast chicken.

Cook's notes

Look for a floury type of potato for this dish so that the creamy sauce can be absorbed by the potatoes during cooking – Desirée or King Edwards, for example.

345

Salmon and Leek Filo Pie

Filo pastry is easy to use and baking on the floor of the Aga roasting oven ensures a crisp finish. It is always best served straight from the oven.

For the pastry
50g/2oz butter, melted
100g/3¹/₂ oz filo pastry

For the filling
50g/2oz butter
2 medium leeks, halved
*   lengthways and finely sliced*

300ml/¹/₂ pint milk
35g/1¹/₂ oz flour
salt and pepper
1 tablespoon lemon juice
1 tablespoon chopped parsley
1 kg/2lbs 4oz skinless salmon
*   fillet*
200g/7oz scallops or prawns

Serves 6–8

Butter the base and sides of a 20 x 30cm/8 x 12-inch shallow ovenproof dish.

Brush 6 sheets of filo pastry with butter and use to line the shallow dish. This should give a double layer. Cut the salmon into bite-sized pieces and place in the dish with the scallops or prawns.

Melt 25g/1oz butter in a saucepan and add the sliced leeks. Cover with a lid and cook on the simmering plate until soft. Remove from the pan and set aside. Put the milk, remaining 25g/1oz butter and the flour in the saucepan. Stand on the simmering plate and whisk constantly until a thick sauce has formed. Cook for 1–2 minutes, beating well. Remove from the heat and season with salt and pepper. Add the parsley and lemon juice and mix in well. Stir in the reserved leeks.

Pour the sauce over the fish. (If making in advance and not baking immediately allow the sauce to cool before pouring over the fish).

Fold over any edges of filo pastry and then brush 4 more sheets of pastry with melted butter and lay over the top to form a lid. Trim any excess pastry or fold over to tidy up the edges. Brush well with any remaining butter.

Place directly on the floor of the roasting oven and bake for 20–25 minutes until golden and crisp.

Cook's notes
This same pie can be made with a variety of fish; pollock and smoked haddock, for example, makes a good combination.

October
13

Warm Spiced Roast Duck Salad

Duck cooked in the roasting oven is crisp and not at all fatty and doesn't become dry. Here it is served warm, which is a much nicer way to eat it than cold. Duck always works so well with fruit; we used always to serve it with orange or cherry – now we are more exotic and use figs, though blackberries work well in autumn as well.

2 duck breasts, skin on
2 tablespoons clear honey
1 tablespoon balsamic vinegar
zest and juice 1 orange
1 tablespoon olive oil
4 fresh figs, halved
1 bag lambs lettuce

Serves 2

Put the rack in the small roasting tin and lay the duck breasts on it, skin side uppermost. Slide the tin onto the second set of runners from the top of the roasting oven and cook for 20–25 minutes, until crisp and golden brown. Remove the duck from the oven and leave to rest for 5 minutes.

Pour off any fat from the pan and reserve the juices.

Whisk the honey, vinegar, zest and juice of the orange and the olive oil together in a bowl. Toss in the fig halves. Tip into the small roasting tin and heat through until the figs are just soft and glossy, about 2 minutes.

Carve the duck breasts into thin slices and toss with the salad leaves. Spoon onto two plates and spoon over the pan juices and the figs.

Cook's notes
It is very easy to make this dish for more than two as all the cooking is done in the oven.

October
14

Tomato and Pepper Soup

I return to this recipe time and time again. I don't like straight tomato soup but I find the addition of the red pepper adds a good flavour and texture. It is quick to make and delicious to eat and very good on those chilly autumnal days when the evenings are beginning to draw in. Have some good bread with it, and good butter of course!

25g/1oz butter
1 onion, peeled and chopped
1 red pepper, seeded and chopped
1 tablespoon tomato purée
1 x 400g can tomatoes
pinch sugar
1 bay leaf
sprig parsley or mint, finely chopped
600ml/1 pint vegetable stock
salt and pepper

Serves 4 small portions

Melt the butter in a saucepan and add the onion. Cover and sweat over a low heat until the onion is soft but not brown. Stir in the chopped pepper and cook for 2–3 minutes. Add the tomato purée, the canned tomatoes, the sugar, bay leaf, herbs and stock. Bring to the boil and cover. Put the pan in the simmering oven for 20–30 minutes. Remove the bay leaf and blend the soup together. Taste and add salt and pepper if needed.

Cook's notes
A swirl of cream and some shredded basil leaves would make this soup suitable to serve to guests.

Apple Custard Tart

This is a variation on apple pie and custard! You can of course make your own custard.

1.25kg/2lb 12oz cooking apples, peeled, cored and sliced
400g carton readymade custard sauce
75g/3oz butter
500g pack puff pastry
1 egg yolk, beaten
2 tablespoons milk
icing or caster sugar for dusting

Serves 8

Produced by a small deciduous tree, apples are among the most common commercially grown fruits throughout the world. There is a huge variety grown in UK orchards – red, yellow, green, sweet apples, sharp apples, soft-and firm-fleshed, some perfect for eating and some suited to cooking. A member of the rose family, the apple tree produces flowers in spring at the same time as its budding leaves. The fruit is harvested throughout autumn and winter.

Melt the butter in a saucepan and add the apples. Cook gently until just softening. Remove from the heat and cool.

Cut the pastry in half. Roll each piece into a circle to fit a shallow pie plate. Line the pie plate with one circle of pastry.

Stir the custard into the apples and spoon into the pastry-lined dish. Lay the remaining circle of pastry over the apples. Seal the pastry well. Decorate the edges.

Beat together the egg yolk and milk and glaze the top of the pie. Cut a small air hole in the middle

Hang the shelf on the third set of runners from the top of the roasting oven. Slide in the apple pie and bake for 20 minutes, until the pastry is risen and a pale golden colour. Move the pie to the floor of the oven for 10–15 minutes. If the top of the pie is browning too much, slide in the cold shelf two runners above to allow the pastry on the bottom to crisp through.

Dust with sugar and serve warm.

Cook's notes
Puff pastry needs the heat from the top of the roasting oven to puff and rise, so start the pie near the top of the oven but watch that it doesn't burn if your oven is on the hot side.

October
16

Pheasant with Button Mushrooms

Pheasant has become much more readily available in butchers and supermarkets over the last few years. This is a traditional way to cook jointed pheasants. The length of cooking time will depend upon the age of the birds. A larger cock bird should serve four, while two hen birds should serve six.

1 tablespoon vegetable oil
50g/2oz butter
2 onions, sliced
3 carrots, sliced
1 pheasant, jointed
1 tablespoon brandy
a bouquet garni
450ml/$^3/_4$ pint red wine
salt and pepper

8 shallots, peeled
8 button mushrooms
2 tablespoon double cream
15g/$^1/_2$ oz butter cut into cubes

Serves 4–6

Heat the oil and half the butter in a frying pan and sauté the onion and carrots until softening. Drain and place in a casserole dish. Brown the pheasant portions in the hot pan and when browned all over pour on the brandy. When the brandy is hot, ignite with a match. Allow the flames to die down then transfer the pheasant to a casserole dish.

Pour the wine into the frying pan and bring to the boil, scraping all the sediment from the base of the pan. Season and pour over the pheasant. Add the bouquet garni. Cover, bring to the boil and transfer to the simmering oven for 3–4 hours. Towards the end of cooking time, heat the remaining butter in a frying pan and fry the shallots and mushrooms until lightly golden. Lift the pheasant joints from the casserole and keep warm. Boil the liquid to reduce and whisk in the butter to make a shiny sauce. Stir in the shallots, mushrooms and cream. Bubble gently for 2–3 minutes. Taste and adjust the seasoning. Pour over the pheasant.

Cook's notes
The bouquet garni can be made from any herbs that you have to hand in the garden, such as bay leaves, sage and thyme. If you have parsley on the windowsill, add that as well. Tie the herbs together with string and leave a long end to tie onto the handle of the casserole and to use to fish the bouquet garni out of the casserole when its job is done.

With autumn comes the rich and varied game season in the UK, representing a wealth of traditional British cooking. Pheasant season in the UK runs from 1st October to 31st January. Due to its rich, full-bodied flavour, pheasant is commonly paired with fresh flavours such as citrus, apples, blackberries and redcurrants. The flavour is greatly enhanced once hung – anything between 3 and 10 days. The longer a bird is left to hang, the more the flavour will increase.

17

Beetroot and Red Wine Risotto

Beetroot gives the rice the most amazing colour as well as flavour. When you serve this it will certainly be a talking point. I have converted many people to eating beetroot with this recipe.

2 tablespoons olive oil
1 red onion, peeled and diced
500g/1 lb 2oz arborio rice
2 beetroot, peeled and diced
225ml/8 fl oz red wine
1 litre/1³/₄ pints light chicken or vegetable stock, hot
grated rind and juice ¹/₂ lemon
shavings of Parmesan cheese

Serves 4 as a main course, 6–8 as a starter

Heat the oil in a large sauté pan and add the onion and cook until softening but not browning. Add the rice and beetroot and stir to coat in the oil. Pour in the wine and cook, stirring, until all the wine has been absorbed. Gradually add the stock, a ladle full at a time. Stir and cook until the rice is creamy and al dente.

Remove from the heat and stir in the lemon juice and rind. Season with salt and pepper.

Serve with shavings of Parmesan.

Cook's notes
Wear rubber gloves when peeling beetroot, unless you want to parade around with pink hands for a day or two.

Aga *year*

October
18

Coffee Cake

A traditional teatime treat looking spectacular with a fluffy, butter icing. Chopped walnuts can be added for variety and to add texture.

4 eggs	***For the icing***
225g/8oz self-raising flour	*225g/8oz icing sugar*
225g/8oz caster sugar	*110g/4oz soft butter*
225g 8oz soft butter	*1 tablespoon Camp coffee*
2 tablespoons Camp Coffee	

Base-line 2 x 20cm/8-inch Victoria sandwich tins. Butter the sides lightly and set aside.

Put the eggs, flour, sugar, butter and coffee essence in a mixing bowl and beat together until light and fluffy. Use either a wooden spoon or an electric mixer.

Divide the mixture between the two prepared tins and level the surfaces.

Bake the cakes.

For a two-oven Aga, put the oven shelf on the floor of the roasting oven. Put in the cakes and slide the cold shelf onto the second set of runners from the bottom of the oven. Bake for 25 – 30 minutes.

For a three- or four-oven Aga, put the shelf on the bottom set of runners of the baking oven and put in the cakes. Bake for 25–30 minutes.

The cakes will be cooked when they are risen, evenly golden brown and springy when lightly pressed in the middle.

Run a table knife round the edge of the tin to loosen the cakes and then turn out to cool on a cooling rack.

Make the butter icing. Sieve the icing sugar into a roomy mixing bowl and add the soft butter. Beat together using a wooden spoon or electric mixer until light and fluffy and then beat in the Camp coffee. Cover with clingfilm until needed.

Place one cake, upside-down, on a serving plate. Smooth over one third of the icing, going right to the edge of the cake. Place the second cake on top and use the remaining icing to decorate the top. Swirl over with a knife.

Cook's notes

This cake can also be made in the small roasting tin to make a tray bake. Use all the icing on the top and cut into squares to serve. If you don't have Camp coffee make up strong instant coffee instead.

October
19

Kedgeree

Traditionally this dish was eaten for breakfast, nowadays it is usually eaten for lunch or supper. I think it makes a wonderful contribution to brunch, a popular weekend meal.

1 large fillet of undyed smoked haddock
300ml/$^1/_2$ pint milk
salt and pepper
300ml/$^1/_2$ pint measure basmati rice
4 eggs
50g/2oz butter
2 tablespoons chopped parsley
150ml/$^1/_4$ pint single cream

Serves 4

Put the fillet of smoked haddock in a shallow ovenproof dish and pour over the milk. Season with a little pepper. Put the shelf on the bottom set of runners of the roasting oven and put in the fish. Poach the fish for 12–15 minutes. Then remove from the oven and set aside until cool enough to handle.

Meanwhile cook the rice. Measure the rice and 450ml/$^3/_4$ pint water and a pinch of salt into a saucepan. Cover and bring to the boil. As the rice starts to boil put the saucepan in the simmering oven for 12–15 minutes.

Put the eggs in a saucepan and cover with cold water. Stand on the boiling plate and bring to the boil. When boiling remove the pan from the heat and stand on the back of the Aga for 10 minutes.

Pour off the hot water and cover the eggs with cold water. When cool enough to handle peel the eggs carefully. Chop 2 of the eggs and quarter the remaining 2 eggs. Set aside.

Carefully remove the fish from the milk and remove any skin and bones from it. Break the fish into large flakes. Strain the milk onto the cooked rice and add the butter, chopped parsley and cream.

Finally, gently stir in the flaked fish and the chopped egg. Spoon into a warmed serving dish and decorate with the quartered eggs.

Serve warm.

Cook's notes
I learnt this method of boiling eggs at college – rarely do the eggs break. Covering with cold water as soon as they are cooked will prevent a black sulphur ring forming round the yolk.

October
20

Chicken Tikka Skewers

Chicken tikka is said to be one of Britain's favourite dishes. I'm not so sure about that but I do know that these delectable, spicy morsels are always very popular and disappear in a flash whenever I serve them to guests!

4 large boneless and skinless chicken breasts,
*   cut into 2¹/₂cm/1-inch chunks*
juice 2 lemons
salt
110g/4oz plain yoghurt
25g/1oz chilli paste
1 teaspoon ground coriander
1 teaspoon garam masala
1 teaspoon crushed garlic
1 teaspoon chopped fresh ginger
¹/₂ teaspoon turmeric

Serves 4

Cut the chicken into even-sized cubes and put in a non-metallic dish and sprinkle with the lemon juice and salt.

Mix together the yoghurt, chilli paste, coriander, garam masala, garlic, ginger and turmeric. Pour over the chicken, mix well and leave to marinate for at least 2 hours.

Thread the chicken onto skewers or bamboo sticks. Line a large baking tray with Bake-O-Glide and space out the chicken tikka skewers. Allow some space between the skewers so that the meat can cook evenly.

Slide the tray onto the second set of runners from the top of the roasting oven and cook for about 15 minutes, turning once.

Cook's notes
Keep a wary eye on the chicken as you do not want to cook it for too long lest the meat begins to dry out.

Mango Chutney

I firmly believe that an Indian style curry has to have a good mango chutney to accompany it, but some of the commercial ones just don't taste of much. Making your own couldn't be simpler and you can add as much chilli as you like for extra heat!

25g/1oz fresh ginger, peeled
6 cloves garlic, peeled
3 fresh chillies, stalks and seeds removed
3 large mangoes, peeled and chopped
1 teaspoon salt
300ml/$^1/_2$ pint white wine vinegar
450g/1 lb granulated sugar

Put the ginger, garlic, chillies and salt together in a blender or pestle and mortar and grind to a paste.

Put all the ingredients in a roomy saucepan, stand on the simmering plate and stir until the sugar has dissolved. Bring to the boil and then move to the simmering oven, uncovered. Cook for 1–1$^1/_2$ hours, until the mango is well cooked and the chutney is beginning to thicken.

Pot into clean and sterile jars. When cold seal the tops and label.

Store in a cool dark place for at least 2 weeks before eating.

Cook's notes
This chutney thickens as it cools, so be careful not to overcook.

October
22

Sea Bass en Papillote

Sea bass is a popular fish rightly noted for its flavour and texture. This method of cooking is very moist, producing a small amount of sauce which goes well with the potatoes. The parcels are always a talking point when served, just take care that the juice doesn't dribble down your guests' front when the parcel is opened!

3 stems lemongrass, very finely chopped
1$^1/_2$ tablespoons finely chopped lemon thyme
finely grated zest 3 limes plus some juice
6 tablespoons extra-virgin olive oil
50g/2oz butter, softened
salt and pepper
6 sea bass fillets

Serves 6

Mix together the lemongrass, thyme, lime zest, juice from 1$^1/_2$ limes and the olive oil.

Cut six oblongs of greaseproof paper long enough to wrap each fillet of fish. Use half the butter to rub over one side of each greaseproof sheet.

Lightly season the flesh side of the fish and lay one fillet, skin side down, on each paper sheet. Spread the lemongrass mixture over the fillets. Fold over the long ends of the paper and twist the short end together to make a parcel. Place on a baking tray.

Hang the tray on the third set of runners from the top of the roasting oven and bake the fish for 12–15 minutes. The parcels will be puffed up. Open one parcel and check that the fish is cooked.

Cook's notes
If I can only find tough-looking stalks in the shop then I tend to use lemongrass from a jar instead.

Roast Beetroot with Goat's Cheese

Beetroot roasted in the Aga is something quite special and this recipe combines it with goat's cheese - a wonderful combination.

100g/3$^1/_2$ oz cherry tomatoes
salt and pepper
2 large or 4 small beetroot, peeled
2 tablespoons olive oil
200g/7oz goat's cheese (a firm variety is easier to handle)
a bunch of rocket
100ml/3$^1/_2$ fl oz extra virgin olive oil
2 tablespoons balsamic vinegar

Serves 6

Line 2 small baking trays with Bake-O-Glide.

Cut the tomatoes in half round the 'equator' and lay cut side up on a lined baking tray. Hang in the middle of the simmering oven until the tomatoes are semi-dried, about 2 hours. Set aside to cool.

Cut the beetroot into bite-sized wedges and toss in the olive oil. Season lightly with salt and spread out on a lined baking tray.

Hang the tray on the third set of runners from the top of the roasting oven and roast the beetroot for 20–30 minutes, until tender. Remove from the oven and set aside.

Chop the goat's cheese into chunks. Roughly slice the rocket. Lay the beetroot wedges on a large platter, scatter over the rocket followed by the goat's cheese and the dried tomatoes. Mix the oil and balsamic vinegar together and sprinkle over the salad. Grind over some pepper.

Cook's notes
Beetroot is readily available in shops, though you should have a go at growing your own – it's very easy.

At its best from June to October, beetroot is a highly nutritious and colourful vegetable with a fresh earthy flavour and fragrance. The flesh of beetroot is sweet and succulent and can be used in a variety of dishes, cooked and raw. The beetroot's leafy green stalks can also be cooked in a similar way to spinach. Having one of the highest sugar contents of any vegetable, beetroot offers added sweetness to a dish.

October
24

Lamb in Ale and Chedder Croûtes

In the cold weather, casseroles cooked in the Aga come into their own. That slow and gentle cooking really brings out the flavour of the ingredients.

1kg/2lbs 4oz diced lamb
1 tablespoon flour
2 tablespoons vegetable oil
3 onions, peeled and sliced
500 ml bottle ale
150ml/¹/₄ pint vegetable or lamb stock
4 stalks celery, chopped
2 bay leaves, 2 sprigs thyme and 2 sprigs rosemary, tied together

4 teaspoons soft brown sugar
4 teaspoons Worcestershire sauce
1 tablespoon tomato paste
salt and pepper

For the topping
12 slices french bread, toasted
wholegrain mustard
110g/4oz Cheddar cheese, grated

Serves 6

Toss the lamb in the seasoned flour. Heat the oil in a frying pan and cook the onions until soft but not brown. Drain the onions and put in a flameproof casserole.

Re-heat the frying pan and brown the meat, in batches (if you are in a hurry you don't need to do this). Transfer the meat to the casserole and stir in the ale, stock, celery, herbs, brown sugar, Worcestershire sauce, tomato paste and a seasoning of salt and pepper. Cover and bring to the boil. Heat for 4 or 5 minutes and then move the casserole to the simmering oven.

Cook the casserole for 1–1¹/₂ hours.

The casserole can be made in advance and chilled for a day or two or frozen at this stage. Reheat thoroughly, bring to the boil on the simmering plate and move to the simmering oven for 30 minutes.

To make the topping, spread one side of the bread slices with mustard. Lay over the top of the casserole, mustard side up. Sprinkle over the cheese and bake on the second set of runners from the bottom of the roasting oven, for 20–25 minutes, until the topping is crisp and golden.

Cook's notes
Liquids do not evaporate much in the simmering oven so make sure that you do not have too much liquid in the casserole at the beginning.

October
25

Italian Beef Burgers

Beef burgers have a mixed reputation in some quarters. We tend to think of them as being fatty and made from poor quality meat. That need not be the case! Have a go at making your own to see what gastronomic heights a burger can actually reach. You can make them any size you like but it is advisable to cook them thoroughly.

500g/1lb 2oz best quality lean minced beef
1 small onion, peeled and finely chopped
1 clove garlic, crushed
2 tablespoons basil pesto
125g/ 5oz Mozzarella, chopped
vegetable oil

Serves 4

Put the beef in a large bowl with the onions, garlic, pesto and Mozzarella. Season with salt and pepper. Using your hands mix all the ingredients together. Shape into 4 burgers. Brush with a little oil and then chill for at least 20 minutes.

Heat the ridged pan on the floor of the roasting oven. When the pan is really hot put in the burgers and cook for 6–8 minutes on each side, until the juices run clear and there is no pink meat.

Serve in a bread roll with tomato slices or roast tomatoes.

Cooks notes
Make sure the burgers are chilled well, otherwise they will fall apart during cooking.

Classic Quiche Lorraine

'A quiche' has become the name for any pastry case filled with something savoury! It is easy to forget what constitutes a classic 'Quiche Lorraine'.

For the pastry
225g/8oz plain flour
115g/4oz butter, chilled and cut
*   into cubes*
pinch salt
iced water

1 onion, peeled and chopped
4 rashers streaky bacon, rind
*   removed and diced*
3 eggs
300ml/$\frac{1}{2}$ pint single cream
salt and pepper
75g/3oz mature Cheddar cheese
*   or Gruyère, grated*

Serves 6

Make the pastry. Put the flour in a mixing bowl and add the diced butter and the salt. Using fingertips rub the butter into the flour until the mixture resembles breadcrumbs. Using a table knife stir in enough cold water to bind the mixture to a firm dough. Start with 2 tablespoons of water and gradually add more until there is no dry mixture in the base of the bowl. Knead lightly to bring it together as a smooth dough.

Place the pastry on a lightly floured work top and shape into a round. Roll the dough to a circle. Make one roll away from you and then turn the circle a quarter turn, pinching the edges if there are any cracks. Continue to roll the dough until it is large enough to fit the base and sides of a 28cm/11-inch flan tin. Lift the pastry onto a rolling pin and gently lower into the flan tin. Press lightly from the centre to the outside, pressing the pastry over the base and up the sides of the tin. This helps to remove airlocks but take care not to stretch or tear the pastry. Flip any excess pastry over the edge of the dish and roll off with the rolling pin. Put to chill well.

Prepare the filling. Put the onion and bacon in a frying pan and stand on the simmering plate or on the floor of the roasting oven. Allow the fat to run from the bacon. Stir occasionally until the onions are cooked, but not brown and the bacon just starting to crisp. Spoon the pan contents onto kitchen paper. Cool.

Beat together the eggs, cream and a seasoning of salt and pepper.

Spoon the onion and bacon mixture into the chilled pastry case. Pour over the egg mixture and scatter over the grated cheese.

Cook the quiche directly on the floor of the roasting oven for 25 minutes until the quiche is golden brown on top and firm in the middle when gently shaken. The pastry will have shrunk slightly from the sides of the tin. Serve hot or warm.

Cook's notes
Take care not to overcook the tart. The filling should be smooth and creamy against the crisp pastry base. If your Aga cooks quickly then slide the cold shelf onto the third set of runners from the top, this will allow the filling to cook more gently but at the same time allow the pastry to become crisp. You may need to remove the cold shelf for the last five minutes of cooking time to allow the top to brown.

Blueberry Pancakes

Blueberries are often thought of as exclusively American, but they are grown in this country and crop from July to October. Blackcurrants can be substituted and give a similar sharp flavour. Make the pancakes on the simmering plate.

150g/5oz plain flour
225ml/8fl oz milk
1 teaspoon vanilla sugar
1 tablespoon melted butter
pinch of salt
3 eggs, separated
1 teaspoon caster sugar
225g/8oz blueberries
4 teaspoons caster sugar mixed with 1 teaspoon cinnamon
vegetable oil, for greasing

Serves 4

Place the flour in a mixing bowl and whisk in the milk, vanilla sugar, butter, salt and egg yolks to make a smooth batter. Whisk the egg whites with the caster sugar until stiff and then fold into the batter.

Oil the simmering plate lightly and ladle half the batter into 2 portions on the oiled plate to make pancakes about 2 cm/$^3/_4$-inch thick. Sprinkle a quarter of the blueberries over each pancake and allow the batter to set. Carefully turn over and brown for 1–2 minutes.

Continue to cook the remaining 2 pancakes. Serve on individual plates and dust with the cinnamon sugar.

Cook's notes
This batter can be made into smaller pancakes if you prefer. If you are making small pancakes then folding the blueberries into the batter before cooking may be easier.

October
28

Onion and Cream Tart

Where would we be without onions? They add so much flavour to our food and although we usually buy white onions the different varieties do have subtly different flavours. Unfortunately I only have to look at an onion and I start crying, but I still think they are worth it! The onions at this time of year will be juicy and full of flavour, and good for tears!

225g/8oz shortcrust pastry or
*   500g pack readymade pastry*
700g/1^1/$_2$ lbs onions, peeled
1 tablespoon olive oil
3 egg yolks
125ml/^{1}/$_4$ pint double cream
salt and pepper

Serves 4-6

Slice the onions as finely as possible, discarding the root end. Heat the olive oil in a frying pan or shallow saucepan. Add the onions. Stir well and cover with a lid. Move the pan to the floor of the roasting oven and cook the onions until soft, stirring occasionally. When cooked remove from the oven and allow to cool.

In a basin, beat together the egg yolks, the cream and a seasoning of salt and pepper.

Roll out the pastry to line a 23cm / 9 inch flan dish or tin. Spoon the onions into the pastry case and pour over the egg mixture.

Put the dish directly onto the floor of the roasting oven and bake until the pastry is golden brown and the filling is set, about 20-25 minutes.

Serve hot.

Cooks notes
Keep an eye on the onions cooking in the frying pan, they contain sugar and can burn easily - the lid helps keep them moist and will help stop them burning.

Venison Beef and Cranberry Pie

Pies can be a little fiddly to make so this is a bit of a cheat – the pastry is served as a separate piece.

700g/1$^1/_2$ lbs stewing venison, cubed
300g/ 10oz braising steak, cubed
1 level teaspoon black peppercorns, crushed
6 juniper berries, crushed
3 bay leaves
1 teaspoon chopped thyme
150ml/$^1/_4$ pint Marsala
2 cloves garlic, peeled and crushed
4 tablespoons olive oil

200g/7oz streaky bacon, chopped
1 tablespoon tomato purée
2 tablespoons flour
300ml/$^1/_2$ pint beef stock
225g/8oz button onions, peeled
225g/8oz chestnuts, vacuum packed
110g/4oz cranberries
1 orange
375g/13oz pack ready-rolled puff pastry
1 egg, beaten, to glaze

Serves 6

Put the venison, beef, peppercorns, juniper berries, bay leaves, thyme, Marsala, garlic and olive oil in a large non-metallic bowl and mix well. Cover and leave to marinate for several hours or overnight.

Place the bacon in a flameproof casserole and heat gently until the fat runs and the bacon begins to crisp. Add the drained meat to the pan and sprinkle over the flour. Stir in. Add the tomato purée and the beef stock. Pour over the reserved marinade. Stir in the onions, chestnuts and the cranberries. Using a vegetable peeler, remove a long strip of rind from the orange and add this to the meat. Squeeze the juice and pour over the meat. Season with a little salt and bring the casserole contents to the boil. Cover and simmer for 5 minutes before transferring to the simmering oven. Cook for 2–3 hours, or until the meat is tender.

Unroll the pastry and lay on the large baking tray. Cut the pastry into six even rectangles. Mark the top with the back of the knife to decorate. Brush with the beaten egg. Hang the tin on the second set of runners from the top of the roasting oven and bake the pastry shapes for 15 minutes, until risen and golden brown.

Divide the meat and sauces between the serving plates and top with a pastry shape.

Cook's notes
If you want to make this into a conventional pie, I suggest cooking the meat one day and then cooling it before putting the pastry on the day of serving.

Savoury Fish Crumble

Savoury crumbles are delicious for family meals. Use any fish that takes your fancy – cod, haddock, whiting or whatever is at a good price at the fishmonger. A dish like this is perfect to try out some of those different fish we are being offered to replace the over-fished and threatened stocks of cod and haddock.

450g–700g/1–1^1/$_2$ lbs white fish
25g/1oz butter
*4 leeks, trimmed, washed and
    sliced*
*4 sticks celery, scrubbed and
    sliced*
*175g/6oz button mushrooms,
    wiped and halved*
*4 hard-boiled eggs, peeled and
    quartered*

For the sauce
450ml/^{3}/$_4$ pint milk
40g/1^1/$_2$ oz flour

40g/1^1/$_2$ oz butter
salt and pepper

For the crumble topping
*175g/6oz wholemeal
    breadcrumbs*
110g/4oz Cheddar cheese, grated
*2 tablespoons chopped fresh
    herbs or 2 teaspoons mixed
    dried herbs*
25g/1oz butter

Serves 4

Cut the fish into chunks and put in the bottom of an ovenproof baking dish, removing any skin and bones.

In a saucepan, heat the butter and gently sauté the leeks and celery. When softening, add the mushrooms and cook until soft. Do not allow to colour too much or the leeks will have a bitter flavour. Add the leeks, celery and mushrooms to the fish. Pour the milk into the saucepan and add the flour and butter and stand the pan on the simmering plate. Whisk constantly to make a creamy white sauce. Bubble for 1–2 minutes and season with salt and pepper. Pour the sauce over the fish and stir through gently to mix. Bury the egg quarters in the sauce.

Mix the breadcrumbs, grated cheese and herbs together and sprinkle over. Dot with slivers of butter.

Put the oven shelf on the bottom set of runners of the roasting oven for 30–40 minutes until golden brown and bubbling hot.

Cook's notes
If you prepare this in advance of cooking, stir the raw fish into the vegetables and sauce when they have cooled down. I recommend adding 5 minutes to the cooking time if baking from cold.

Pumpkin Pie

A few years ago my family went to America in October with my youngest son who was on a choir tour with Westminster Cathedral Choir. It was amazing to see the preparations for Hallowe'en over there. Everywhere we went with the children they were given Hallowe'en presents and tons of jelly babies and other sweets when 'trick or treating'. Although everyone seemed to put out pumpkin lanterns we were never offered pumpkin pie! This recipe makes very good use of the flesh of the pumpkin lantern.

375g/13oz packet dessert pastry or 225g/8oz
  homemade sweet pastry
225g/8oz caster sugar
3 eggs
200ml/7fl oz milk
$1^1/_2$ teaspoons ground cinnamon
$^1/_2$ teaspoon ground ginger
$^1/_2$ teaspoon grated nutmeg
the cooked and mashed flesh of 1 medium
  pumpkin or a 425g can of pumpkin flesh

Serves 8–10

Line a 28cm/11-inch flan tin with the dessert pastry. Chill.

   Beat together the eggs, sugar, spices and milk. Gradually beat in the pumpkin flesh. Pour into the prepared pastry case. Stand the pie on the floor of the roasting oven and bake for 35–40 minutes until set and golden brown. Serve warm or cold with cream or yoghurt.

Cook's notes
If you have a particular liking for cinnamon you can increase the amount used by an extra teaspoon.

November

1st Buckwheat Cake 2nd Tagliatelle Siciliana
3rd Chocolate Amaretti Pudding 4th Spicy Carrot
Soup 5th Slow Roasted Duck Legs with Puy Lentils
6th Simple Herb Pâté 7th Leek and Potato Soup with
Camembert Croûtes 8th Sephardic Chocolate Cake
9th Pheasant with Peas 10th English Treacle Tart
11th Poussin with Black Pudding 12th Vegetarian
Sheperd's Pie 13th Lemon Meringue Pie
14th Wensleydale and Leek Slice 15th Lamb's Liver
with Mushrooms 16th Celeriac, Whisky and Thyme
Soup 17th Apricot Chutney 18th Guinea Fowl with
Prunes and Apples 19th Leamington Festival Cake
20th Pumpkin Pancakes 21st Mincemeat
22nd Yoghurt Cake with Grapes in Syrup
23rd Mixed Roast Vegetables 24th Apple and Raisin
Pizza 25th White Stilton Torte with Roast Vegetables
26th Miso Beef Stir-Fry with Noodles
27th Granny's Christmas Pudding 28th Roast Partridge
with Apricot Stuffing 29th Smoked Haddock with
Bubble and Squeak 30th Rich Sticky Gingerbread

November

1

Buckwheat Cake

The use of buckwheat flour adds a nuttiness to the cake and would give it quite a firm texture if it wasn't for the egg whites which are whisked in, giving a lightness to the cake.

110g/4oz shelled almonds, toasted and then finely ground
110g/4oz caster sugar
110g/4oz butter, softened
3 eggs, separated
110g/4oz buckwheat flour
2 level teaspoons baking powder
pinch salt
1 teaspoon grated lemon rind
$1/_4$ teaspoon ground cinnamon
about 350g/ 12oz blackcurrant jam
icing sugar to finish

Butter the sides of a 20cm/ 8-inch spring-release cake tin. Line the base with Bake-O-Glide.

Put 75g/ 3oz caster sugar into a bowl and add the butter. Beat together well and then beat in the egg yolks. Fold in the buckwheat flour, baking powder, salt, lemon rind, cinnamon and ground almonds. Fold in thoroughly.

Whisk the egg whites to the soft peak stage and slowly add in the remaining 25g/1oz caster sugar. Gently fold the meringue mixture into the almond mixture.

Spoon the mixture into the prepared tin and level the surface.

For a two-oven Aga, put the oven shelf on the floor of the roasting oven and put in the cake. Hang the cold shelf on the third set of runners from the top of the oven and bake for 30–35 minutes.

For a three- and four-oven Aga, put the shelf on the bottom set of runners of the baking oven and slide in the cake. Bake for 35–40 minutes.

When the cake is cooked a skewer inserted in the middle will come out clean. Release the side of the tin carefully and cool the cake.

Cut the cold cake in half horizontally and fill with the blackcurrant jam. Dust generously with the icing sugar.

Cook's notes
Any jam you have to hand can be used here but blackcurrant adds a richness that stands up well to the buckwheat in the cake.

Tagliatelle Siciliana

As the days rapidly shorten, a little taste of Italy will bring back welcome thoughts of warm summer days and give us hope for those days to come around again next year. I like this on its own for a non-meat day, but you could always serve an oily fish such as sardines or mackerel with this.

50g/2oz raisins

50g/2oz sultanas

4 tablespoons olive oil

2 fennel bulbs, trimmed and
   roughly chopped

200g/7oz shallots, peeled and
   diced

2 x 400g cans chopped tomatoes

4 cloves garlic, peeled and
   crushed

150ml/^{1}/$_4$ pint red wine

150ml/^{1}/$_4$ pint vegetable stock

3 tablespoons tomato purée

pinch sugar

salt and pepper

500g/1lb 2oz tagliatelle

110g/4oz pine nuts

110g/4oz fresh breadcrumbs

2 tablespoons chopped parsley

Serves 6

Soak the raisins and sultanas in a little water until plump. Drain. Heat 2 tablespoons olive oil in a saucepan and add the fennel and shallots. Toss in the hot oil and then add the garlic. Cook gently for 5 minutes and then add the tomatoes, wine, stock, tomato purée, pinch of sugar, the drained sultanas and raisins and a seasoning of salt and pepper. Stir well and bring to the boil and move to the simmering oven for an hour.

Ten minutes before serving, bring a large pan of water to the boil. Add a pinch of salt and plunge in the tagliatelle and cook according to pack instructions or until al dente. Drain well.

In a frying pan, heat the remaining 2 tablespoons of olive oil and fry the pine nuts until just colouring. Add the breadcrumbs and the parsley. Cook until golden.

Return the pasta to the cooking pan and pour over the sauce. Toss well. Spoon into serving dishes and scatter over the pine nut mixture.

Cooks notes
The pine nut topping can be made and stored in the fridge or freezer and used to add crunch to other pasta dishes.

Chocolate Amaretti Pudding

This pudding can be served warm but I find it easier to slice at room temperature with the hot sauce poured over. Alternatively, make individual puddings and serve the sauce separately.

For the pudding
225g/8oz butter
225g/8oz plain chocolate
4 eggs
225g/8oz dark soft brown sugar
110g/4oz ground almonds
25g/1oz plain flour
1 teaspoon baking powder

4 tablespoons Amaretto liqueur
10 amaretti biscuits

For the sauce
150ml/$^1/_4$ pint double cream
150g/5$^1/_2$oz golden syrup
100g/3$^1/_2$oz plain chocolate
2 tablespoons amaretto liqueur

Serves 10

Butter, flour and base-line a 900g/2lb loaf tin.

Put the butter and chocolate in a basin and stand at the back of the Aga to melt.

Mix together the ground almonds, flour and baking powder. Put the amaretti biscuits on a plate and dribble over 1 tablespoon of the liqueur.

Put the eggs and sugar in a large bowl and whisk until thick and foamy. Gently fold the melted butter and chocolate mixture into the eggs followed by the flour mixture and the remaining 3 tablespoons of liqueur.

Spoon some of the chocolate mixture into the prepared tin, scatter over the biscuits and then the remaining mixture. Cover the top loosely with foil. Stand the tin in the small roasting tin and pour round boiling water.

Hang the tin on the bottom set of runners of the roasting oven and slide the cold shelf onto the third set of runners from the top. Bake for 40–50 minutes. The pudding is ready when a skewer inserted in the middle comes out clean.

Make the sauce. Place all the ingredients in a saucepan and stand on the simmering plate, stirring occasionally, until smooth and the sugar has dissolved.

Loosen the edges of the pudding in the tin and invert onto a serving plate. Pour over the sauce. Serve in slices.

Cook's notes
This pudding can be made up to 2 days in advance and re-heated or frozen for up to 1 month. I find it best to freeze already sliced. Freeze the sauce separately.

November
4

Spicy Carrot Soup

This recipe is good to make in the winter when there are plenty of main crop carrots and you need a little inner warmth from the red chilli!

3 tablespoons olive oil
2 onions, peeled and diced
1 clove garlic, peeled and chopped
1 tablespoon finely chopped ginger
1 small red chilli, seeded and chopped
1 bunch coriander, roughly chopped
 (reserve a few leaves for garnish)
1 teaspoon ground coriander
1 kg/2$^1/_4$ lbs carrots, peeled and roughly chopped
1 litre/1$^3/_4$ pints good chicken or vegetable stock
salt and pepper
250ml/$^1/_4$ pint crème fraîche

Serves 6

Heat the oil in a large saucepan and stir in the onion, garlic, ginger and chilli. Stir and gently cook for about 10 minutes until soft and pale golden.

Add the chopped coriander, ground coriander and the carrots to the pan and stir well. Cook for 2–3 minutes and then stir in the stock. Cover and bring to the boil and move the pan to the simmering oven for 30–40 minutes, or until the carrots are very soft.

Purée the soup and then stir in three quarters of the crème fraîche. Adjust the seasoning. Reheat if needed but do not boil.

Pour into bowls and garnish with the remaining crème fraîche and a few coriander leaves.

Cook's notes
Do not be tempted to leave the soup cooking too long in the simmering oven as the carrots will tend to loose their fresh flavour.

Slow-Roasted Duck Legs with Puy Lentils

I love duck and am very fond of Puy lentils as well, so this recipe is an ideal combination for me. Reading the recipe it may seem fiddly but it really is straightforward once you start.

350g/12oz Puy lentils
bouquet garni
1 onion, peeled and quartered
1 onion, peeled and chopped
2 carrots, peeled and chopped
2 sticks celery, chopped
500g/1 lb 2oz carrots, peeled and sliced diagonally
6 duck legs
2 cloves garlic, chopped
large glass white wine
chopped parsley to garnish

Serves 6

Rinse the lentils and put in a saucepan. Pour over enough water to just cover. You must not add salt as this will make the lentils hard. Add the bouquet garni and the quartered onion, one of the chopped carrots and half of the chopped celery. Cover with a lid and bring to the boil. Move to the simmering oven for 40 minutes to 1 hour. Drain the lentils, remove and discard the bouquet garni and the vegetables and set aside.

Stand the rack in the roasting tin and place on the duck legs. Season with salt and pepper. Hang the tin on the bottom set of runners of the roasting oven and roast the duck for 1 hour.

Remove the duck from the oven and drain off and reserve the fat. Toss the carrots in 1–2 tablespoons of the duck fat and put in the bottom of the roasting tin. Return the duck to the tin and then return to the oven. Cook for a further 20–30 minutes, until the duck is tender and the carrots roasted.

Put 1 tablespoon of duck fat in a saucepan and sauté the chopped onion, carrot and celery and cook until soft and lightly coloured. Stir in the garlic, wine and lentils. Bring to the boil and transfer to the simmering oven. Cook for about 15 minutes, or until the vegetables are cooked. Season with salt and pepper, stir in the parsley and serve with the roast duck and carrots.

Cook's notes
Always cook duck on a rack so that the fat can drain from the joint and then it will be crispy on the outside and moist in the middle. Save the fat for roasting potatoes.

Aga *year*

Simple Herb Pâté

Pâtés are easy to make and yet I find them quite expensive to buy. This one is fairly smooth and is good with bread or as a sandwich filling.

450g/1lb pig's liver
350g/12 oz streaky bacon
1 small onion, chopped
salt and pepper
$^{1}/_{4}$ teaspoon ground coriander
a grating of nutmeg
1 good tablespoon chopped fresh
  herbs or $^{1}/_{4}$ teaspoon dried herbs
1 egg, beaten

Trim the rind from the bacon and put it in a small frying pan on the simmering plate. Allow the fat to run and then add the onion. Fry the onion until cooked. Discard the bacon rind.

Put the liver and bacon either through a mincer or a food processor and then mix in all the remaining ingredients.

Spoon the mixture into a buttered $^{1}/_{2}$kg/1lb loaf tin. Cover with foil.

Stand the tin in the small roasting tin and pour round a kettle full of boiling water.

Hang the tin on the bottom set of runners of the roasting oven and cook for 30 minutes. After the first 30 minutes, slide the cold shelf on to the second set of runners from the top of the roasting oven for 40 minutes.

Remove the tin from the oven and lift the pâté out of the bain marie to cool. Lay some weights on to the pâté as it cools. Chill before slicing.

Cook's notes
If you don't have a loaf tin this can be made in a soufflé dish or other ovenproof dish, just make sure it will fit in the roasting tin before you fill it.

November
7

Leeks are in season throughout autumn and winter and make a fantastic alternative to onions when used in soups and stews for their slightly sweeter flavour. Due to their subtle flavour, leeks pair brilliantly with potatoes and cream-based soups. Their close relationship to onions and garlic also means that they offer the same health benefits such as promoting the function of the blood and heart.

Leek and Potato Soup with Camembert Croûtes

Leek and potato soup is an excellent potato standby. Using different toppings adds variety and in this recipe Camembert – or indeed any soft cheese – leftover from a dinner party may be used to delicious effect.

4 leeks, trimmed, washed and sliced
350g/12oz potatoes, peeled and roughly chopped
1 tablespoon vegetable oil
600ml/1 pint vegetable stock
1 bag or bunch washed watercress, thick stalks removed
150g/5oz Camembert, chopped
100ml/4 fl oz milk
salt and pepper
croûtes
8 thin slices French bread
100g/4oz Camembert, sliced into 8 slices

Serves 4

Heat the oil in a large saucepan and add the leeks and the potatoes. Toss in the oil and cook over gentle heat, with the lid on the pan, for 2–3 minutes. Stir in the stock. Bring to the boil and move to the simmering oven for 30 minutes.

Remove the pan from the simmering oven to the simmering plate and add the watercress to the soup. Cook for 2–3 minutes. Remove from the heat and blend the pan ingredients together with the Camembert and the milk. Return to the rinsed out pan. Season and gently heat through.

Place the slices of French bread on a baking tray. Top each slice with a slice of cheese and bake on the third set of runners from the top of the roasting oven for 5 minutes, until the cheese is melting.

Ladle the soup into bowls and place one croûte on the soup and one alongside.

Cook's notes
If the Camembert has developed a dry rind then remove it before adding it to the soup.

November 8

Sephardic Chocolate Cake

This has come to be one of my all time favourite cakes. It is moist, easy to make and always tastes wonderful whether eaten as a dessert or as a cake. Should there be any left, it keeps well for a day or two.

225g/8oz plain chocolate
25g/1oz butter at room temperature
5 eggs, separated
175g/6oz caster sugar
125g/5oz ground almonds
2 tablespoons milk
1 teaspoon wine vinegar
icing sugar, to decorate
cocoa powder, to decorate

Serves 8–10

Butter the sides of a 25cm /10-inch spring-release cake tin. Line the base with Bake-O-Glide.

Place the chocolate in a basin and stand at the back of the Aga until melted. When the chocolate has melted stir in the butter.

Whisk the egg whites until white and peaking. Whisk in the caster sugar followed by the egg yolks. Fold in the almonds. Fold in the chocolate mixture followed by the milk and wine vinegar.

Spoon the cake mixture into the prepared tin. Bake.

For a two-oven Aga, put the shelf on the floor of the roasting oven. Put in the cake and then slide the cold shelf onto the third set of runners from the top. Bake the cake for 30–40 minutes, until a skewer inserted in the middle comes out clean.

For a three- or four-oven Aga, put the shelf on the bottom set of runners of the baking oven. Put in the cake and bake for 40–45 minutes, until a skewer inserted in the middle comes out clean. Cool in the tin.

To serve, dust the top with icing sugar and cocoa.

Cook's notes
If you would like to drizzle some chocolate over the top, simply melt a few squares of chocolate in a small jug when the cake is cooking. Decorate before serving by holding the jug high above the cake and pouring 'drizzles' of chocolate back and forth over the cake.

Pheasant with Peas

At the start of the pheasant season the birds will be tender and just need simple cooking to avoid smothering their delicate flavour. This easy method of cooking pheasant is popular with those that have a lot of birds to deal with. There should be a generous amount of sauce, so be sure to serve some boiled or mashed potatoes.

110g/4oz butter
4 young pheasants
600ml/1 pint double cream
450g/1lb frozen peas
salt and pepper

Serves 6

In a large pan with a closely fitting lid melt the butter on the simmering plate. Season the birds and put breast side down into the pan of melted butter. Cover with a lid and put on the floor of the roasting oven for 10 minutes. Turn the pheasants onto their other breast side and re-cover. Return to the floor of the roasting oven for a further 10 minutes.

Turn the pheasants onto their backs and pour over the cream. Cover with a lid. Place the pan on the simmering plate until the cream has heated through and then place the pan in the simmering oven for 30–40 minutes.

Cook the peas and arrange on a carving dish. Remove the birds from the pan and whisk the pan juices together to mix the cream and pan juices. Check the seasoning and allow the sauce to bubble slightly and to thicken.

Carve the birds and arrange the meat on the peas, pour over the sauce.

Cook's notes
Remember to get the pan contents hot before putting in the simmering oven as otherwise the pheasant won't be cooked in time.

Ensure that you baste the meat regularly during cooking to avoid the meat becoming dry.

English Treacle Tart

I am sure this treacle tart will bring back memories of childhood for many. My mother made delicious treacle tarts but the ones we had at school were called 'tombstones' – impossible to cut and to eat! Take care not to overcook.

1 x 500g packet dessert pastry
250g/9oz golden syrup
75g/3oz fresh white breadcrumbs
Grated rind and juice 1 lemon

Serves 6

Prepare the filling. Measure the golden syrup into a basin and stand at the back of the Aga to heat gently. Stir in the breadcrumbs and the lemon zest.

Roll out the pastry and use to line an 20cm/8-inch fluted flan tin. Chill the pastry case well or pop into the freezer for 15 minutes.

Stir the lemon juice into the syrup mixture and then spoon into the pastry case.

To bake in a two-, three- or four-oven Aga, put the tart directly on the floor of the roasting oven and bake for 20 minutes, until pale golden brown and the pastry has slightly shrunk from the sides of the flan tin.

Cook's notes
You can use plain short crust pastry if you prefer a less sweet version.

Poussin with Black Pudding

Black pudding isn't to everyone's taste – if you prefer you can substitute a tasty pork sausage. Whatever you use will add flavour and moistness to these little birds that look so attractive and devourable when served.

Serves 6

For the stuffing	For the barley risotto
50g/2oz butter	*50g/2oz butter*
$^1/_2$ onion, peeled and chopped	*1 tablespoon olive oil*
300g /10$^1/_2$oz black pudding, chopped	*2 leeks, trimmed and cut into fine rings*
300g/10$^1/_2$oz cooking apple, peeled and chopped	*1 litre/1$^1/_4$ pints chicken stock*
$^1/_2$ teaspoon thyme leaves, chopped	*450g/1 lb pearl barley*
salt and pepper	*4 tablespoons chopped parsley*
	150g/5$^1/_2$oz smoked bacon lardons
	salt and pepper

6 poussins

Make the stuffing. Heat 25g/1oz butter in a pan and sauté the onion until soft but not browned. Add the black pudding and the apple and cook briskly for 2–3 minutes. Remove from the heat and add the thyme and a seasoning of salt and pepper.

Season the inside of each poussin and then stuff each poussin with the stuffing mixture. Smear the remaining butter over the poussin and stand them in a roasting tin.

Hang the roasting tin on the third set of runners from the top of the roasting oven and roast the poussin for 30–40 minutes, until golden and the juices run clear.

Make the risotto. Heat the butter and the olive oil in a sauté pan and add the leeks. Cook until the leeks are soft but not coloured. Heat the stock in a saucepan. Add the barley to the leeks and stir well to coat the grains in the butter. Gradually add the stock, stirring well between each addition. Gradually the barley will soften and become creamy. This can take 30 minutes. Stir in the parsley and season the risotto.

Put the bacon lardons in a frying pan and place on the floor of the roasting oven and cook until crisp. When cooked, stir the bacon into the risotto.

Adjust the seasoning and serve the risotto with the poussin.

Cook's notes
The risotto will keep covered in the simmering oven for 30 minutes or so. Add the crispy bacon just before serving or else it will go soft.

Vegetarian Shepherd's Pie

Any dish that has mashed potato on top seems to be a winner with my family. You can of course vary the vegetables in this dish to suit the season, or whatever you have available. This recipe makes a good warming everyday meal.

For the topping
700g/1½ lbs potatoes, peeled and
  cut into chunks
50g/2oz butter
150ml/¼ pint milk
175g/6oz Wensleydale cheese,
  crumbled
salt and pepper

For the filling
1 tablespoon vegetable oil
1 onion, peeled and finely
chopped
1 stick celery, chopped
1 clove garlic, peeled and crushed
1 leek, trimmed and sliced
1 carrot, peeled and sliced
1 x 400g mixed beans, drained
1 x 400g can chopped tomatoes
1 tablespoon fresh herbs, chopped
  or 1 teaspoon dried mixed
  herbs
1 tablespoon tomato purée
salt and pepper

Serves 4

Put the potatoes into a saucepan and add water to come 2.5cm/1–inch up the side of the pan. Add a pinch of salt, cover and bring to the boil. Boil for 1 minutes and then drain off all the water. Put the pan of potatoes in the simmering oven for 30–40 minutes until soft. Mash the potatoes with the butter and milk and then add half the cheese.

For the filling, heat the oil in a saucepan and cook the onion, garlic, celery, leek and carrot for about 10 minutes until softening but not browning. Stir in the beans, tomatoes, herbs, tomato purée and a seasoning of salt and pepper. Stir well and add a little water if the filling is dry. Simmer for 5 minutes and then spoon into an ovenproof dish.

Carefully top the vegetables with the mashed potatoes and scatter over the remaining cheese.

Hang the oven shelf on the bottom set of runners of the roasting oven, slide in the pie and bake for 20–25 minutes, until the pie is hot and golden brown on the top.

Cook's notes
Different beans, or even lentils, can be used according to your preference.

13

Lemon Meringue Pie

This has to be my husband Geoff's' favourite pudding though with all the testing that goes on in our house he doesn't get it very often. We love the contrast between the sweet meringue and the tangy lemon filling.

375g/13oz packet dessert shortcrust pastry
*   or 225g/8oz homemade sweet pastry*
2 tablespoons cornflour
50g/2oz caster sugar
finely grated rind and juice 2 lemons
150ml/$^1/_4$ pint water
2 egg yolks

For the Meringue
2 egg whites
110g/4oz caster sugar

Roll the pastry to fit a 20cm/8-inch flan tin. Chill.

Put the cornflour, sugar and lemon rind into a small saucepan. Blend in the water and stand on the simmering plate, stirring, until a thick sauce is made. Remove from the heat and beat in the lemon juice and then the egg yolks. Pour into the pastry case.

Whisk the egg whites until stiff white peaks are formed and then whisk in the caster sugar one teaspoon at a time. Carefully pile the meringue on to the pie filling, covering right to the edge.

Stand the lemon meringue pie on the floor of the roasting oven and slide the cold shelf onto the third set of runners from the top of the oven.

Bake for 20–25 minutes, until the pastry is golden and the meringue tinged with colour.

Cook's notes
Have the lemons at room temperature or slightly warm to extract the maximum flavour and juice from them.

384   Aga *year*

November
14

Wensleydale and Leek Slice

I know Wallace and Gromit are great fans of Wensleydale cheese –
I am too! I love that crumble and tanginess. It is as good as Feta in a
salad and brings a slight sharpness to the leeks in this dish.

2 x 375g/13oz packs ready-rolled puff pastry
500g/1lb 2oz leeks, trimmed and finely sliced
50g/2oz butter
1 scant tablespoon honey
2 teaspoons chopped rosemary
salt and pepper
250g/8oz Wensleydale cheese
beaten egg, to glaze

Serves 6

*Wensleydale is a cheese,
produced exclusively in
Hawes, Wensleydale, North
Yorkshire. Known and used
for its mild flavours or wild
honey and slight acidity,
Wensleydale is a popular
addition to many savoury
dishes and is also enjoyed
on its own. It has a
crumbly, slightly moist
texture, not dissimilar in
style to Caerphilly.
Originally produced by
French monks who had
settled in the region many
years ago, Wensleydale
remains a popular cheese
in Britain today.*

Wash the leeks. Melt the butter in a saucepan and add the leeks. Cook
the leeks until soft but not brown, about 10 minutes. Remove from the
heat and stir in the honey and rosemary and season with salt and
pepper. Cool.

Line a large baking tray with Bake-O-Glide and lay on one sheet of
pastry.

Crumble the Wensleydale into the leeks. Spread the leek mixture over
the sheet of pastry, leaving a 1cm/^{1}/$_2$-inch border all round. Brush the
pastry border with beaten egg. Lay the remaining sheet of pastry on top
and seal the edges.

Crimp the edges and decorate the top with the back of a knife blade.
Cut three slashes in the top to allow steam to escape. Brush well with
beaten egg.

Put the baking tray on the third set of runners from the top of the
roasting oven and bake for 20 minutes. Check after 15 minutes to see
if the tray needs turning round for even browning. Move the tray to the
floor of the roasting oven to crisp the base for 5 minutes.

Cook's notes
The Wensleydale won't need grating, just crumble it into the leeks.

Lamb's Liver with Mushrooms

Lamb's liver has a subtle flavour and needs cooking quickly – a perfect dish for when you are in a hurry to get a meal on the table.

50g/2oz butter
1 onion, peeled and chopped
700g/1$^1/_2$ lbs lamb's liver
2 tablespoons seasoned flour
200g/7oz mushrooms
200ml/7fl oz chicken or vegetable stock
4 large-ish tomatoes, skinned and chopped
3 tablespoons Worcestershire sauce
salt and pepper
250ml/9 fl oz soured cream or crème fraîche

Serves 6

Melt the butter in a large frying pan and add the onion. Cook the onion gently to soften but not brown.

Cut the liver into strips and coat in the seasoned flour. Slice the wiped mushrooms.

Add the liver and the mushrooms to the pan. Fry for 5 minutes until the liver is browning and the mushrooms collapsing. Stir in the stock and bring the pan contents to the boil.

Stir in the tomatoes and Worcestershire sauce and check the seasoning. Stir in the soured cream or crème fraîche, heat through without boiling and serve with tagliatelle.

Cook's notes
I love to serve this very speedy and delicious dish with tagliatelle.

Celeriac, Whisky and Thyme Soup

Celeriac makes wonderful soup and brilliant mash!

1 large celeriac, peeled and
   chopped
50g/2oz butter
1 medium onion, chopped
pinch of mace or nutmeg
1 parsnip, peeled and chopped
225g/8oz potatoes, peeled and
   chopped
2 sprigs thyme
700ml/1¼ pints vegetable stock
salt and pepper
150ml/¼ pint milk
2 tablespoons whisky

75ml/3 fl oz double cream
lemon juice

For the croûtons
2 thick slices bread, crusts
   removed
75ml/3 fl oz olive oil
1 tablespoon finely chopped
   thyme leaves
coarse sea salt

Serves 6

Thyme appears in many varieties, and ones such as lemon and orange thyme are named after their particular fragrance. Due to thyme's perfume and flavour, it is a highly potent herb when eaten fresh or dried. It grows and can be picked throughout the year, and complements meats such as chicken, pork and lamb very well indeed. In ancient Greek times it was believed to be a source of courage, and sprigs were used in incense, burning in temples and sacred places.

Melt the butter in a large saucepan and add the onion and nutmeg and cook until the onion is soft but not brown. Add the celeriac, parsnip, potatoes, thyme sprigs and stock. Cover and bring to the boil. When boiling move the pan to the simmering oven and cook for 40 minutes, or until the vegetables are soft.

Meanwhile make the croûtons. Toss the bread cubes in the oil along with 1 teaspoon chopped thyme. Spread the croûtons on a baking tray and hang the tray on the second set of runners from the top of the roasting oven. Bake for 5–10 minutes until golden brown. Remove from the oven and sprinkle with sea salt and the remaining thyme. When cold these can be stored for 1 week in a sealed container.

When the soup is cooked liquidise the soup until very smooth. Return to the rinsed-out pan, add the milk and the whisky and bring to the boil on the simmering plate. Stir and then add the cream. Remove from the heat. Check the seasoning and add lemon juice to taste.

Serve with the thyme croûtons scattered on the top.

Cook's notes
Keep a supply of homemade croûtons handy in a sealed box or in the freezer to go on soups or to add crunch to a salad. The soup can also be frozen. Follow the method above but stop short of adding the cream and lemon juice. Allow to cool and fill suitable portion-sized containers. Stir in the cream after you have re-heated, add lemon juice to taste and then adjust the seasoning.

Apricot Chutney

This is a recipe with which to stock the cupboard, ready to have some chutney to hand either for home use or gifts.

225g/8oz dried apricots, soaked in
*   water overnight*
450g/1lb cooking apples, peeled,
*   cored and chopped*
1 onion, peeled and finely chopped
grated rind and juice 1 orange
1 teaspoon salt
600ml/1 pint white wine vinegar
450g/1lb granulated sugar

Drain the apricots well and place in a large pan. Add all the remaining ingredients and stand on the simmering plate. Stir to dissolve the sugar and then bring to the boil. When boiling move the pan uncovered, to the simmering oven.

After 1 hour remove the pan – the apricots should be cooked and the mixture thick. If there is still a lot of moisture, stand the pan in the simmering plate and allow the chutney to bubble and the liquid to evaporate for a few minutes.

Spoon the chutney into warm sterile jars.

When cold cover the jars and seal and label. Store in a cool dark place for 2 weeks before using.

Cook's notes
Buy the cheaper dried apricots for this, not the 'ready to eat' variety as they will be already soaked.

Guinea Fowl with Prunes and Apples

Guinea fowl may be available from your butcher or supermarket but I suggest ordering in advance. If you are unable to source guinea fowl you could substitute pheasant or poussin.

1 large onion, peeled and
    chopped
1 large carrot, peeled and
    chopped
2 sticks celery, peeled and
    chopped
8 guinea fowl joints
500ml/1 pint red wine
1 tablespoon thyme, chopped
2 bay leaves
175g/6oz ready-to-eat prunes
2 tablespoons vegetable oil

3 cloves garlic, crushed
1 teaspoon harissa paste
1 tablespoon tomato purée
1 tablespoon flour
150ml/^{1}/$_4$ pint chicken or
    vegetable stock
225g/8oz streaky bacon rashers,
    cut into quarters
2 eating apples, cored and sliced

Serves 8

Put the onion, carrot, celery and guinea fowl in a large, non-metallic bowl. Pour over 400ml/^{3}/$_4$ pint red wine. Add the thyme and the bay leaves and a seasoning of pepper. Cover and leave to marinate for 4 hours or overnight.

Place the prunes in a basin and pour over the remaining wine. Cover and leave to marinate.

Drain the joints and dry on kitchen paper. Reserve the marinade and vegetables. Heat the vegetable oil in a flameproof casserole and brown the guinea fowl joints. Remove from the casserole and add the vegetables to the pan. Cook for 4–5 minutes and then add the garlic, harissa paste and the tomato purée. Stir in the flour and cook for 1 minute before adding the reserved marinade and the stock. Return the meat to the pan, bring to the boil, cover and then move to the simmering oven for 1 hour.

Place the bacon in a frying pan and place either on the simmering plate on the floor of the oven and cook until the fat is running and the bacon is crisping. Add the apples to the pan and cook until golden.

Remove the casserole from the oven. Remove the guinea fowl to a plate and keep warm. Strain the sauce through a sieve. Return the meat to the pan and add the strained sauce, the prunes and their marinade, the bacon and the apples. Warm through on the simmering plate.

Cook's notes
If freezing, pack into a plastic box when cold and freeze. Thaw in the fridge overnight. Reheat in the roasting oven for 30–40 minutes or a little longer if still frozen.

Leamington Festival Cake

This is the recipe that I started making when I was training as a home economics teacher in Gloucester. My tutor, Jean Jackson, gave us the recipe and I have used it ever since. I later discovered from an Aga owner that the recipe was originally in a book called *To Love and To Nourish, A Cookery Book for Brides* published in 1963!

2 oranges, grated rind and juice	*4 eggs, beaten*
75ml/ 3 fl oz brandy	*175g/6oz self-raising flour*
100g/3$^{1}/_{2}$oz glacé cherries,	*110g/4oz plain flour*
halved and washed	*pinch salt*
275g/10oz raisins	*50g/2oz ground almonds*
350g/12oz sultanas	*2 heaped teaspoons ground*
225g/8oz currants	*mixed spice*
50g/2oz chopped almonds, toasted	*2 tablespoons black treacle*
225g/8oz butter, softened	*2 tablespoons golden syrup*
175g/6oz Demerara sugar	*50 ml/2 fl oz milk*

The quantities make one 8-inch/20cm cake

The day before making, mix together the orange rind and juice, brandy, cherries, raisins, sultanas and currants. Cover and leave to soak overnight.

Butter and line the inside of the cake tin.

Cream together the sugar and butter until light and fluffy. Sieve together the flours, salt and mixed spice. Beat in the eggs, one at a time, with 1 teaspoon flour, to the butter mixture. Fold in the remaining flour mixture and ground almonds. Add the toasted chopped nuts and soaked fruit. Mix the treacle, golden syrup and milk together and stir into the cake mixture. Stir well. When thoroughly mixed, spoon into the prepared tin. Level the top.

For a two- or three- oven Aga, put the shelf on the floor of the simmering oven and put in the cake. For a four-oven Aga, put the cake on the floor of the simmering oven. Bake the cake for 6–8 hours, but don't be surprised if the cake takes up to 12 hours.

The cake is cooked when a warm skewer inserted into the middle of the cake comes out clean and the cake has shrunk from the sides of the tin. Cool in the tin. Decorate with marzipan, icing or as liked.

Cook's notes
If this is the first time you have made a rich fruit cake in the Aga I suggest you make the cake one day and then bake the cake the next day so that you can keep a close eye on timings. Make a note below on how long it took to bake. I know how long mine takes – I put the cake in and go to bed.... But I do leave myself a reminder note on the breakfast table so that I remember to take it out the next morning!

Pumpkin Pancakes

Pumpkins have become very popular in the autumn and if you don't grow your own there are always plenty in the shops. I have visited some growers who have had the most amazing variety of pumpkins. It can be so tempting to come away with a huge selection and then, having got home, wonder in desperation what to do with them! Here is a change to the usual pumpkin pie.

225g/8oz pumpkin purée
50g/2oz plain flour
$^1/_2$ teaspoon allspice
$^1/_2$ teaspoon baking powder
1 large egg, beaten
a little oil to lightly grease the
*   simmering plate, or Bake-O-Glide*

To serve
butter
cinnamon syrup

For the cinnamon syrup
150g/5oz caster sugar
1 100ml/3$^1/_2$ fl oz water
small cinnamon stick

Pumpkin is a member of the squash family in various colours, shapes and sizes, but typically with green to orange skin, with bright orange to yellow flesh.
The flesh is succulent and sweet, with a slightly earthy taste, and marries with other flavours very well, especially warm spices such as cinnamon and nutmeg. It can be roasted, stuffed into pies and pasta and is perfect for sweet, warming winter soups.

Put the pumpkin purée in a large mixing bowl. Sieve together the allspice, baking powder and the flour. Stir into the pumpkin purée and beat well until smooth. Beat in the egg and when smooth leave to stand for 30 minutes.

Dampen a piece of kitchen roll with a little vegetable oil and wipe over the simmering plate.

Drop 1 tablespoon of batter onto the plate to make a pancake. Allow to bubble and become golden brown and then flip over and cook the second side for 2–3 minutes. Keep warm on a plate – several pancakes can be cooked at a time. Repeat with the remaining batter.

Serve with butter and cinnamon syrup.

To make the syrup, put the sugar, ground cinnamon and water in a saucepan. Stand on the simmering plate until the sugar has dissolved. Add the cinnamon stick and then boil the syrup rapidly until thick, about 5 minutes. Pour over the pancakes.

Cook's notes
Make sure the purée is fairly dry for this recipe. If necessary, heat the purée in a pan to dry it out before making the pancakes.

Mincemeat

I originally developed a sugar-free mincemeat recipe for my mother when she developed diabetes. I have used the idea since but added a few different flavours. Heating the mincemeat in the simmering oven means that the mincemeat will keep well without being chilled. Indeed, it will keep through to next year to make puddings with if you have any left over.

225g/8oz dried apricots, soaked in
*   water overnight and dried*
450g/1lb apples, cored, peeled
*   and grated*
225g/8oz suet
350g/12oz raisins
350g/12oz sultanas
350g/12oz currants
grated rind and juice 2 oranges
grated rind and juice 2 lemons
50g/2oz slivered almonds
4 teaspoons mixed spice
1 teaspoon ground cinnamon
$^{1}/_{2}$ grated nutmeg
6 tablespoons brandy

Makes about 2.5 kg/5$^{1}/_{2}$ lbs

Chop the soaked apricots to the size of a sultana. Place in a big mixing bowl along with all the other ingredients except the brandy. Mix really well, this is easiest done with your hands! Cover and leave to stand for 24 hours, stirring occasionally.

Make sure the mincemeat is not in a plastic basin. Cover with foil. Put the shelf on the floor of the simmering oven and put in the bowl of mincemeat. Leave to gently heat for 4 or 5 hours and then remove from the oven. Stir well and allow to go completely cold. Stir in the brandy and pot into clean sterile jars. Seal and label.

Cook's notes
Pot some of the mincemeat into pretty jars to use as gifts for friends.

Yoghurt Cake with Grapes in Syrup

This soft and light cake uses yoghurt instead of butter in an attempt to be healthy! I'm not so sure about the health aspects but the yoghurt certainly gives the cake a wonderfully distinctive flavour and texture.

For the cake
4 eggs, separated
110g/4oz caster sugar
3 tablespoons plain flour
400g/14oz Greek yoghurt
finely grated rind and juice 1 lemon

For the grapes in syrup
110g/4oz sugar
1 tablespoon lemon juice
500g/1lb 2oz seedless grapes, red or white

Serves 8

Grease and base-line a 23cm/ 9-inch spring-release cake tin.

Beat the egg yolks with the sugar until pale and creamy. Fold in the flour, yoghurt, lemon rind and juice.

Whisk the egg whites until white and stiff and fold into the egg mixture. Spoon the mixture into the prepared tin. Bake.

For a two-oven Aga, hang the shelf on the bottom set of runners of the roasting oven and put in the cake tin. Slide the cold shelf on to the third set of runners from the top of the oven and bake the cake for 40–45 minutes.

For a three- or four-oven Aga, hang the shelf on the bottom set of runners of the baking oven and slide in the cake. Bake for 45–50 minutes.

The cake will rise like a soufflé but then subside. When the cake is cooked it will be brown on the top and firm when shaken .

Cool in the tin.

For the grapes, put the sugar, lemon juice and 150ml/$^1/_4$ pint water in a saucepan. Stand on the simmering plate and heat until the sugar is dissolved. Bring to the boil, add the grapes stripped from their stalks and simmer gently for 5 minutes. Cool.

Serve slices of cake with the grapes spooned over.

Cook's notes
Don't be alarmed by the collapsing cake – as it cools just pile some of the grapes into the middle.

November
23

Mixed Roast Vegetables

Roast vegetables at any time of year are delicious from the Aga but in the winter I like to add sprouts towards the end. All the vegetables can be served in one dish and the range of colours together looks wonderful.

450g/1 lb shallots, peeled
900g/2lbs carrots, peeled and sliced into chunks
1 large beetroot, peeled, cut into chunks and dipped in lemon juice
4–5 tablespoons olive oil
700g/1$\frac{1}{2}$ lbs sprouts, trimmed
1 tablespoon balsamic vinegar
salt and pepper

Serves 6–8

Line a large baking tray with Bake-O-Glide.

Put the shallots, carrots and beetroot in a bowl and pour on the olive oil. Toss well and tip the contents onto the baking tray. Season with salt and pepper. Hang the tray on the second set of runners from the top of the roasting oven and roast for 20 minutes.

Put the sprouts in a saucepan and add enough water to come 2.5 cm/ 1 inch up the side of the pan. Bring to the boil and fast boil for 4–5 minutes. Drain well and add to the tray of roasting vegetables. Toss the vegetables together and return to the oven for a further 15 minutes. Sprinkle the vegetables with balsamic vinegar and serve immediately.

Cook's notes
The beetroot is tossed in lemon juice to stop the colour leeching into the other vegetables.

November
24

Apple and Raisin Pizza

Make this dessert when you have been making bread and can steal a little excess dough. Apples and raisins are perfect for late autumn and early winter, they seem made to go together.

110g/4oz plain bread dough
1 good tablespoon crème fraîche
1 eating apple, quartered, cored and thinly sliced
1 small handful raisins
pinch ground cinnamon
2 teaspoons caster sugar

Makes 1 pizza for 2 people

Roll the dough out to just a little smaller than the circle of Bake-O-Glide cut for the simmering plate. It is easiest to do this directly on the Bake-O-Glide. The dough should be very thin.

Spoon on the crème fraîche and spread over the base, leaving a small border. Lay on the apple slices and scatter over the raisins. Sprinkle the cinnamon and sugar over the pizza.

Place the pizza, on the Bake-O-Glide, directly on the simmering plate. Put the lid down and cook for 5 minutes.

The base will become very crisp, but the topping will not brown. Serve immediately.

Cook's notes
Mix the cinnamon in with the sugar, it will then be easier to sprinkle evenly over the pizza.

White Stilton Torte with Roast Vegetables

I have used white Stilton here, a neglected cheese beside its big blue brother. It has a creaminess that isn't always noticeable in blue Stilton. Most white Stilton is flavoured with fruits such as apricots and even strawberries – not to my personal taste! If you can't find plain white Stilton, then substitute Wensleydale or Caerphilly.

For the base
175g/6oz Caerphilly cheese, crumbled
75g/3oz butter, softened
175g/6oz self-raising flour
1 tablespoon mustard, smooth for preference
3 eggs, beaten
60ml/4 tablespoons boiling water

150g/5oz white Stilton, crumbled
1 tablespoon sesame seeds

For the topping
selection of vegetables (such as carrots, peppers, red onions)
6 cherry tomatoes
olive oil
salt

Prepare the vegetables for roasting: peel the carrots and cut into thick slices, de-seed and cut the peppers into chunky pieces and finally peel and quarter the onions. Place on a shallow roasting tray. Drizzle with 2–3 tablespoons of olive oil and season with salt. Set aside.

Butter a deep 24cm/9$\frac{1}{2}$-inch spring release cake tin.

Mix together the Caerphilly and the butter. Add the flour, mustard and eggs and stir in. Add the boiling water and gently stir in to make a smooth mixture. Spoon half the mixture into the base of the buttered tin. Level off. Cover with the crumbled white Stilton and then spread the remaining mixture on top. Sprinkle over the sesame seeds.

Hang the baking tray of vegetables on the second set of runners from the top of the roasting oven.

Place the oven shelf on the bottom set of runners of the roasting oven and put in the tin with the torte mixture, taking care not to slide it under the roast vegetable tin as it will mask the heat.

Bake for 30–35 minutes until golden brown and firm to the touch. Remove from the tin and top with the roast vegetables and the cherry tomato halves.

Serve hot.

Cook's notes
Use vegetables that are in season and then add some extra colour with the tomatoes. Carrots are deliciously sweet when roasted.

398   Aga *year*

Miso Beef Stir-Fry with Noodles

I am often asked if it is possible to cook a stir-fry on an Aga. The answer is 'yes', but it needs a little planning. Preheat the wok, completely empty, for 5–10 minutes on the boiling plate and have warm plates ready to keep the food warm. As with any stir-fry, prepare all the food before starting to cook.

35g/1¹/₄oz miso paste
5 tablespoons mirin
3 tablespoons soy sauce
2 tablespoons Thai fish sauce
2 cloves garlic, peeled and
* crushed*
2 teaspoons runny honey
700g/1¹/₂lbs fillet steak, cut into
* slivers*
2 tablespoons sunflower oil

2.5cm/1-inch piece peeled and
* chopped*
175g/6oz oyster mushrooms,
* sliced*
2 tablespoons sesame oil
3 tablespoons fresh coriander

To serve
medium noodles
steamed vegetables

Serves 6

Mix together the miso paste, mirin, soy sauce, Thai fish sauce, garlic and honey. Add the beef, stir well and leave to chill for 15 minutes.

Heat the wok on the boiling plate for 5 minutes and then add the sunflower oil and the ginger. Stir-fry the ginger for 1 minute and then add the beef and the marinade. Stir-fry for 1 minute and then add the mushrooms. Cook for 1–2 minutes and then remove from the heat. Stir in the sesame oil and coriander.

Serve with noodles and steamed vegetables.

Cook's notes
Noodles can be 'cooked' on the back of the Aga. Pour boiling water over them, cover with a lid and leave in a warm spot so they are ready to drain as the stir-fry is cooked.

November
27

Granny's Christmas Pudding

This recipe, from my *Traditional Aga Party Book* is the best recipe for Christmas pudding that I have ever tried. Traditionally, puddings are made on the first Sunday of Advent, also known as 'Stir-up Sunday' when everyone is at home to have a stir and a wish. I usually make mine a month or so earlier than this, but we all still enjoy the tradition.

250g/9oz suet (I use 'vegetable suet', suitable for vegetarians)	pinch salt
	grated rind and juice 1 lemon
350g/12oz Demerara sugar	grated rind and juice 1 orange
500g /1lb 2oz sultanas	300ml/$^1/_2$ pint Guinness
500g/1lb 2oz currants	300ml/$^1/_2$ pint water
500g/1lb 2oz raisins	60ml/2 fl oz brandy
1 cooking apple, peeled and grated	30ml/1 fl oz sherry
	30ml/1 fl oz rum
15g/$^1/_2$oz ground mixed spice	5 eggs, beaten
15g/$^1/_2$oz ground ginger	350g/12oz fresh breadcrumbs

**Makes either 2 large (2 litre/4 pint)
or 3 medium (1 litre/2 pint) puddings**

Put all the ingredients except the eggs and the breadcrumbs in a large mixing bowl and mix thoroughly. Cover and leave to stand somewhere cool for 3 to 4 days, stirring occasionally. When you are ready to cook the puddings, add the eggs and breadcrumbs to the soaked fruit mixture and stir thoroughly. Get the family or friends to 'Stir and Wish'. Spoon the mixture into basins. Level the top. Then cover with a fitted lid, if using boilable plastic basins, or a circle of greaseproof paper and a double layer of foil, if using a traditional basin.

Stand each pudding on a trivet or an old plate and place on the base of a saucepan. (It is useful to stand the basin in a strap of foil, so it can be easily lifted from the hot pan.) Pour in enough water to come 5cm/2-inch up the side of the pudding basin. Cover the pan with a lid and bring to the boil. Move to the simmering plate and simmer for 20 minutes. (You may need to pull the pan half off the plate to keep to a simmer.) Move the puddings to the simmering oven and leave to cook for 11–12 hours. Remove from the oven and allow to completely cool. When cold, replace the greaseproof paper and foil with fresh pieces and then store the puddings somewhere cool.

On Christmas Day, return the pudding to a saucepan with a trivet in the base. Pour in enough water to come 2.5cm/1-inch up the side of the saucepan. Bring to the boil and move to the simmering oven for 1 hour. Cool for 10 minutes before turning out onto a warm serving plate.

Cook's notes
On Christmas day if the simmering oven is not full put the pudding in at the back in the basin with no saucepan for 3–4 hours.

Roast Partridge with Apricot Stuffing

It is now possible to buy partridge in supermarkets as well as from game dealers, so there's no excuse for not trying this wonderful roast.

8 rashers of streaky bacon
4 young partridges
225g/8oz pork sausagemeat
50g/2oz dried apricots, diced
2 tablespoons chopped parsley
salt and pepper
1 tablespoon flour
300ml/$^1/_2$ pint chicken stock

Serves 4

There are two types of partridge, the English partridge (otherwise known as the grey partridge) and the French partridge. The English partridge is far superior in flavour. It should be hung for one or two days before cooking, and tastes wonderful both roasted and grilled. Its season runs from October through to January.

Wrap 2 bacon rashers in a cross over the breasts of the partridge. Put the partridge in the small roasting tin and hang the tin on the third set of runners from the top of the roasting oven and roast for 40 minutes.

Mix the sausagemeat, apricots, parsley and salt and pepper with your hands and then form into 8 even-sized balls.

After 10 minutes of roasting, place the stuffing balls round the partridges. At the end of cooking time the birds should have a golden skin and any juices from the insides of the legs should run clear.

Place the partridges on a warm serving plate with the stuffing balls. Stand the roasting tin on the simmering plate. Using a wire whisk, stir in the flour and allow to thicken before slowly adding the stock to make a smooth gravy. Adjust the seasoning and serve with the partridge.

Cook's notes
Should you not be able to find partridge, you can use poussins instead.

29

Smoked Haddock with Bubble and Squeak

This may seem a complicated recipe to prepare but it can be done in stages and really is quite delicious!

2 fillets of un-dyed smoked haddock
1 kg/2½ lbs Desirée potatoes
400g/14oz cabbage, finely shredded
2 tablespoons goose fat or
    vegetable oil
2 bunches spring onions,
    trimmed and finely chopped

25g/1oz butter
1 tablespoon flour
300ml/½ pint milk
25g/1oz butter, melted
200g/7oz grated Cheddar cheese
1 teaspoon mustard
1–2 tablespoons milk

Serves 4

Peel the potatoes and put into a saucepan. Add enough water to come 2.5cm/1-inch up the side of the pan. Cover and bring to the boil. After 2–3 minutes fast boiling drain the potatoes well and put into the simmering oven until soft enough to mash, about 30 minutes.

Place the cabbage on a small baking tray and pour over the fat or oil. Season with salt and pepper and hang the tray on the bottom set of runners of the roasting oven for 10 minutes. Then move the cabbage to the simmering oven while the potatoes cook.

Cut the haddock into 4 even portions and place in a shallow ovenproof dish. Add the milk. Put the shelf on the bottom set of runners of the roasting oven and put in the fish. Cook for 10 minutes. Reserve the poaching liquid for the sauce.

Melt the butter in a saucepan and then cook the spring onions until just softening. Remove the onions from the pan, leaving the buttery juices in the saucepan for the sauce.

Mash the cooked potatoes until smooth and fluffy and then stir in the cabbage and the drained spring onions. Shape the potatoes into 4 potato cakes. Brush with the melted butter and stand on a baking tray. Place the tray on the floor of the roasting oven and cook the potato cakes for 8–10 minutes, turning over half way through, until hot and crisp.

Remove the fish from the oven and carefully place the fillets on a clean baking tray. Mix together the grated cheese, the mustard and the 1 tablespoon of milk and divide this rarebit between the fish fillets. Pop into the roasting oven for 3–4 minutes to melt the cheese and glaze the fish.

Make a fish sauce. Pour the reserved fish poaching liquid into the buttery juices in the saucepan and whisk in the flour. Stand on the simmering plate and whisk while coming to the boil. Season with pepper.

Put a potato cake on a serving plate and top with a fillet of fish. Pour round a little fish sauce.

Cook's notes
The potato cakes can be made in advance and kept in the fridge until needed.

Rich Sticky Gingerbread

This is an enriched version of the gingerbread to be found in my first book, *The Traditional Aga Cookery Book*. I have tried many alternatives over the years, but in the end always come back to this one. At Christmas time I add crystallised ginger to the basic recipe, which gives it a nice seasonal edge.

300ml/¹/₂ pint milk
2 level teaspoons bicarbonate of soda
350g/12oz plain flour
2 level teaspoons ground ginger
2 level teaspoons ground cinnamon
225g/8oz butter
225g/8oz soft brown sugar
110g/4oz golden syrup
110g/4oz treacle
2 eggs
6 balls crystallised ginger, finely chopped

Line the small roasting tin with Bake-O-Glide. Measure the milk into a jug and add the bicarbonate of soda and place on the back of the Aga to warm. Sieve the flour, ginger and cinnamon into a large mixing bowl. Put the butter, sugar, golden syrup and treacle in a saucepan and stand on the simmering plate. Heat and stir until the butter has melted. Remove from the heat and pour into the flour and spices. Mix together well and then beat in the eggs, one at a time. Next, stir in the warmed milk mixture followed by the crystallised ginger. Pour the gingerbread batter into the prepared tin. Bake.

For a two-oven Aga, hang the roasting tin on the bottom set of runners of the roasting oven and put the cold shelf on the third set of runners from the top of the oven.

For a three- or four-oven Aga,

hang the roasting tin on the second set of runners from the bottom of the baking oven. Bake the gingerbread for 30–40 minutes until risen and a cake tester or fine skewer inserted in the middle come out clean. Cool and store in the tin.

This gingerbread is at its best a day or two after baking.

Cook's notes
Even when the cake is thoroughly baked it sometimes sinks a little in the middle on cooling.

December

1st Gnocchi and Mozzarella Bake 2nd Celery Baked in Cream 3rd Chocolate Tea Loaf 4th Bean and Tomato Casserole 5th Brussels Sprouts with Chestnuts 6th Chicken and Prune Casserole 7th Mince Pies with Brandy Cream 8th Clementines with Caramel 9th Pork Stew with Dumplings 10th Dried Orange Slices with Cinnamon 11th A Farmers Wife's Fruit Tart 12th Leek and Stilton Soup 13th Double Chocolate Puddings 14th Gougere Cheese Choux Puffs 15th Sherry Sauce 16th Pork, Walnut and Sausage Rolls 17th Cabbage with Juniper Berries 18th Gingerbread and Butter Pudding 19th Christmas Pear Tart 20th Devils on Horseback 21st Apricot and Almond Stuffing 22nd Roast Turkey 23rd Chocolate Shortbread Torte with a Cranberry Glaze 24th Bread Sauce 25th Roast Goose with Prune and Apricot Stuffing 26th Gammon and Chutneys 27th Turkey and Hazelnut Soup 28th Christmas Nut Loaf 29th Whisky-Baked Fruit with Marmalade Ice Cream 30th Salmon Fishcakes with Lemon Butter Sauce 31st Hare Stew with Whisky

Gnocchi and Mozzarella Bake

This is one of my quick 'after work' meals that can be put on the table in no time at all when energy is low and the thought of all the Christmas preparation yet to come gets me down. Gnocchi bought from the chill counter in the supermarket has a reasonable shelf life so it is a good standby when you know you are going to be busy.

2 x 500g packs gnocchi
130g/4^1/$_2$oz cubed pancetta
1 small onion, peeled and chopped
2 teaspoons sun-dried tomato paste
400g can chopped tomatoes
salt and pepper
6 basil leaves, roughly chopped
150g/5oz Mozzarella

Serves 4

Bring a large pan of salted water to the boil and cook the gnocchi. When it floats to the top of the pan it is cooked, about 3 minutes. Drain.

Meanwhile, heat the pancetta in a frying pan and gradually the fat will run. Add the chopped onion and cook until the pancetta is browning and the onion cooked. Add the chopped tomatoes and the tomato paste. Season with salt and pepper and cook until thickening.

Put the gnocchi in a buttered, shallow ovenproof dish. Pour over the tomato sauce, scatter over the basil leaves.

Drain and cube the Mozzarella and scatter over the gnocchi.

Hang the shelf on the third set of runners from the top of the roasting oven, put in the gnocchi dish and bake for 15–20 minutes, until golden and bubbling.

Cook's notes
Mozzarella freezes well – if you don't have any fresh to hand grate it while still frozen and scatter over the top of the dish.

December
2

Celery Baked in Cream

Celery is often used as a flavouring in casseroles and soups or eaten raw as a salad vegetable but not often cooked. Try this gentle method of baking it. It tastes really good with a simply cooked piece of fish. British celery has a much better flavour and texture than imported varieties.

1 large head of celery, trimmed
$^1/_4$ teaspoon allspice
2 cloves garlic, crushed
300ml/$^1/_2$ pint single cream
salt and pepper
25g/1oz fresh breadcrumbs

Harvested from the same plant that also produces celeriac, celery was originally regarded as a medicinal plant rather than a vegetable. It is harvested between September and January and is part of the umbellifer family which also includes carrots. It is cultivated for its fresh and juicy pale green stems which can be eaten raw or cooked. Celery is also harvested for its seeds which are used either as a spice or ground and mixed with salt to produce celery salt.

Reserve a few celery leaves for garnish. Break off the sticks and wash and dry well. Cut the sticks into strips and then into lengths about 10cm/4-inch long. Put the celery strips into a shallow ovenproof dish. Mix together the allspice, garlic, cream and salt and pepper. Pour over the celery. Sprinkle over the breadcrumbs.

Put the shelf on the bottom set of runners of the roasting oven and put in the dish. Bake for 20–30 minutes until browning and then move to the simmering oven for a further 1 hour, until the celery is cooked.

Garnish with the reserved celery leaves.

Cook's notes
If you don't have allspice try some nutmeg or mace.

December
3

Chocolate Tea Loaf

Tea loaves are always popular. This one is a little different because it has chocolate added to the fruit. You can vary the flavours by trying different teas or different dried fruits.

110g/4oz mixed dried fruit
50g/2oz soft brown sugar
200ml/7 fl oz tea
1 egg
1 tablespoon dark marmalade
225g/8oz self-raising flour
1 teaspoon mixed spice
50g/2oz chocolate, roughly chopped

The day before making, put the fruit, sugar and tea in a basin and leave to soak overnight.

Butter or line a 500g/1 lb loaf tin.

Beat the egg and the marmalade together. Pour into the soaked fruit mixture and stir well. Sieve over the flour and the mixed spice. Add the chocolate and mix in with the other ingredients. Spoon into the prepared tin.

For a two-oven Aga, put the shelf on the floor of the roasting oven. Put in the loaf and bake for 15 minutes. Then slide in the cold shelf on the second set of runners from the top of the oven and bake for 40–45 minutes.

For the three- or four-oven Aga, put the shelf on the second set of runners from the bottom of the baking oven, slide in the loaf and bake for 45–50 minutes.

Bake until the loaf is risen and springy to the touch and a skewer inserted in the middle comes out clean.

Cook's notes
This recipe doesn't have any fat in it so it is best to serve the slices buttered unless the loaf is very fresh.

December
4

Bean and Tomato Casserole

Having hated butterbeans at school, where we had too many hard ones, I am now very fond of them. If you don't care for them, use another bean.

1 x 400g can kidney beans
1 x 400g can black-eyed beans
1 x 400g can butter beans
1 large onion, chopped
2 sticks celery, chopped
2 tablespoons olive oil
1 clove garlic, crushed
400g can chopped tomatoes
150ml/$^1/_4$ pint vegetable stock
$^1/_4$ teaspoon chilli powder
salt and pepper
75g/3oz wholemeal breadcrumbs
110g/4oz tasty cheese, grated

Serves 4

Drain and rinse all the beans.

Heat the oil in a pan and cook the onion and celery until they begin to soften. Add the garlic and fry until soft. Stir in the tomatoes and stock, chilli powder, beans, salt and pepper to taste. Bring to the boil, cover and move to the simmering oven for 30–40 minutes. Spoon into an ovenproof dish.

Mix the breadcrumbs and cheese and scatter over the bean mixture. Put the shelf on the second set of runners from the bottom of the roasting oven and put in the bean dish for 10–15 minutes until golden brown and crusty.

Cook's notes
This is a really tasty casserole and comes into its own when served with good quality sausages for a hearty winter meal.

December
5

Brussels Sprouts with Chestnuts

So many people buy sprouts for just one day of the year – Christmas! They don't know what they are missing. Cook Brussels sprouts for as short a time as possible to keep their colour and flavour and then toss in butter. I also like them shredded raw into a salad.

500g/1lb 2oz Brussels sprouts
200g/7oz cooked chestnuts
25g/1oz butter

Brussels sprouts are in season throughout the winter, with a peak in the mid-winter months, which makes them an ideal dish to prepare as part of a Christmas dinner. Literally, Brussels sprouts are miniature heads of cabbage, closely related to savoy and white cabbages.

Trim the sprouts and put in a saucepan with a pinch of salt. Add enough water to come 2.5cm/1-inch up the pan. Cover and bring to the boil on the boiling plate. Boil the sprouts rapidly for about 5 minutes so that the sprouts are just cooked when tested with the point of a sharp knife. Drain the sprouts well and return to the hot pan. Add the butter and the chestnuts and toss well to melt the butter and heat through the chestnuts. Serve immediately.

Cook's notes
Do not cut a cross in the bottom of the sprouts, they will become water-logged during the fast boiling.

December
6

Chicken and Prune Casserole

Prunes add a real richness to dishes such as this wonderful casserole, a particular favourite of mine. It is so easy to make. I find it a very comforting dish for cold winter days.

6–8 chicken portions
4 garlic cloves
2 level teaspoons dried mixed herbs
2 tablespoons red wine vinegar
100ml/4 fl oz olive oil
225g/8oz pitted, ready to eat prunes
salt and pepper
300ml/$^1/_2$ pint dry white wine
25g/1oz Demerara sugar
1 level teaspoon cornflour
150 ml/$^1/_4$ pint chicken stock

Serves 6–8

Place the chicken in a large, non-metallic bowl. Add the sliced garlic cloves, mixed herbs, wine vinegar, oil, prunes and a seasoning of salt and pepper. Cover and marinate in the fridge overnight.

Remove the chicken from the marinade and fry it until golden brown in a little oil skimmed from the marinade. Transfer to a flameproof casserole dish. Add the marinade mixture and the wine. Sprinkle in the sugar.

Bring to the boil on the simmering plate. Boil for 2–3 minutes, cover and place in the roasting oven on the shelf on the floor of the oven for 45 minutes.

Blend the cornflour and the chicken stock. Remove the casserole from the oven. Place the chicken on a serving plate and keep warm in the simmering oven. Add the stock mixture to the marinade and heat it on the simmering plate, stirring until thickened. Pour the sauce over the chicken.

Garnish with chopped parsley and serve.

Cook's notes
Pop some potatoes to bake in the roasting oven while the casserole cooks.

Aga *year*

December
7

Mince Pies with Brandy Cream

With the arrival of December then so begins the mince pie making season. No matter how many I make they always seem to be consumed with relish, so I like to have a few dozen stored away in the freezer ready to bake when unexpected visitors pop in. For the cookery demonstrations I do in Aga shops around the country I tend to use readymade dessert shortcrust pastry, which is excellent. If I have time I like to make the pastry.

300g/10½ oz plain flour
50g/2oz ground almonds
75g/3oz icing sugar
175g/3oz butter, chilled and
  cubed
grated rind ½ lemon
1 egg yolk
3–4 tablespoons milk

For the filling
225g/8 oz mincemeat
icing sugar to dust after baking

For the brandy cream
150ml ¼ pint double cream,
  whipped to soft peak stage
1 tablespoon caster sugar
2 tablespoons brandy

Makes 24

In a mixing bowl mix together the flour, ground almonds and the icing sugar. Add the butter and rub in until the mixture resembles fine breadcrumbs. Stir in the lemon rind and then bind the pastry together with the egg yolk and enough milk to make a firm dough.

Flour the work top and roll two thirds of the pastry out. Stamp out enough rounds to make 24 mince pies. Put the circles in the bun or mini-muffin tins. Fill each case with mincemeat. Roll the remaining pastry out and cut out star shapes to fit the tops. Place the stars on the filling. Chill the mince pies well, or freeze at this stage.

Bake the mince pies. Put the tray of mince pies directly on the floor of the roasting oven and bake for 12–15 minutes until pale golden brown. Cool slightly before removing from the tin or the pastry will bake.

Fold the sugar and the brandy gently into the whipped cream and serve a spoonful with each mince pie.

Cook's notes
Make the mince pies in bun tins or mini-muffin tins. Freeze the mince pies raw and, if you need the tins, flip the mince pies from the tins when frozen and store in boxes in the freezer. Return to the tins to bake as above.

December
8

Over the Christmas period I often fancy something simple to prepare and fresh to eat. These clementines fit the bill perfectly and, of course, they are at their best now.

8 clementines
200g/ 7oz caster sugar

A variety of mandarin, and a close relative of the satsuma and tangerine, clementines are widely cultivated and exported from the Mediterranean and northern African countries such as Morocco. In such regions of high heat, the clementine matures rapidly and is a popular early variety throughout these regions. There are two clones of the clementine, the 'common ordinary' and the 'Montreal' whose flavours are virtually indistinguishable, and are both, like other citrus fruits, high in vitamin C, potassiam, and natural fibres

Peel the clementines and remove any excess pith. Cut in half horizontally and arrange on a heatproof plate.

Put the sugar in a small frying pan or saucepan and stand on the simmering plate until the sugar has melted. Do not stir the sugar, just shake the pan.

As soon as the sugar has melted and is golden brown, drizzle the caramel over the clementines in a narrow stream. A teaspoon can be used to pull strands of the sugar to decorate the tops. If left, the caramel will dissolve over the clementines and form a sauce.

Cook's notes

Don't be tempted to stir the sugar while it is dissolving and caramelising otherwise it will become crystalline and you won't get a good caramel. When all the caramel has been used, allow the saucepan to cool down before putting to soak, it will be very hot!

December
9

Pork Stew with Dumplings

On a cold-snap day in December I'm afraid diets go out of the window and some warming dishes come in through the front door. Packed with vegetables this is a fairly healthy option, the dumplings apart! Any seasonal root vegetables can be used for this hearty stew. Serve with a bright vegetable to add colour to the plate.

25g/1oz dripping or lard
2 large onions, peeled and chopped
700g/ 1¹/₂ lb potatoes, diced
225g/8oz turnips, diced
4 sticks of celery, chopped
8 pork chops
25g/1oz seasoned flour
600ml/1 pint chicken or vegetable stock
1 bay leaf

For the suet dumplings
225g/8oz plain flour
¹/₂ teaspoon baking powder
salt
110g/4oz shredded suet

Serves 8

Melt the dripping in a frying pan and fry the onions, potatoes, turnips and celery until softening. Drain and transfer to a flameproof casserole dish. Dip the chops in the seasoned flour and brown in the hot frying pan. Lay the chops on top of the vegetables. Add the stock to the pan, bring to the boil and pour over the meat. Add the bay leaf. Cover the casserole and bring to the boil and then transfer to the simmering oven for 1–1¹/₂ hours.

Make the suet dumplings: place all the ingredients in a mixing bowl. Mix with enough water to make a soft but manageable dough and then form into 8 dumplings.

Remove the casserole from the oven and place the dumplings on top of the gravy. Replace the lid and put the casserole on the shelf on the floor of the roasting oven for 20–30 minutes, until the dumplings have risen.

Cook's notes
I have used pork chops in this recipe, but you could ask your butcher for a cheaper cut if you like.

December
10

Dried Orange Slices with Cinnamon

I make these at Christmas time to use as decorations and add a seasonal aroma to the house. When drying the orange slices do not be alarmed if a puddle of water appears on the floor in front of the Aga. Sometimes the flue can't cope with the amount of moisture that is being driven off from the oranges.

oranges, fairly thinly sliced
cinnamon sticks
string or raffia

Put the rack inside the large roasting tin. Slice the oranges fairly thinly and lay out on the rack in a single layer. Hang the tin on the middle set of runners of the simmering oven and allow the oranges to dry out for 4–6 hours, or overnight if your Aga is not too hot. If you have a four-oven Aga you can put the oranges overnight in the warming oven.

Remove the dried orange slices from the oven and allow to cool completely. When cold, tie a cinnamon stick to each orange slice using string or raffia. Use for tree decorations, parcel ties or hang in the kitchen.

Cook's notes
For a lovely, evocative Christmas aroma, put a handful of cloves in a small bowl and pour on water. Stand at the back of the Aga. Top up the water when filling the kettle.

December
11

A Farmer's Wife's Fruit Tart

I have no idea why this is a farmer's wife's tart because it really isn't a tart at all. I know it has its origin as an Italian dessert and a whole variety of fruits can be used. I wonder who the Farmer'a wife was? It is a cross between a cake and a clafoutis and very easy to make.

2 eggs
4 tablespoons milk
225g/8oz caster sugar
salt
175g/6oz plain flour
900g/2lbs eating apples, peeled, quartered and sliced
butter for smearing on tin and dotting on the tart

Serves 6

Butter a 23cm/9-inch round cake tin.

Place the flour in a mixing bowl. Add the sugar and then beat in the eggs and milk to make a smooth batter. Slice in the apples and turn to coat in the batter. Spoon into the prepared tin and level off. Dot the top with a little butter.

Place the oven shelf on the bottom set of runners of the roasting oven. Put in the tart and slide the cold shelf onto the second set of runners from the top of the oven and bake for 55–60 minutes. The tart will be golden brown on the top and the fruit soft.

Turn onto a plate and serve while warm.

Cook's notes
If you have some blackberries in the freezer, leftover from the autumn, then use them with the apples in this tart – apples and blackberries are just made for each other.

Leek and Stilton Soup

Many moons ago, I worked for the Milk Marketing Board and at Christmas we were given a lot of Stilton. I love Stilton and so do my family and friends but at the end of the Christmas season there was always some left! This was one of the recipes I put together then and still use today.

50g/2oz butter
350g/12oz leeks, washed, trimmed and sliced
2 medium potatoes, peeled and cut into chunks
2 bay leaves
250g/9oz blue Stilton
4 tablespoons plain yoghurt
pepper

Serves 4–6

Put the butter in a roomy saucepan and put on the simmering plate to melt. Add the leeks and stir in the melted butter. Cover with a lid and cook, stirring occasionally, until softening but not browning. Add the potatoes and the bay leaves and toss in the butter. Pour in 1 litre/ $1^3/_4$ pints water. Cover, bring to the boil and move to the simmering oven for 30–40 minutes, or until the potatoes are cooked.

Remove the bay leaves and crumble in most of the cheese, reserving a little for garnish. Purée the soup in a blender. Season with pepper. Stir in the yoghurt. Crumble over the remaining cheese.

Cook's notes
If you wish, you can freeze this soup before the yoghurt is added.

December 13

Double Chocolate Puddings

This terrific recipe came from David Pengelly, an Aga demonstrator in Cornwall. It has become a great favourite in my family because of the hidden treasure in the middle of the hot pudding. Beware, it is very rich!

50g/2oz cocoa powder
6 tablespoons boiling water
125ml/4fl oz milk
3 eggs
175g/6oz self-raising flour
1 teaspoon baking powder
110g/4oz soft butter or margarine
280g/10oz caster sugar
200g/7oz plain chocolate
icing sugar for dusting

Makes 8

Butter the base and sides of 8 x 200ml/7 fl oz ramekins.

Put the cocoa in a mixing bowl and blend in the boiling water to make a paste. Add the milk, eggs, flour, baking powder, soft butter and the caster sugar. Beat well to form a smooth batter. Divide the mixture between the buttered ramekins.

Break the chocolate into squares and stack 4 squares in the centre of each filled ramekin. Stand the ramekins on a baking tray.

Bake the puddings.

For a two-oven Aga, put the shelf on the floor of the roasting oven, slide in the puddings and put the cold shelf on the second set of runners from the top of the oven. Bake for 15–20 minutes.

For a three- or four-oven Aga, put the shelf on the bottom set of runners in the baking oven, put in the puddings and bake for 20 minutes, until risen and firm to the touch.

Dust with icing sugar and serve immediately.

Cook's notes
Blending the cocoa powder with boiling water stops the pudding becoming dry.

December
14

Gougère Cheese Choux Puffs

I often make these as a hand-around starter for a supper party. They are best straight from the oven, but can also be eaten cold. The roasting oven needs to be up to temperature for their baking, so if the oven needs to be full, bake them in advance and then warm them through before serving.

3oz/75g plain white flour
1/4 teaspoon salt
shake of pepper
2oz/50g butter, cut into cubes
2 eggs, beaten
3oz/75g grated Gruyère

Makes about 12

Sieve flour, salt and pepper onto a sheet of greaseproof paper.

Put the butter into a saucepan with 1/4pint/150ml water. Stand the pan on the simmering plate and allow the butter to melt. Bring to the boil. Tip in the flour and beat well with a wooden spoon until the mixture leaves the sides of the pan clean. Cool.

Beat in the eggs – I use an electric mixer – until the mixture is smooth and glossy. Add the grated cheese and beat well.

Grease a baking tray. Spoon about 12 dessertspoons of mixture. Bake on the third set of runners from the top in the roasting oven for 15–20 minutes. Check that the puffs are not browning too much – if they are, move the oven shelf to the floor of the oven. If not too brown, leave them nearer the top. Bake for a further 10 minutes. Serve warm or cold.

Cook's notes
Serve immediately or warm through for 4–5 minutes in the roasting oven before serving. Do not add any salt to the mixture as Gruyère can be quite salty when cooked.

December
15

Sherry Sauce

This creamy sauce is remarkably light to eat. It goes perfectly with
'Granny's Christmas Pudding' on page 400, as many Aga customers
will verify. It is a lighter option to brandy butter. If preferred, you can
replace the sherry with brandy.

600ml/1 pint single cream
50g/2oz butter
50g/2oz flour
50g/2oz caster sugar
6 tablespoons sweet sherry or more,
  to taste

Serves 8–10

Pour the cream into a milk pan. Add the flour and the butter. Stand the
pan on the simmering plate and whisk the mixture continuously until
the sauce has thickened. Bubble gently for 2–3 minutes. Remove from
the heat and stir in the sherry. If the sauce is to be served immediately,
whisk in the sugar and pour into a warm serving jug. If you are not
serving immediately, you can prevent a skin forming by scattering the
caster sugar over the surface of the sauce in the jug. Whisk the sugar
into the sauce just before serving.

Cook's notes
This creamy sauce is best made in a non-stick pan as it has a tendency
to catch quite easily on the bottom of a stainless steel pan.

December
16

Pork, Walnut and Sausage Rolls

At Christmas time I love to serve sausage rolls. They are so easy to make at home and can be cut to any size to suit your requirements. Here the Stilton adds a seasonal flavour and the walnuts add a little crunch. This is one of my favourite sausage roll fillings.

8 pork and herb sausages, skinned
*   or 500g/1lb 2oz sausagemeat*
50g/2oz walnuts, chopped
150g/5oz blue Stilton, crumbled
1 tablespoon chopped parsley
1 x 325g pack ready-rolled puff pastry
1 egg, to glaze

Put the sausage meat in a bowl and add the nuts, Stilton, parsley and a seasoning of pepper. Mix together well with your hands.

Unroll the pastry onto a large sheet of Bake-O-Glide. Cut into two long strips using a table knife. Divide the sausage mixture in half and roll each half into a sausage shape the length of each sheet of pastry. Lay the sausages on to one side of a sheet of pastry each. Brush one edge of the pastry with the beaten egg and fold over the pastry. Seal and knock up the edges.

Cut the sausage rolls to the desired sizes. Brush well with beaten egg.

If you like you can freeze the sausage rolls at this stage. Open freeze and then put into bags and label.

To bake, put onto a baking tray lined with Bake-O-Glide. Hang the baking tray on the third set of runners from the top of the roasting oven and bake the sausage rolls for 15–20 minutes (20–25 minutes if frozen) until crisp and golden brown.

Serve warm.

Cook's notes
There will be some oozing of the cheese in the filling during cooking, so make sure that you line the baking tray well.

Cabbage with Juniper Berries

Cabbages of all different varieties are available throughout the winter, so I find it very useful to have a few different recipes to hand. In this recipe the juniper berries, which release a wonderful aroma when crushed, add a gentle flavour to the cabbage.

25g/1oz butter
1 onion, peeled and chopped
1 clove garlic, crushed
6 juniper berries, crushed
450g/1lb cabbage, finely shredded
salt and pepper

Serves 4

Cabbages are one of those rare vegetables that come in different shapes and forms all through the year. The winter harvest are generally ball- or drum-headed and either green or white, and they are all suitable for immediate cooking. The white varieties are suitable for coleslaw, and all are perfect ingredients for warming winter dishes such as soups and casseroles, or served simply with just a knob of butter, a touch of mustard, or a sprinkle of chorizo or other chopped meat.

Melt the butter in a roomy saucepan and add the onion. Cook gently in the butter for a minute before adding the garlic and juniper berries. Continue to cook for another 5 minutes until the onion is soft.

Add the cabbage to the pan and stir to coat with the butter, season with salt and pepper. Cover with a lid and move to the simmering oven for 10 minutes until the cabbage is cooked, but still crunchy.

Cook's notes
Any type of cabbage can be cooked in this way.

December
18

Gingerbread and Butter Pudding

A great twist on a classic dish that fits the warming, comfort food needs of the Christmas period. The gingerbread cake gives more of a sponge-like texture than the more traditional use of bread would.

300g/10$^{1}/_{2}$oz gingerbread
25g/1oz butter, softened
25g/1oz crystallised ginger, chopped
2 eggs
2 egg yolks
1 tablespoon caster sugar
450ml/$^{3}/_{4}$ pint full-fat milk
1 teaspoon vanilla essence
1 tablespoon Demerara sugar
good pinch ground cinnamon

Serves 6

Cut the gingerbread into slices and spread each with butter. Arrange in a shallow, buttered ovenproof dish, buttered side up. Scatter over the chopped ginger.

In a basin, beat together the eggs, egg yolks, sugar, milk and vanilla essence. Strain through a sieve into a jug and then pour over the gingerbread. Leave to sit for 30 minutes.

Sprinkle over the Demerara sugar and cinnamon.

Stand the dish in a small roasting tin and pour boiling water round the pudding.

For a two-oven Aga, hang the tin on the bottom set of runners of the roasting oven and bake for 10 minutes. Move to the simmering oven for 30–40 minutes.

For a three- or four-oven Aga, hang the tin on the bottom set of runners of the baking oven and cook for 35–45 minutes.

Bake until the custard is set.

Cook's notes
The gentle cooking in a bain marie gives a lovely smooth custard base to the gingerbread.

Christmas Pear Tart

A delightful change from the usual mincemeat filling but still with a hint of traditional Christmas flavours. I have tried to make this a simple dessert to cook at a busy time of the year.

2 x 325g packs ready-rolled puff
    pastry
1 egg white
caster sugar to dust

For the pear and raisin syrup
1 medium pear, peeled, cored
    and diced
50g/2oz caster sugar
50g/2oz raisins
150ml/¼ pint water

1 vanilla pod, split or a few
    drops vanilla extract added
    after blending

For the filling
4 pears, peeled, cored and diced
50g/2oz raisins
50g/2oz sultanas
pinch cinnamon
zest 1 orange

Serves 8

Unroll 1 packet puff pastry and lay on a baking tray lined with Bake-O-Glide.

Mix together the filling ingredients in a mixing bowl and spread over the pastry sheet, leaving a border. Brush the border with the beaten egg white. Unroll the second sheet of pastry and carefully lay over the filling. Seal the edges decoratively.

Brush the top of the pastry with the egg white and dust the top with sugar. Make a few slits in the top of the pastry to allow steam to escape.

This can be frozen at this point. Open freeze and then wrap and label. The syrup can also be frozen and thawed gently in a saucepan.

To bake, hang the baking tray on the third set of runners from the top of the roasting oven and bake for 15 minutes then move to the floor of the roasting oven to crisp the base. If cooking from frozen, allow 5–10 minutes extra baking time.

Make the syrup. Put all the ingredients into a saucepan and bring slowly to the boil on the simmering plate. Move to the simmering oven for 30 minutes. Blend the contents of the pan and then strain through a sieve.

Serve the tart warm with the syrup and cream.

Cook's notes
If freezing this tart, remember to use chilled and not previously frozen pastry.

December
20

Devils on Horseback

A favourite from my *Traditional Aga Christmas* book. A classic combination of prunes and bacon that always proves popular at parties. Although slightly fiddly to make, these little devils can be prepared up to 24 hours in advance and kept chilled until ready for cooking.

12 rashers good streaky bacon
24 ready-to-eat prunes
24 cocktail sticks

Makes 24

Cut the bacon rashers in half, lengthways. Wrap a piece of bacon round each prune and secure with a skewer. Lay each wrapped prune on a baking tray lined with Bake-O-Glide.

To cook, hang the tin on the second set of runners from the top of the roasting oven and cook for 15 minutes, then turn over and cook for a further 5 minutes until the bacon is crisp.

December
21

Apricot and Almond Stuffing

This recipe has become an absolute favourite for stuffing chicken or turkey. Remember to only stuff the neck end of a bird and to add the weight of the stuffing on to the weight of the bird when calculating cooking times.

15g/$\frac{1}{2}$oz butter
1 large onion, peeled and finely chopped
1 kg/2lbs 4oz fresh sausage meat
225g/8oz streaky bacon, rind removed and finely chopped
salt and pepper
110g/4oz ready-to-eat dried apricots, finely chopped
50g/2oz whole almonds, skinned and roughly chopped

Heat the butter in a frying pan and cook the onion until soft but not brown. Cool. Put the sausage meat and bacon into a large bowl and mix well.

Add the apricots, almonds and a seasoning of salt and pepper. Mix very well together (I find the easiest way of doing this is with my hands). Use this to stuff the neck end of the bird, or to form into stuffing balls.

Cook's notes
This can be frozen for up to one month. Thaw in the fridge overnight before using.

December
22

Roast Turkey

I have included this recipe here, just three days before Christmas, for those who cannot conceive of Christmas without turkey. So, if you're not going to celebrate with the goose that appears on page 433, then this is the recipe for you! And even if you do prefer to cook goose on the big day, it might be that you would like turkey for some of the days following – cold turkey is always popular and a friend to all sorts of accompaniments on a cold buffet table.

Turkey simmering oven cooking times (for all Agas)

8–12lb/3.6–5.4kg
3–5 hours
12–16lb/5.4–7$\frac{1}{2}$ kg
5–7$\frac{1}{2}$ hours
16–20lb/7$\frac{1}{4}$–9kg
7$\frac{1}{2}$–10 hours
20–24lb/9–10.8kg
10–12$\frac{1}{2}$ hours
24–28lb/10.8–12.6kg
12$\frac{1}{2}$–15 hours

Cook's notes

The turkey needs to be taken out of the fridge at least half an hour before roasting. Always remember to add on the weight of any stuffing to the weight of the bird. If you have a two-oven Aga you may prefer to use the simmering oven and free up the roasting oven for roasting vegetables. Another thing to remember is that the turkey will need to rest for half an hour between coming out of the oven and being carved.

To prepare the turkey for the oven, remove the wishbone (your butcher can do this for you), as this makes carving easier, though it's not essential. Stuff the neck end and fix the skin with a skewer. Do not stuff the cavity – with a bird heavily stuffed, there is a danger of it not cooking thoroughly. If you prefer, you can put an onion, lemon and some bay leaves in the cavity to add flavour.

Put the turkey in a large roasting tin. If liked, you can lattice some streaky bacon rashers over the breast and tops of the legs. This looks attractive and keeps those areas that are particularly prone to dryness, moist. Sometimes the flesh immediately under the bacon can develop a pink tinge, this is perfectly harmless. A little softened butter may be smeared over the exposed skin. Put a small piece of foil or a butter paper over the top of the turkey. Remove it half an hour before the turkey is cooked to allow the bacon to crisp. I don't like the idea of tenting foil over my turkey to keep it moist because it can cause the meat to steam rather than roast – after alll the Aga ovens are renowned for the way they keep food moist. This also means there is no need to baste. Anyway, it's so difficult to remove a heavy turkey from the oven without being splashed with fat!

All roasting times given are approximate and you must check that the turkey is cooked through. If in doubt, return the turkey to the oven for a further 30 minutes and then re-check.

Hang the roasting tin on the bottom set of runners of the roasting oven for one hour. This is essential to get the turkey up to 60C (140F) for safe cooking. Then move the turkey to the simmering oven and cook according to the times for each weight of bird in the margin, left.

Test to see if the turkey is cooked. I think the best method is to insert a sharp knife between the leg and the breast and look to see that the meat has cooked and the tip of the blade comes out hot. The joint should also be able to freely wiggle when moved.

When you are sure that the turkey is cooked through, remove it from the oven and lift onto a warm serving platter. Cover the bird loosely with foil and stand either on the warming plate or on a trivet on top of the boiling plate lid. While the turkey rests, all the juices will settle in the meat, making it juicier and easier to carve. This half-hour should give you time to make a gravy and finish cooking all other accompaniments.

Aga *year*

December 23

Chocolate Shortbread Torte with a Cranberry Glaze

This is one of my favourite desserts for Christmas. It is so easy to make in advance and chill or freeze before topping with the cranberries. I sometimes make this in the summer and top with raspberries.

For the shortbread
175g/6oz butter, melted
225g/8oz plain flour
25g/1oz cocoa powder
75g/3oz caster sugar

For the filling
200g/7oz cream cheese
5 tablespoons double cream
150g/5oz plain chocolate, melted
2 eggs, beaten
1 egg yolk

1 teaspoon coffee essence
2 tablespoons rum

For the topping
75g/3oz granulated sugar
3 tablespoons water
175g/6oz cranberries
142ml (small carton) soured
  cream
icing sugar, to dust

For the shortbread, put the flour, cocoa and caster sugar in a bowl and add the melted butter. Stir to make a dough. Press the shortbread into the base of a 20cm/8-inch spring-release cake tin. Set aside.

Make the filling. Beat the cheese and cream together until smooth. Beat in the melted chocolate and then the beaten eggs, coffee essence and the rum. Pour over the shortbread base.

Put the shelf on the floor of the roasting oven. Put in the cake tin and slide the cold shelf onto the third set of runners from the top of the oven. Bake the torte for 25–30 minutes, until the filling is set. Cool.

For the topping, put the sugar and water in a saucepan and stir until dissolved. Add the cranberries, cover and bring to the boil. Cook until the fruit is glazed. Cool.

Spread the soured cream over the cooled torte and then spread over the glazed cranberries. Dust with icing sugar.

Cook's notes
Cooking this torte towards the bottom of the roasting oven helps the shortbread base to cook while the filling is cooking and saves a separate stage of baking.

December
24

Bread Sauce

There are certain things I see on the supermarket shelves and simply cannot work out why they are bought instead of being made from scratch at home. Bread Sauce is one, along with crumble mix and batter mix!

1 large onion, peeled
6–8 cloves
1 bay leaf
6 whole peppercorns
600ml/1 pint whole milk
110g/4oz fresh breadcrumbs
50g/2oz butter, diced
1–2 tablespoons single cream
salt

Serves 8

Stick the cloves into the onion and place in a milk pan. Add the bay leaf and the peppercorns. Pour in the milk. Stand on the simmering plate and bring slowly to the boil. Remove from the heat and stand at the back of the Aga for 30 minutes to allow the flavours to infuse.

Strain the milk through a sieve and rinse out the pan. Return the infused milk to the pan and heat gently. Add the breadcrumbs and the butter to the warm milk and stir well until the butter has melted. Add the cream and adjust the seasoning.

Pour into a serving dish and cover with foil to keep warm either on the back of the Aga, or in the warming oven, or serve immediately.

Cook's notes
This rich and slightly spicy sauce can be made on Christmas Eve and warmed through on the big day.

December
25

Roast Goose with Prune and Apricot Stuffing

Goose is my Christmas Day meal of choice. Traditional, rich and special. Goose roasts really well in the Aga and the fat should, of course, be saved for roasting vegetables for weeks to come.

4–5.5kg/9–12lb oven ready goose

For the fruit stuffing
110g/4oz stoned prunes, roughly chopped
110g/4oz dried apricots, roughly chopped
85ml/3fl oz port
2 eating apples, cored and chopped
1 small onion, peeled and chopped
½ teaspoon cinnamon
a few gratings of nutmeg
salt and pepper

For the forcemeat stuffing
1 small onion, peeled and chopped
the goose liver, chopped (if in the goose)
grated rind and juice 1 orange
225g/8oz pork sausagemeat
1 teaspoon chopped thyme leaves
3 tablespoons chopped parsley
50g/2oz fresh breadcrumbs
1 egg, beaten
salt and pepper

Goose roasting times
4 kg /9lbs 2½ hours
4–5kg /10–11lbs 3 hours,
5.5kg/12lbs 3½ hours

Make the fruit stuffing. Soak the prunes and apricots in the port overnight. Mix all the stuffing ingredients together. Do not worry if this is a sloppy stuffing mix.

Make the forcemeat stuffing. Mix all the ingredients together, adding enough egg to bind all together.

Remove any excess fat from the goose and stuff the neck end of the goose with the forcemeat stuffing. Tuck the neck flap over the stuffing. Secure with skewers.

Put the fruit stuffing in the body cavity.

Prick the skin of the goose all over with a fork. Stand the rack inside the roasting tin and place the goose on it. Hang the tin on the second set of runners from the bottom of the roasting oven (if space allows) and roast the goose for the times suggested in the left-hand column.

Periodically check the fat level in the tin, it may need emptying if the goose is fatty. If the meat is browning too much, slip a piece of foil loosely over the top. To test if the goose is cooked, pierce the fattest part of the thigh with a skewer. If the juices run clear, the goose is cooked. Allow to stand, covered, in a warm place, for up to 30 minutes before carving.

Serve a tart apple sauce with the goose and a selection of roast vegetables.

Cook's notes
Buy the goose from a good butcher to ensure that you have plenty of meat on the bird.

26

Gammon and Chutneys

I love having home-cooked ham in the house at Christmas, It is always so useful for eking out meals for unexpected guests. Once you have cooked a gammon at home you won't be satisfied with the bought variety.

gammon joint
water, cider or apple juice
English mustard
cloves
Demarera sugar

chutneys
Mango Chutney (see page 309)
Indian Chutney (see page 124)
Apricot Chutney (see page 388)

Gammon cooking times
1–$1^1/_2$ kg/2–$3^3/_4$lb
$2^1/_2$ hours
$1^3/_4$–$2^1/_4$kg/4–5lb
3 hours
$2^1/_2$–$3^1/_4$kg/$5^1/_2$–7lb
$3^1/_2$ hours
$3^1/_2$–4kg/8–9lb
$4^1/_2$ hours
$4^1/_2$–5kg/10–11lb
$5^1/_2$ hours
$5^1/_2$–6kg/12–13lb
$6^1/_2$ hours
$6^1/_2$–7kg/14–15lb
$7^1/_2$ hours
$7^1/_4$kg and over/16lb and over
overnight or 12 hours

Cook's notes
Find a butcher who cures his own gammons and ask him how long he thinks the joint needs to soak in order to remove excess salts prior to cooking.

Soak the joint in cold water for 2–3 hours, or as recommended by your butcher (see Cook's notes). Drain. Put a trivet or old plate in the base of a saucepan large enough to take the joint. Pour in enough water, cider or apple juice, to come no more than 5cm/2"up the side of the pan. Cover with a lid.

Stand on the simmering plate and slowly bring to the boil. Simmer for 30 minutes and then move to the simmering oven. (For weights and cooking times, see left-hand column for details.)

Remove the pan from the oven and the gammon from the pan. When cool enough to handle, strip off the skin and score a diamond pattern on the fat. Spread the fat with mustard and stud the centre of each diamond with a clove. Press Demarera sugar all over the mustard.

Stand the ham on a baking tray lined with Bake-O-Glide. Hang the tray on the second set of runners from the bottom of the roasting oven and allow a crust and glaze to form for 20–30 minutes, keeping an eye on it so that it doesn't burn. Allow it to rest for 20–30 minutes before carving, if serving hot, otherwise allow to cool.

If you choose a joint on the bone, the chances are that you won't have a saucepan large enough to cook it in, following this method. In which case, put the rack on its lowest setting. Put the joint in the roasting tin and place on the rack, pour in enough water to come just around the meat. Cover as tightly with foil as possible, remembering that the foil will tear if put on the runners. Put the tin on the floor of the roasting oven and cook for 1 hour before moving to the simmering oven for the appropriate time. When the ham is cold, wrap it in greaseproof paper – not foil or clingfilm – and keep in the fridge or somewhere cool. It will keep well for at least a week. Serve with a selection of chutneys.

December 27

Turkey and Hazelnut Soup

If you are stuck for interesting ideas to use up the inevitable leftover turkey at Christmas, do try this soup. Strip the bird of meat and make stock from the carcass. This is a pleasingly light soup after all the richness of Christmas.

75g/3oz hazelnuts
25g/1oz butter
1 onion, finely chopped
$^1/_2$ teaspoon paprika
225g/8oz cooked turkey meat, diced
1.2 litres/2 pints turkey stock
1 egg yolk
150ml/$^1/_4$ pint single cream
1 tablespoon chopped parsley or chervil
salt and pepper

Serves 6

Put the hazelnuts on a baking tray and place towards the top of the roasting oven for 2–3 minutes until browned. Watch! They burn easily. Cool for 1–2 minutes and then coarsely chop in a food processor.

Heat the butter in a roomy saucepan and fry the onion and paprika until soft but not too brown. Add the stock and bring to the boil, then add the turkey meat and simmer for 3–4 minutes, until hot.

Purée the soup in a food processor and return to the rinsed pan. Blend the egg yolk and cream and add to the soup. Heat gently but do not boil. Add the hazelnuts and herbs and adjust the seasoning.

Cook's notes
Cook the carcass in the simmering oven to make a really rich stock – essential for this soup!

Christmas Nut Loaf

This is a terrific recipe for the much-maligned nut loaf – I have cooked it many times at Christmas for both vegetarians and nut-lovers to great acclaim. Even meat-eaters love it!

1 tablespoon olive oil
1 medium onion, peeled and finely chopped
25g/1oz butter
110g/4oz button mushrooms, sliced
225g/8oz chestnuts
50g/2oz brazil nuts
110g/4oz fresh wholemeal breadcrumbs
1 tablespoon chopped fresh parsley
110g/4oz blue Stilton
salt and pepper
150ml/¹/₄ pint vegetable stock

Serves 4

Heat the oil in a frying pan and cook the onion until soft but not brown. Tip into a bowl and melt the butter in the pan. Stir in the mushrooms and fry until just colouring. Set aside.

Chop the nuts. I use a food processor for this to get a mixture of very finely chopped and some chunky nuts. Stir in the breadcrumbs, parsley, and a seasoning of salt and pepper. Crumble in the Stilton. Mix in the cooked onion and the stock.

Grease and line a ¹/₂kg/1lb loaf tin. Spoon half the nut mixture into the base of the tin and smooth off. Spoon over the mushrooms to form a layer. Top with the remaining nut mixture. Smooth the top and cover loosely with foil.

Put the shelf on the bottom set of runners of the roasting oven and put in the nut loaf. Bake for 30 minutes. Remove the loaf and allow it to rest for 5 minutes before turning out onto a serving plate. Serve warm.

Cook's notes
Use any variety of mixed nuts – brazils and chestnuts are seasonal but I often use walnuts, pretty green pistachios or peanuts.

Whisky-Baked Fruit with Marmalade Ice Cream

I love the sensuous contrast of hot fruits with ice cream. Although I choose to serve the fruit hot in this recipe, it could also be served at room temperature if preferred.

4 eating apples
4 pears
12 plums
200ml/7fl oz whisky
150ml/5fl oz white wine
juice 1 lemon
110g/4oz soft brown sugar

For the ice cream
500ml/18fl oz double cream
350g/12oz Seville orange
  marmalade
25g/2oz icing sugar
juice ¹/₂ lemon
2 tablespoons whisky

Serves 6

Quarter and core the apples and pears and thinly slice. Put into a shallow ovenproof dish. Halve and quarter the plums and add to the dish. Pour over the whisky, wine and lemon juice. Sprinkle over the brown sugar.

Hang the shelf on the bottom set of runners of the roasting oven and put in the dish of fruit. Bake for 30–40 minutes, until the fruit is just soft and the liquid is reduced.

Make the ice cream. Whisk the cream, marmalade and icing sugar together. Using an electric whisk will help break up the marmalade. Whisk until the cream is just floppy, then add the lemon juice which will thicken the cream. Add the whisky. Pour into an ice cream machine and churn until set. If you make this in advance and want to keep it in a freezer the ice cream will set hard, so remove from the freezer 20–30 minutes before serving.

Spoon the fruit into small dishes and serve with a scoop of ice cream.

Cook's notes
If the marmalade has coarse shreds, cut it up a little for a silkier finish to the ice cream.

Salmon Fishcakes with Lemon Butter Sauce

The lemon butter sauce in this recipe is a delicious addition to one of my favourite leftover dishes.

350g/12oz salmon fillet, cooked
350g/12oz cooked and mashed
   potato
1 tablespoon tomato ketchup
1 teaspoon mustard
2 tablespoons finely chopped
   parsley
plain flour
1 tablespoon olive oil
25g/1oz butter

For the lemon butter sauce
3 tablespoons lemon juice
40g/1$\frac{1}{2}$oz butter
125ml/$\frac{1}{4}$ pint double cream
2 tablespoons finely chopped
   chives
salt and pepper

Serves 6

Flake the cooked salmon, removing any skin and bone. In a mixing bowl, add half the salmon to the potato, tomato ketchup, mustard and parsley. Mix well together and season with salt and pepper. Add the remaining salmon and mix in, but take care to keep the salmon unbroken. Divide into 6 even-sized portions. Flour your hands and shape each portion into a fishcake. Chill for at least half an hour.

Using a frying pan that can fit into the oven, heat the butter and the olive oil and put in the fishcakes. Put the pan on the floor of the roasting oven and cook for about 5 minutes. They should be golden on the underside. Turn over and cook for a further 10 minutes, until crisp and heated through.

To make the lemon butter sauce, melt the butter in a saucepan, add the cream and heat through. Whisk in the lemon juice and chives, taking care not to boil the sauce. Adjust the seasoning. Serve with the fishcakes.

Cook's notes
Don't be tempted to add milk or butter to your mashed potato, as you might normally – it will only make the cakes more difficult to shape and may cause them to fall apart.

December
31

Hare Stew with Whisky

It's New Year's Eve, and whether you are Scottish or not, whisky is called for at some point in the celebrations. Here it is hidden in a wonderfully rich game stew. If you aren't able to find hare, use rabbit, stewing venison or older game birds. Try to use reasonable quality whisky in this recipe as the flavour of the whisky still has to stand up after the alcohol is cooked out of the dish.

1 hare, jointed
25g/1oz flour, seasoned with salt and paprika
50g/2oz butter
110g/4oz bacon, each rasher quartered
2 large onions, finely chopped
4 celery stalks, chopped
2 sprigs thyme and mint
2 teaspoons Worcestershire sauce
150ml/¼ pint whisky
450ml/¾ pint stock, either from
*   hare trimmings or good beef stock*

Serves 6–8

Whilst rabbit is commonly available from most butchers, farmers' markets and game dealers, hare is somewhat less common. Its season runs from October through to February. Unlike rabbit, which has pale delicate meat reminiscent of chicken, hare has deeper-coloured flesh with a rich gamy flavour. Hare meat is rich in protein and is commonly used in dishes such as casseroles and stews.

Coat the joints of hare with the seasoned flour. In a frying pan heat the butter and bacon, and when the fat has run from the bacon add the hare joints. Fry until browned all over, then transfer the hare and bacon to a casserole dish.

Add the onions to the frying pan and cook until softened and then add the celery. Cook until the celery is softened and the onion is golden brown. Stir in the whisky, stock and Worcestershire sauce. Bring to the boil and pour over the hare. Tuck in the fresh herbs, cover with a lid and bring back to the boil. Move the casserole to the simmering oven for about 3–4 hours.

When the meat is tender, remove the joints from the casserole and keep warm. Remove the herbs from the liquor and if needed reduce the liquid by boiling on the boiling plate for 2–3 minutes.

Serve with creamy mashed potato to soak up the juices.

Cook's notes
Hare and venison are very filling meats so don't serve too much to start with – there's a long night ahead!

Index

a

Aga lemon curd 257
Aga-dried tomatoes 250
ale and Cheddar croûtes, Lamb in 360
almonds
   Almond-crusted salmon fillet 56
   Almond marmalade tart 72
   Almond Swiss roll 182
   Almond and white chocolate tart 102
   Apricot and almond stuffing 428
   Plum and almond puddings with bay-scented custard 292
Amaretti meringues with raspberry coulis 266
apples
   Apple crumble tart 316
   Apple custard tart 349
   Apple porridge 17
   Apple and raisin pizza 396
   Apple strudel 325
   Farmer's wife's fruit tart 417
   Fudge and pistachio baked apples 320
   Guinea fowl with prunes and apples 389
   Plum and Apple chutney 303
   Roast rack of pork with roast apples 334
apricots
   Apricot and almond stuffing 428
   Apricot and cherry crumble 277
   Apricot chutney 388
   Apricot and walnut biscotti 203
   Chicken and apricot koresh 207
   Fruity glazed chicken 268
   Roast goose with prune and apricot stuffing 433
Aromatic Asian pesto with chicken 198
artichokes
   Artichoke and wild mushroom pie 340
   Individual white pizzas 299
asparagus
   Asparagus, Serrano ham and Taleggio tart 123
   Asparagus soup 165
   Aubergine and asparagus bruschetta 177
   Cheese and asparagus tart 160
   Salmon with grilled asparagus 172
aubergines
   Aubergine and asparagus bruschetta 177
   Aubergine and goat's cheese rounds 183
   Grilled tuna with aubergine 167
   Oriental aubergines 304
   Oven-roasted vegetable moussaka 344
   Penne with aubergine and pine nuts 265
   Tian of aubergines 226

b

Baby leaf risotto with lemon 171
bacon
   Devils on horseback 427
   Quail in bacon 201
Baked pears with cassis 327
Baked stuffed mushroom caps 91
Baked tomatoes on brioche 271
Bakewell tart 21
bananas
   Breakfast bars 272
   Hot banana brioche 173
Barley risotto 381
basil
   Cheese, basil and pine nut triangles 245
beans
   Bean and tomato casserole 409
   Broad bean and bacon soup 192
   Butterbean vinaigrette 157
   Provençal bean stew 135
beef
   Beef stroganoff pies 308
   Beef tagine with prunes 14
   Braised and spiced topside-of beef 141
   Classic beef casserole 46
   Italian beef burgers 361
   Miso beef stir-fry with noodles 399
   Pot roast beef in red wine 107
   Venison, beef and cranberry pie 365
see also veal
beetroot
   Beetroot and red wine risotto 351
   Roast beetroot with goat's cheese 358
biscuits
   Apricot and walnut biscotti 203
   Butter digestive biscuits 57
   Cherry and white chocolate cookies 19
   Devon flats 106
   Easter biscuits 144
   Ethel's shortcake biscuits 110
   Hazelnut and chocolate chunk cookies 228
   Soft and chewy cranberry biscuits 16
black pudding, Poussin with pudding 381
blackberry sauce, Duck breast with 322
Blackcurrant slump 323
Blue Stilton soup 42
blueberries
   Blueberry butter cake 237
   Blueberry muffins 293
   Blueberry pancakes 363
   Fig and blueberry clafoutis 302
Braised carrots with Parmesan 61
Braised chicken and chicory 99
Braised chicken legs in red wine 343
Braised five-spice pork with pak choi 169
Braised peppers with olives 243
Braised sausages with chestnuts 32
Braised and spiced topside of beef 141
Bread and butter pudding 47
Bread sauce 432
breads
   Aubergine and asparagus bruschetta 177

Bread with olives and tomatoes *230*
Cheese and walnut loaf *298*
Chelsea buns *69*
Chocolate bread *168*
Fougasse Farci *174*
Goat's cheese croustade *50*
Hot cross buns *138*
Malthouse bread *86*
Raisin bread for cheese *20*
Roast garlic bread *295*
Scones *132*
Seed and grain loaf *116*
see also brioche; muffins
Breakfast bars *272*
brioche
Baked tomatoes on brioche *271*
Figs on brioche *339*
Hot banana brioche *173*
Broad bean and bacon soup *192*
Broccoli quiche *84*
Brussels sprouts with chestnuts *410*
Buckwheat cake *370*
butter
Butter digestive biscuits *57*
Fennel saffron butter *13*
butterbeans
Butterbean vinaigrette *157*
Sugar-glazed gammon with
butterbean mash *93*
cabbage
Cabbage with juniper berries *424*
Cheesey bubble and squeak cakes *96*
Spicy red cabbage *33*
see also pak choi

C

cakes
Blueberry butter cake *237*
Buckwheat cake *370*
Cherry and marzipan cake *208*
Chocolate brownies *105*
Cider Cake *306*
Coffee cake *353*
Cup cakes *53*
Ginger cake *112*
Guinness cake *98*
Leamington festival cake *390*
Lemon and seed drizzle cake *194*
Orange drizzle tray bake *31*
Orange and white chocolate sponge
37
Passion cake *60*
Pear upside-down cake *311*
Plum and oatmeal Madeira cake *337*
Polenta shortcake with raisins *11*
Rhubarb cake *140*
Rich sticky gingerbread *403*
Sephardic chocolate cake *378*
Simnel cake *142*
Strawberry crumble cake *286*
Strawberry meringue roulade *219*
Yoghurt cake with grapes in syrup
394
calamari *see squid*
Caramelised onion, Pan fried lamb's
liver with *180*
Caramelised pineapple with raspberries
259

carrots
Braised carrots with Parmesan *61*
Spicy carrot soup *373*
Summer vegetable flan *291*
Cauliflower soufflés *59*
Celeriac, Whisky and thyme soup *387*
celery
Celery baked in cream *407*
Celery soup *130*
cheese
Asparagus, Serrano ham and Tallegio
tart *123*
Aubergine and goat's cheese rounds
183
Blue Stilton soup *42*
Cheese and asparagus tart *160*
Cheese, basil and pine nut triangles
245
Cheese ramekins *77*
Cheese soufflés *117*
Cheese and walnut loaf *298*
Cheesey bubble and squeak cakes *96*
Couscous, tomato, and haloumi salad
231
Fennel gratin *235*
Gnocchi and Mozzarella bake *406*
Gorgonzola risotto *111*
Jerusalem artichokes with cheese *23*
Lamb in ale and Cheddar croûtes
360
Leek and potato soup with
Camembert croûtes *377*
Lemon Ricotta puddings *43*
Macaroni cheese *27*
Plaice baked with cheese *128*
Roquefort feuilleté *70*
Smoked haddock au Gratin *145*
Smoked salmon and goat's cheese
roulade *195*
Stuffed peppers with Brie *313*
Wensleydale and leek slice *385*
see also Feta; goat's cheese; Gouda;
Gruyère; mascarpone; Parmesan;
Ricotta; Stilton
Chelsea buns *69*
cherries
Apricot and cherry crumble *277*
Cherry and marzipan cake *208*
Cherry and white chocolate cookies
19
chestnuts
Braised sausages with chestnuts *32*
Brussels sprouts with chestnuts *410*
Chestnut soup *35*
chicken
Aromatic Asian pesto with chicken
198
Braised chicken and chicory *99*
Braised chicken legs in red wine *343*
Chicken and apricot Koresh *207*
Chicken and egg oriental rice *52*
Chicken and mango stir-fry *276*
Chicken noodle soup *68*
Chicken and prune casserole *411*
Chicken in red wine with raisins *36*
Chicken in sherry sauce *85*
Chicken with sparkling wine *103*
Chicken tikka skewers *355*
Chicken with watercress sauce *126*
Chilled lemon chicken *234*

Friceaséed chicken with rosemary
and lemon juice *26*
Fruity glazed chicken *268*
Herby chicken with lemon and herb
butter *156*
Mediterranean chicken with lemon
and olives *264*
Paella *205*
Poussin with black pudding *381*
Spice-crusted chicken with rose
harissa *58*
Spring chicken with lemon rice *164*
Warm chicken salad *289*
see also goose; guinea fowl; pheasant;
poussin; quail; turkey
chickpeas
Seared tuna with chickpea and
pepper salad *278*
Spiced crusted leg of lamb with
chickpeas *305*
chicory, Braised chicken and chicory *99*
Chilli salt squid *49*
chocolate
Chocolate Amaretti pudding *372*
Chocolate bread *168*
Chocolate brownies *105*
Chocolate and Cointreau soufflés *149*
Chocolate meringue *241*
Chocolate mousse *34*
Chocolate shortbread torte with a
cranberry glaze *431*
Chocolate tea loaf *408*
Chocolate tea pots *137*
Double chocolate puddings *419*
Hazelnut and chocolate chunk
cookies *228*
Pistachio and chocolate torte with
summer fruits *233*
Sephardic chocolate cake *378*
Three-chocolate millefeuille *41*
see also white chocolate
chorizo
Chorizo, pepper and tomato
macaroni *338*
New potato, chorizo and roast
pepper salad *246*
Christmas decorations *416*
Christmas nut loaf *436*
Christmas pear tart *426*
Christmas pudding, Granny's *400*
chutneys
Apricot chutney *388*
Gammon and chutneys *434*
Indian chutney *124*
Mango chutney *356*
Pear, prune and walnut chutney *317*
Plum and Apple chutney *303*
cider
Cider cake *306*
Pot-roast lamb in cider *82*
Somerset cider hotpot *22*
cinnamon, Dried orange slices with *416*
Classic quiche Lorraine *362*
Clementines with caramel *414*
coconut
Coconut lamb *232*
Coconut rice pudding with papaya
274
Haddock, sweetcorn and coconut
chowder *270*

Index

cod, fillet with fennel saffron butter, Wrapped *13*
Coffee cake *353*
Cointreau soufflés, Chocolate and *149*
Compôte de tomates *248*
cookies *see biscuits*
corn *see sweetcorn*
courgettes
    Courgette Tart *212*
    Marinated courgettes *281*
    Potato and courgettes with pistou *236*
    Roast leg of lamb with roasted peppers and courgettes *119*
    Roast salmon with courgettes and pine nuts *294*
    Tomato and courgette salsa *191*
couscous
    Couscous with roast summer vegetables and goat's cheese *273*
    Couscous, tomato, and Haloumi salad *231*
    Couscous-crusted fish fingers with mint peas *214*
    Lamb tagine with minted couscous *159*
    Mediterranean chicken with lemon and olives *264*
crab, Corn, crab and prawn chowder *335*
cranberries
    Chocolate shortbread torte with a cranberry glaze *431*
    Soft and chewy cranberry biscuits *16*
    Venison, beef and cranberry pie *365*
Crema catalana *152*
Crêpe Caribe *83*
Crumbed tomatoes *204*
cucumbers, Thai fishcakes with cucumber relish *262*
Cup cakes *53*
Curried sweet potato soup *315*
damsons, Sweet pickled damsons *309*

d

desserts
    Almond marmalade tart 72
    Almond and white chocolate tart 102
    Amaretti meringues with raspberry coulis *266*
    Apple crumble tart 316
    Apple custard tart 349
    Apple and raisin pizza *396*
    Apple strudel *325*
    Apricot and cherry crumble *277*
    Baked pears with cassis *327*
    Bakewell tart 21
    Blackcurrant slump *323*
    Bread and butter pudding *47*
    Caramelised pineapple with raspberries *259*
    Chocolate Amaretti pudding *372*
    Chocolate and Cointreau soufflés *149*
    Chocolate meringue *241*
    Chocolate mousse *34*
    Chocolate shortbread torte with a cranberry glaze *431*

Chocolate tea pots *137*
Christmas pear tart 426
Clementines with caramel *414*
Coconut rice pudding with papaya *274*
Crêpe Caribe *83*
Double chocolate puddings *419*
Elderflower fritters with elderflower mousse *199*
English treacle tart 380
Farmer's wife's fruit tart 417
Fig and blueberry clafoutis *302*
Figs on brioche *339*
French rice pudding *24*
Fruit flan *187*
Fudge nut tranche *65*
Fudge and pistachio baked apples *320*
Individual ginger puddings *29*
Italian rhubarb tart 92
Gingerbread and butter pudding *425*
Gooseberry and raspberry crumble *221*
Granny's Christmas pudding *400*
Honeyed fig kebabs with lemon tzatziki *324*
Hot banana brioche *173*
Lemon meringue pie *383*
Lemon Ricotta puddings *43*
Lemon roulade with passion-fruit cream *215*
Orange and vanilla custard tart 76
Pecan tarts 196
Pineapple upside-down puddings *249*
Pistachio and chocolate torte with summer fruits *233*
Plum and almond puddings with bay-scented custard *292*
Pumpkin pancakes *391*
Pumpkin pie *367*
Queen of Pudingds *279*
Raspberry cheesecake *213*
Rhubarb and ginger crumble *120*
Rosemary and raspberry pavlovas *223*
Spiced fruit with mascarpone cream *331*
Steamed jam sponge *175*
Steamed lemon and pistachio puddings *127*
Strawberries and lemon curd with filo pastry *290*
Strawberry meringue roulade *219*
Summer fruit torte *252*
Tarte au citron et aux armandes 158
Three-chocolate millefeuille *41*
Whisky-baked fruit with marmalade ice cream *437*
Devils on horseback *427*
Devon flats *106*
Double chocolate puddings *419*
Dried orange slices with cinnamon *416*
duck
    Duck breast with blackberry sauce *322*
    Honeyed duck and vegetable stir-fry *310*Slow-roasted duck legs with puy lentils *374*
    Warm spiced roast duck salad *347*

dumplings
    Gnocchi and Mozzarella bake *406*
    Gnocchi with sun-dried tomatoes, rocket and lemon *197*
    Pork casserole with herb dumplings *129*
    Pork stew with dumplings *415*
    Venison casserole with parsley dumplings *62*

e

Easter biscuits *144*
eggs
    Aga lemon curd *257*
    Chicken and egg oriental rice *52*
    Smoked fish risotto with poached egg *64*
Elderflower fritters with elderflower mousse *199*
English treacle tart *380*
Ethel's shortcake biscuits *110*
Exotic fruit salad *254*

f

Falafel and tomato salsa *258*
Farmer's wife's fruit tart *417*
fennel
    Fennel gratin *235*
    Grilled fennel with Feta *190*
    Roast sea bass with fennel *155*
    Wrapped cod fillet with fennel saffron butter *13*
Feta
    Cheese, basil and pine nut triangles *245*
    Grilled fennel with Feta *190*
figs
    Fig and blueberry clafoutis *302*
    Figs on brioche *339*
    Honeyed fig kebabs with lemon tzatziki *324*
    Polenta shortcake with raisins and dried figs *11*
filo pastry
    Apple strudel *325*
    Cheese, basil and pine nut triangles *245*
    Salmon filo tart *240*
    Salmon and leek filo pie *346*
    Strawberries and lemon curd with filo pastry *290*
fish
    Almond-crusted salmon fillet *56*
    Couscous-crusted fish fingers with mint peas *214*
    Grilled lemon and pepper mackerel with lemon pilaf *90*
    Grilled tuna with aubergine *167*
    Haddock, sweetcorn and coconut chowder *270*
    Herb-crusted fish *109*
    Herrings in oatmeal *113*
    Japanese-style salmon *10*
    Kedgeree *354*

Marinated sea bass fillets *330*
Monkfish stir-fry *94*
Plaice baked with cheese *128*
Salmon fishcakes with lemon butter
   sauce *438*
Savoury fish crumble *366*
Smoked cod pasta bake *307*
Smoked fish risotto with poached
   egg *64*
Thai fishcakes with cucumber relish
   262
Trout baked in red wine *161*
West Indian fish curry in coconut
   cream sauce *200*
Wrapped cod fillet with fennel
   saffron butter *13*
see also salmon; sea bass; seafood;
   smoked haddock; squid; tuna
five-spice powder
Braised five-spice pork with pak choi
   169
Five-spice lamb *122*
Fougasse farci *174*
French onion soup *342*
French rice pudding *24*
Fried scallops with pak choi and peanut
   sauce *206*
fruit
Duck breast with blackberry sauce
   322
Exotic fruit salad *254*
Fruit yakitori *285*
Fruity glazed chicken *268*
Guinness cake *98*
Leamington festival cake *390*
Mincemeat *392*
Passion cake *60*
Pigeon and peach salad with
   hazelnut dressing *275*
Sweet pickled damsons *309*
see also apples; apricots; blackcurrants;
   cherries; coconuts; cranberries; figs;
   fruit desserts; lemons; mangoes;
   oranges; pears; pineapples;
   plums; prunes; raisins;
   raspberries; strawberries
fruit desserts
Clementines with caramel *414*
Coconut rice pudding with papaya
   274
Exotic fruit salad *254*
Fruit flan *187*
Hot banana brioche *173*
Pistachio and chocolate torte with
   summer fruits *233*
Pumpkin pie *367*
Spiced fruit with Mascarpone cream
   331
Summer fruit torte *252*
Whisky-baked fruit with marmalade
   ice cream *437*
Fruity glazed chicken *268*
Fudge nut tranche *65*
Fudge and pistachio baked apples *320*

g

game
Hare stew with whisky *439*
Pheasant breasts with orange and
   walnut *30*
Pheasant with peas *379*
Quail in bacon *201*
Rabbit in Dijon mustard *134*
Venison, beef and cranberry pie *365*
Venison casserole with parsley
   dumplings *62*
gammon/ham
Gammon and chutneys *434*
Roast gammon with plums and
   redcurrant glaze *300*
Sugar-glazed gammon with
   butterbean mash *93*
garlic
Garlicand mint stir-fried noodles *153*
Roast garlic bread *295*
Wild garlic soup *184*
ginger
Chicken noodle soup *68*
Ginger cake *112*
Gingerbread and butter pudding *425*
Individual ginger pudding *29*
Rhubarb and ginger crumble *120*
Rich sticky gingerbread *403*
Seared salmon with ginger and lime
   dressing *284*
gnocchi
Gnocchi and Mozzarella bake *406*
Gnocchi with sun-dried tomatoes,
   rocket and lemon *197*
goat's cheese
Aubergine and goat's cheese rounds
   183
Couscous with roast summer
   vegetables and goat's cheese *273*
Goat's cheese croustade *50*
Goat's cheese and rocket slice *225*
Roast beetroot with goat's cheese
   358
Smoked salmon and goat's cheese
   roulade *195*
goose
Roast goose with prune and apricot
   stuffing *433*
Gooseberry and raspberry crumble *221*
Gorgonzola
Gorgonzola risotto *111*
Mascarpone and Gorgonzola tart
   with balsamic onions *74*
Granny's Christmas pudding *400*
Grilled fennel with Feta *190*
Grilled lemon and pepper mackerel
   with lemon pilaf *90*
Grilled tuna with aubergine *167*
Gruyère
French onion soup *342*
Gruyère cheese choux puffs *420*
Gruyère and watercress roulade *131*
Guinea fowl with prunes and apples *389*
Guinness cake *98*

h

haddock
Haddock, sweetcorn and coconut
   chowder *270*
see also smoked haddock
ham *see gammon/ham*
hare
Hare stew with whisky *439*
Rich casserole of hare *80*
harissa
Harissa prawns *210*
Spice-crusted chicken with rose
   harissa *58*
hazelnuts
Fudge nut tranche *65*
Hazelnut and chocolate chunk
   cookies *228*
Pigeon and peach salad with
   hazelnut dressing *275*
Turkey and hazelnut soup *435*
herbs
Herb-crusted fish *109*
Herb pancakes with smoked salmon
   178
Herby chicken with lemon and herb
   butter *156*
Simple herb pâté *376*
Herrings in oatmeal *113*
Honeyed duck and vegetable stir-fry *310*
Honeyed fig kebabs with lemon tzatziki
   324
horseradish, gratin Potato and *345*
Hot banana brioche *173*
Hot cross buns *138*

i

Indian chutney *124*
Individual white pizzas *299*
Italian beef burgers *361*
Italian rhubarb tart *92*

j

Jerusalem artichokes with cheese *23*
juniper berries, Cabbage with juniper
   berries *424*

k

Kedgeree *354*

l

lamb
Coconut lamb *232*
Five-spice lamb *122*
Lamb in ale and Cheddar croûtes *360*
Lamb tagine with minted couscous *159*
Lamb's liver with mushrooms *386*
Lemon and lamb meatballs *267*
Middle Eastern shepherd's pie *67*
Mustard and herb-rubbed leg of lamb
   136

Index   *443*

Pan-fried lamb's liver with caramelised onions *180*
Pot-roast lamb in cider *82*
Roast leg of lamb with roasted peppers and courgettes *119*
Slow cooked lamb with puy lentils *176*
Spiced crusted leg of lamb with chickpeas *305*
Spring lamb stew *146*
Thai-style red lamb curry *217*

leeks
Leek and potato soup with Camembert croûtes *377*
Leek and saffron risotto *89*
Leek and Stilton soup *418*
Leek tart *108*
Potato gratin with leeks *148*
Salmon and leek filo pie *346*
Seafood and leek tart *216*
Turkey and leek crumble *40*
Wensleydale and leek slice *385*
Leamington festival cake *390*

lemons
Aga lemon curd *257*
Baby leaf risotto with lemon *171*
Chilled lemon chicken *234*
Grilled lemon and pepper mackerel with lemon pilaf *90*
Herby chicken with lemon and herb butter *156*
Honeyed fig kebabs with lemon tzatziki *324*
Lemon and lamb meatballs *267*
Lemon meringue pie *383*
Lemon Ricotta puddings *43*
Lemon roulade with passionfruit cream *215*
Lemon and seed drizzle cake *194*
Mediterranean chicken with lemon and olives *264*
Salmon en croute with watercress and lemon butter *166*
Spring chicken with lemon rice *164*
Strawberries and lemon curd with filo pastry *290*
Taglioni in a lemon cream sauce *186*
Tarte au citron et aux armandes *158*

lentils
Pork fillet with Puy lentils *222*
Slow cooked lamb with Puy lentils *176*
Slow-roasted duck legs with puy lentils *374*
Lettuce and watercress soup *209*
liver with mushrooms, Lamb's *386*
liver with caramelised onions, Pan-fried lamb's *180*

m

Macaroni cheese *27*
Malthouse bread *86*
mangoes
Chicken and mango stir-fry *276*
Mango chutney *356*
Marinated courgettes *281*
Marinated sea bass fillets *330*

marmalade
Almond marmalade tart *72*
Seville orange marmalade *25*
Whisky-baked fruit with marmalade ice cream *437*
mascarpone
Mascarpone and Gorgonzola tart with balsamic onions *74*
Spiced fruit with Mascarpone cream *331*
meats *see individual types*
Mediterranean chicken with lemon and olives *264*
Middle eastern shepherd's pie *67*
Mince pies with brandy cream *413*
Mincemeat *392*
Minestrone with pesto croutons *18*
mint
Couscous-crusted fish fingers with mint peas *214*
Garlic and mint stir-fry noodles *153*
Lamb tagine with minted couscous *159*
Mint sauce *163*
Miso beef stir-fry with noodles *399*
Monkfish stir-fry *94*
moussaka, Oven-roasted vegetable *344*
Mozzarella bake, Gnocchi and *406*
muffins, Blueberry *293*
mushrooms
Artichoke and wild mushroom pie *340*
Baked stuffed mushroom caps *91*
Pheasant with button mushrooms *350*
Lamb's liver with mushrooms *386*
mussels
Oriental 'paella' *71*
Quick seafood linguine *314*
mustard
Mustard and herb-rubbed leg of lamb *136*
Rabbit and Dijon mustard *134*

n

New potato, chorizo and roast pepper salad *246*
noodles
Chicken noodle soup *68*
Garlic and mint stir-fry noodles *153*
Miso beef stir-fry with noodles *399*
nuts
Christmas nut loaf *436*
Fudge nut tranche *65*
Pecan tarts *196*
Sultana and nut pilaf *73*
see also almonds; hazelnuts; pistachios; walnuts

o

oats
Apple porridge *17*
Herrings in oatmeal *113*
Plum and oatmeal Madeira cake *337*
olives
Braised peppers and olives *243*

Bread with olives and tomatoes *230*
Mediterranean chicken with lemon and olives *264*
onions
French onion soup *342*
Mascarpone and Gorgonzola tart with balsamic onions *74*
Onion and cream tart *364*
Onion and gorgonzola pizza *100*
orange(s)
Dried orange slices with cinnamon *416*
Orange drizzle tray bake *31*
Orange and vanilla custard tart *76*
Orange and white chocolate sponge *37*
Pheasant breasts with orange and walnut *30*
Rhubarb and orange meringue *88*
Oriental aubergines *304*
Oriental 'paella' *71*
Oven-roasted vegetable moussaka *344*

p

paella
Oriental 'Paella' *71*
Paella *205*
pak choi
Braised five-spice pork with pak choi *169*
Fried scallops with pak choi and peanut sauce *206*
pancakes
Blueberry pancakes *363*
Crêpe Caribe *83*
Herb pancakes with smoked salmon *178*
Pumpkin pancakes *391*
Thin pancakes with lemon *51*
Parmesan
Braised carrots with Parmesan *61*
Parmesan and mustard parsnips *12*
parsley dumplings, Venison casserole with *62*
parsnips
Parmesan and mustard parsnips *12*
partridge, Roast partridge with apricot stuffing *401*
Passion cake *60*
passionfruit cream, Lemon roulade with *215*
pasta
Chorizo, pepper and tomato macaroni *338*
Macaroni cheese *27*
Penne with aubergine and pine nuts *265*
Quick seafood linguine *370*
Smoked cod pasta bake *307*
Tagliatelle Siciliana *371*
Taglioni in a lemon cream sauce *186*
pâté
Pâté maison *101*
Simple herb pâté *376*
pears
Baked pears with cassis *327*
Christmas pear tart *426*
Pear, prune and walnut chutney *317*

Pear upside-down cake *311*
Pears in red wine *447*
peas
    Couscous-crusted fish fingers with
      mint peas *214*
    Pea soup *229*
    Pea and spinach soup *181*
    Pheasant with peas *379*
Pecan tarts *196*
Penne with aubergine and pine nuts *265*
peppers
    Braised peppers with olives *243*
    Chorizo, pepper and tomato
      macaroni *338*
    New potato, chorizo and roast
      pepper salad *246*
    Roast leg of lamb with roasted
      peppers and courgettes *119*
    Roasted pepper tartlets *263*
    Seared tuna with chickpea and
      pepper salad *278*
    Stuffed peppers *288*
    Stuffed peppers with Brie *313*
    Tomato and pepper soup *348*
    Turkish ratatouille *329*
    Twice-cooked red pepper soufflés *319*
pesto
    Aromatic Asian pesto with chicken
      198
    Roast tomatoes with Ricotta pesto
      253
    Winter minestrone with pesto
      Croutons *18*
pheasant
    Pheasant breasts with orange and
      walnut *30*
    Pheasant with button mushrooms
      350
    Pheasant with peas *379*
pigeon
    Pigeon and peach salad with
      hazelnut dressing *275*
    Pigeon with raisins *336*
pine nuts
    Cheese, basil and pine nut triangles
      245
    Penne with aubergine and pine nuts
      265
    Roast salmon with courgettes and
      pine nuts *294*
pineapples
    Caramelised pineapple with
      raspberries *259*
    Pineapple upside-down puddings *249*
    Pork tenderloin roast with pineapple
      227
pistachios
    Fudge and pistachio baked apples
      320
    Pistachio and chocolate torte with
      summer fruits *233*
    Steamed lemon and pistachio
      puddings *127*
pizzas
    Apple and raisin pizza *396*
    Individual white pizzas *299*
    Onion and Gorgonzola pizza *100*
plums
    Plum and almond puddings with bay-

scented custard *292*
    Plum and apple chutney *303*
    Plum and oatmeal Madeira cake *337*
    Roast gammon with plums and
      redcurrant glaze *300*
Polenta shortcake with raisins and
    dried figs *11*
pork
    bacon, Broad bean and bacon soup
      192
    Braised five-spice pork with pak choi
      169
    Pork casserole with herb dumplings
      129
    Pork fillet with Puy lentils *222*
    Pork stew with dumplings *415*
    Pork tenderloin roast with pineapple
      227
    Pork, walnut and sausage rolls *423*
    Roast rack of pork with roast apples
      334
    Slow roast pork *55*
    Somerset cider hotpot *22*
    Sweet and sour pork *283*
    See also gammon/ham
    See also sausage
Pot-roast beef in red wine *107*
Pot-roast lamb in cider *82*
potatoes
    Cheesey bubble and squeak cakes *96*
    Leek and potato soup with
      Camembert croûtes *377*
    New potato, chorizo and roast
      pepper salad *246*
    Potato and courgettes with pistou
      236
    Potato gratin with leeks *148*
    Potato and horseradish gratin *345*
    Vegetarian shepherd's pie *382*
Poussin with black pudding *381*
prawns
    Corn, crab and prawn chowder *335*
    Corn and prawn cakes with
      Vietnamese dipping sauce *121*
    Harissa prawns *210*
    Oriental 'Paella' *71*
    Thai-spiced scallop and prawn salad
      239
Provençal bean stew *135*
prunes
    Beef tagine with prunes *14*
    Chicken and prune casserole *411*
    Devils on horseback *427*
    Guinea fowl with prunes and apples
      389
    Pear, prune and walnut chutney *317*
    Roast goose with prune and apricot
      stuffing *433*
puddings *see desserts*
puff pastry
    Christmas pear tart *426*
    Pork, walnut and sausage rolls *423*
pumpkin
    Pumpkin pancakes *391*
    Pumpkin pie *367*

q

Quail in bacon *201*
Queen of Puddings *279*
quiche
    Broccoli quiche *84*
    Classic quiche Lorraine *362*
    Spinach quiche *282*
Quick seafood linguine *314*

r

Rabbit in Dijon mustard *134*
raisins
    Apple and raisin pizza *396*
    Chicken in red wine with raisins *36*
    Pigeon with raisins *336*
    Polenta shortcake with raisins and
      dried figs *11*
    Raisin bread for cheese *20*
raspberries
    Amaretti meringues with raspberry
      coulis *266*
    Caramelised pineapple with
      raspberries *259*
    Gooseberry and raspberry crumble
      221
    Raspberry cheesecake *213*
    Rosemary and raspberry Pavlovas
      223
redcurrants
    Fruit flan *187*
    Roast gammon with plums and
      redcurrant glaze *300*
rhubarb
    Italian rhubarb tart *92*
    Rhubarb cake *150*
    Rhubarb and ginger crumble *120*
    Rhubarb and orange meringue *88*
rice
    Baby leaf risotto with lemon *171*
    Beetroot and red wine risotto *351*
    Chicken and egg oriental rice *52*
    Coconut rice pudding with papaya
      274
    French rice pudding *24*
    Gorgonzola risotto *111*
    Grilled lemon and pepper mackerel
      with lemon pilaf *90*
    Kedgeree *354*
    Leek and saffron risotto *89*
    Oriental 'Paella' *71*
    Smoked fish risotto with poached
      egg *64*
    Spring chicken with lemon rice *164*
    Sultana and nut pilaf *73*
    Three tomato risotto *242*
Rich sticky gingerbread *403*
Ricotta
    Cheese, basil and pine nut triangles
      245
    Lemon Ricotta pudding *43*
    Roast tomatoes with Ricotta pesto
      253
risottos *see rice*
Roast beetroot with goat's cheese *358*
Roast gammon with plums and
    redcurrant glaze *300*

Index

445

Roast garlic bread *295*
Roast goose with prune and apricot
  stuffing *433*
Roast leg of lamb with roasted peppers
  and courgettes *119*
Roast rack of pork with roast apples *334*
Roast salmon with courgettes and
  pine nuts *294*
Roast sea bass with fennel *155*
Roast swede *54*
Roast tomatoes with Ricotta pesto *253*
Roast turkey *429*
Roasted pepper tartlets *263*
rocket slice, Goat's cheese and *225*
Roquefort feuilleté *70*
Rosemary and raspberry Pavlovas *223*

S

saffron risotto, Leek and *89*
salads
  Couscous, tomato and Haloumi salad
    231
  New potato, chorizo and roast
    pepper salad *246*
  Pigeon and peach salad with
    hazelnut dressing *275*
  Seared tuna with chickpea and
    pepper salad *278*
  Seared tuna Niçoise *255*
  Thai-spiced scallop and prawn salad
    239
  Warm chicken salad *289*
  Warm spiced roast duck salad *347*
salmon
  Almond-crusted salmon fillet *56*
  Herb pancakes with smoked salmon
    178
  Japanese-style salmon *10*
  Roast salmon with courgettes and
    pine nuts *294*
  Salmon en croûte with watercress
    and lemon butter *166*
  Salmon filo tart *240*
  Salmon fishcakes with lemon butter
    sauce *438*
  Salmon with grilled asparagus *172*
  Salmon and leek filo pie *346*
  Salmon pie *318*
  Seared salmon with ginger and lime
    dressing *284*
  Smoked salmon and goat's cheese
    roulade *195*
sauces
  Bread sauce *432*
  Chicken with watercress sauce *126*
  Corn and prawn cakes with
    Vietnamese dipping sauce *121*
  Duck breast with blackberry sauce
    322
  Fried scallops with pak choi and
    peanut sauce *206*
  Mint sauce *163*
  Sherry sauce *422*
  West Indian fish curry in coconut
    cream sauce *200*
sausages
  Braised sausages with chestnuts *32*
  New potato, chorizo and roast

pepper salad *246*
Spicy sausage and tomato ragu *97*
Savoury fish crumble *366*
scallions *see spring onions*
scallops
  Fried scallops with pak choi and
    peanut sauce *206*
  Salmon pie *318*
  Thai-spiced scallop and prawn salad
    239
Scones *132*
sea bass
  Marinated sea bass fillets *330*
  Roast sea bass with fennel *155*
  Sea bass en papillote *357*
seafood
  Chilli salt squid *49*
  Corn, crab and prawn chowder *335*
  Oriental 'Paella' *71*
  Paella *205*
  Quick seafood linguine *314*
  Seafood and leek tart *216*
  Squid Provençal *139*
see also fish; prawns; scallops; tuna
Seared salmon with ginger and lime
  dressing *284*
Seared tuna with chickpea and pepper
  salad *278*
Seared tuna Niçoise *255*
Seed and grain loaf *116*
Sephardic chocolate cake *378*
Seville orange marmalade *25*
Shepherd's pie, Middle Eastern *67*
sherry
  Chicken in sherry sauce *85*
  Sherry sauce *422*
shortbread torte with cranberry glaze,
  Chocolate *431*
shortcake
  Ethel's shortcake biscuits *110*
  Polenta shortcake with raisins and
    dried figs *11*
Simnel cake *142*
Simple herb pâté *376*
Slow cooked lamb with puy lentils *176*
Slow roast pork *55*
Slow-roasted duck legs with puy lentils
  374
Smoked cod pasta bake *307*
smoked haddock
  Smoked haddock au gratin *145*
  Smoked haddock with bubble and
    squeak *402*
  Smoked haddock vichyssoise *81*
Smoked salmon and goat's cheese
  roulade *195*
Somerset cider hotpot *22*
soups
  Asparagus soup *165*
  Blue Stilton soup *42*
  Broad bean and bacon soup *192*
  Celeriac, whisky and thyme soup
    387
  Celery soup *130*
  Chestnut soup *35*
  Chicken noodle soup *68*
  Corn, crab and prawn chowder *335*
  Curried sweet potato soup *315*
  French onion soup *342*
  Haddock, sweetcorn and coconut

chowder *270*
  Leek and potato soup with
    Camembert croûtes *377*
  Leek and Stilton soup *418*
  Lettuce and watercress soup *209*
  Pea soup *229*
  Pea and spinach soup *181*
  Smoked haddock vichyssoise *81*
  Spicy carrot soup *373*
  Spinach soup *220*
  Sweet potato and ham soup *38*
  Tomato and pepper soup *348*
  Turkey and hazelnut soup *435*
  Wild garlic soup *184*
  Winter minestrone with pesto
    croûtons *18*
Spice-crusted chicken with rose harissa
  58
Spiced crusted leg of lamb with
  chickpeas *305*
Spiced fruit with Mascarpone cream *331*
Spicy carrot soup *373*
Spicy red cabbage *33*
Spicy sausage and tomato ragu *97*
spinach
  Pea and spinach soup *181*
  Spinach soup *220*
  Spinach quiche *282*
Spring chicken with lemon rice *164*
Spring lamb stew *146*
squid
  Chilli salt squid *49*
  Squid Provençal *139*
Steamed lemon and pistachio puddings
  127
Steamed jam sponge *175*
Stilton
  Blue Stilton soup *42*
  Leek and Stilton soup *418*
  White Stilton torte with roast
    vegetables *397*
stir-fries
  Chicken and egg oriental rice *52*
  Chicken and mango stir-fry *276*
  Fried scallops with pak choi and
    peanut sauce *206*
  Garlic and mint stir-fry noodles *153*
  Honeyed duck and vegetable stir-fry
    310
  Miso beef stir-fry with noodles *399*
  Monkfish stir-fry *94*
strawberries
  Strawberries and lemon curd with
    filo pastry *290*
  Strawberry crumble cake *286*
  Strawberry meringue roulade *219*
Stuffed peppers *288*
Stuffed peppers with Brie *313*
stuffing, Apricot and almond stuffing *428*
Sugar-glazed gammon with butterbean
  mash *93*
Sultana and nut pilaf *73*
Summer fruit torte *252*
Summer vegetable flan *291*
swede, Roast *54*
Sweet pickled damsons *309*
sweet potatoes
  Curried sweet potato soup *315*
  Sweet potato and ham soup *38*
Sweet and sour pork *283*

sweetcorn
Corn, crab and prawn chowder *335*
Corn and prawn cakes with
Vietnamese dipping sauce *121*
Haddock, sweetcorn and coconut
chowder *270*
Sweetcorn relish *244*

t

Tagliatelle Siciliana *371*
Taglioni in a lemon cream sauce *186*
Tarte au citron et aux armandes *158*
Thai fishcakes with cucumber relish
262
Thai-spiced scallop and prawn salad
239
Thai-style red lamb curry *217*
Thin pancakes with lemon *51*
Three tomato risotto *242*
Three-chocolate millefeuille *41*
Thyme Yorkshire puddings *326*
Tian of aubergines *226*
tomatoes
Aga-dried tomatoes *250*
Baked tomatoes on brioche *271*
Bean and tomato casserole *409*
Bread with olives and tomatoes *230*
Chorizo, pepper and tomato
macaroni *338*
Compôte de tomates *248*
Couscous, tomato and Haloumi salad
231
Crumbed tomatoes *204*
Falafel and tomato salsa *258*
Gnocchi with sun-dried tomatoes,
rocket and lemon *197*
Roast tomatoes with Ricotta pesto
253
Spicy sausage and tomato ragu *97*
Three tomato risotto *242*
Tomato and courgette salsa *191*
Tomato and pepper soup *348*
Treacle tart, English *380*
Trout baked in red wine *161*
tuna
Grilled tuna with aubergine *167*
Seared tuna with chickpea and
pepper salad *278*
Seared tuna Niçoise *255*
turkey
Roast turkey *429*
Turkey and hazelnut soup *435*
Turkey and leek crumble *40*
Turkish ratatouille *329*
Twice-cooked red pepper soufflés *319*

v

vegetables
Baby leaf risotto with lemon *171*
Broccoli quiche *84*
Brussels sprouts with chestnuts *410*
Cauliflower soufflés *59*
Couscous with roast summer
vegetables and goat's cheese *273*
Goat's cheese and rocket slice *225*

Honeyed duck and vegetable stir-fry
310
Jerusalem artichokes with cheese *23*
Mixed roast vegeatbles *395*
Oven-roasted vegetable moussaka
344
Roast swede *54*
Summer vegetable flan *291*
Thai fishcakes with cucumber relish
262
Turkish ratatouille *329*
Vegetarian shepherd's pie *382*
White Stilton torte with roast
vegetables *397*
see also asparagus; aubergines; beans;
beetroot; butterbeans; cabbage;
carrots; courgettes; fennel; leeks;
pak choi; parsnips; peas;
peppers; salads; soups;
sweet potatoes;
sweetcorn; tomatoes
Vegetarian shepherd's pie *382*
venison
Venison, beef and cranberry pie *365*
Venison casserole with parsley
dumplings *62*

w

walnuts
Apricot and walnut biscotti *203*
Cheese and walnut loaf *298*
Pear, prune and walnut chutney *317*
Pheasant breasts with orange and
walnut *30*
Pork, walnut and sausage rolls *423*
Warm chicken salad *289*
Warm spiced roast duck salad *347*
watercress
Chicken with watercress sauce *126*
Gruyère and watercress roulade *131*
Lettuce and watercress soup *209*
Salmon en croûte with watercress
and lemon butter *166*
Wensleydale and leek slice *385*
West Indian fish curry in coconut cream
sauce *200*
whisky
Celeriac, whisky and thyme soup
387
Hare stew with whisky *439*
Whisky-baked fruit with marmalade
ice cream *437*
white chocolate
Almond and white chocolate tart *102*
Cherry and white chocolate cookies
19
Orange and white chocolate sponge
37
Three-chocolate millefeuille *41*
White Stilton torte with roast
vegetables *397*
Wild garlic soup *184*
wine
Beetroot and red wine risotto *351*
Braised chicken legs in red wine *343*
Chicken in red wine with raisins *36*
Chicken with sparkling wine *103*
Pears in red wine *447*

Pot-roast beef in red wine *107*
Trout baked in red wine *161*
Winter minestrone with pesto croûtons *18*
Wrapped cod fillet with fennel saffron
butter *13*

y

Yoghurt cake with grapes in syrup *394*
Yorkshire puddings, Thyme *326*

Index